Global Lives

This is a fascinating and unique account of Britain's rise as a global imperial power told through the lives of over forty individuals from a huge range of backgrounds. Miles Ogborn relates and connects the stories of monarchs and merchants, planters and pirates, slaves and sailors, captives and captains, reactionaries and revolutionaries, artists and abolitionists from all corners of the globe. These dramatic stories give new life to the exploration of the history and geography of changing global relationships, including settlement in North America, the East India Company's trade and empire, transatlantic trade, the slave trade, the rise and fall of piracy, and scientific voyaging in the Pacific. Through these many biographies, including those of Anne Bonny, Captain Cook, Queen Elizabeth I, Pocahontas and Walter Ralegh, early modern globalisation is presented as something through which different people lived in dramatically contrasting ways, but in which everyone played a part.

MILES OGBORN is Professor of Geography at Queen Mary, University of London. His previous books include *Spaces of Modernity: London's Geographies, 1680–1780* (1998) and *Indian Ink: Script and Print in the Making of the English East India Company* (2007).

Cambridge Studies in Historical Geography 41

Series editors:
ALAN R. H. BAKER, RICHARD DENNIS, DERYCK HOLDSWORTH

Cambridge Studies in Historical Geography encourages exploration of the philosophies, methodologies and techniques of historical geography and publishes the results of new research within all branches of the subject. It endeavours to secure the marriage of traditional scholarship with innovative approaches to problems and to sources, aiming in this way to provide a focus for the discipline and to contribute towards its development. The series is an international forum for publication in historical geography which also promotes contact with workers in cognate disciplines.

For a full list of titles in the series, please see
www.cambridge.org/historicalgeography

Global Lives

Britain and the World, 1550–1800

——

MILES OGBORN

CAMBRIDGE
UNIVERSITY PRESS

CAMBRIDGE UNIVERSITY PRESS
Cambridge, New York, Melbourne, Madrid, Cape Town, Singapore, São Paulo, Delhi

Cambridge University Press
The Edinburgh Building, Cambridge CB2 8RU, UK

Published in the United States of America by Cambridge University Press, New York

www.cambridge.org
Information on this title: www.cambridge.org/9780521607186

First published 2008

Printed in the United Kingdom at the University Press, Cambridge

A catalogue record for this publication is available from the British Library

Library of Congress Cataloguing in Publication data
Ogborn, Miles.
Global lives : Britain and the world, 1550–1800 / Miles Ogborn.
   p.   cm. – (Cambridge studies in historical geography ; 41)
Includes bibliographical references.
ISBN 978-0-521-84501-4 – ISBN 978-0-521-60718-6 (pbk.)
1. Great Britain – Commerce – History.   2. Great Britain – Foreign relations – History.
3. Great Britain – Colonies – History.   4. Great Britain – Economic conditions.
5. Great Britain – Civilization.   6. Imperialism – History.   I. Title.   II. Series.
DA16.O33   2008
327.41009′03 – dc22   2008025897

ISBN 978-0-521-84501-4 hardback
ISBN 978-0-521-60718-6 paperback

Contents

Figures

Tables

Acknowledgements

I would like to thank Brian Graham and Catherine Nash for asking me to contribute a chapter on global historical geography to their book *Modern Historical Geographies* (Longman, 2000) just as I was beginning to think about teaching and writing on the subject. I am very grateful to all those who have said that they found that chapter useful, and even enjoyable. In particular, I owe a debt to Alan Baker who encouraged me to turn the chapter into a book (although unfortunately I was unable to live up to his ambitions for what spans of space and time it might contain). Subsequent thanks are due to my editors at Cambridge University Press: Richard Fisher, who encouraged the project and agreed to a long initial deadline, and Michael Watson who has seen the book to completion. I have appreciated their help, and the comments of the Press's readers, on the shape the venture should take.

Thanks are also due to the Leverhulme Trust whose Philip Leverhulme Prize (2001) provided the time to write a full proposal and sample chapter. I am very grateful to Edward Oliver for drawing such a large number of maps and diagrams with such speed and skill, to Karen Anderson Howes for her sensitive and careful copy-editing, and to all the libraries, galleries and archives who have allowed me to reproduce material from their collections. Every effort has been made to secure the necessary permissions to reproduce copyright material in this work, though in some cases it has proved impossible to trace copyright holders. If any omissions are brought to my notice, I will be happy to include appropriate acknowledgements in any subsequent edition. I would also like to acknowledge all the final-year students who have taken GEG315 'Global Historical Geography, 1492–1800' at Queen Mary, University of London, in particular, Sam Garnett, Matthew Gent, James Lewis, Mary Madike, Hannane Naciri, Juliz Reddy, Takenori Sato, Deen Sharp, Rajinder Thind and Iain Watson. They are a remarkable group of citizens of the contemporary world who have been willing to take on its past.

Finally, I must thank Catherine once again for her never-ending enthusiasm for the telling of these lives, and her insistence that each life is given its due. And I can now also thank Eve in print for the very first time. She was born the day after the first draft was finished, and she has changed our world.

Brief lives

All of the individuals whose lives are briefly sketched out here are also put together on a timeline on page xx. They all subsequently reappear in the chapters that follow, where their biographies are retold in detail and in relation to Britain's changing place in the world.

Sarah Affir, also known as Affy b. 1767, d. after 1832. An enslaved woman who was born and worked all her life in the fields, house and laundry on the Barham family's Mesopotamia sugar plantation in Westmoreland parish, Jamaica. She gave birth to six children.

Anonymous, Slave in Revolt, 1789 Date of birth unknown, date of death uncertain. This enslaved African, taken on board from Sierra Leone, was probably killed during the revolt on the American slave ship *Felicity* in the mid-Atlantic in 1789 during which he himself shot and killed the ship's captain.

Edward Barlow b. 1642, d. 1706. Seaman who sailed on many naval and merchant vessels in the Atlantic and Indian Oceans and the Mediterranean and Caribbean Seas.

La Belinguere, also known as Marie Mar and Maguimar Dates of birth and death unknown. A powerful Luso-African woman merchant and daughter of a local ruler, who operated around the mouth of the Gambia River in West Africa in the late seventeenth century, trading with both European and other African merchants.

Anne Bonny b. 1698, d. 1782. The Irish-born illegitimate daughter of a lawyer, who grew up in South Carolina and sailed as a pirate from New Providence in the Bahamas in 1720. Though she was captured and tried in Jamaica for piracy, pregnancy saved her from execution and she returned to South Carolina.

Thomas Clarkson b. 1760, d. 1846. English-born anti-slave trade activist and writer who pursued the cause through extensive travels around Britain to gather information from those involved in the slave trade and to generate extra-parliamentary support. Also travelled to post-revolutionary France.

James Cook b. 1728, d. 1779. Yorkshire-born officer of the Royal Navy. Had served in the Seven Years' War (1756–1763) and undertaken surveying along the St Lawrence River, Canada, before being appointed to command the *Endeavour* for a voyage to the Pacific (1768–1771). Undertook two subsequent extensive Pacific voyages (1772–1775 and 1776–1779). His voyaging ended when he was killed on a beach in Hawai'i.

Archibald Dalzel (formerly Dalziel) b. 1740, d. 1811. Scottish-born surgeon who worked at the Royal African Company's slaving fort at Anoumabu (Gold Coast) from 1763 and became the director of the fort at Ouidah (Dahomey) in 1767. Retired from the Company in 1770 and worked organising and captaining slaving voyages from London until he was appointed governor of Cape Coast Castle (Gold Coast) in 1791.

William Dampier b. 1651, d. 1715. English-born buccaneer and privateer whose voyages took him around the world three times, including crossing the Pacific from Central America to the Philippines, and a landing on the north Australian coast. Well known for his journal recording plants, animals and indigenous peoples.

Elizabeth I b. 1533, d. 1603. Queen of England from 1558. Her reign involved war with Spain, the beginnings of England's involvement in the transatlantic slave trade, colonial settlement in Ireland and North America and the establishment of the English East India Company.

Olaudah Equiano, also known as Gustavus Vassa b. c. 1745, d. 1797. A slave of a Royal Navy officer who served in the Seven Years' War (1756–1763), crossing the Atlantic several times, and also living in London. Sold to a merchant on Montserrat, he bought his freedom and travelled to the Arctic, Turkey, North America and the Caribbean. Became a prominent activist in the movement to abolish the slave trade and travelled extensively in Britain and Ireland promoting the cause via the *Interesting Narrative* of his life that he first published in 1789.

William Freeman b. 1645, d. 1707. Caribbean-born plantation-owner, merchant and Royal African Company agent for the Leeward Islands. Moved to London in 1674 to pursue his own mercantile activities and to operate as a commission agent buying and selling for planters and merchants still in the Caribbean.

Briton Hammon Dates of birth and death unknown. An African-American sailor (and later ship's cook) from New England who sailed on naval and merchant vessels to Virginia, the Caribbean and Europe in the middle of the eighteenth century.

John Hawkins b. 1532, d. 1595. Devon-born merchant, maritime adventurer, slave-trader and naval commander and administrator. Operated in the Atlantic and particularly in the Caribbean in the 1560s.

William Hodges b. 1744, d. 1797. Artist trained in Richard Wilson's studio who was employed on Cook's second voyage to the Pacific (1772–1775). Completed a range of pictures during and after the voyage, from small sketches to large oil paintings shown at the Royal Academy. Later travelled extensively as an artist in British India (1780–1783).

John Jea b. 1773, d. after 1815. Born in Old Calabar, West Africa, and sold into slavery in New England, he gained his freedom and became a preacher. Travelled as a ship's cook and preacher along the North American coast, through the Caribbean and to Europe.

William Jones b. 1746, d. 1794. Barrister and later judge in both Britain and British India, including appointment to the Bengal Supreme Court. Tutor and scholar of classical and 'Oriental' languages. Founder of the Asiatick Society of Bengal (1784).

Robert Keayne b. 1595, d. 1656. Puritan merchant tailor who migrated from London to Massachusetts in 1635. Became a prominent Boston merchant who imported goods from Europe and traded with the Caribbean.

William Kidd b. c. 1645, d. 1701. A Scottish-born buccaneer in the late seventeenth-century Caribbean who set sail from New York in 1696 to capture the pirates who were disrupting shipping in the Indian Ocean. He was himself hanged for piracy in London in 1701.

Mai, also known as Omai b. c. 1753, d. c. 1780. Born on the island of Ra'iatea in the Pacific, moved to Tahiti after dispossession by invaders from Borabora. Joined Cook's companion ship *Adventure* at Huahine on the second voyage and sailed to Britain where he stayed for two years (1775–1776). Was introduced to the king and to high society and travelled around the country. Returned to Tahiti to stay on the third voyage.

Streynsham Master b. 1640, d. 1724. English East India Company employee who served in Ahmedabad and Surat and traded to the Persian Gulf. He later travelled back to India to become the governor at Fort St George (Madras), charged with reorganising the company's business, before losing his position in 1681.

Hannah More b. 1745, d. 1833. English-born author of plays, poetry and educational tracts who was known as 'Saint Hannah'. Published *Slavery: A Poem* (1788) as a contribution to the movement for the abolition of the slave trade. Later published conservative tracts to counter the radical political ideas of the 1790s.

Essa Morrison Dates of birth and death unknown. Inhabitant of a Wapping lodging house near the banks of the River Thames in London. Convicted at the Old Bailey in 1765 of the theft of money from a sailor and transported to North America.

Hugh O'Neill (Aodh Ó Néill), Second Earl of Tyrone b. c. 1550, d. 1616. Lord of extensive lands in Ulster, courtier and leader of an extensive but unsuccessful rebellion against English authority in Ireland (1595–1604).

Richard Oswald b. c. 1705, d. 1784. Scottish-born merchant who worked in Glasgow, Virginia and Jamaica before moving to London in 1746. With a group of associates he operated a very extensive and lucrative set of trading, shipping, planting, slaving and military supply operations around the Atlantic world.

Pocahontas, also known as Matoaka, Amonute and Rebecca Rolfe b. c. 1596, d. 1617. Daughter of the paramount chief Powhatan, and go-between for the Jamestown colony (Virginia). Kidnapped by the English colonists. Married an Englishman, John Rolfe. Travelled to England where she died.

Charles Price b. 1708, d. 1772. Jamaican sugar plantation-owner, speaker of the Jamaican Assembly and judge of the Supreme Court. Born in Jamaica, educated in England, returned to Jamaica in 1730. Became probably the largest land-owner and slave-holder in Jamaica after the Seven Years' War (1756–1763).

Walter Prideaux b. 1676, date of death unknown. Born in Devon into a family that included merchants and sea captains. Undertook one slave-trading voyage from 1700 to 1701 as merchant in charge of the cargo of the *Daniel and Henry* from Dartmouth to the Gold Coast to Jamaica and back to Dartmouth.

Radhakanta Tarkavagisa Date of birth unknown, d. 1803. Scholar of Sanskrit texts on history, botany, chess, drama, religion and law who worked in Bengal under both Indian and British patronage. Appointed as a legal expert for the civil courts in British Bengal.

Walter Ralegh b. 1554, d. 1618. Soldier, courtier, adventurer and writer. Fought in France and Ireland, attempted to found a colony in Virginia and undertook expeditions up the Orinoco River in South America in 1595 and 1616.

Bartholomew Roberts b. c. 1682, d. 1722. Welsh-born pirate captain who is said to have captured four hundred merchant ships in a two-year (1720–1722) campaign of terror from Newfoundland to Brazil, and from the West African coast to the Caribbean. He was killed in an engagement with a Royal Navy ship off the African coast.

Ancona Robin Robin John Dates of birth and death unknown. Member of the Efik ruling family in the Old Town slave-trading centre of Old Calabar (Bight of Biafra). Enslaved in 1767 along with his kinsman Little Ephraim Robin John, and lived as a slave in Dominica and Virginia before being taken to Bristol in 1773. Gained his freedom and returned to Old Calabar in 1774.

Little Ephraim Robin John Dates of birth and death unknown. Member of the Efik ruling family in the Old Town slave-trading centre of Old Calabar (Bight of Biafra). Enslaved in 1767 along with his kinsman Ancona Robin Robin John and lived as a slave in Dominica and Virginia before being taken to Bristol in 1773. Gained his freedom and returned to Old Calabar in 1774.

John Sassamon b. c. 1620, d. 1675. Interpreter, translator, scribe, preacher, teacher and go-between for both New England colonists and Amerindians.

John Smith Bap. 1580, d. 1631. Fought as a soldier for various armies across Europe, captured and enslaved by the Turks. Went as a colonist to Virginia in 1607, became a cartographer, governor of Jamestown, and promoter in print of North American colonisation.

William Spavens b. 1735, d. 1799. English-born seaman who sailed merchant vessels to northern Europe and the East Indies, and served in the Royal Navy around the Atlantic world during the Seven Years' War (1756–1763).

Tacky Date of birth unknown, d. 1760. An enslaved African of Akan origin, and almost certainly born in Africa, who led an extensive slave revolt on Jamaica in 1760. He was killed by a maroon sharpshooter during the revolt.

Thomas Thistlewood b. 1721, d. 1786. Born in Lincolnshire and settled in Jamaica in 1750. Worked for thirty-six years as an overseer and slave-owner on sugar plantations and livestock pens in St Elizabeth's and Westmoreland parishes, first for others, then on his own land.

Toussaint L'Ouverture, also known as Toussaint Bréda b. 1743, d. 1803. A former slave on Saint Domingue who became the leader of a successful slave rebellion that began in 1791. He was a formidable military strategist whose troops fought off both the British army and the French army. Tricked by the French, he died a captive in France the year before the Republic of Haiti was proclaimed.

Tupaia Date of birth unknown, d. 1770. A navigator, high priest, warrior and artist from the island of Ra'iatea who was displaced to Tahiti in about 1760 and formed an alliance with politically powerful Tahitians. He joined Cook's ship *Endeavour* intending to go to England, and travelled with Cook to the Society Islands, New Zealand and Australia. He died at Batavia (Indonesia).

Kasi Viranna, also known as Hasan Khan Date of birth unknown, d. 1680. Merchant, property-owner, judge and tax-farmer operating from Madras. Had extensive mercantile investments and connections across the Indian Ocean trading world, and conducted substantial trade with the English East India Company.

Eunice Williams, also known as Marguerite, Waongote and Kanensten-hawi b. 1696, d. 1785. Daughter of the Deerfield (Massachusetts) minister John Williams. Taken captive aged seven by Mohawks from Kahnawake (Canada) in a raid in 1704. Married a Mohawk and made her life at Kahnawake.

Life lines

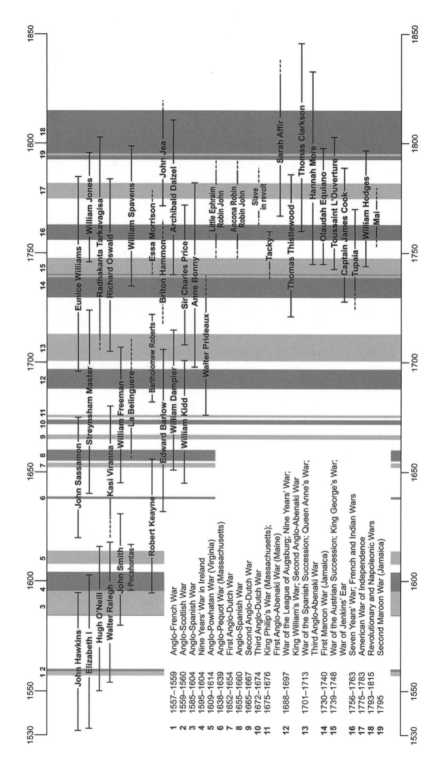

1	1557–1559	Anglo-French War
2	1559–1560	Anglo-Scottish War
3	1585–1604	Anglo-Spanish War
4	1595–1604	Nine Years' War in Ireland
5	1609–1614	Anglo-Powhatan War (Virginia)
6	1638–1639	Anglo-Pequot War (Massachusetts)
7	1652–1654	First Anglo-Dutch War
8	1655–1660	Anglo-Spanish War
9	1665–1667	Second Anglo-Dutch War
10	1672–1674	Third Anglo-Dutch War
11	1675–1676	King Philip's War (Massachusetts); First Anglo-Abenaki War (Maine)
12	1688–1697	War of the League of Augsburg; Nine Years' War; King William's War; Second Anglo-Abenaki War
13	1701–1713	War of the Spanish Succession; Queen Anne's War; Third Anglo-Abenaki War
14	1730–1740	First Maroon War (Jamaica)
15	1739–1748	War of the Austrian Succession; King George's War; War of Jenkins' Ear
16	1756–1763	Seven Years' War; French and Indian Wars
17	1775–1783	American War of Independence
18	1793–1815	Revolutionary and Napoleonic Wars
19	1795	Second Maroon War (Jamaica)

1 | Global lives

The world changed between the sixteenth and eighteenth centuries. It changed in directions that can be described using some of our current ideas of globalisation. Parts of the world that were previously disconnected became connected in novel ways; important reconfigurations of empires and trade routes were established that operated beyond the confines of nation-states; the lives of many people were increasingly shaped by the decisions made by others who lived far away in new centres of power and control; cultures and landscapes were reworked as people, ideas and material objects were transported and recombined elsewhere in unprecedented ways. It was a world that offered striking possibilities for power and profit for some and new dangers and forms of oppression and exploitation for others. The processes that created this world were shaped by many people, and, in turn, these processes themselves changed many lives.

Contemporary mapmakers sought to interpret this changing geography. Herman Moll, a late seventeenth-century migrant to London from war-torn northern Europe, presented to a British audience *A New Map of the Whole World* (Figure 1.1) that was simultaneously one of confidence and trepidation. It offered a globe whose geography was ordered by the trade winds that could carry merchant and naval ships to its four corners. Yet what is known to Europeans is obviously incomplete. There are many gaps on the map. The different implications of this new world of trade for people, real and imagined, are also illustrated on the map. Engraved at the bottom are allegorical male figures representing each of the four continents: America, Europe, Asia and Africa. Each is dressed as if for war, with weapons to hand. Between them is the Roman goddess Fortuna. Held with her right arm, a cornucopia pours forth symbols of sovereignty and wealth. On her left, she also brings to the world the instruments of violence and terror: a dagger, a whip, a hatchet, shackles and the hangman's noose. Lives would now be bound together across the lands and seas of the world by trade, war, money, power and pain.

This book sets out to demonstrate the ways in which these historical and geographical changes happened. It weaves together accounts of the making of this new world of global connection and, in order to bring that to life, the

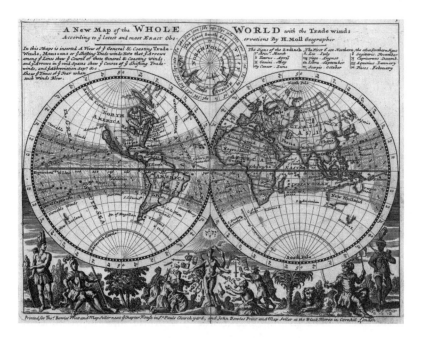

Figure 1.1 *A New Map of the Whole World*, by Herman Moll, 1736. This was one of many maps that were drawn, printed and sold to a broad European audience from the late seventeenth century onwards. Using the latest cartographic information and a range of allegorical figures it offered its viewers a vision of their place in the world.

biographies of some of those whose work, ideas, relationships and struggles made all of this come about. In what follows the histories and geographies of trade, settlement, colonisation, empire building, piracy, slavery and science are set out to demonstrate the variety of forms of global connection that made this world. The organisation and the implications of these histories and geographies are traced out through the lives of figures both well known – such as Queen Elizabeth, Captain Cook and Toussaint L'Ouverture – and previously more obscure – La Belinguere, Anne Bonny and Tupaia. Telling the tales of their lives as part of these global changes sheds new light on how we think of their biographies, and it offers a renewed perspective on the history of globalisation and on global history.

Questioning global history

Global history – or world history, or universal history – takes many forms. It has been around for a long time, but has gained a new life in the context of an expanding interest in processes of contemporary globalisation within both the social sciences and the wider media. Social theorists and media commentators have propounded views of a new globalised economy, society and culture emerging in the late twentieth century. At the same time those concerned with the past have engaged in efforts to put these contemporary forms of globalisation into a longer-term – and sometimes very long-term indeed – history of modes of global connection. Globalisation, it is stressed, has a past. It has a history. The world of increasing global connections and interconnections involving trade, violence and cultural encounter is not something unprecedented. What is going on now can be understood on the basis of what happened in the past. Yet giving globalisation a history also means recognising that it changes over time. There are different sorts of globalisation. There are different global histories that have to be set out, and there are comparisons that can be made to illuminate the implications of these histories.

Much global history needs to operate on the largest scales of space and time in order to make evident the connections and comparisons that it seeks to draw out. Its advantage is that it operates beyond the scale of the locality, the region or the nation-state, drawing comparisons between world regions, civilisations or empires, or tracing the connections made by warfare, long-distance trade or disease across oceans and continents. These entities and these connections arise, change and decline on the timescale of centuries. It must also be said that global history cannot avoid questions of geography. In seeking to be truly global, and in aiming to transcend the blinkers of the taken-for-granted geographies of smaller spatial scales, particularly that of the nation-state, historians have to redefine the geographies that they are working with. The two most prominent forms of global history – the tracing of connections and the making of comparisons – are both defined geographically. The argument that history proceeds through long-term webs of connection, either positive or negative, which produce economic, political, social and cultural change requires the recognition of both the 'political frontiers, spatial units and geographical boundaries' that are crossed, and the shape, scale and impact of the networks or webs of connection that do the crossing.[1] Comparative global history, by contrast, has to establish a new (or renewed) geographical basis for comparison. Once again, this is a geography that is beyond the scale of the nation-state. In one of the most celebrated cases, this involves comparing the economic histories of China and Europe over four centuries in order to demonstrate the relatively recent 'Great Divergence' between them, and its basis in the contingent circumstances of the availability of sources of energy rather than in long-term social or cultural structures.

The long chronologies and large scales of these forms of global history have often demanded big arguments too. A central debate has been over the 'Rise of the West', with global historians disagreeing over the reasons for the growing hegemony, achieved by the nineteenth century, of 'the West' over 'the rest'. Here global history necessarily intersects with, and even becomes, the history of empires, particularly the history of European empires and their rise and fall. Recent debates among imperial historians have taken a global perspective to debate the legacies of the British Empire across the globe, and its role in the making of the modern world. Interpretations of the 'rise of the West' have also been caught up in debates over the historical development of capitalism. For historians, social theorists and anthropologists seeking a central motor for global history and a central organising principle for global geography, the organisation of production, distribution and consumption through capital's profit-seeking forms of economic activity since at least the sixteenth century seems to fit the bill. As Karl Marx, the nineteenth century's keenest critic of capitalism, put it, drawing the histories of four continents together in characteristically dramatic and ironic terms, 'The discovery of silver and gold in America, the extirpation, enslavement and entombment in mines of the aboriginal population, the beginning of the conquest and looting of the East Indies, the turning of Africa into a warren for the commercial hunting of black-skins, signalised the rosy dawn of the era of capitalist production. These idyllic proceedings are the chief momenta of primitive accumulation. On their heels treads the commercial war of the European nations, with the globe for a theatre.'[2] Using these ideas it has been argued that global history can be told in terms of the development of a single capitalist world system whose changing geography of core, periphery and semi-periphery defines the fortunes of different parts of the globe.

Yet these big arguments are also unsubtle and unstable ones. The grand narratives both of the 'Rise of the West' and of singular economic explanations have been undermined in various ways. Their assumptions of singularity have been challenged by increased attention to the histories of other parts of the world – to the dependence of European development on broader Afro-Eurasian changes, and to the multiple origins of capitalism – and by a questioning of whether categories such as 'the West' or 'capitalism' are not just terms of convenience, used by people now and in the past for particular purposes, which obscure a multiplicity of differences. There are two connected implications of this: first, gathering in the different trajectories that can be traced in arenas as diverse as material life, warfare, religion, culture, gender and politics under the broad umbrella headings of 'the West' or 'capitalism' seems to do damage to the different ways in which they might be explained and used to write global histories. Second, seeking a single global historical geography – the West's 'rise' or the capitalist world system – that eventually operates across the whole globe seems to do equal damage to the range of spatial forms, relationships and connections that might be studied, so that new ways of describing these geographies need to be found.

This is, perhaps, unsurprising. After a flurry of apocalyptic or utopian pronouncements about contemporary globalisation as heralding 'the end of geography': either as the dream of a world in which distance no longer mattered, and local differentiation no longer stood in the way of global flows, or as the nightmare of a world made homogeneous by the domination of finance capital and American culture, a different picture has emerged. Contemporary globalisation is understood not as singular and undifferentiated but as partial, multiple and diverse. There are different relationships and varied geographies to be traced depending on where we look and what we look at. Economic analyses of trade and money look different from cultural analyses of religion or language. Different places and different people are involved in particular ways in globalising processes. The imperative is to trace the specific and distinct relationships and the forms of connection that are made over time and space.

For many, understanding global changes in the past – for example, tracing histories of migrations, the development of trade, the building of empires or the uses of technologies – is also a matter of the many geographies of globalisation. Thinking about this can usefully develop ideas of networks or webs of global connection that are built in various ways to link people, places, ideas and objects together in dynamic configurations. The advantage of thinking in this way is that it allows for multiple webs or networks to come into view, all with different shapes and different sorts of connections, rather than trying to construct a single big picture into which all must fit. It allows for many different ways of being global, or of doing globalisation. For instance, the set of connections formed by merchants trading over long distances could be quite different from that made by imperial administrators governing overseas territories, although they also intersected at some points. Each web or network can also be seen as connecting different sorts of things in different ways, with particular implications for those involved. They can also be seen to have meshed or clashed with each other in ways that might be either complementary or contradictory. This means that we can be attentive to complex processes of change over time, and also to the shifting geographies of where people are located within and between these different webs or networks. This produces much more nuanced historical geographies than ones that speak simply of core and periphery. Thinking in this way means that the accounts produced by those undertaking global history are themselves becoming increasingly diverse and differentiated. They may no longer speak of the whole world as one, or even of the whole world, but their intentions are no less global for all that.

Geographies of global connection

Global Lives aims to provide just this sort of history. The time-span that it covers is a long one, but at the same time it is also limited to the two and half centuries between around 1550 and about 1800 during which Britain became a global power with well-developed connections to Africa, the Americas, Asia and the Pacific. This means that the geographical scope of this global historical geography is a wide one, but one that is delimited by the focus on England's, and then Britain's, involvement with the wider world. These considerations of scale and scope mean that this is, therefore, a book in which the concerns of global history and the history of empire closely intersect. Quite simply, the British 'empire' became a global matter during this period. In the middle of the sixteenth century England had significant extra-territorial interests only in the British Isles, especially over Ireland, and some claims to pockets of territory in France. By the end of the eighteenth century an empire had been gained and then lost in North America (although Canada remained within the fold); a new empire was being created in large parts of India; there were imperial designs on the Pacific; and the vast wealth of the sugar-producing islands of the Caribbean was integrated into a network of Atlantic trade which shipped unprecedented numbers of enslaved Africans across the ocean on British ships.

This extensive empire was put together through warfare, primarily through those wars fought in the eighteenth century against the French and the Spanish. Britain was at war for much of that century. The balance of European power and the control over territories beyond Europe shifted between these great powers as a result of the War of the Spanish Succession (1701–1713), the War of the Austrian Succession (1740–1748), the Seven Years' War (1756–1763), the American War of Independence (1775–1783) and the Revolutionary and Napoleonic Wars (1793–1815). In general, and over time, power and territory shifted in favour of the British Empire. One of the main aims of the book is to show how this particular history and geography was created. By attending to the many forms of connection forged between Britain and other places it shows how new and often fragile relationships were established, how these links were made routine, and how they were integrated in a way that pulled Britain away from the margins and into the centre of a global network.

This requires a global historical geography, but *Global Lives* is only one of the many global historical geographies that might be written. It is left to others to use this account of Britain and the world to help provide a comparative history of European empires, or to evaluate Britain's global connections and forms of social, cultural and economic change in relation to what was happening elsewhere in the world or in other time periods. What this book aims to do is to set out the changing historical geographies of Britain's modes of global connection and engagement in these crucial centuries. Each chapter takes as its focus a particular process or set of processes explored through their changing geographies: Elizabethan England's forays into trade, empire and colonialism; settlement in early North America; trade with the East Indies; trade in the Atlantic world; the organisation of maritime labour; the changing forms of piracy; the transatlantic slave trade; plantation slavery in the Caribbean; the movement to abolish the slave trade; and the voyages of 'discovery' in the Pacific Ocean. These are judged to be the most significant processes and relationships involved in shaping Britain's engagement with the world. The intention has not been to cover all geographical areas, so there is nothing here, for example, on Britain's relationship with China or with northern Europe. Neither is the intention to provide a political or administrative history of the British Empire. There is no chapter on the American Revolution and its implications. Overall, in my choice of subject matter I have tried to combine the thematic and the geographical. I have sought out constellations, networks or configurations of people, ideas and things whose organisation and movements shaped Britain's changing place in and involvement with the rest of the world.

Each chapter sets out the shifting dimensions and shape of the history and geography of the processes under consideration. Each aims to outline the ways in which that form of global connection worked, and how it changed over time and space. Who was involved? What were their relationships to each other? How were places connected? How did relationships, connections and places change? Each chapter's intention is global, its geographical coverage stretching as far as the relationships discussed take it. Yet it is also partial, concerned with only one of the many webs or networks. What are being followed are particular forms of connection and engagement. This means that each chapter can easily be read separately: each is relatively self-contained. While the book as a whole is organised in a broadly chronological order the reader can switch back and forth between chapters, reading thematically as much as chronologically.

This focus on different modes of global connection also means that the forms of interpretation shift between chapters. Some are undoubtedly more focused on questions of economics, such as the discussion of the dynamics of merchant involvement in the Atlantic trades. Others pay more attention to social and cultural questions, such as the analysis of the organisation of maritime labour, or the questions of intercultural relationships in the settlement of North America. Another, the discussion of the abolition of the slave trade, centres on questions of politics. This is in recognition of the differences between the subject matter of each chapter, and what is required for understanding and interpretation in each one. There is an intention here to treat each process in parity with the others, not prioritising one over the other, but exploring how each works. Yet at the same time this differentiation of focus between the chapters is never exclusive. The overall intention to explain the historical geography of a particular form of global connection or engagement means that this cannot be simply an economic history, or a social, cultural or political one. This breadth of approach is also an outcome of the book's focus on the individual lives of those involved in these processes.

Telling global lives

The shift of global history away from singular 'master narratives' focused on the longest spans of time, the largest scales and the broadest comparisons opens up a variety of new questions. Once the emphasis is on the differentiation of global processes, networks and webs these forms of history are opened more fully to other modes of historical enquiry, such as the history of empire or the history of slavery. They are also opened up to the question of the actions of the people who were part of these processes. While it is important not simply to associate the large scale with the constraints imposed by political, economic and social structures, it is easier to see the effects of human action, and the effects on human action, once that global scale is understood as the on-going organisation of different and partial relationships, networks and webs. These modes of connection may stretch across vast areas, but they always do so via particular forms of action, perhaps the translation between languages, the filling in of an account book, the sailing of a ship or the signing of a petition. They also meet particular forms of action understood as collaboration or resistance.

What makes this book distinctive is that it gives due weight to the actions of all sorts of people in exploring these global histories and geographies. It does so by setting out the 'global lives' of over forty different individuals across the different chapters (those chosen are also summarised in the 'Brief lives' section at the beginning of the book, and displayed all together, against the background of Britain's history of warfare, on the chronological 'Life lines' diagram, p. xx). This biographical approach serves to give some life to the accounts presented in each chapter, first, by dramatising the issues for the reader by introducing them to specific individuals and, second, by animating the more abstract processes, histories and geographies through showing that they involved all those things that make up individual lives: personal relationships, difficult choices, the making of identities and the conditions and implications of action. Indeed, another main aim of this book is to emphasise the role of the actions – what we call the 'agency' – of all people involved in these global processes. People can and do make a difference for themselves and others.

Global Lives deploys the tools of biography to explore and understand global and imperial history. In many ways this is nothing new. The biographies of powerful and prominent figures have long been used to chart the histories of exploration and discovery, of empire building, of piracy and of global warfare. Some of these figures feature in this book too: Sir Walter Ralegh, the Elizabethan adventurer who is supposed to have brought tobacco and the potato back from the Americas; Sir William Jones, the 'father' of the Western study of Oriental languages; Captain William Kidd, the pirate hunter turned pirate; and Captain James Cook, whose three voyages charted the Pacific Ocean. Yet there is also a more recent trend amongst historians and others to tell a different set of life stories. This has emerged where global and imperial history meets social and cultural history. Here the lives of those who might otherwise have been left in obscurity, or have slipped back into it, are retold in great detail and situated within the broader sweep of events, and within the complex economic, political and cultural contexts of which they were a part. These are often dramatic stories, and some are retold in what follows: the New England preacher's daughter Eunice Williams's captivity among the native Americans in Kahnawake; the capture, enslavement and freedom of Little Ephraim Robin John and Ancona Robin Robin John, African slave-traders who became slaves; the everyday violence perpetrated by the Jamaican slave overseer Thomas Thistlewood; and the many travels of the former slave and political activist Olaudah Equiano. In turn, this form of life writing has produced new approaches to the biographies of the powerful and prominent too, moving away, as in recent treatments of Captain Cook, from individual motivation to careful anthropological con-textualisation. However, in contrast to all these biographies – old, new and renewed – which tell the world through a single life, *Global Lives* offers a variety of lives through which multiple worlds can be told.

The aim is to present the world as seen from many points of view: masters and slaves; men and women; indigenous people and newcomers; the powerful and those who helped or resisted them; the upholders of the law and its breakers. The intention is to use these lives to draw out the implications of different locations and positions within the networks and webs set out in accounting for the histories and geographies of global connection. It gives life to what were often the situations of many, or at least what shaped the situations of many, by focusing on a few. Alongside variety, the other aim is parity. Each life is given roughly the same amount of attention regardless of the prominence accorded to it in other histories or in the surviving sources. All of the chapters are then organised around four or five of these biographical sketches, each one of which is recounted under the heading 'The world of . . . '.

The chapters are, however, organised differently to make use of these lives to explore how individuals fitted into the global processes under consideration, and how their actions shaped them. A few examples will suffice. Chapter 2 offers a more historically grounded introduction to the book than does this one. It shows through the biographies of Walter Ralegh, John Hawkins (England's first slave-trader) and Hugh O'Neill (the Irish rebel lord) that they each responded to a different dimension of the policy towards the world beyond continental Europe produced by Elizabeth I's unique situation as a Protestant queen. In their responses, the tentative, partial, fragile and compromised beginnings of Britain's later global history can be seen. In turn, chapter 4 pairs an English and an Indian merchant who worked together in seventeenth-century Fort St George (later Madras) – Streynsham Master and Kasi Viranna – and then a British and an Indian lawyer – William Jones and Radhakanta Tarkavagisa – who also worked together in late eighteenth-century Bengal, to demonstrate the changing balance of power in India over two centuries of British involvement. Finally, chapter 5 selects merchants operating at different times and in different places in the Atlantic world – William Freeman and Richard Oswald in London, Robert Keayne in Boston and La Belinguere at the mouth of the Gambia River – to show the similarities and differences between their attempts to profit from increasingly transoceanic trades.

Therefore, in different ways in different chapters the intention is always to use these lives to draw comparisons between those in different positions. Sometimes it is to demonstrate the differences between people, such as the contrast drawn in chapter 10 between the different political positions taken on the abolition of the slave trade (and of slavery itself) by the political organiser Thomas Clarkson, the writer Hannah More, the ex-slave Olaudah

Equiano and the leader of a successful slave revolt on the island of Saint Domingue, Toussaint L'Ouverture. In other chapters it is to emphasise what are perhaps unexpected similarities, such as the parallel processes of navigation, discovery and the representation of unfamiliar situations being undertaken in the Pacific and beyond by Captain Cook, William Hodges (the artist on Cook's second voyage), Tupaia (the navigator and high priest from the Society Islands) and Mai (the first Polynesian to visit London).

Overall, the benefit of understanding global processes through the lens of biography, and of understanding individual lives in the context of global and imperial history, is the focus it provides on the role of human action in the making of the world. In each life, in each instance of 'The world of . . .', individuals are seen acting in situations that, in varying degrees, are not of their own choosing. This may be a matter, as described in chapter 9, of how enslaved women such as Sarah Affir got by on Caribbean plantations, or how the slave-owners such as Sir Charles Price tried to make that same land, labour and capital pay. It may also be a matter, as related in the same chapter, of Thomas Thistlewood's decisions to use violence to make the plantation system work, or of the slave rebel Tacky's use of violence against it. The conditions of action, and its potential effects and implications, look different from different locations, and can be told via different lives. For example, the interplay of freedom, oppression and exploitation in the world of maritime labour depends upon the differences between Royal Navy vessels and merchant ships, the differences between black sailors and white sailors and the differences between men and women. The lives on ships and on quaysides, of Edward Barlow, William Spavens, Briton Hammon, John Jea and Essa Morrison, as told in chapter 6, aim to demonstrate that there are actions and choices even under the strictest constraints. Restoring this sense of agency within the big picture of global and imperial history allows the rewriting of important parts of that history. For example, the discussion of Pocahontas and John Smith in early seventeenth-century Virginia revisits a story told many times as a romance, but the purpose here is to emphasise the political nature of the Amerindian woman's actions in the context of the colonial encounter. One of the central aims of *Global Lives* is, therefore, to demonstrate that everyone is trying to have an effect by acting in and on their world and the worlds of others.

There are, of course, dangers and difficulties in adopting this biographical approach to global history. *Global Lives* has to find a way between the opposite perils of tokenism, using particular individuals to stand only for generic positions or types rather than for themselves, and exceptionalism, the danger that those individuals who left enough evidence of themselves in the surviving sources are so singular that they cannot be used to stand for the lives of others. Whether it succeeds or not readers will have to judge for themselves. The attempt has certainly been made to illuminate particular issues using particular lives. This has meant finding, for example, a woman pirate (Anne Bonny in chapter 7) or a particular slave in revolt upon a slave ship (in chapter 8) to set against the other lives told in those chapters, and to open up a different facet of the story. Yet the attempt has also been made to offer up the details of those lives, as far as they are known, and even when no name can be found, to show how that particular person made, inhabited and lived out the position they found themselves in. It is perhaps too glib to say that everyone is both typical and exceptional, but there is some truth in it too.

Other difficulties are presented by the source material from which these biographies are written. Any work of history is dependent upon the creation of some sort of record at the time, and then the subsequent survival of that material down to the present so that it can be put to new uses. At each step the making or survival of source material is more or less likely depending upon who or what the subject matter is. Men and women, the rich and the poor, the literate and the illiterate, property-owners and those owned as property differed in the degree to which their lives, actions or words were recorded. When elements of their lives were actually written down rather than just remembered as stories these different sorts of people had very different levels of control over what was recorded about them. They also figured in different sorts of documents which included different degrees of detail. Overall, the lives of the more powerful can often be more easily documented than the lives of the less powerful, both because more was written about them at the time and because more of it either survives in private collections or has been kept in public archives. Someone somewhere had to have a reason to value that material and the means necessary to keep it safe so that the memory of what it contained would be preserved for future use.[3] Yet, as the biographies presented here show, it is possible to reconstruct the lives, or at least parts of the lives, of a very wide range of people, even from several centuries ago. Sometimes this is a matter of the routine recording of everyday events from which biographies can be drawn out, such as, for example, the annual accounting of the enslaved workers on a Caribbean plantation or the recording of judgments passed in London's criminal courts. Sometimes it is a matter of exceptional cases drawing attention to themselves: the life of a woman pirate, or the autobiography of an African written by himself in the cause of the abolition of the slave trade.

Reconstructing this range of biographies has, therefore, involved drawing on a wide variety of different sorts of sources, and on other scholars who have used those sources. Wherever possible the aim has been to use sources that are readily available in printed form or online, so that the short accounts presented here can easily be followed up on by those who want to fill the stories out further. For some of these biographies the sources would fill library shelves; for others there is barely a paragraph in a letter or a legal document. The response has been to recognise that no life can be told in full. For some that has meant spinning a story from the little that we do know. For others it has meant careful selection of what to tell from the wealth of material available. There are also great differences in the nature of the source material, and this has to be negotiated too. There are the differences between the everyday and the exceptional. There are also differences between whether sources purport to offer the direct voice of the subject or not. For some of those whose lives are set out here there are extensive collections of letters, journals, published accounts or autobiographies in which they discuss their own actions, and sometimes their motives. Some lives, in contrast, appear to us only through the words of others, either sympathetic or unsympathetic, sometimes with motives and intentions attributed and either criticised or lauded, and sometimes entirely ignored.

There are obvious but difficult-to-resolve dangers in taking any of these sources at face value. What purposes did the buccaneer William Dampier's own journal serve in establishing his distance from the world of piracy? How far can we credit the accounts of Bartholomew Roberts and Anne Bonny that appear in the part fact, part fiction of Captain Charles Johnson's *History of the Pyrates*? How far can we reconstruct the motives and intentions, let alone the emotions, of the slave-trader Walter Prideaux in chapter 8 from a set of account books and ledgers, or those of the go-between John Sassamon (chapter 3) from fragmented legal and governmental sources? Again, the approach taken is shaped by the main aims of this book. On the one hand, putting these lives – however well documented they may be – in the broader context of the variety of forms of global connection allows the 'everyday' elements of the 'exceptional' lives to be drawn out, and sets limits on assertions of agency, motive and intention. On the other, considering these lives in terms of the agency of all the people involved in these global processes focuses on the singular locations of those only dimly available to us through fragmented and often unrevealing sources, and suggests the need to reconstruct their active role in trying to shape their circumstances. Doing both means that these brief biographies give equal weight and attention to the lives of an array of people that the documentary record has treated very differently.

This eclecticism and breadth of coverage mean that *Global Lives* is primarily a work that draws upon and draws together the work of others across a wide interdisciplinary field. The discussions of the histories and geographies of the processes in each chapter are drawn from the excellent recent work in global history and imperial history that has appeared in increasing volume over the past ten or twenty years. The lives discussed have also often been those that have featured in this work. I am deeply indebted to all the works that I have drawn upon and I hope to have accurately represented with my broad brush what others have presented through painstaking depictions based on careful archival work. I have not, however, taken it as my duty to set out the debates between scholars that each of these chapters raises, and to which more specialist work responds. These debates will easily be found by those who wish to discover more through the further reading at the end of each chapter. My intention has been to write for those considering Britain's changing place in the early modern world for the first time. I have aimed to provide an account which combines the broad sweep of a varied history and geography with the intimate detail of an array of differentiated and contrasting biographies. It stresses the ways in which global connections, networks and webs changed, solidified and consolidated, shifting Britain from a position of marginality to one of centrality by the end of the eighteenth century. It also emphasises the many forms of human action that brought those changes about. By combining global historical geographies with these multiple biographies, *Global Lives* aims to breathe some new life into the history and geography of globalisation.

Further reading

For contrasting forms of global history, see William H. McNeil (1963) *The Rise of the West: A History of the Human Community* (University of Chicago Press, Chicago) and Kenneth Pomerantz (2000) *The Great Divergence: China, Europe, and the Making of the Modern World* (Princeton University Press, Princeton). For Marxist perspectives, see Immanuel Wallerstein (1974) *The Modern World System I: Capitalist Agriculture and the Origins of the European World-Economy in the Sixteenth Century* (Academic Press, London) and Eric R. Wolf (1982) *Europe and the People Without*

History (University of California Press, Berkeley). There is a useful general discussion of the current state of global history in the first issue of the *Journal of Global History* 1 (2006). For quite different ways of renewing the study of the history of the British Empire, see Niall Ferguson (2003) *Empire: How Britain Made the Modern World* (Allen Lane, London) and Kathleen Wilson (ed.) (2004) *A New Imperial History: Culture, Identity and Modernity in Britain and the Empire, 1660–1840* (Cambridge University Press, Cambridge). The renewed use of biographical approaches in imperial and global history can be seen in John Demos (1996) *The Unredeemed Captive: A Family Story from Early America* (Papermac, London), Randy L. Sparks (2004) *The Two Princes of Calabar: An Eighteenth-Century Atlantic Odyssey* (Harvard University Press, Cambridge, Mass.), Trevor Burnard (2004) *Mastery, Tyranny, and Desire: Thomas Thistlewood and His Slaves in the Anglo-Jamaican World* (University of North Carolina Press, Chapel Hill), Vincent Carretta (2005) *Equiano, the African: Biography of a Self-Made Man* (University of Georgia Press, Athens), David Lambert and Alan Lester (eds.) (2006) *Colonial Lives Across the British Empire: Imperial Careering in the Long Nineteenth Century* (Cambridge University Press, Cambridge) and Linda Colley (2007) *The Ordeal of Elizabeth Marsh: A Woman in World History* (HarperCollins, London).

Notes

1 Patrick O'Brien (2006) 'Historiographical traditions and modern imperatives for the restoration of global history', *Journal of Global History* 1 p. 4.
2 Quoted in Immanuel Wallerstein (1974) *The Modern World System I: Capitalist Agriculture and the Origins of the European World-Economy in the Sixteenth Century* (Academic Press, London) p. xv.
3 Miles Ogborn (2003) 'Finding historical data', in Nicholas Clifford and Gill Valentine (eds.) *Key Methods in Geography* (Sage, London) pp. 101–115.

2 | The Elizabethan world

It was during the reign of Queen Elizabeth, between 1558 and 1603, that England stepped – or rather, sailed – on to the global stage. Yet the English did so as minor players in a world which, in those parts where Europeans mattered at all, it was the empires of Spain and Portugal that were important. Looking to the west from the Iberian peninsula, the Spanish and Portuguese had been driven by the crisis of the feudal economy to push further into the Atlantic from the middle of the fifteenth century onwards in search of new lands and fishing grounds. In the process they had encountered, conquered and settled the island groups of the Canaries and the Azores. Then, with the voyage of Christopher Columbus in 1492, the Kingdom of Castile's representatives happened not, as anticipated, upon a route to the riches of the East gained by sailing west across Atlantic but on a whole continent new to early modern Europeans. The subsequent establishment of a Spanish empire in the Americas was built upon the violent conquests of Mexico (1521) and Peru (1533) for the king of Spain and the Catholic church, as well as the colonisation of the larger islands of the western Caribbean – Cuba, Hispaniola and Jamaica. Spain's empire was devoted to shipping Mexican gold and Peruvian silver back to Europe in huge annual treasure fleets (figure 2.1).

This New World wealth was used to buy, among other things, luxury goods from Africa and the East supplied by the Portuguese. The ships of King Henry the Navigator and his successors had reached Guinea by the 1440s, and by the late fifteenth century had settled islands and established trading relations along the West African coast. They traded for gold, ivory and pepper and had, by 1444, begun exporting African slaves to supply labour to their American empire in Brazil and to the Spanish in the Caribbean. By 1487 Bartholomeu Dias had rounded the Cape of Good Hope and entered the Indian Ocean, and by 1557 the Portuguese empire had established trading posts from the Cape to Macao, and demanded that all shipping pay for *cartazas* (or licences) to sail the oceans over which it claimed control. The Estado da India, an arm of the Portuguese state, had also challenged the long-established overland trade in pepper, spices, textiles and porcelain across the Eurasian landmass by bringing these commodities directly back

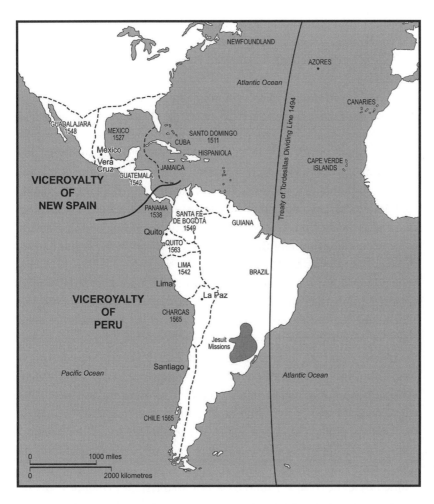

Figure 2.1 The Iberian empires in the Americas. The areas claimed by the Spanish and Portuguese empires were divided by a line established in the Treaty of Tordesillas in 1494. The Spanish empire in the Americas was divided into two viceroyalties which were themselves organised as a series of *audiencia*s.

around the Cape. By the sixteenth century, then, it seemed that the Iberians had things covered. In 1494 Castile-Aragón and Portugal had signed a treaty at Tordesillas that divided the world between their two crowns. The lands to the west of a line drawn 370 leagues west of the Cape Verde Islands were claimed by Spain. The lands to the east (which included much of Brazil) went to Portugal. They had developed their overseas interests along those duopolistic lines and, when Portugal was annexed by Spain in 1580, and the crowns were unified upon the head of King Philip II, it seemed that the Spanish idea of a universal monarchy might actually be realised.

Looked at in other ways, however, this world was full of holes. Europe was wracked by religious wars prompted by the Protestant challenge to the Catholic church. The broad claims to control made by the Spanish and Portuguese, based as they were on their own treaties and the bulls and donations of various popes, were neither accepted by others nor able to be enforced in practice. European activity in the Atlantic world, and at least in maritime Asia if not inland, had opened up borderlands and unstable frontiers where things were in flux. In these places, for all involved, possessions and loyalties were only temporary, alliances were contingent, and support and supplies to colonists, traders and officials could not be guaranteed. Into these gaps, along these frontiers and exploiting these weaknesses came adventurers from France, the Netherlands and England who sought to carve out some profit for themselves from the flows of treasure and goods through the veins of the Iberian empires.

The English were late-comers to all this. In 1558, when Elizabeth was crowned queen, the vast bulk of English maritime activity was in European waters and the only overseas possessions to which the new queen laid claim were Ireland and the Channel Islands. Earlier monarchs had involved themselves with long-distance exploration, but Henry VII's sponsoring of John Cabot's voyages from Bristol to Newfoundland in 1497 and 1498 did not produce precious metals or new trades and colonies. English merchants, where they did see opportunities further afield, were primarily focused on the Oriental trades. This had led to the establishment of the Muscovy Company (1555), the Venice and Turkey Companies (merged to form the Levant Company in 1592) – which brought cotton and silk, carpets, sweet wines, oils and currants from the eastern Mediterranean – and finally the English East India Company (1600). The many sixteenth-century attempts to find a northwest or northeast passage were attempts to get round the Spanish via an Arctic route to China. Since this proved impossible, other adventurers operated in the interstices of Iberian control. English voyages to Guinea from the 1530s founded no permanent trading posts and relied upon renegade Portuguese pilots and runaway Portuguese traders. Francis Drake's circumnavigation of the globe between 1577 and 1580 began as an attempt to both plunder and trade with Spanish settlements on South America's Pacific coast, and continued via a cruise through the islands of the East Indies, promising English trade and military support against Spain. However, it was in and around the Caribbean where the Spanish empire was at its richest and most vulnerable. It was here that Englishmen such as Drake, Walter Ralegh and John Hawkins sought to profit both through the undeclared war with Spain waged outside Europe from the 1560s, and in the open war from 1585 to 1604. Overall, it is the case that all the Elizabethan innovations in overseas activity – the English East India Company, involvement in the transatlantic slave trade, the beginnings of settlement in the Americas, and voyages to the Pacific (the so-called Spanish lake) – were attempts to try to get something out of a world dominated by Spain.

This chapter sets the scene for the more specific studies of particular processes and regions that follow by offering a historical introduction that sits alongside the thematic introduction presented in chapter 1. It shows, through the varied lives of Hawkins, Ralegh and Hugh O'Neill, that these tentative early steps in the making of England's new relationships with the rest of the world need to be understood as a product of the particular circumstances and concerns of the reign of Queen Elizabeth.

The world of Queen Elizabeth I

Elizabeth was born in 1533, the daughter of Henry VIII and Anne Boleyn (figure 2.2). It was Henry's desire for a son that had led him to divorce Catherine of Aragon to marry Anne – separating the English church from Rome in the process – and then prompted Anne's execution when she failed to provide a male heir. It therefore seemed unlikely that the young Elizabeth would ever succeed to the throne. However, after the brief reigns of Mary I, who was Catherine's daughter, and Edward VI, the son of Henry's third wife Jane Seymour, were cut short by illness, it was Elizabeth who became queen against the claims of her Catholic cousin Mary, Queen of Scots. Despite the later reputation of her reign, and despite Edmund Spenser's styling of her in *The Faerie Queene* (1596) as 'Queene of England Fraunce and Ireland and of Virginia', Elizabeth's primary concern was not with building an overseas empire, but with securing her position as queen and ensuring the security of her realm within the power struggles of western Europe.[1] Those concerns did, however, give a particular shape to England's engagement with the world beyond its borders.

Elizabeth needed to manage England's place within the shifting balance of power between France and the Habsburg empire ruled from Spain. The complex machinations of diplomacy, warfare and dynastic marriage proposals were all deployed towards this end. Initially, France was considered to be the primary threat. The two countries were at war in 1557–1559, and

Figure 2.2 Queen Elizabeth I. In this portrait, commissioned by a courtier who had returned to the queen's favour, the monarch is depicted as a powerful and commanding woman. The elaborate richness of her dress and jewellery speak of her wealth and importance. She is shown standing upon, and ruling over, a map of England and Wales against a stormy background.

Elizabeth considered marriage proposals from Philip II of Spain, who had previously been married to Mary I (although strictly limited in his powers as consort), and from an Austrian Habsburg archduke. Gradually, and through a tense period of isolation for England in Europe, Spain came to be considered the main danger. As relationships with the Habsburg empire deteriorated during the 1570s Elizabeth negotiated, more or less seriously, marriage alliances with, in turn, the duc d'Anjou and duc d'Alençon. The threats of war, invasion and regime change were very real and shaped international relations close to home. Elizabeth's war with Scotland (1559–1560) aimed to counter French influence in Scottish politics (what was called the 'auld alliance'), and Catholic Ireland was constantly seen as an opportunity for Spain. As the vast Armada fleet sailed towards the English Channel in 1588, intending to ferry the duke of Alba's army across the narrow seas from the Spanish Netherlands, the fear in England of an invasion was very real indeed.

These concerns could never be separated from the other big question facing Elizabeth: that of religion. This also combined domestic and international politics. The Protestant Reformation and the Catholic Counter-Reformation were continually reshaping the religious map of Europe, and sparked a series of bloody religious wars throughout the sixteenth century. England itself was divided between the old church and the new. On Elizabeth's accession to the throne it was unclear what form the religious settlement would take. Her attempt to tread a careful path between extremes was, perhaps inevitably, rejected both by 'the papish sect' and by those who saw her compromise as 'a cloaked papistry or a mingle-mangle'.[2] Elizabeth certainly did not favour a Protestant holy war against Catholicism, and was perhaps even more wary of strident Protestantism itself. Yet, events such as Pope Pius V's bull *Regnans in excelsis* (1570), which excommunicated Elizabeth and denied her legitimacy as queen in the context of a pro-Marian conspiracy, and the reaction of Puritans both inside and outside parliament to such events made religion a matter of life and death in England.

Elizabeth ruled through her Privy Council and through the court. Politics was a very personal matter of intimate connections based on friendship and favour, and of the management of patronage and interest. The queen had her powerful councillors and her favourites – men such as William Cecil (Lord Burghley), Robert Dudley (the earl of Leicester), Walter Ralegh and Robert Devereux (the second earl of Essex) – whose networks of political patronage shaped access to power and influence. Lands, titles and rights to control various revenue streams (such as the customs duty on sweet wines) could be distributed to those in favour. The monarch's own revenue was only around £300,000 per year in the 1590s, so resources had to be carefully husbanded. Wars and other overseas ventures were an expensive business that could not be entered into lightly.

Like all monarchs Elizabeth faced important questions of policy and serious challenges to her legitimacy as ruler. Unlike most others she also had to face the question of her right to rule as a woman. Mary I had been the only other English queen since the troubled reign of Matilda in the twelfth century. Despite Elizabeth's overall popularity there were always those who questioned her rule. This came both from the educated pens of men such as John Knox, whose *First Blast of the Trumpet Against the Monstrous Regiment of Women* (1558) greeted her accession, and the mouths of those such as Joan Lyster of Cobham who argued in 1585 that 'the [Privy] Counsayle makes a foole of the Queenes Majestie, and bycause she is but a woman she owght not to be governor of a Realm'.[3] Her position as a queen in a patriarchal society posed a general problem of authority. More specifically, her failure to marry and to provide an heir of her body, and her refusal even to name her successor (a sensible move given the way that might divide the kingdom), provoked concern over the succession and fears of civil war. These anxieties were often projected on to the queen herself. Despite her public image as the Virgin Queen, there was much malicious gossip about her and her favourites, and the heirs she might have given birth to and concealed.

All of this gave a particular shape to Elizabethan overseas endeavours. They were certainly subordinate to European power politics both strategically and financially. If English ships had to be kept at home to protect the coasts from the Spanish then this came at the cost of Atlantic voyages. Unless overseas ventures were likely to yield a quick and tangible return in captured bullion, customs revenue or power at sea, they were of little interest to the crown. As a result, although Elizabeth invested in such ventures, and sometimes reaped substantial profits, she did so as one (albeit important) investor among many. The governance of the ventures was organised via the familiar mechanisms of patronage and clientage, and the pursuit of private profit. Whether the networks were mercantile or courtly or both, England's colonial and commercial adventures were in the hands of private adventurers with little interest in long-term planning. Indeed, their immediate interests meant that attempts at trade and colonisation meshed with, and easily mutated into, quests for plunder when the rewards from that were greatest. In general, therefore, Elizabethan England's overseas ventures were tentative and ill funded and often ended in failure; they had multiple and contradictory objectives; they were focused on short-term profit seeking; and they relied upon violence. What follows in this chapter shows how these facts shaped the lives and worlds of John Hawkins, Walter Ralegh and Hugh O'Neill. The rest of the book traces the ways in which these uncertain beginnings became something more solid and enduring.

The English at sea

The nature of England's involvement with the sea, and with overseas ventures, in the early sixteenth century meant that the distinction between the Royal Navy and the merchant navy was far less clear than it would later become. The Elizabethan navy, counted in terms of ships owned by the queen, was very small. She owned only twenty-five ships of various sizes and seven smaller pinnaces among the fleet of 182 ships that faced the Armada in 1588. The Navy Royal's primary role was to defend England's coasts and to wage war in west European waters. Royal ships rarely sailed to the south and west of the Azores, and did not operate in the Indian Ocean until the eighteenth century. Moreover, in any battle fleet, royal ships always represented the minority of vessels until the middle of the seventeenth century. The bulk of ships were private vessels going to war in pursuit of profit. Indeed, the organisation of Elizabethan sea power was a public–private partnership right to its very core. The Admiralty officers – both those in the administration of the navy and its commanding admirals – were also merchants, ship-owners, ship-builders and naval contractors who built, sold and lent ships to the queen as well as kitting them out with guns, ropes, provisions and men. Wars, particularly the sea war with Spain from 1585, were pursued by licensing 'privateers', private vessels authorised by the crown to fight and capture enemy shipping for a share of the value of those ships and their cargoes (see chapter 7). Privateering attracted investment from landed gentlemen, and even the queen herself, since such ventures smacked of martial glory and national service. But they also promised substantial rewards and were carefully organised, often by merchants who traded overseas, as hardheaded business ventures. In the Atlantic, and particularly in the Caribbean, the war against Spain became a private affair pursued by men, such as Francis Drake, who plundered cities and captured ships. It was also pursued by merchants formerly in the Iberian trades whose ships had been captured by the Spanish in 1585 and who saw privateering as a way of continuing to supply luxury goods to north European consumers. In the East, it was the case that private enterprises such as the East India Company, given a royal charter by Elizabeth, took on the military and diplomatic functions that the state could not provide at so great a distance. The Company fought battles against Portuguese fleets and entered into diplomatic negotiations with Eastern rulers. Whether to the west or to the east, English merchants entered these trades as interlopers on the monopolies that the Iberians claimed. As a result, English merchant vessels were armed and willing to use violence, and their commanders were always ready to divert a peaceful commercial voyage into one of plunder.

These changing uses were reflected in the ships and armaments with which they were pursued, and the skills needed to deploy them. Before the 1570s the Navy Royal mainly consisted of galleys with one big gun in the bows (and sometimes the stern) which would be expected to fire one round per battle, and needed to make it count. English ships were either small and unspecialised or large and unwieldy, with top-heavy castles at the bows and stern. They were dangerous and difficult to handle, especially on the deep oceans, being heavily dependent upon favourable winds. The new ships that replaced them were streamlined galleons with an efficient sail plan and long, low gun decks. The use of these ships increasingly far afield meant that English masters had to learn from their Iberian counterparts the skills of navigation by the sun and stars, and the use of charts, rather than relying on the 'coasting' that had previously served them well enough. These masters also took on more powers over their men on more heavily manned ships, decreasing the degree of consultation with the crew over the course and duration of voyages (see chapter 6). Finally, there were advances in gunnery. By the 1580s improvements in iron founding had brought the price of heavy guns down so substantially that they were no longer the preserve of kings and princes. Overall, therefore, faster, more manoeuvrable ships which could spend longer at sea, with cheaper ordnance and skilled masters, made England more powerful on the oceans than on land. English ships were ready to fight and, commanded by men such as John Hawkins, they contributed significantly to the rising level of maritime violence across the sixteenth century.

The world of John Hawkins

John Hawkins was born in Plymouth in 1532, the son of a merchant, sea captain and ship owner (figure 2.3). He had killed another man, a barber named White, in a fight by the time he was twenty but was cleared of murder. With his elder brother William he put his time and effort into developing the family shipping business. Together they traded with France, engaged as privateers during the Anglo-French war of 1557–1558, and built connections with substantial merchant families in the Canary Islands, trading textiles for sugar. Hawkins was becoming an accomplished ship commander and a well-connected merchant, and it was upon this expertise and these connections that he launched a series of three trading voyages in

Figure 2.3 John Hawkins. This portrait, published after Hawkins's death, celebrates in English and Latin his achievements against enemies at sea and his work in naval administration. Dressed in the clothing of a gentleman he is said to be the very symbol of 'Advauncement by dilligence'.

the 1560s. These voyages were novel in that they sought for the first time to use English ships to transport enslaved Africans to the Caribbean. This meant defying both the Portuguese on the Guinea coast where the cargo was gathered and the Spanish in the West Indies where the slaves were to be sold. Each of Hawkins's three voyages was on a larger scale than the previous one, as investors saw the profits that could be made selling people. The first voyage, with three small ships, was backed by naval administrators – including Hawkins's father-in-law William Gonson, and substantial London merchants, Sir Lionel Ducket and Sir Thomas Lodge – who were already active in the Guinea gold trade. The second voyage attracted investment from three privy councillors, including Robert Dudley, and from the queen herself who allowed one of her largest ships, the 700-ton *Jesus of Lubeck*, to be chartered for the voyage and permitted Hawkins to fly the royal ensign. The influential Ponte family of the Canary Islands also contributed their share. The third voyage combined the national and the mercantile even further, with the queen continuing as an investor and contributor of two ships, Hawkins styling himself as a naval commander, Francis Drake in command of the other ship and William Cecil masterminding the planning of what was a heavily armed trading venture and a warning to Spain.

Trading on the Guinea coast combined barter, intimidation and violence in interactions with both the Portuguese merchants and the African rulers. With no established base and no secure local contacts there could be no real basis for trust on any side. Hawkins certainly took ships and goods from the Portuguese by force. He also landed armed men to take slaves, and fought with local people armed with deadly poisoned arrows. These contests were not, however, simply loaded in the Europeans' favour. At a town called Bymba, Hawkins's men barely escaped back to their boats. They had taken ten slaves, but at the cost of seven of their own men killed and another thirty injured. Another strategy was to forge provisional alliances. On the third voyage, Hawkins joined with two local kings, Sheri and Yhoma, on the coast of Sierra Leone to fight their enemies Sacina and Setecama, having agreed to divide the resulting captives between them. The successful assault, with Hawkins's men using their boats to attack from the river, yielded several hundred prisoners. But when the African rulers took the lion's share there was little Hawkins could do about it.

Yet Hawkins was able to fill his ships with African men and women. He was also able to do so sufficiently cheaply that the deaths of around a quarter of them during the horrendous eight weeks chained below decks at sea between Africa and the Americas did not hamper the profitability of the voyage for him and his investors. In part this was a matter of supply and demand in the Spanish Indies. Hawkins sought out ports at the edges of Spanish control, those that were less well supplied from Seville, and where he could expect the demand for his human cargo to be strong, and the will to abide by the letter of Spanish imperial law correspondingly weak. In this way he profited from small ports such as those on the more isolated north coast of Hispaniola, and Borburata in what is now Venezuela.

All of this was a direct challenge to the power and profits of Spain. As a result, Hawkins used various strategies: he stretched the truth, saying that he had been blown off course and needed to sell some slaves to cover his expenses; he colluded with Spanish merchants against Spanish local officials, by arranging to trade by night, or to take them 'hostage' so that they could claim to have been forced to trade; and he collaborated with Spanish local officials against their superiors, trading under the cover of ransom payments and the reimbursal of damages. It was, therefore, only when a storm during the third voyage (1567–1569) forced his fleet into San Juan de Ulúa, the port town for the substantial settlement of Vera Cruz on the Mexican coast, and when his fleet was joined by a sizeable Spanish fleet carrying Martín Enríquez, the recently appointed viceroy of New Spain, that things went awry. Their initial stand-off collapsed into a battle in the harbour, and Hawkins, having been deserted by Drake, was lucky to escape in a badly overloaded ship. He had most of his valuables but insufficient food. He also left many dead men in the harbour; others were taken prisoner; and still more died on the return voyage as supplies ran out and they were reduced to eating rats, the parrots they had caught as pets and pieces of leather. In justifying his actions back in England, Hawkins wrote to Cecil that 'yf I shold wryt of all our calamytes I ame sure a volome as great as the byble wyll scarcly suffice'.[4]

Hawkins's actions were guided by the changing relationship between England and Spain in the 1560s and 1570s, and they also shaped that relationship. In 1568 Philip II warned his English ambassador Guerau de Spes of 'the English pirate John Hawkins, who had gone through the Indies committing great robberies and destruction'.[5] Like Drake, Hawkins contributed to Anglo-Spanish enmity. Yet things were more complicated than that. Hawkins wanted to gain freedom for his men who were still held captive by Spain after the battle at San Juan de Ulúa. His religious affiliations were also unclear, and that meant that his loyalties were in doubt. In the early 1570s he was certainly implicated in a Spanish plot to depose Queen Elizabeth and to put Mary, Queen of Scots, on the throne. There was an agreement for him to use his sixteen ships in the service of Spain. He certainly reported his dealings with the Spanish to Cecil when the time came, but he also reported much to de Spes too. Whether he was acting as a double agent, whether agreements had been made in his name without his consent or whether he was simply keeping his options open, there was a suspicion of treachery around him that was not finally removed until the defeat of the Spanish Armada in 1588.

Hawkins's role in this crucial event in the relations between England and Spain was a significant one. It was also a double one. He was a member of the war council and served as the commander of 20 ships in Lord Howard's fleet of 120. Indeed, he owned three of those ships. He was knighted for his part in the battles that had harassed the Armada along the English Channel and finally – along with substantial help from the winds, the tides and the panic sown by English fireships – dispersed the Spanish fleet off Calais. Yet, more importantly, he had helped prepare a navy that could do the job. As treasurer of marine causes from 1577 he demonstrated himself to be a highly competent administrator. He was certainly criticised for profiting from his post, and he often saw it as more trouble than it was worth, yearning to return to a sea command. However, he created the conditions within which the lower, faster English ships designed by the royal shipwrights Peter Pett and Matthew Baker could transform the Elizabethan navy. By 1588 two-thirds of the navy's ships had been built on the new design. In addition, he pioneered new methods of sheathing, introduced the chain pump and established a social insurance scheme for mariners (the 'Chatham Chest'). He also formulated plans for the defence of the realm via a privateering fleet that would pay for itself by blockading Spanish shipping between Spain and the Azores.

Fittingly, Hawkins died on board ship in the Caribbean in 1595. He was sixty-three years old. Unfortunately, this final voyage was marred by confused aims – Elizabeth kept changing her mind – and conflicts of authority. Splitting command between the impetuous Drake and the pragmatic Hawkins was a recipe for disaster, and they could rarely agree. They also found that new Spanish fortifications put plunder out of their reach. Things had changed between the 1570s and the mid-1590s, and the expedition was abandoned when Drake died too.

Hawkins's world was a world of maritime, mercantile and political pragmatics. He was an effective merchant who knew how to deploy the stick as well as the carrot. He was a well-organised bureaucrat who, in the particular circumstances of the Elizabethan navy, was able to work for his own profit and to make a more effective fighting force. He was a political operator who could form alliances with African kings, Spanish officials and privy councillors. He may have been caught out once or twice but he was a survivor. His was a world of profit and loss, and in exploiting that he had to be able to read the economic and political balance sheet of Spanish power. He did that as a Plymouth ship-owner's son would. It was for others to take a more scholarly interest in what lay beyond Europe's shores.

Encountering the world

What did medieval and early modern European scholars know of the rest of the world, and how did that shape their practical and intellectual engagement with it? The key foundations of European knowledge were Christianity

Figure 2.4 The world before America. Andrea Bianco's map, 1436. Europe, Africa and Asia are shown as a single landmass surrounded by a world ocean, and as home to disparate peoples inhabiting different climates. The Indies, here the site of earthly paradise, are due east of Europe.

and the Renaissance rediscovery of classical learning. Geographical knowledge was based on classical writings, especially those of Ptolemy and Strabo. Ptolemy's *Geography* was a first-century Alexandrian compilation which was translated into Latin in the early fifteenth century and printed in 1475, and which passed on a model of the world as a globe whose land masses were divided into three continents – Europe, Asia and Africa – surrounded by a world ocean. The globe was also divided from top to bottom into climatic or environmental zones defined as frigid, temperate and equatorial. Medieval Christians had, in turn, conceived this as coextensive with Christ's body and as symbolically centred on the holy city of Jerusalem. Each continent was associated with one of Noah's sons and the earthly paradise was located to the east in the 'Indies' (figure 2.4). These sources were supplemented by the writings of European explorers such as Marco Polo, who had travelled into Asia from the thirteenth century and left accounts of the wonders they had encountered.

These works and these ideas directly shaped the voyages of exploration. Christopher Columbus, a humble weaver's son who was born in Genoa in 1451 and who worked as a book-seller and mapmaker in the 1480s, read Ptolemy's *Geography* as suggesting that the distance between Europe and Asia was one that could be traversed by a ship going westwards across the Atlantic. He is said to have annotated his copy with the words 'every ocean can be navigated'.[6] But such a reading of the ancients could not be simply taken as truth. Others disagreed, arguing that the distance was too great ever to be crossed. Indeed, the uncertainties of geographical knowledge left a great deal of room for speculation and debate over the size of the globe and the disposition of land and sea on its surface. For example, the Florentine cosmographer Paolo del Pozzo Toscanelli argued in 1474 that the distance across the ocean was 5,000 miles (Columbus disagreed), but that the journey could be broken either at the island of 'Antillia' or at Chipangu (Japan) which Marco Polo had said lay 1,500 miles from China.[7] Columbus, who had read an early printed edition of Marco Polo's travels and learned about the lands of the Great Khan and the island empire of Chipangu, seized upon the idea of these islands off the coast of the Indies, and saw no need to drop it when he sailed into the Caribbean. Sometimes the New World challenged classical geographical knowledge, and sometimes it seemed to confirm it.

Columbus's motivations were varied, as was his reading. He may have been searching for the earthly paradise in the 'Indies'. He certainly believed himself to have a divine mission, which included the recapture of Jerusalem for Christianity, as well as a strong social ambition that could also be fed by claiming overseas territories and finding gold. Alongside his Ptolemy, Columbus, like many of his contemporaries, was drawn to the descriptions of the exotic marvels and wonders of far-off lands in books such as *The Travels of John Mandeville* of the middle of the fourteenth century and Pierre d'Ailly's *Imago Mundi* (1410). Mandeville's *Travels* was a ghost-written mélange of real and imagined travel writings that was widely read across Europe and up and down the social scale. It set out in its wondrous multiplicity the diversity of the earth's inhabitants. This included the so-called monstrous races described in Pliny the Elder's *Natural History* (also read by Columbus) and in Strabo's geography. These included Amazons (women who lived without men), cannibals, the Blemmyae (people whose

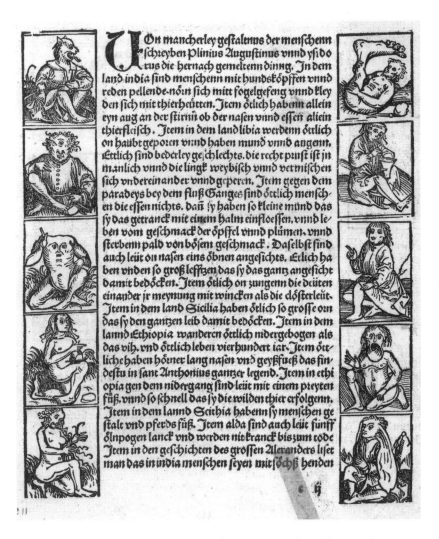

Figure 2.5 The monstrous races. This page from a German chronicle printed in 1500 shows a variety of 'races' as described by the classical authority Pliny. Cyclops, Blemmyae and Sciapods are all identifiable here, alongside figures who are part human, part animal, and figures with curious body parts.

heads were in their chests), Cynocephali (dog-headed people), pygmies, giants, Troglodytes (cave dwellers) and those who sheltered from the sun under their one vast foot (Sciapods) (figure 2.5). These wondrous peoples were always associated with faraway places whose locations on the map were hazy to medieval and early modern Europeans – India, Ethiopia, Cathay – and which conjured up an air of mystery. In these forms of knowledge human diversity was social and cultural (cannibals) as well as physiological (Sciapods). Following the authority of classical authors once again, those beyond the margins of civilisation were defined as 'barbarians'. Characterised, as they had been for the classical world, by their lack of towns, settled agriculture, manufactures and a sophisticated spoken and written literary culture, they helped to define how 'civilised' peoples understood themselves.

Once again, however, there was plenty of room for debate. The existence of the 'monstrous races' was hotly disputed. Significantly, these exotic creatures were not always defined or understood in negative terms. Mandeville was strikingly non-judgemental about the differences he described, even cannibalism. His readers might be so too. One of them was Menocchio, a miller in sixteenth-century northern Italy who mainly travelled in his mind. He said at his trial for heresy that it was 'having read that book of Mandeville about many kinds of races and different laws that sorely troubled me'. It clearly excited him too, and led him to question his own beliefs by showing him 'many islands where some lived in one way and some in another'.[8] He was eventually executed for his unorthodox beliefs, but others continued to debate how savages and barbarians should be seen. In these discussions of classical authors bestiality and innocence ran side by side as competing characterisations. Tacitus' *Germania* supported a vision of barbarian innocence and freedom existing in a state of nature outside the corruption of Roman civilisation. Yet Aristotle's *Politics* held that because barbarous races had weak, irrational minds and bodies made only for labour they should be ruled by others.

Upon the 'discovery' of the New World these ideas were pressed into service right from the start. Columbus, who heard and did not discount stories of people with tails and of Amazons, reported that the 'Indians' were innocents who would make good slaves. Others argued that the American 'savages' were under the sway of the devil and should be in permanent bondage to their Spanish masters. In contrast, Bartholomé de Las Casas, the defender of the Amerindians, argued in the 1550s that 'Not all barbarians are either lacking in reason or slaves by nature'.[9] As practical exercises in trying to resolve these questions, Europeans brought representatives of native peoples from Arctic America, the Caribbean and Brazil to the Old World. An Inuk, who had been kidnapped by Martin Frobisher from among the Inuit of Newfoundland, was displayed with his kayak in London in 1576, and was drawn clothed and naked in attempts to resolve questions about how American people should be judged. Geographical and ethnographic knowledge was an important part of Europe's encounter with the Americas. It was woven in different ways into various projects and schemes.

The world of Walter Ralegh

One Elizabethan adventurer for whom knowledge looked to be the route to power and wealth was Sir Walter Ralegh. His voyage up South America's Orinoco River in 1595 and his presentation of it in his book *The Discoverie of the Large, Rich and Bewtiful Empyre of Guiana* (1596) were part of a process of geographical and ethnographic encounter that was shaped by Ralegh's position in relation to Queen Elizabeth and England's relationship with Spain, as well as by Europe's relationship with the Americas.

Ralegh was the youngest of four surviving sons in a modest, if well-connected and long-established, Devon gentry family. His ambitions for himself and his family were ones that he sought to fulfil primarily as a soldier and a courtier, but also as a writer. Military service in France and Ireland brought him to the attention of Queen Elizabeth and her court. In the 1580s he became one of Elizabeth's favourites, balanced and challenged by her growing affection for Robert Devereux, Second Earl of Essex. The story of Ralegh covering a muddy puddle with his fine cloak so that Elizabeth could cross it is probably just court gossip, but as such it sits alongside both the persistent rumours of sexual intimacy between them and the love poetry that he wrote to the queen, which was widely read at court. As a courtier Ralegh made enemies – the company he kept certainly led to rumours of his atheist sympathies – but he was also able to garner from the monarch a series of honours, offices, patents and leases on lands from which he could live. He became captain of the Guard and lord lieutenant of Cornwall, and held the patent for the sale of wine (worth £700 a year), as well as being granted extensive lands in Ireland. However, all of this came at the queen's pleasure, and all of it could be taken away again. Ralegh's involvement in overseas adventures needs to be understood as part of attempts to guarantee the queen's continued favour, and as a way to provide himself with some independent income.

The basis of these adventures in the world of Elizabeth's court, and the rivalry between England and Spain, is evident in various ways. Ralegh's expeditions to Virginia (named for the Virgin Queen) in the mid-1580s aimed, first of all, to establish a privateering base from which to launch raids on Spanish shipping in the Caribbean (see chapter 3). However, unlike the ventures of Drake and Hawkins, Ralegh also sought to establish an agricultural colony of 'citizen-planters' on Roanoke Island under a patent that gave him supreme power, derived from the queen, to govern as he wished (although he never visited Virginia himself). These ventures ended in failure largely because the Armada crisis meant that the queen and Privy Council prevented any voyages from visiting the colony until 1590, by which time it had been abandoned.

Ralegh was fervently anti-Spanish, and wrote that he had 'consumed the best part of my fortune hating the tirranus sprosperety [sic] of that estate'.[10] Indeed, the voyage to Guiana in 1595 was presented as a challenge to both Spain's tyranny and its prosperity. Ralegh argued that the land of the Epuremei, 'the Empyre of Guiana', was such that 'whatsoever Prince shall possesse it, that Prince shall be Lorde of More Gold, and of a more beautifull Empire, and of more Cities and people, then eyther the king of Spain, or the great Turke'.[11] Moreover, due to his good offices the English would be welcomed by the indigenous people as their liberators from the Spanish tyrants and as their allies against the Epuremei invaders. As he had travelled up the Orinoco River he had spread word of Queen Elizabeth's 'greatnes, her justice, her charity to all oppressed nations, with as manie of the rest of her beauties and virtues, as either I could expresse, or they conceive'. He had told them of the defeat of the Armada, and of Elizabeth's power, so that the Orinoqueponi, the people of the river, called her '*Ezrabeta Cassipuna Aquerewana*, which is as much as *Elizabeth*, the great princesse or greatest commaunder'.[12] Yet this was as much a matter of the personal politics of the court as of the geopolitics of European rivalries in the Americas. In 1592, Elizabeth had discovered that Ralegh had secretly married Elizabeth Throckmorton, one of the young ladies attendant at court, and that they had had a son. Elizabeth was furious over this loss of control over her interwoven networks of political and personal power, just as she had been in other similar cases. She separated husband and wife, and imprisoned them both in the Tower of London for several months. The commission for the voyage to Guiana several years later was a sign of her returning favour. It presented Ralegh with a chance to get back into the queen's good books.

Indeed, he did so by writing a book himself. Ralegh's *Discoverie* dramatised the story of his difficult explorations in South America. It presented what he had found and, more importantly, since no land had been claimed and little gold brought back, what remained to be found and what could be brought under the queen's control in the future. This was a story of failure dressed up as one of success and it was told as an encounter with new-found lands and their peoples. As Ralegh concluded, '*Guiana* is a Countrey that hath yet her Maydenhead.'[13] It was, he said, virgin land ready for the English Virgin Queen. It was also full of golden promises and strange wonders. He retold the tales of El Dorado ('the golden one'), a ruler who was worshipped by being covered in gold dust; the rich cities of the Epuremei, Incas displaced from Peru by the Spanish invasion; and of Amazons, cannibals and the headless Ewaipanoma, with their faces in their chests.

The *Discoverie* was, therefore, part of the broader European attempt to get to grips with the Americas. However, it cannot be dismissed simply as the colonisers' wish-fulfilment, either of limitless gold or of monstrous races that required only removal by any means necessary. For the Amerindian peoples that Ralegh met this was certainly no first encounter. Their cultural and political lives had been shaped by a hundred years of living with the Spanish presence. For example, the larger pre-Columbian 'empires' (*ararewana*) had been replaced by smaller 'states' run by *caciques* or 'captaynes' which responded better to Spanish power. Also, the division between *caribes* (Caribs) and *arauacas* (Arawaks), which many later observers assumed was an ethnic division, is better explained by the political choice of resistance or accommodation to the Spanish. Ralegh had to operate within this on-going process of engagement. Much of what he knew, or thought he knew, about Guiana he had learned from Spanish books or captured Spaniards. The Spanish presence also meant that indigenous peoples had to be treated as potential political allies against Spain rather than simply demonised as devils or celebrated as innocents. Ralegh's alliance with Topiawari, the 'King of Arromaia', involved Topiawari's son (named Iwaikanarie Gualtero as a sign of allegiance to Ralegh) returning to England and two young Englishmen, Frauncis Sparrow and Hugh Goodwin, staying in Guiana. The discussions between Ralegh and Topiawari were represented as a courtly act of diplomacy between nations, with its attendant ceremonies and dangers (figure 2.6). In addition, the stories that Ralegh collected were ones that were forged in a meeting of European and Amerindian beliefs. He had to learn from 'aged men, & such as were greatest travelers', just as he needed indigenous pilots and guides such as '*Martyn* the *Arwacan*' to take his men through 'that laborinth of rivers'.[14] So, it was from the evidence of long-distance exchanges between elites who shared a culture of the ritual use of gold that Ralegh and others constructed the notion of a Golden Empire. It was also from the existence in both Amerindian and European cultures of Amazons (the locals called them Aikeam-Benano, women-who-live-alone, or Cougnantaisecouima, women-without-men), Acephali (headless people), Sciapods and cannibals (Ralegh reported that the Orinoqueponi thought the English would eat them because the Spanish

Figure 2.6 Walter Ralegh meets Topiawari. The English adventurer is shown as being fêted by the Arromaian king and his people, while his ship lies at anchor in the river. There are, however, also signs of danger. The group by the shore carry clubs, and Ralegh's men keep their guns, pikes and swords at the ready.

had told them so) that conversations about the limits of humanity were formed that were not simply the imposition of one side's views on the other. Ralegh remained sceptical but was prepared to take the locals' word for such wonders. He needed to be interested in these people and the detail of their lives, histories and beliefs because it was only through them that he could offer any challenge to the power of Spain and any promise of wealth and power to his queen.

Ralegh left his mark on Guiana. His return was expected and Waterali was reported as being used as an honorific title in the eighteenth century. The Americas also left its mark on him if only because he had taken up smoking tobacco and experimenting with American medicines. Yet the voyage had been a disappointment. It was not until 1616, in a final desperate attempt to gain the favour of Elizabeth's successor, James I, that Ralegh returned to Guiana. But his old alliances were of no use and his search for gold was fruitless. The venture cost the lives of Ralegh's son Wat, and close friend Lawrence Keymis. Unable to fulfil his rash promise to the king, it was not long before Ralegh found himself facing execution. He told the crowd gathered around the scaffold on 29 October 1618 that he had lived 'a sinful Life, in all sinful Callings, having been a Souldier, a Captain, a Sea-Captain, and a Courtier'.[15] Indeed, it was as a captain and a courtier that he had ventured to the Americas. It was also as an author that he had brought that place home again in ways that showed how European representations of the Americas were shaped by an on-going encounter that was at least two-sided. In his pocket on that last day was a golden idol from Guiana. Whether it was there as a token of a fortune in bullion that never materialised, or whether it had become a cross-cultural symbol which might bring another sort of good fortune we do not know.

Empire on the doorstep: Elizabethan Ireland

Ralegh's imperial career had begun closer to home, in Ireland, and England's empire began there too. During the sixteenth century Ireland became both a separate kingdom and a colony. Originally conquered and claimed for the English crown by Henry II at the end of the twelfth century, it was incorporated as a kingdom by Elizabeth's father Henry VIII. Parliamentary legislation in 1541 declared him king (rather than lord) of Ireland. Before the middle of the sixteenth century English kings had little power over Ireland, and were represented there by feudal lords who ruled through established forms of local prestige and patronage. They were either Old English noblemen (the descendants of Anglo-Norman settlers of the Middle Ages) in the area around Dublin known as the Pale where English rule was most established, or Gaelic chiefs who controlled the rest of the island (figure 2.7). Neither, independent as they were, had too much difficulty acknowledging the distant authority of whichever English monarch was on the throne.

Ireland's incorporation as one kingdom within a composite 'British' monarchy (that conjoined it with England and Wales, and would include Scotland after 1603) brought new pressures and a desire to bring 'order' to the independent and 'uncivilised' fringes of the realm. Judging that Ireland offered itself as a land of opportunity for the English (particularly for otherwise landless younger sons), but that it also threatened to drain the treasury through mismanagement, Henry and Elizabeth, neither of whom ever visited their other kingdom, both sought to reform its government. Prompted by the Protestant Reformation, and fearing that Ireland could become a foothold for Spanish power and the Counter-Reformation too close to home, they also sought to reform its religion. A series of

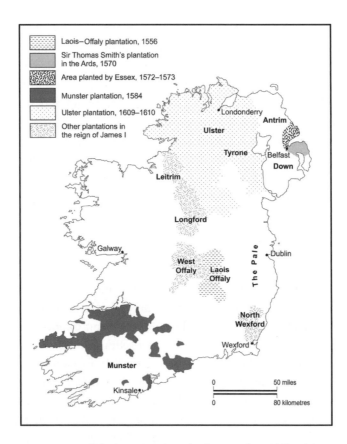

Figure 2.7 English plantations in Ireland. From the middle of the sixteenth century there were a variety of schemes to establish English settlers in various parts of Ireland. The most extensive plantations, in Munster and Ulster, followed the military defeat of rebellions led by Irish lords and were intended to transform the country and its people.

sixteenth-century governors, and their appointees in newly established provincial presidencies, sought to institute a reform agenda in both administration and religion. In political terms this was an attempt to bring existing Gaelic chieftains under the rule of the English common law and the authority of the crown through them surrendering their lands and powers and having them regranted by the English monarch. This was pursued instead of a process of direct conquest of their lands, which would have been far too costly both in lives and gold, and in the loss of legitimacy involved in a monarch overturning existing forms of – professedly loyal – authority rather than supporting them. The appeal of these surrender and regrant schemes to the Gaelic chiefs was that they offered security of tenure on their lands, but the insistence on inheritance (of land and titles) through primo-geniture cut against their traditions of partible inheritance and tanistry (the Gaelic mode of political succession), and threatened to undermine their established authority. There were many Gaelic chieftains who saw that they would lose out and were willing to fight to restore their powers, and many Old English nobles who resented paying the cost of administrative reforms and the military forces needed to back them up.

The reformation of religion – and the attempts to change the language, dress and manners of the Irish that went with it – was also a failure. Rejected by both the Gaelic chiefs and the Old English nobles, it meant that there would be no Irish sister kingdom ruled by an already established, but newly Protestant, elite. Ireland became unusual in Europe in that the religion of its populace was not the religion of its ruler or, indeed, of its administrators who were, increasingly, required to be English-born rather than just of English blood. This concern that the Old English of the Pale had become Gaelicised and could not promote reform further alienated them from the New English settlers, administrators, clergy and army captains who were increasingly muscling their way in. Importantly, however, the existing feudal lords were not powerless to derail efforts at reform. They did so by professing loyalty to the queen and concern at the actions (and corruption) of her servants in Ireland. Each governor was part of the patronage politics of the English court and Privy Council, and Irish lords had influence there too. Their appeals, over the heads of the governor in Ireland, to the queen and her councillors were effective in undermining the authorities in Ireland and their policies.

Unfortunately, for many of the English, both in England and in Ireland, the alternative to reform was not to leave Ireland alone but to use force to bring it into line. The Pale was already hedged around with military settlements and forms of martial law in the middle of the sixteenth century. Armed resistance to reformist surrender and regrant arrangements had been met with militarised settlements in the Irish Midlands (in Counties Laois and Offaly) in the 1540s and 1550s. Indeed, the failure of reform efforts meant that the trend was towards more interventionist government. For example, plantation schemes – militarised impositions of settlers from England on Irish lands – were pursued, albeit unsuccessfully, in Ulster in the 1570s by the first earl of Essex and Sir Thomas Smith, with the support of the queen and investment from men such as John Hawkins. When the earl of Desmond rose up in rebellion against the reforms in Munster in 1579, and attempted to draw support both in Ireland and outside by declaring that Elizabeth – who had been excommunicated by papal bull in 1570 – was not a legitimate ruler, he brought down upon himself and his allies a concerted and unforgiving military response from the English crown. It was as part of the suppression of Desmond's rebellion that Walter Ralegh went to Ireland and gained notoriety leading the massacres of Spanish mercenaries, Irish rebels and women and children.

What followed Desmond's rebellion in Munster was something quite new. The English government was aware that it would be impossible to meet the claims over Desmond's confiscated lands from both the loyal Irish lords (such as the queen's cousin, the earl of Ormond) who had helped put down the rebellion and the English military leaders. The alternative was the first extensive state-sponsored and scientifically organised colonisation scheme proposed by the English. Drawing upon Roman precedents for the planting of colonies, the Munster plantation would create a new geography in Ireland, one that would have a significant influence on colonisation schemes there and in North America in later years. Claiming that warfare had meant that this was empty land (the Roman law justification of *res nullius*; see chapter 3), with no existing social order to be reformed, what was proposed was the establishment of sixty-two seignories (feudal domains) each with a fortified mansion and a series of model English agricultural villages, each complete with a church and a mill. The imposition of English settlers tilling the land, speaking English and living an 'ordered' religious, political and economic life would, it was anticipated, act as a humanist moral lesson for the Irish who would be brought to comparable forms of civility once released from the sway of their tyrannical and rebellious lords. Ralegh himself was given one of the largest grants of land and attracted to it some of those who had been involved in his failed Roanoke venture.

Matters in Munster did not quite work out as anticipated. The colonisation turned out to be more military than civil. There were also conflicts over land assignments, including claims by Irish lords – backed by the law, encouraged by Ormond and supported by the queen – that their lands had been illegitimately included in the plantation. Finally, many incoming tenants (both Irish and English) chose to move on, seeking better lands and tenancy agreements, including those offered by native lords of the province rather than New English land-owners. By the 1590s the plantation was seen by the New English as hopelessly compromised. It had left Irish lords with too much power and failed in the dramatic and total transformation of Ireland sought by propagandists for conquest such as the poet and Munster planter Edmund Spenser. His *View of the Present State of Ireland* (1596) had advocated the use of force to create a unitary state with one religion, language and law: 'a union of manners and conformity of minds, to bring them to be one people'.[16] Indeed, the matter was all the more urgent because by the late 1590s the future of the plantation, and of the English in Ireland as a whole, was threatened by the extensive rebellion led by Hugh O'Neill, Second Earl of Tyrone.

The world of Hugh O'Neill (Aodh Ó Néill)

Hugh O'Neill, born around 1550, was the son of Matthew O'Neill, the first baron of Dungannon and heir designate to the earldom of Tyrone in Ulster, a feudal title that had been created by Henry VIII only in 1542. Hugh became the third baron of Dungannon, but his succession to the earldom was disputed by other Gaelic lords, particularly Shane O'Neill, in contravention of a surrender and regrant agreement. It was, however, supported by the English. Hugh's claim was based on primogeniture, and he seemed to offer what the English wanted: a loyal and reformed government of an increasingly Anglicised Ulster on a shoestring budget. Hugh seemed to have been brought up for this. His earliest years were spent fostered among the households of O'Neill families in Tyrone, but he also spent several years of his childhood in the Dublin household of Sir Henry Sidney and with the family of Giles Hovenden, a settler and soldier, who was a member of a less fervently Protestant part of New English settler society, which had been integrated by marriage into the established Old English gentry of the Pale. Like many other young Gaelic noblemen, Hugh O'Neill's experience of the culture and politics of English and Irish lordship gave him the resources to build a power base during what was a period of transition.

By the 1580s the English government's plan seemed to be to install Hugh O'Neill on a reduced portion of the old O'Neill lands, and to institute a provincial presidency and the English common law within which he would govern his tenants. His Catholicism and his appeal to the traditions of Gaelic lordship were not a problem as long as he remained loyal to the queen and could see off the competing claims of Turlough Luineach O'Neill and the sons of Shane O'Neill. Hugh had commanded a company of cavalry as part of the earl of Essex's plantation, and Essex referred to him as 'the only man of Ulster . . . meet to be trusted and used'. Queen Elizabeth called him 'a creature of our own', and Hugh himself admitted to being 'raised from nothing by her Majesty'.[17] Indeed, Hugh travelled to the English court in 1587 to meet Elizabeth and to argue, successfully as it turned out, that he should be granted all his grandfather's lands. He charmed the queen and she must have felt her influence on him to have been successful when, a year later, he ordered the execution of around 500 survivors from Spain's Armada who had washed up along the Ulster coast.

Yet this attempt to effect state centralisation through Gaelic lordship was full of contradictions and conflicts. It provided the basis for Hugh O'Neill, as the earl of Tyrone, to build up his own powerful position. Via the marriages of himself, his sisters and his children throughout the 1580s and early 1590s he created a series of strategic alliances. Hugh sought to govern Ulster for the queen as a palatinate, which would put him in sole control and halt what he felt to be increasing restrictions on his traditional privileges. Yet as his authority grew it began to challenge that of the English officials who also sought power and profit in Ulster. Nicholas Bagenal, an influential English settler, had supported Hugh O'Neill in the 1560s and 1570s, but turned against him in the 1580s because Hugh's increasing power as earl of Tyrone conflicted with his own aim of becoming the first lord president of Ulster. Hugh's response was to try and merge their interests by asking for the hand of Bagenal's only daughter Mabel. When this was refused Hugh and Mabel eloped in 1591, earning them the lasting opposition of her brother Henry whose own ambitions to become the chief commissioner in the province of Ulster were based on his promise that he could curb 'the two great barbarous governments' of Hugh and Turlough Luineach O'Neill.[18] Part of this was Henry's charge, which Hugh answered before the Privy Council in England, that the Irishman had opened a treasonous correspondence with Philip II of Spain and James VI of Scotland to help restore a Catholic monarch to the English throne.

It was these local tensions over autonomy and authority combined with the cementing of an unprecedented alliance with Hugh Roe O'Donnell, the earl of Tirconnell – another great Gaelic lord and a former rival – that gave Hugh O'Neill the motive and the means to rebel against English authority in 1595. O'Neill's actions reflected all the complexities of Irish politics, and his place within them. This was, at least initially, a rebellion not against royal authority, but against the queen's officials in Ireland. O'Neill had no wish to alienate the Old English, and his protestations of loyalty as earl of Tyrone as well as his political manifesto were designed to appeal to them. He demanded the restoration of Catholicism, the repeal of laws discriminating against the Irish and the filling of all posts in the civil government below governor (to be renamed viceroy) with Irishmen. Against the competing local claims of Gaelic lordship he stressed faith and fatherland: a common religion and a common land. Yet he also drew upon those local claims. He was inaugurated as 'the O'Neill' in September 1595, the head of a clan with the right to appoint subordinate lords. As the Protestant bishop of Limerick put it, clearly disagreeing with the conclusion: 'the whole Irishry are taught now a new lesson: O'Neill is no traitor. Tyrone was one, but O'Neill none.'[19] Finally, he increasingly sought the support of international Catholicism. At first he was simply keeping his options open. Later, as the war progressed, he appealed unsuccessfully to the pope to excommunicate those who still supported Elizabeth, and he made stronger overtures to the Spanish. He wanted 6,000 of their soldiers. The final recompense would be the transfer of Irish sovereignty to Philip II. This was an idea supported by reviving the story from the twelfth-century 'Book of invasions' (*Leabhar Gabhála*) that the Gaels were descended from the northern Spanish king Milesius. It was also perfectly consistent with an attempt to maintain the autonomy of Gaelic chiefdoms under a monarch to whom they might swear conditional loyalty, rather than seeing themselves as subjects of one ruler in perpetuity. As one Spaniard put it in 1600, 'Most nations dislike Spain – the Irish love it'.[20] Hugh sent his second son Henry to Spain to cement the alliance.

Hugh O'Neill's intermittent military campaign in Ireland was a great success between 1595 and early 1599. Initially, this was more because the Elizabethan regime was slow to understand and respond to the threat than because of Tyrone's skills on the battlefield. His English-trained, and some-times even English, soldiers were, however, able to take the government forces by surprise with their 'perfect use of firearms'.[21] He gained a strik-ing victory in August 1598 at Yellow Ford where Henry Bagenal (an even less accomplished military commander) was killed. In the same year the Munster plantation collapsed completely and rapidly when faced with a force sent south by Tyrone. By then it was clear that the rebellion repre-sented a serious threat to the English presence across the whole island, and Elizabeth's attention had to be focused there as never before.

In response, the queen appointed – very much against his will – her favourite, Essex, as lord lieutenant and dispatched him to Ireland with 17,600 troops. Although this was the largest army she was ever to send beyond England's borders, its commander sought a truce and was vilified for it at home. The military resources were subsequently increased under Sir Charles Blount. In turn, the Spanish eventually sent 3,000 men in 1601. Tyrone and Tirconnell managed to reach them at Kinsale, and to engage the English army and the loyal Irish lords who were fighting with them, but the battle was lost. Tyrone finally surrendered in 1603, after nine years at war, unaware that the queen who had spent £2,000,000 to gain her victory had died shortly before. Although he had to swear allegiance to the new king, and promise to sever all contact with Spain, he was reinstalled in his earldom. Despite continued challenges to his property rights and his authority by army captains, royal officials, churchmen and former subordinates, it was a surprise when he joined Tirconnell and others in fleeing the country in 1607 (what is called 'the flight of the earls'). If he had expected to gather Spanish support and return triumphantly to regain his autonomy as a Catholic Gaelic lord on his ancestral lands that was never to be. England and Spain were now at peace, and his cause was something of an embarrassment to the Spanish king. Hugh O'Neill died in Rome in 1616.

Queen Elizabeth's concerns centred on her own position as monarch, the difficulties of forging a religious settlement and the fiscal, military and diplomatic manoeuvres associated with the west European balance of power. Where these concerns became matters of overseas ventures she got involved, either directly or indirectly. The queen invested in John Hawkins's trading voyages in the 1560s, and her Privy Council oversaw his efforts to create a more effective navy. It was in her name, and seeking her favour as a courtier, that Walter Ralegh voyaged to Guiana in search of gold. And it was in the pursuit of reform and Reformation in her other 'kingdom' that Elizabeth first raised up Hugh O'Neill, the earl of Tyrone, as a subordinate lord and later declared him a rebel against her authority. In each case what was at issue was the power and wealth of Spain. This provided the context for Elizabethan England's engagement with the wider world in terms of trade in the Atlantic, direct military confrontation at home, imperial land claims in the Americas and the politics of religion and rebellion in Europe.

In each case the beginnings of a new set of relationships, and geographies, can be traced. Hawkins's voyages inaugurated a trade in slaves from Africa to the Americas in English ships as part of a more general demonstration that substantial profits could be made trading in the Atlantic world. Significantly, the tonnage of the English merchant marine almost doubled between 1550 and 1630, largely due to the privateering war with Spain which also provided ships and capital for the English East India Company. Ralegh, in both Roanoke and Guiana, was part of an English intellectual and practical engagement with American lands and people. The defeat of Hugh O'Neill, perhaps most dramatically, allowed the establishment of functioning English sovereignty over Ireland and, with the Ulster plantation, substantially increased the establishment of permanent overseas settlements of English and Scots. What began in Ireland established a pattern for settlement in the Atlantic world.

All of these later developments will be explored in the chapters that follow, and each had significant implications for Britain's relationship with the rest of the world. It is, however, important to stress how fragile and full of failures those beginnings were. With little direction and support from the state, overseas ventures were left to fend for themselves. John Hawkins might have thrown his lot in with Philip II. Walter Ralegh's colony at Roanoke was abandoned and his search for El Dorado came to nothing and eventually cost him his head. Hugh O'Neill came close to driving the English (at least the New English) from Ireland. Things might have turned out very differently. For these uncertain beginnings to become anything of significance a great deal had to be done. The next two chapters demonstrate what was required, and how this turned out, in the different contexts of North America and India. In both cases it can be seen that Britain's engagement with other parts of the world meant a new set of relationships being made with their existing inhabitants, relationships in which questions of dependence and independence were the key.

Further reading

The best general texts are Kenneth Andrews (1984) *Trade, Plunder and Settlement: Maritime Enterprise and the Genesis of the British Empire, 1480–1630* (Cambridge University Press, Cambridge) and Nicholas Canny (ed.) (1998) *The Oxford History of the British Empire*, vol. I, *The Origins of Empire* (Oxford University Press, Oxford). There are excellent short biographies of all the main characters here in the *Oxford Dictionary of National Biography*, and longer treatments in Harry Kelsey (2003) *Sir John Hawkins: Queen Elizabeth's Slave Trader* (Yale University Press, New Haven, Conn.) and Hiram Morgan (1993) *Tyrone's Rebellion: The Outbreak of the Nine Years War in Ireland* (Royal Historical Society, Boydell Press, Woodbridge), as well as the many biographies of Elizabeth I and Walter Ralegh. For Ralegh's account of Guiana, Neil L. Whitehead (ed.) (1997) *The Discoverie of the Large, Rich and Bewtiful Empyre of Guiana by Sir Walter Ralegh* (Manchester University Press, Manchester) reprints the whole text with an extensive introduction and accompanying notes. For a concise summary of the transformation of early modern Ireland, see Nicholas Canny (1989) 'Early Modern Ireland, c. 1500–1700', in Roy Foster (ed.) *The Oxford History of Ireland* (Oxford University Press, Oxford) pp. 88–133.

Notes

1 Quoted in David Armitage (2000) *The Ideological Origins of the British Empire* (Cambridge University Press, Cambridge) p. 53. The claim to France was based on the disputed city of Calais.

2 Quoted in the entry for Elizabeth I in the *Oxford Dictionary of National Biography*, p. 32.

3 Quoted in Carole Levin (1998) '"We shall never have a merry world while the Queene lyveth": gender, monarchy and the power of seditious words', in Julia M. Walker (ed.) *Dissing Elizabeth: Negative Representations of Gloriana* (Duke University Press, Durham, N.C.) p. 89.

4 Quoted in Harry Kelsey (2002) *Sir John Hawkins: Queen Elizabeth's Slave Trader* (Yale University Press, New Haven, Conn.) p. 99.

5 Quoted ibid., p. 76.

6 Quoted in Anthony Grafton (1995) *New Worlds, Ancient Texts: The Power of Tradition and the Shock of Discovery* (Harvard University Press, Cambridge, Mass.) p. 77.

7 Felipe Fernández-Armesto (1991) *Columbus* (Oxford University Press, Oxford) p. 30.

8 Quoted in Carlo Ginzburg (1980) *The Cheese and the Worms: The Cosmos of a Sixteenth-Century Miller* (Johns Hopkins University Press, Baltimore) pp. 42 and 45.

9 Quoted in Grafton, *New Worlds, Ancient Texts*, p. 137. See also J. H. Elliott (1992) *The Old World and the New* (Cambridge University Press, Cambridge).

10 Quoted in the entry for Sir Walter Ralegh in the *Oxford Dictionary of National Biography*, p. 845.

11 Quoted in Neil L. Whitehead (ed.) (1997) *The Discoverie of the Large, Rich and Bewtiful Empyre of Guiana by Sir Walter Ralegh* (Manchester University Press, Manchester) p. 136.

12 Quoted ibid., pp. 173 and 134.

13 Quoted ibid., p. 196. See also Louis Montrose (1993) 'The work of gender in the discourse of discovery', in Stephen Greenblatt (ed.) *New World Encounters* (University of California Press, Berkeley) pp. 177–217.

14 Quotations from Whitehead, *Discoverie*, pp. 149, 157 and 166.

15 Stephen J. Greenblatt (1973) *Sir Walter Ralegh: The Renaissance Man and His Roles* (Yale University Press, New Haven and London) p. ix.

16 Quoted in Nicholas Canny (2001) *Making Ireland British, 1580–1650* (Oxford University Press, Oxford) p. 52.

17 Quoted in the entry for Hugh O'Neill in the *Oxford Dictionary of National Biography*, p. 838.

18 Quoted in Canny, *Making Ireland British*, p. 81.

19 Quoted in Hiram Morgan (1993) 'Hugh O'Neill and the Nine Years War in Ireland', *Historical Journal* 36:1 p. 35.

20 Quoted ibid., p. 34.

21 Quoted in Hugh O'Neill entry in the *Oxford Dictionary of National Biography*, p. 841.

3 | Savage tales: settlement in North America

The different lives and concerns of Queen Elizabeth, John Hawkins, Walter Ralegh and Hugh O'Neill all help indicate why the thoughts of many of the propagandists of overseas ventures, and the eyes of many ordinary men and women, as well as of clergymen, financiers and statesmen, were turned towards the establishment of colonies in North America in the late sixteenth century. In the *Discourse of Western Planting* (1584), one of the best-known, and earliest, works promoting colonisation by the English, Richard Hakluyt the younger argued that such settlements would serve many useful purposes. His report, commissioned by Francis Walsingham and read by Elizabeth I, argued that English colonies in what he called Norumbega would create the stability and order at home that the queen desired by providing somewhere that the vagrants and masterless men who roamed the English countryside and filled the towns could be put to work. Indeed, their labour growing olive, lemon and orange trees, vines and sugarcane, and making salt and casting iron, would also save on the customs duties and dependence paid to southern Europe's princes. These colonies planted in the Americas would also have benefits on the international stage, as Ralegh and Hawkins desired, frustrating the ambitions of the Spanish king by preventing him 'from flowinge over all the face of that waste firme of America', and by providing a base from which English privateers could prey on his treasure ships.[1] Finally, they would continue the work begun in the 'civilising' and settling of Ireland, both by generating maritime trades that would tie that island's ports more closely into the English economy, and by extending the process of exporting Protestant civilisation overseas to the New World. Yet, as Ralegh's venture on Roanoke Island showed, all this political and economic promise could very easily come to nothing.

It is clear from Hakluyt's *Discourse of Western Planting* that what was intended was to establish a significant and lasting English presence in North America. Once the dreams of emulating Spanish discoveries of vast stores of precious metals had faded, thoughts turned to more prosaic commodities. The colonists were to take wheat, rye and barley seeds to grow for food, as well as breeding pairs of pigs, rabbits, doves, chickens and ducks. The cane, vine and olive planters and the pitch, tar and soap makers were to be accompanied by artisans – carpenters, brickmakers, tilers, thatchers and sinkers of wells, who would build them English-style dwellings and workplaces – and by the captains, soldiers and fortification and weapons experts who would protect them. Hakluyt's plan was, of course, an idealised vision of a productive and civilised colonial venture designed to whet the appetite of statesmen and investors. What came to pass up and down the Atlantic coast over the next century was never so neat and complete and not so immediately prosperous, and turned out radically to depart from Hakluyt's plan in very different ways in different places. America was not to become Europe's supplier of citrus fruits, olive oil and wine. It did, however, become the permanent home for very many English men and women, and they significantly transformed its landscape in the process.

After Roanoke and Sagahadoc (Maine), where the colonies did not survive, there were shaky starts at Jamestown in Virginia in 1607 and at Plymouth (1620) and Massachusetts Bay (1630). Failure looked as likely as success, and the settlers survived only where the Amerindians allowed them to. Yet by the end of the seventeenth century 160,000 people had moved from the British mainland to North America (in the same period, 190,000 migrated to the Caribbean Islands (see chapter 9) and 180,000 to Ireland). Of these 116,000 moved to the Virginian settlements where a new economy was being constructed based on tobacco cultivation for export, and a new society was being made which combined Europeans (often as indentured servants, poor people whose passage across the ocean was paid for by seven years of labour for their masters), Amerindians and enslaved Africans. Many of the rest (perhaps 21,000 between 1630 and 1642) joined the Great Migration of Puritans to escape religious persecution and economic decline to set up on family farms in their promised land of New England.

In both of these contexts, and in the others that developed right along the Atlantic coast, the issue was *settlement*. This raised questions of what sort of society, landscape and material culture should or could be constructed. It raised questions of the place of English colonies alongside, and in competition with, those of Spain to the south and France to the north: questions of the rights of empires to plant colonies. Perhaps most important of all it raised the question of the people who were already there and what these settlements meant for them. In one sense the answer is obvious: it was absolutely devastating. Old World diseases – measles, smallpox, typhoid – against which the indigenous people had no immunity spread like wildfire amongst them. Estimates are that around 90 per cent of the one million people who lived between the Mississippi River and the Atlantic coast in 1600 died from diseases brought by the newcomers. Those who were left had to negotiate changing social structures, an altered political landscape, new goods and technologies, different notions of land and land use, different ideas of property and different conceptions of the savage and the civilised. These engagements often ended in violence.

What this chapter aims to do is to set out the ways in which these different, changing and conflicting forms of settlement developed in North America between the newcomers and those who had been there for some time. In doing so it starts with the early, troubled years of the colony at Jamestown, and its political engagement with the Powhatan empire of the Chesapeake Bay, before moving on to consider the questions of land and land use, and of empire, culture and identity, in late seventeenth- and early eighteenth-century New England. In each case the biographies through which this history is told are those who lived closest to the boundary (and therefore often crossed it) between the English and the Amerindians, the newcomers and the natives: John Smith and Pocahontas, each of whom was taken captive by the other side; John Sassamon who mediated between the two and suffered for it; and Eunice Williams, an English girl who made her life with the 'savages'. That's the ending – now, where do we begin?

Taking possession at Jamestown

Before the three ships sent by London's Virginia Company made landfall in the Chesapeake Bay in May 1607 that land had already been claimed by more than one empire. What was to become Virginia lay within the vast area claimed by the king of Spain on the basis of a papal bull of 1494 (see chapter 2). Consequently, in 1570 the Spanish had sponsored a Jesuit mission from Cuba to the bay which included a Pamunkey Indian called Paquiquineo who was returning home, having been away a long time. He had previously been taken to Europe by Spanish explorers, and then travelled to Havana and Mexico City. The Spanish hoped that on his return Paquiquineo, now renamed Don Luís de Velasco, would teach the Pamunkey Indians the Castilian language and help convert them to Christianity. Instead he rejoined his people and led them in an attack that wiped out the missionaries and put an end to the mission. The Spanish were in no hurry to return, but remained attentive to and wary of other Europeans' claims on that Atlantic coast.

More significantly, shortly before the English arrived the area had come under the sway of an Algonquian Indian 'empire' led by a chief named Powhatan (or Wohunsonacock). Quite unlike most other parts of North

America, where the largest political unit was the village, the Chesapeake Bay had seen the consolidation of a new indigenous paramount chiefdom. Born some time in the 1550s, Powhatan had inherited the six chiefdoms of Powhatan, Arrohateck, Appamattuck, Pamunkey, Mattaponi and Chiskiack. By the early seventeenth century he had extended his empire eastwards towards the coast through warfare and intimidation. The Powhatan empire, whose inhabitants called it Tsenachomacoh, was bounded geographically and politically (figure 3.1). Its northern boundary was the Potomac River down which occasionally came marauding bands of Iroquoian-speaking Massawomecks. The southern limit was the Great Dismal Swamp (on the current North Carolina/Virginia border) and peace agreements with the Algonquian-speaking Pamlicos and Chowanocs. Inland to the west the limit of Powhatan's dominion was marked by the line of waterfalls along the great rivers that cut deep into the country, and the warriors of the Siouan-speaking Mannahoacs and Monacans who lived in the hills beyond.

Tsenachomacoh was peopled by somewhere between 13,000 and 22,000 Algonquian Indians living on 6,000 square miles of land in about 150 villages. Just prior to the arrival of the English only the Chesapeakes (the tribe for whom the bay was named) of Cape Henry and the Chickahominies remained independent. The hereditary tributary chieftains (*weroances*) of the other thirty or so tribes of the region (including the Paspaheghs on whose land the English planted themselves) expressed their obedience to Powhatan and paid him tribute in high-status foods (venison and cornmeal), deer hides, strings of pearls and shells, and antimony ore. In return, as paramount chief or *mamanatowick*, Powhatan monopolised the small local supplies of copper and used it, as gifts or payment, to manage the military services provided by those *weroances* (who could be male or female). Indeed, these *weroances* were often his relatives or close counsellors. Powhatan had more than a hundred wives in his lifetime and, by having only one child with each wife, he created a dense network of half-siblings connected to each other but without the means to create strong alliances against him. Powhatan had the power to enforce his will. He destroyed the Chesapeakes and the Piankatanks in 1608 for holding out against him. Inevitably, of course, different parts of this empire were held more or less strongly than others. The Chickahominies maintained their independence while making enough judicious payments to keep Powhatan happy, and the Accomacs and Occohannocks of the eastern shore, and furthest from Powhatan's heartlands, remained only very loosely under his control.

The origins of Powhatan's empire lay in the recent changes in the region. This paramount chiefdom was constructed in response to the implications

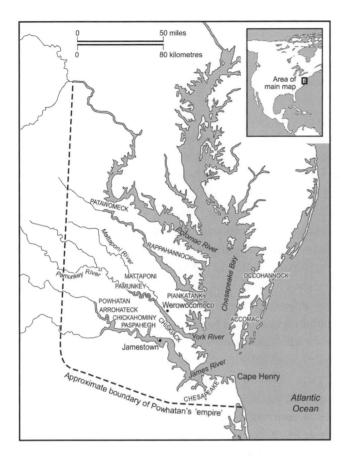

Figure 3.1 Powhatan's empire, c. 1600. Established on the lands around the Chesapeake Bay in what became Virginia, Powhatan ruled an empire made up of a complex confederation of different peoples. The Jamestown settlement was established by the Virginia Company at the heart of this empire, just south of Powhatan's 'capital' at Werowocomoco.

of early European contact and the military threats from other indigenous groups in a region where warfare (as raids and ambushes) was endemic. Powhatan's dominion was intended to provide social and political cohesion in the face of the deadly epidemics which had spread well in advance of the Europeans themselves along traditional routes for Amerindian traders, warriors and peace-makers. It also sought the creation of a stronger bargaining position in relation to desirable European goods: metal axes and fish-hooks, which replaced stone and bone; copper kettles which were to be used for making ritual gifts and jewellery rather than for cooking in; and woollen cloth which replaced laboriously prepared skins and furs. For Powhatan, the English trade goods available through Jamestown promised to be new sources of wealth which, controlled and judiciously distributed among his *weroance*s, could further consolidate his empire. Initially, to Powhatan, these new European settlers did not look much of a threat and they might, he must have thought, have promised both some useful trade and perhaps new allies and weapons to use against his local enemies.

However, as well as seeking alliances with Powhatan, these few English-men also thought to take possession of his land for the English king and their masters the Virginia Company, and to establish their settlements upon it. For Europeans, claiming possession of parts of the Americas and rule over their peoples was no small matter. These new-found lands could not simply be taken by force. The Europeans wanted to establish their rule as legitimate, and that required intricate justifications of the claims that were being made and careful observation of the formalities through which it was argued that those claims could become rights. Each of the main colonising powers relied upon different ways of claiming possession which involved particular rituals and ceremonies. The Spanish depended upon elaborate ceremonies of arrival with flags, crosses and ritual invocations of the crown of Castile and the papacy. After 1512 these all-important speeches were codified into what was called the Requirement (*requerimiento*) which had to be read to the natives, but did not need to be understood by them. The Portuguese, as well as justifying their claims in terms of the need to convert the natives to Catholicism, relied upon the planting of crosses and stone pil-lars which announced their prior arrival to other Europeans, and upon the establishment of agreements to trade, formal or informal, with the people they encountered. The English, more interested in land than people, placed their faith in establishing their occupation of the land and their intent to stay. They used flags and crosses, and the renaming of places, but also con-structed symbolic buildings, fences and boundary markers. In many ways, for them, just being Englishmen with the proper authorisation from the monarch and being there on the land was enough.

These rituals had different audiences. Sometimes they were directed at the indigenous peoples, sometimes at other Europeans. Inevitably their claims were contested by the other imperial powers which did not hold with rights established in ways different from their own, and they were ignored or rejected by Amerindians for whom they made little sense. There were also significant debates within any imperial power over what it took to claim legitimate possession. In 1607–1608 the Council of the Virginia Company met with the aim of providing for its stockholders a strong justification of its rights to both imperial rule over American peoples (*imperium*) and ownership of American lands (*dominium*). They wanted justifications that had 'not only comparatively to be as good as yᵉ Spaniards . . . but absolutely to be good against yᵉ Naturall people'.[2] Unsurprisingly, they rejected Spanish claims based on the papal bulls, arguing that they could not be the basis for denying the rights of an English empire in the Americas. However, they also carefully reviewed the Spanish difficulties in establishing a case for dispossessing the natives. They concluded that the uncivil and non-Christian state of the inhabitants, and the civilised Christianity of those who would take possession, might provide justification for imperial rule but could not confer property rights on to the Europeans.

In the face of such problems they decided not to present a formal written justification. This left the arena open to an eclectic array of promoters and propagandists to make a range of competing justifications by drawing on a contradictory set of ideas about America and its inhabitants. Some argued that conversion to Christianity and civilisation was justification enough; others put their faith in trade, the sword, or in the right to take 'waste' land from those who weren't using it productively. The ideas drawn upon ranged from the crudest stereotypes of innocent or ignoble savagery to the much more sophisticated accounts of Amerindian land and life produced from the experiences at Roanoke. For every reiteration of the idea that the land was empty and ready for the taking – 'a plaine wilderness as God first made it', or that the natives had 'only a generall residencie there, as wild beasts have in the forest' – there was the contrary evidence of Amerindian agriculture, settlement and civil society.[3] Thomas Harriot's *Report of the New Found Land of Virginia* with John White's striking images of Algonquian people, villages and fields was widely circulated in print from 1590 (figure 3.2). In the earliest years of the Jamestown settlement there was no secure way of taking possession.

This also helps to explain what Englishmen were doing in Virginia. Captain Christopher Newport and his men had established themselves in Paspahegh territory on a low-lying piece of land beside one of the rivers flowing into Chesapeake Bay. They assumed that because there was no village there, and because they had been welcomed on their arrival, they could simply take that land with no further negotiation or recompense. It was not a particularly desirable spot. They had valued the deep-water moorage just off-shore, but had not identified the mosquito-infested swamp nearby, the poor corn-growing land or the propensity for the river to become brackish at that point in the summer months. Moreover, it was Paspahegh hunting land and the English settlement was an intrusion. As well as physical possession the settlers engaged in a bit of ceremony. They renamed the watercourse the

Figure 3.2 Secotan village, Roanoke. This printed version of one of the drawings by John White shows an Amerindian village near the English settlement at Roanoke. Along with his other drawings it shows both an autonomous and well-ordered agricultural settlement of fields, gardens, dwellings and hunting lands which would have been familiar to English viewers, and some of the unfamiliar Amerindian rituals.

James River after their king, and in the presence of an Amerindian guide they planted a wooden cross inscribed 'Jacobus Rex. 1607' and gave a 'great shout'.[4] Yet the aim was *imperium* and the audience was an absent Spanish one. Captain Newport's explanation to their guide of what they were doing suggests that these Englishmen knew, both as a matter of law and as a matter of practicality, that they could not claim *dominion* over these Paspahegh lands. Newport told the guide that the two arms of the cross represented Powhatan and himself, the join where they met was their peace agreement and that the shout was the reverence they paid to Powhatan.

This mixture of English hubris, weakness and deceit was characteristic of Jamestown's early years. Just as Powhatan saw the English – whom his people called the Tassantasses – both as a problem that needed to be contained, and as a potential source of valuable goods and military assistance, so the English knew that they needed the Amerindians' corn and continuing goodwill if they were not to be removed from the land. In these early years the issue was less about settling the land than about food, sovereignty and identity as the intertwined lives of John Smith and Pocahontas serve to show.

The worlds of John Smith and Pocahontas

John Smith, baptised in 1580, was the son of a Lincolnshire yeoman farmer who beat his ploughshare into a sword in a bid to become a gentleman. After an unsuccessful apprenticeship to a King's Lynn merchant he set off to serve as a soldier in the religious wars in the Low Countries. Later adventures took him to the Mediterranean and, at the beginning of the seventeenth century, he joined the Austrian army fighting the Turks in Transylvania. Wounded in a skirmish with Tatars, he was taken captive and sold into slavery. By his own, later, account of his life he became the possession of a woman called Charatza Trabigzanda, but escaped from a future as a Christian slave of a Muslim mistress by killing her brother and making his way, via Morocco, back to England. A few years after his return, and having spent some time promoting overseas ventures, he sailed once again. This time he was part of the Virginia Company's first fleet which landed in Chesapeake Bay in the spring of 1607.

Pocahontas, born in 1595 or 1596, was one of Powhatan's many daughters. According to Algonquian practice she had several names. At birth she was named Matoaka or Amonute (the various Englishmen who recorded her life were not agreed), but was then given a nickname to keep her birthname a secret. She was to be known as Pocahontas – 'little wanton' or 'playful one' – a name which sought to describe her, and which might be changed as she changed. As a Powhatan girl, and one of the paramount chief's favourite daughters, she was born into a society of matrilineal descent where women could be important political figures (*weroansqua*), and where they were responsible for the vital and valued work of growing and gathering food. It was women who planted and tended the corn that their god Okeus had shown them how to grow (as well as the squashes, pumpkins and beans with which it was intercropped), and which was the measure of a village's wealth. Women also owned the houses that they constructed from bent saplings and closely woven mats. While men might have many wives, women exercised choice over which husband they married and were not expected to be faithful only to them.

According to Smith, he and Pocahontas first met in December 1607. The English captain was on one of several expeditions by boat up the rivers into Powhatan territory to chart the land and the disposition of the native peoples (his instructions from the Virginia Company ordered him to 'have great care not to offend the naturals').[5] His companions were killed and he was captured by a hunting party led by Powhatan's brother Opechancanough, and eventually taken to the emperor's stronghold at Werowocomoco. Impressed by the emperor's 'grave and majestical countenance' and subject to divining rituals by Powhatan priests to reveal his intentions, Smith found himself threatened by what he thought was imminent execution.[6] His head on a block of stone in front of the emperor, surrounded by warriors, he was, he thought, saved when Pocahontas rested her cheek on his, and the danger of death was averted. That this may, contrary to Smith's interpretation, have been some kind of adoption ritual, is perhaps supported by Powhatan's subsequent insistence that he call John Smith 'son', and be referred to by him as 'father'.

It was certainly the case that the early years of Anglo-Powhatan relations were marked by attempts by each side to assimilate the other to its politics and culture. They swapped symbolic 'sons' who might learn the language and act as intermediaries: Thomas Savage came to live with the Powhatans and Namontacke went to England. Powhatan sought to make Smith a *weroance* and, unsuccessfully, encouraged him to move the English to a site closer to Werowocomoco where they might make metal tools and jewellery for the Amerindians. On the orders of the Virginia Company, Captain Newport attempted (against Smith's better judgement and the emperor's unwillingness to bend his knee) to crown Powhatan as a vassal of king James I. The colonists' continual demands for food, and the Powhatans' attempts to contain them while benefiting from trade, meant that each side was testing the other as well as studying them for what they could learn about the strangers and themselves. Both newcomers and natives were also probing for weaknesses and exploiting those they found, as well as experimenting with new crops, words and technologies. So, the young Pocahontas could be found delivering gifts of food from her father and playing with the boys at the Jamestown fort: 'making them wheel falling on their hands, turning their heels upwards, whome she would then follow and wheel herself naked as she was all the fort over'.[7] But she could also be found, on Smith's report, negotiating for prisoners taken by the English and warning the colonists of impending attacks. Smith, in turn, was learning Powhatan words, sending colonists to live in their villages to survive the winter and, at the same time, using his military experience to negotiate his way into and out of tense stand-offs with Powhatan and Opechancanough over corn and political control behind which always lay the threat and use of violence (figure 3.3).

By 1609 matters had reached their lowest ebb in Jamestown. In response to the shortages of food Smith had, as governor since 1608, already imposed a strict regime where 'he that will not work shall not eat'.[8] This tried to ensure that the soft-handed gentlemen-colonists whom the Company had sent, and those obsessed only with finding gold, would have to become farmers and foragers to survive. Smith was, however, injured in an explosion and deposed by his numerous enemies; he took a ship for England in October 1609. Powhatan, unaware that Smith had gone, but increasingly alive to the danger the colonists posed, had withdrawn upriver and sought to force the English out by denying them food. He very nearly succeeded. In these 'starving times' the colonists were reduced to eating vermin from their houses, serpents from the forests and, it was said, the dead from their graves. One man was executed for killing and eating his wife. The sixty or so colonists that remained of the five hundred who had started the winter resolved to leave that miserable place. Having packed up, boarded the ships and set sail on 7 June 1610, they met De La Warr's relief ship which had been long delayed by a wreck in the Bermudas. Powhatan's wish to see them gone was not to come to pass.

The new regime imposed an even harsher martial law internally and an increasingly belligerent posture towards the Powhatans. The successive raids, massacres, ambushes and attacks on cornfields, perpetrated on both sides – and which made this the first Anglo-Powhatan war – lasted from 1609 to 1614. It was brought to an end when Captain Samuel Argall convinced Iapassus, the brother of the *weroance* of Patawomeck on the northernmost edge of Powhatan's domain, to trick Pocahontas into boarding his ship. She was used as a hostage to begin negotiations for the men, guns and tools that the Powhatans had captured. Yet there was to be no simple swap. Powhatan seemed reluctant to release what he had gained, and Pocahontas declared that she would, therefore, 'dwell with the Englishmen, who loved

Figure 3.3 John Smith and Opechancanough. Taken from Smith's history of his exploits in Virginia published in 1624, this picture dramatises the conflict between the Amerindians and the English settlers. Smith is shown bravely confronting these dangers and acting decisively by capturing Powhatan's brother. Others saw his actions as unnecessarily provocative.

her'.[9] Eventually, it was decided, with the blessing of both Powhatan and Jamestown's governor Sir Thomas Dale, that she should be allowed to marry one of those Englishmen. John Rolfe had arrived with the ship from Bermuda and had lost his wife and child to sickness. Pocahontas's own husband Kocoum was also conveniently forgotten as this marriage became a political alliance. Their union was embraced by Dale as meaning that the English and the Powhatans were 'now friendly and firmly united together and made one people . . . in the band of love'.[10] It brought a new period of peace and cultural accommodation to Anglo-Powhatan relations. They were able to try and find ways to live together.

For Pocahontas this was more a matter of transformation than accommodation. Her conversion and baptism, and her marriage, involved a significant remaking of her identity. Through it she added a new name to those she already had, becoming Rebecca Rolfe. No doubt her husband changed in some ways too: he grew new crops, ate new food and spoke at least some of a new language. But the change demanded of her was much more dramatic. She had to shed what were seen as the signs of the savage and the heathen (people her teacher Edward Whitaker called 'naked slaves of the divell') for those of the civilised and Christian lady.[11] The degree and significance of the transformation, at least as far as the English were concerned, is evident in Rolfe's soul-searching over a marriage which crossed cultural boundaries. He wrestled with his conscience. Was it really the work of the devil, he asked himself, that 'should provoke me to be in love with one whose education hath been rude, her manners barbarous, her generation accursed, and so discrepant in all nurtriture from myself'? He wished to convince himself, Thomas Dale and God that this was love, and not merely desire. As he said, 'it is not any hungry appetite to gorge myself with incontinency'. Love had him caught in a labyrinth, but God showed him the way out. A voice spoke to him in the night: 'Why dost thou not endeavour to make her a Christian?' For Rolfe, writing to Dale, his marriage, and the transformation of Pocahontas upon which it depended, was 'For his [God's] glory, your honor, our country's good, the benefit of the plantation, and for the converting of one unregenerate to regeneration'.[12] We do not know what Pocahontas thought about crossing these boundaries or what she felt John Rolfe should himself become.

The Virginia Company certainly sought to take advantage of Pocahontas's transformation into Rebecca Rolfe and all it promised for the future of their colony in Virginia. They welcomed the Rolfes to London in 1616, supported them while they were there and organised a range of social entertainments (including dinner with the bishop of London and attendance at the king's Twelfth Night masque). This Virginian princess turned English gentlewoman became the talk of the town, and an engraving of her was rushed out to bring her conversion to a wider audience (figure 3.4). Yet her crossing of cultural boundaries remained troubling for herself and others. While John Smith said he was pleased she had 'become very formall and civill after our English manner',[13] the courtier John Chamberlain interpreted the engraving as 'a fine picture of no fayre Lady'. He saw a contradiction between this 'Virginian woman' lodged at the Belle Savage Inn in Ludgate and 'her tricking up and high stile and titles'.[14] Pocahontas herself also showed signs of the tensions of managing her many identities. She was unwilling to return

Figure 3.4 Pocahontas. In a picture printed to take advantage of Pocahontas's journey to London in 1616 she is simultaneously shown as both Matoaka – the daughter of 'the mighty Prince Powhatan', emperor of Virginia – and as Rebecca Rolfe, the Christian wife of an English settler.

to Virginia, where the Company expected her to lead the effort to convert the Powhatan Indians to Christianity, for which purpose it had provided £100. When she encountered John Smith again, at her new lodgings in Brentford, she refused for several hours to speak to a man she had thought long dead. When she did so she chastised him for failing to meet the obligations he owed to Powhatan as his 'father', and said that she would both 'be forever and ever your countryman' and expressed the opinion that 'your countrymen will lie much'.[15]

Pocahontas died at Gravesend in March 1617 as the ship returning her unwillingly to Virginia began its journey. John Smith turned increasingly to living from the pen rather than the sword until he died in 1631. He wove Pocahontas into his stories of the colonisation of Virginia more and more tightly as time wore on. Indeed, they both had a significant effect on the politics of settlement in North America. Smith with his military mode of negotiation had kept Jamestown fed by confronting Powhatan and resisting his sovereignty. Pocahontas had brokered a crucial peace by agreeing to marry Rolfe. Yet it was her English husband who perhaps had the most significant effects on the future of the colonists and the Amerindians. His introduction of a new strain of fragrant tobacco from Trinidad revolutionised the colonists' economy and society. Between 1619 and 1622, 3,000 colonists landed in Virginia, and their hunger for land for a crop which exhausted the soil after only three years began to push the Amerindians back towards the mountains. As exports of the noxious weed to England grew, the land around the Chesapeake Bay began to look very different from how Hakluyt had envisaged it, and how the Powhatans had known it. Finally, in 1622, the Amerindians rose up under Opechancanough and, aiming to drive the English from the land, killed 347 colonists, a quarter of all those in Virginia at the time. But they did not succeed in expelling the incomers. Retaliation was both brutal and taken as serving a higher purpose. As Edward Waterhouse saw it, this was a just war which gave the right of possession: 'we . . . may now by right of Warre, and law of Nations, invade the Country, and destroy them who sought to destroy us'.[16] Here, as elsewhere in North America, it was conflicts over land, authority and identity that led to violence and dispossession.

Living together in New England

The colonies of New England were not like Virginia. In Massachusetts Bay, Plymouth, Rhode Island, Maine and New Hampshire colonists adopted a town-based settlement pattern, a diversified agrarian economy based on the plough and the cow, and a family labour system rather than the plantations, monoculture and bonded labour further south (figure 3.5). These predominantly Puritan settlers, escaping religious persecution in England, sought the land which would give them religious freedom, economic independence and political autonomy. The colonies only survived their difficult early years with the help of the native people. By 1650, however, there were over forty towns and 23,000 colonists in New England, and they had begun a

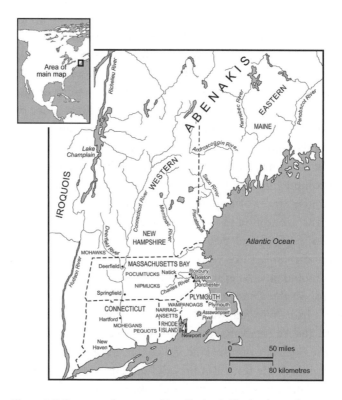

Figure 3.5 Seventeenth-century New England. The lands northwest of the Hudson River were home to a range of Amerindian peoples from the Pequots in the south to the Abenakis in the north. They were also claimed by the English and divided into a series of jurisdictions dotted with newly named towns and villages.

lucrative trade in timber and foodstuffs with the West Indian sugar islands that made New England part of an Atlantic mercantile economy (see chapter 5). By contrast, by the same period devastating epidemics meant that only one in ten of the pre-contact population of 90,000 Amerindians remained, their way of life undergoing substantial transformation. It was land upon which the colonists' and the Amerindians' economy, politics and culture were based, and this increasingly brought them into conflict with each other.

Although the natives and the colonists were similar in many ways, they came to use the land quite differently. Among the Ninnimissinouks, the indigenous term for the peoples of the region – including the Massachusetts, the Narragansetts, the Pokanokets and the Pequots – there were varied ways of fitting into the complex ecology of New England. In the upland regions of oak-hickory forests, lakes and swamps were mobile hunter-gatherers who did not engage in cultivation. On the coast people lived from the rich and varied resources of estuarine and salt marsh environments. They hunted and fished, and gathered large quantities of shellfish, drying them for the winter. They encouraged wild plants and collected berries, nuts and snails. Settlement patterns were very fluid, the inhabitants being neither sedentary villagers nor wandering foragers. Stable social groupings of around two hundred people occupied more or less bounded zones but did so in collective groups or single and extended family campsites as the need arose. After 1300 AD population growth had led to the adoption of corn cultivation at the coast, and a more settled and centralised social system and settlement pattern.

Between the coast and the uplands were the agricultural villages of the river valleys, particularly along the Connecticut River. Here corn was an important staple, and the year was organised around it. Corn was planted in small regularly spaced 'hills' in late April and early May, with beans growing up the stalks, and squashes and pumpkins between the hills (fixing nitrogen and keeping down the weeds). It was harvested in September and October and preserved for winter in large woven and grass-lined baskets sunk into the ground. Women did all the agricultural work, and gathered shellfish from the clam banks. Men grew only tobacco and engaged in hunting and fishing which provided materials for clothing and tools as well as food. Villages moved when necessary, and the annual round – of foraging and hunting trips to the coast or the uplands – meant that people provisioned themselves from a large area, drawing on a variety of resources. While the English and the Amerindians learned from each other – the colonists adopting corn and pumpkins, and the Ninnimissinouks taking to pigs which could be left to forage in the forests – the fixed farmhouse, the fenced fields and the demands of caring for cattle remained as alien to the Amerindians as their seemingly unkempt gardens, shifting villages and foraging for wild foods did to the English.

These two sets of people were forced by the circumstance of the colonists' arrival to live together. Since the English settled on land that had been depopulated by epidemics, and since they bought land from the Amerindians, the peoples often lived side by side. Their different uses of the land then brought them into conflict. The importance of domestic livestock to the colonists meant that they reversed the usual English practice of requiring cattle-owners to keep their herds fenced in. Instead they required agriculturalists to fence their fields. Animals wandering into unfenced Amerindian fields and gardens were a constant source of aggravation. This was returned when the natives killed the trespassing beasts. These conflicts were rooted in different notions of land ownership and land use, and were exacerbated by different understandings of how conflicts should be resolved. For the Amerindians what was crucial was not the ownership of land but its use. In many ways, use was ownership. Amerindian groups gave power to their leaders, or *sachems*, to manage these use rights, allocating planting fields, overseeing forms of conflict resolution through personal revenge, and dealing with the colonists. When *sachems* sold land to the colonists, they did so for the European manufactured goods on which they had come to depend. Thus, in 1649, Massasoit, the Wampanoag *sachem* sold 196 square miles of land for seven coats, nine hatchets, eight hoes, twenty-nine knives, four moose skins and ten and a half yards of cotton. These sales were, however, accompanied by guarantees that Amerindians could still plant, hunt, fish and gather on those lands. Their use rights remained in place.

For the colonists, by contrast, ownership was all important. It could be a use in and of itself, and formed the basis for rights that would be enforced by the colony's law courts. When an Amerindian killed a colonist's wandering cow the native notion of legitimate personal revenge in defence of use rights clashed with the colonists' ideas of individual property rights (in land and beasts) that should be adjudicated by the courts. Early treaties between the Amerindians and the colonists had sought to establish their societies as separate legal and political entities, existing side by side. This was primarily so that the English, in the uncertain early years, could enforce their own laws on their own people. The problems of living together as the colonies grew stronger and more extensive increasingly meant that that autonomy could not be maintained.

This was true in cultural terms as well. Living together meant that both the English and the Amerindians feared losing their distinctive identities. They feared becoming more like each other. The English worried that living in the wilderness would make them wild too. They feared that their adoption of native ways – speaking some of the heathen language, eating different food, wearing buckskin – would rob them of the virtues of Englishness. With this in mind their clothes, their houses, their fields and their cows were much more than a way of living. They were a way of life. One response was to convert the Amerindians, and to convert them to Englishness as much as to Puritanism. The fourteen 'praying towns' established after 1651 by John Eliot for Christian Indians required them to wear English clothes, live in houses of wood and brick and tend cattle, as well as to learn to read the Bible. They were learning to be English. The Amerindians, faced with this and other evidence of the transformation of their world, feared that the settlers would change them forever. The Narragansett *sachem* Miantonomo appealed to the Montauk Indians of Long Island in 1641 in strident terms:

Our fathers had plenty of deer and skins, our plains were full of deer, as also our woods, and of turkies, and our coves full of fish and fowl. But these English having gotten our land, they with scythes cut down the grass, and with axes fell the trees; their cows and horses eat the grass, and their hogs spoil our clam banks, and we shall all be starved.

This was not just the defence of a livelihood, but of a way of life in which land and animals were much more than a matter of mere property and provisions. Miantonomo's solution was a total one, to 'fall on' the English, and to 'kill men, women, and children'.[17] While the New England colonies differed from those of Virginia in many respects, they shared a history of violence and warfare between natives and newcomers over issues of autonomy and encroachment. The bloodiest war was sparked by the death of a man who had tried to serve both sides.

The world of John Sassamon

For much of his life the Christian Indian John Sassamon must have looked to the colonists like a symbol of their success. The Puritan minister William Hubbard noted that Sassamon 'was observed to conform more to the English Manners than any other Indian'.[18] His parents were among the few who survived the epidemic of 1616–1618, but it is likely that they converted to Christianity on their deathbeds during the smallpox outbreak of 1633 and left their son in the care of an English family. By 1637 Sassamon was serving with Sergeant Richard Callicott of Dorchester on the English side in the Pequot War, and he may have been the 'interpreter' who shot dead a Pequot warrior curious enough to ask him the troubling question: 'What are you, an Indian or an Englishman?'[19] After the war he returned to Dorchester with a Pequot captive whom he may later have married. He was well acquainted with John Eliot, who was the minister of nearby Roxbury. Sassamon may indeed have been taught English by Eliot. He certainly assisted the divine in learning the Massachusett language, acting as an interpreter, and in translating the body of Christian texts, including the Bible, into Massachusett with which Eliot hoped to convert the 'savages'. When Eliot founded the first 'praying towns' at Natick Sassamon was there to help build them, and he later worked as a preacher and schoolmaster. In 1653 Eliot found the funds to send Sassamon to Harvard College where his fellow students were the sons of the Puritan elite. On his death John Eliot expressed his sorrow, calling this Christian Indian 'a man of eminent parts & wit'.[20]

There were, however, other worlds in which John Sassamon moved. He disappointed John Eliot as well as pleasing him. In 1654 Eliot had planned a day of examination for the members of the Natick church which would bring the 'praying Indians' into the Puritan community. Ten days before it was due to happen three Natick Indians got drunk and forced alcohol on the young son of a devout Christian Indian. Eliot, angered by his interpreter's involvement, saw in this 'much of Satans venome' and the two became estranged.[21] Indeed, we know little of what happened to Sassamon in the decade after this, but he subsequently reappeared working for the Amerindians. When the Wampanoag *sachem* Massasoit died in 1662 he was succeeded by his eldest son Wamsutta, known to the English as Alexander, and later by Alexander's brother Metacom (whom the English called Philip). Sassamon took his skills in reading and writing English and Massachusett and put them to work for Wamsutta and Metacom. His name appears again and again on treaties and land deals 'for he could write, though the King his master could not so much as read'.[22]

Yet this is not simply a story of someone switching sides. Sassamon was caught in between these two worlds. John Eliot certainly thought that his work with Metacom might help to bring the Wampanoag *sachem* into the Christian fold, and he asked the commissioners of the New England Confederation (of the colonies of Massachusetts, Plymouth, Connecticut and New Haven) 'to give incouragmt to John Sosaman, who teacheth Phillip and his men to read'.[23] But there was no successful conversion here, and many Englishmen believed that Sassamon had instead 'apostatiz[ed] from the profession of Christianity'.[24] At the same time, some Wampanoags clearly thought that Sassamon was working against their *sachem*, and accused him of writing himself into Philip's will, confident that his master's illiteracy would keep his deceit hidden. Philip certainly came to distrust Sassamon. In 1671 the *sachem* accused his go-between of giving false information about the whereabouts of the Wampanoags' Narragansett enemies and of informing the English that Philip was entertaining other Amerindian leaders. In 1675 Sassamon went to the governor of the Plymouth colony, Josiah Winslow, saying that 'Philip . . . was Indeavouring to engage all the Sachems round about in a warr', and that his own life was in danger for passing on this intelligence to the English.[25] Winslow should have believed him rather than sending him off alone on the long walk home through the snowy woods. His body was found, his neck broken and his head swollen, beneath the ice of Assawompsett Pond, a short distance from his destination. John Sassamon had not been able to stay alive between two worlds that were colliding.

Many thought Philip responsible. Yet he explicitly denied it and there was no proof. It was not even clear that Sassamon had been murdered. Eventually a native witness came forward to say that he had seen three men closely connected to King Philip – Tobias, Wampapaquan (Tobias's son) and Mattashunnamo – kill Sassamon and put his body through the ice. The colony's courts took it upon themselves to try the case. The three men were found guilty and sentenced to death by hanging. It was, however, not clear that the courts had the power to do any of this. The principle of Amerindian justice, which had been written into treaties with the English, was that the subjects of a *sachem* were to be dealt with the traditional way. This was a matter of legitimate revenge which might even have sanctioned Sassamon's assassination for the betrayal of Philip. The Wampanoags had as much claim on determining how and why Sassamon had died as the English, who took the view that what happened in their territories was a matter for the colony's law. Like trespassing animals, the murder of a go-between blurred the legal boundaries. Perhaps there was some recognition of the Indians' claim in the impanelling of an odd jury made up of twelve Englishmen, and then six of the 'most indifferentest, gravest, and sage Indians . . . to healp to consult and advice with, of, and concerning the premises'.[26] Yet the conviction on the evidence of a single unreliable witness, and the death by firing squad of Wampapaquan after the hangman's rope had broken, both testify to the willingness of the English to identify Philip's men as Sassamon's murderers and to extend English 'justice' at the expense of native legal and political autonomy. Sassamon's trial marked a new point in the extension of the power of the colonists.

On the land, in the law and in matters of identity there was, by 1675, no way to live together. A few days after the executions King Philip went to war in a bloody conflict that would kill a higher proportion of Americans on both sides than any subsequent war. He complained that it had not been the case that 'when the English boft [bought] land of them that thay wold have kept ther Catell upone ther owne land', and his warriors killed and mutilated the settlers' cows and left them to die in the fields.[27] He also complained 'that they had a great fear to have ani of ther indians should be Caled or forsed to be Christian Indians. [T]hay saied that such wer in everi thing more mischievous, only dissemblers, and then the English made them not subject to ther kings, and by ther lying to rong their kings.'[28] He might well have been thinking of John Sassamon's deceit and the English court's denial of his own sovereignty. He was certainly thinking about how the English had robbed his people and himself of their economic, political and cultural autonomy.

Empires and Indians

King Philip's War not only set the Amerindians against the English, it set Indian against Indian too. The colonists would in all likelihood have been pushed off the land completely had not the Mohegans, Pequots and many of the Christian Indians fought with them against the Narragansetts, Nipmucks, Pocumtucks and Abenakis who joined Metacom's Wampanoags. Each Amerindian group had to make a series of new calculations as to where their allegiances lay and how their interests were best served within long-standing cycles of wars for lands, trade and captives. They had to judge, like Powhatan before them, whether this new element in the politics of North America was one they should ally themselves with, or stand and fight against. Over the seventeenth and eighteenth centuries many, such as the Pequots, were to do both.

From the late seventeenth century onwards, after King Philip's War, there was an added complication. The politics of control over North American land were not just colonial, they were also imperial. To the south of the English territories were the Spanish in Florida, and to the north were the French in New France (Canada). As the great European powers themselves entered a cycle of warfare that was to last from 1688 to 1815, from King William III's accession to the English throne in support of Protestantism to the defeat of Napoleon at Waterloo, these conflicts were also fought out on an increasingly global scale. What was known in Europe as the Nine Years' War (1688–1697), or the War of the League of Augsburg, was fought out on the east coast of North America as King William's War. A brief peace was then disturbed by what the Europeans called the War of the Spanish Succession (1701–1713), which became Queen Anne's War across the Atlantic. The middle of the eighteenth century saw the War of the Austrian Succession (1739–1748) – also known as the War of Jenkins' Ear (although that is another story; see chapter 5), and as King George's War to Amerindians and Europeans in North America – and the Seven Years' War (1756–1763), a truly global conflict with fighting in India, across the world's oceans and in the North American colonies, known as the French and Indian Wars. Despite their localised and often peculiar names these conflicts were all part of a worldwide struggle for imperial supremacy between France and

England. It was only with the capture of Montreal and Quebec, and the surrender of New France, in 1760, that the French had to concede to the English in North America. New France lost out to New England.

Yet all global wars are local wars too. They are fought out in particular places according to local interests, alliances and enmities. New France, with its aristocratic society of landed estates, did not have the extensive population of settlers to draw upon that New England's Puritan villages had, and as a result, in fighting its wars, relied on alliances with the Amerindian groups that lived within and between the territories claimed by the two empires. The English colonists, and their empire, needed native allies too. In each of these conflicts the Amerindians had to make political choices. This is most dramatically illustrated by the formation of the Iroquois League. This alliance of the Mohawks, Oneidas, Onondagas, Cayugas and Senecas enabled these 'Five Nations' to avoid being weakened by internal warfare, and to conduct collective diplomatic negotiations with the French and English. Having fought the French in the middle of the seventeenth century, and having been allied to the English in the Nine Years' War, they signed a treaty at Montreal in 1701 that committed them to neutrality in future imperial conflicts in return for the right to hunt north of the Great Lakes and to trade at the French post of Detroit. Others allied themselves more fully with the French. Many displaced Amerindians had converted to Catholicism and settled in mission villages along the St Lawrence River. There were Hurons at Lorette, Iroquois of the Mountain at La Montagne and, most prominently, the Mohawks at Kahnawake (figure 3.6). This was a village of between 800 and 1,000 people, making it larger than most towns in either New France or New England, where the Christian Indians lived alongside Jesuit priests and practised a form of Catholicism that retained many elements of traditional religious ritual. The Mohawks of Kahnawake were, however, also involved in an extensive fur trade with the English at Albany, against the wishes of the government of New France, and they maintained contact with the Mohawk groups of the Iroquois alliance who had previously fought the French. They were poised between the two empires, and their allegiances could not be taken for granted.

This was even more strikingly the case for the Abenakis. Following their defeat in King William's War they had been pushed north into the area between the two empires. They continued to fight English encroachments from the south, but they were not always convinced that their interests lay in a strong alliance with those other Europeans in New France and Arcadia. As a result the four Anglo-Abenaki wars fought between 1675 and 1727 were sometimes rolled up into other colonial wars (such as King Philip's

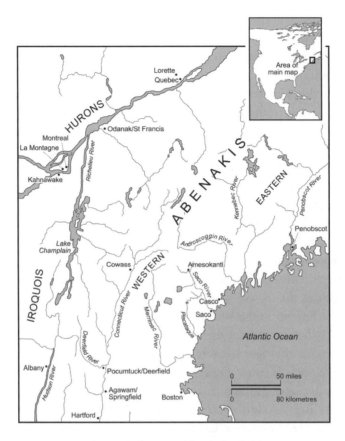

Figure 3.6 North America's imperial borderlands. The mountainous lands between the French empire in Canada and the English empire in New England were an uncertain zone of border settlements which was also inhabited and crossed by Amerindians who traded across the divide, conducted raids and made alliances with the Europeans.

War), sometimes fought when peace had broken out elsewhere (for example, between 1722 and 1727), and sometimes became part of 'global' conflicts. Thus, the third Anglo-Abenaki War overlapped with the War of the Spanish Succession, the Abenakis little caring whether the duc d'Anjou became the king of Spain or not, but seeing that in this case their interests lay in an alliance with the French of New France against the settlers of New England who had taken their land.

Indeed, the English colonies were still growing in population and were seeking new land for their sons and daughters. In doing so they were also negotiating a fine line between independence and imperial control. New

Englanders had initially formed their new society in opposition to much that the English state stood for. They continued to value their independence from its economic, political and religious controls where that could be secured. Yet they also increasingly operated in a world of empires. As their settlements expanded north up the river valleys of Massachusetts, New Hampshire and Maine, they became not only Puritan townships on land bought from the Amerindians, but the last outposts of Protestantism and the English empire. Their position on the frontier was a barrier against the French empire and its native allies. In keeping themselves there, and in dealing with the consequences of being there, the settlers found that they needed to call upon the forces of empire too.

The world of Eunice Williams

In the early years of the eighteenth century the furthest outpost of England's North American empire was Deerfield, Massachusetts. This was a township of about 50 families, around 270 people, who lived by farming and trading. Its location in the valley of the Connecticut River provided good land that had been bought from the Pocumtuck Indians displaced by epidemics and the ravages of warfare since 1675. However, this location also made the town vulnerable. During the Nine Years' War Deerfield had been captured by Amerindians, but then retaken from them. At dawn on 29 February 1704, several years into Queen Anne's War, the town was attacked by a party of several hundred men who had come the three hundred miles over the snow-covered mountains from New France, and down the river to Deerfield. This was a combined French and Amerindian raiding party. It was led by Jean-Baptiste Hertel de Rouville, a young Canadian aristocrat bent on distinguishing himself in military service as his forebears had done. He commanded a small group of professional soldiers from the *troupes de la marine*, and a body of Canadian militia men used to snow-shoeing and surviving in the winter forests. The majority of the warriors were Amerindians: *sauvages domiciliés* from the mission villages, mostly Mohawks from Kahnawake, but also Hurons and Iroquois of the Mountain. They were joined by Abenakis from the mission village at Odanak, but also from the lands nearer Deerfield which lay between the empires. The French aim was to bring death and destruction to the frontier: to remove the township from the map and to spread fear among New England's settlers. They also aimed to cement the alliances between themselves and the Amerindians, and to further drive a wedge between the natives and the English. To do so they had composed a force made up of as many different Amerindian groups as possible. They had also promised those Christian Indians that they would get what they wanted from the raid: captives.

The Amerindians wanted captives for a variety of reasons. They were an economic resource, providing hands that could work in the fields or help on the hunt. By the early eighteenth century English captives could also be ransomed to the French, who sought European as well as native converts to Catholicism and, where that was impossible, English men, women and children to trade for the French prisoners held by their enemies. Yet there was more to captivity than that. Amerindians had long fought what were called 'mourning wars' whose aim was to gather people, not land or trade routes. Prisoners taken in these wars were spiritual substitutes for those who had been lost in other conflicts. As such, they might be adopted into native families as real substitutes for the missing, or they might be subject to violent tortures and death to make good through pain and suffering the loss to those remaining. The raid on Deerfield was thus shaped by many motives. On the French commander's orders, houses were burned and animals were killed along with those who resisted the attack. When the home of the town's prominent minister John Williams was attacked, the raiders immediately killed an African-American slave woman called Parthena and two young children, six-year-old Joshua and baby Jerusha, born only six weeks before, who would have been a burden on the long trek back to Canada. They took captive the minister, his wife Eunice, their male slave Frank, and their children: Samuel (15 years old), Esther (13), Stephen (10), Eunice (7) and Warham (4). Mrs Williams and Frank would not last the journey. Along with many other adult women and small children they were killed by their captors as valueless captives. At most only 89 of the 112 Deerfield settlers who were taken away that morning reached Canada.

Most of those who did were soon ransomed to the French, including the Reverend John Williams. Some found themselves with the Indians. Stephen Williams was taken up into the Abenaki hunting grounds around Cowass. Eunice Williams was taken back to Kahnawake, south of Montreal. Here she eventually crossed two cultural boundaries. The Jesuits put the captives under pressure to convert. Eunice was scared. She told her father when he managed to get to see her that 'They force me to say some prayers in Latin, but I don't understand one word of them. I hope it won't do me any harm'.[29] Eventually she was rebaptised into a new faith that was not her father's, and she took the name Marguerite. She was also adopted into a Mohawk family, and she carried this new status in the name they gave her. Eunice was now Waongote: 'they took her and place her as a member of their tribe'.[30] As a young woman in Kahnawake she would have worked with the other women in the fields around the village and dressed like them in a combination of European blankets, lace and ribbons, and the skins of animals trapped by the villagers. She would have worn her hair greased and tied back with an eelskin, and her face painted. She soon forgot how to speak English, and she began to fit in. At some point she was renamed Kanenstenhawi ('she brings in corn'), and in 1713 she married a Mohawk named Arosen and they began to raise a family. Eunice Williams had settled into another world.

Yet the world from which she came had not totally lost sight of her. The majority of the Deerfield captives ended up in the hands of the French. Some of them converted to Catholicism, married Canadians and chose to make their lives as settlers in New France. The rest became bargaining chips in the great game of imperial diplomacy. Delegations of officials representing Governor Vaudreuil of New France and Governor Dudley of Massachusetts, who themselves stood for King Louis XIV and Queen Anne, shuttled between the empires deciding the fate of the captives. John Williams was back in Deerfield by 1707, and penned *The Redeemed Captive Returning to Zion* on his return to inspire others with his message that he had been delivered by God from his trials. His other children had all returned too. Only Eunice remained. Governor Dudley demanded that his opposite number get her back from what he called the 'French Indians'. Governor Vaudreuil argued that he had no power except that of persuasion, and that even that was of no use if captives had decided that they wanted to stay. And to the shock and dismay of her family, the residents of Deerfield, and the colonial and imperial authorities, Eunice did want to stay with the Indians. A delegation led by John Schuyler was able to put the question to her directly in 1713, after Queen Anne's War was over. As he reported back, they talked to her for two hours and, like Pocahontas with John Smith, she remained silent, 'harder than Steel in her Breast'. Finally she spoke, 'wch was after long Solicitations (Jaghte oghte) which words being translated into the English Tongue their Signification [is] maybe not but the meaning thereof among the Indians is a plaine denyall'.[31] Her polite 'Jaghte oghte' – 'Maybe not' – meant no. She was not going back, even with the promise that she would be safe and could return when she wanted. Eunice was staying put.

Eunice Williams did eventually cross back into the English empire to see her New England family, but not until 1740. By that time, thirty-six years after she had been carried away, her father was dead and her brothers and sisters were grown up too (all of them with children called Eunice in memory of their dead mother and their 'captive' sister). She came back then, and several times afterwards, with her husband, children and grandchildren. She travelled with them along the fur trade routes, via Albany, and across the shrinking native lands that had always made the border a space of crossings and recrossings. She could only speak to the Williamses via an interpreter but, despite their pleadings and bribes, she always made it clear that she was not coming back to stay. In her final letter to her brother Stephen she said 'I am now growing old and can have but little hopes of seeing you in this wor<u>l</u>d.'[32] She was buried at Kahnawake in 1785, having lived for eighty-nine years. Just as the Amerindians had made choices of how to live with the empires that came to take their lands away, so Eunice, now Kanenstenhawi, had made a choice of how to live with those who had come to take her away.

This chapter began with the first faltering steps of English settlers disembarking from ships in North America and has ended with the achievement of English imperial hegemony over the continent's east coast by the middle of the eighteenth century. This was not simply a matter of fulfilling the hopes and plans embodied in the projections of men such as Richard Hakluyt and the investors of the Virginia Company. The North American colonies turned out differently from what had been expected or desired: a plantation-based slave society producing tobacco for export to Europe to the exclusion of all else grew up in Virginia; and an independent society founded on political and religious dissent was founded in New England. In both cases, however, what was sought was control over land. This was imperial control forged against the claims of other European powers who also sought possession of the Americas. It was also colonial control which in all parts of North America dispossessed the native peoples who had inhabited the land when the Europeans arrived.

This dispossession was not a simple process either. It was the Amerindians who kept the colonists alive in the early years of settlement, hoping to incorporate them into their way of life and to benefit from what they brought with them. Amerindians tried to weave the English into their politics. In turn, the colonists tried to convert the natives – both to Christianity and to settled agriculture. As the natives and the newcomers lived together there was much that they shared, and much that they had to learn from each other. All of the lives told in this chapter bear witness to these cultural crossings and mixings: John Smith and Pocahontas found some common ground. He certainly thought that she had helped him, and he had tried to understand her. John Sassamon and Eunice Williams both crossed between peoples: changing religions, identities and their most intimate connections. Yet all of these lives were also marked by the violence and savagery that came with the hunger for land, the desire for possession and the fear of losing autonomy and identity. John Smith faced off against Powhatan, and threatened to bring destruction down on his people. Pocahontas was tricked into captivity and offered in trade for soldiers and weapons. John Sassamon died because the middle ground between the English and the Amerindians which he inhabited was fast eroding in the tense times of early 1670s Massachusetts. Eunice Williams, having been captured on a night of fire and bloodshed, was forced to choose one side or the other. In the end, settlement on the land made living together impossible and meant that the tales of North America that are told are often savage ones.

Westwards towards settlement in North America was only one direction in which Britain's engagement with the world developed. Looking east towards Asia matters looked, as we shall see in the next chapter, quite different. The creation of extensive colonies of agricultural settlements peopled by Europeans was never an option in places such as India. Instead of supposedly 'empty' land, it was the rich and extensive production systems and trading networks that already existed around the Indian Ocean which provided the lure. Yet there are similarities when looking east too. Trading, like settling, also necessitated constructing close relationships with the people who were already there. As in the Americas, these relationships of dependence and independence were also ones that changed over time to the disadvantage of the indigenous people.

Further reading

The Powhatan empire is well documented in Helen C. Rountree (1990) *Pocahontas's People: The Powhatan Indians of Virginia Through Four Centuries* (University of Oklahoma Press, Norman and London). A selection of early colonisation literature is available in Peter C. Mancall (ed.) (1995) *Envisioning America: English Plans for the Colonization of North America, 1580–1640* (Bedford/St Martins, Boston) and the legitimacy of possession is dealt with in Patricia Seed (1995) *Ceremonies of Possession in Europe's Conquest of the New World* (Cambridge University Press, Cambridge). For the process of encounter in North America, see James Axtell (2001) *Natives and Newcomers: The Cultural Origins of North America* (Oxford University Press, Oxford) and the chapters by Nicholas Canny, James Horn, Virginia DeJohn Anderson and Peter Mancall in Nicholas Canny (ed.) (1998) *The Oxford History of the British Empire*, vol. I, *The Origins of Empire* (Oxford University Press, Oxford). There are very different versions of John Smith and his relationships with the Powhatans in Philip L. Barbour (1969)

Pocahontas and Her World (Robert Hale & Co., London) and Martin Quitt (1995) 'Trade and acculturation at Jamestown, 1607–1609: the limits of understanding', *William and Mary Quarterly*, 52:2 pp. 227–258. Also, for different understandings of the relationships between the natives and the newcomers, see Bernard W. Sheehan (1980) *Savagism and Civility: Indians and Englishmen in Colonial Virginia* (Cambridge University Press, Cambridge) and Karen Ordahl Kupperman (2000) *Indians and English: Facing Off in Early America* (Cornell University Press, Ithaca). Many of the original documents relating to John Smith and Pocahontas are available in modern editions such as Edward Wright Haile (ed.) (1998) *Jamestown Narratives: Eyewitness Accounts of the Virginia Colony. The First Decade: 1607–1617* (Roundhouse, Champlain, Va.). The Indians of New England, the death of John Sassamon and the outbreak of King Philip's War are dealt with by Kathleen J. Bragdon (1996) *Native People of Southern New England* (University of Oklahoma Press, Norman), Yasuhide Kawashima (2001) *Igniting King Philip's War: The John Sassamon Murder Trial* (University Press of Kansas, Lawrence) and Jill Lepore (1999) *The Name of War: King Philip's War and the Origins of American Identity* (Vintage Books, New York). The story of Eunice Williams and the Deerfield raid are beautifully told by John Demos (1996) *The Unredeemed Captive: A Family Story from Early America* (Papermac, London) and put in a broader imperial context by Evan Haefeli and Kevin Sweeney (2003) *Captors and Captives: The 1704 French and Indian Raid on Deerfield* (University of Massachusetts Press, Amherst and Boston).

Notes

1 *Discourse of Western Planting*, reprinted in Peter C. Mancall (ed.) (1995) *Envisioning America: English Plans for the Colonization of North America, 1580–1640* (Bedford/St Martins, Boston) quotation on p. 50.
2 Quoted in David Armitage (2000) *The Ideological Origins of the British Empire* (Cambridge University Press, Cambridge) p. 93.
3 John Smith quoted in Jess Edwards (2005) 'Between "plain wilderness" and "goodly corn fields": representing land use in early Virginia', in Robert Applebaum and John Wood Sweet (eds.) *Envisioning an English Empire: Jamestown and the Making of the North Atlantic World* (University of Pennsylvania Press, Philadelphia) p. 217, and Robert Gray (1609) *Good Speed to Virginia* quoted in Michael Leroy Oberg (1999) *Dominion and Civility: English Imperialism and Native America, 1585–1685* (Cornell University Press, Ithaca and London) p. 52.
4 Quoted in James Axtell (2001) *Natives and Newcomers: The Cultural Origins of North America* (Oxford University Press, New York and Oxford) p. 240.
5 Quoted in Oberg, *Dominion and Civility*, p. 50.

6 Quotations from documents reprinted in Edward Wright Haile (ed.) (1998) *Jamestown Narratives: Eyewitness Accounts of the Virginia Colony. The First Decade: 1607–1617* (Roundhouse, Champlain, Va.) p. 161.

7 Ibid., p. 630.

8 Ibid., p. 314.

9 Ibid., p. 844.

10 Ibid., p. 833.

11 Quoted in Karen Ordahl Kupperman (2000) *Indians and English: Facing Off in Early America* (Cornell University Press, Ithaca) p. 51.

12 All quotations from Haile, *Jamestown Narratives*, pp. 853 and 855.

13 Quoted in Kupperman, *Indians and English*, p. 199.

14 Quoted in Karen Robertson (1996) 'Pocahontas at the masque', *Signs: Journal of Women in Culture and Society*, 21:3 p. 554.

15 Quoted in Haile, *Jamestown Narratives*, p. 864.

16 Quoted in Robertson, 'Pocahontas at the masque', p. 556 n. 11.

17 Quoted in Yasuhide Kawashima (2001) *Igniting King Philip's War: The John Sassamon Murder Trial* (University Press of Kansas, Lawrence) p. 35.

18 Quoted in Jill Lepore (1999) *The Name of War: King Philip's War and the Origins of American Identity* (Vintage Books, New York) p. 43.

19 Quoted in Kawashima, *Igniting King Philip's War*, p. 77.

20 Quoted ibid., p. 87.

21 Quoted in Lepore, *The Name of War*, p. 34.

22 Quoted ibid., p. 39.

23 Quoted in Kawashima, *Igniting King Philip's War*, p. 79.

24 Quoted in Lepore, *The Name of War*, p. 39.

25 Quoted ibid., p. 21.

26 Quoted in Kawashima, *Igniting King Philip's War*, p. 107.

27 Quoted in Virginia DeJohn Anderson (1994) 'King Philip's herds: Indians, colonists, and the problem of livestock in early New England', *William and Mary Quarterly*, 51:4 p. 621.

28 Quoted in Lepore, *The Name of War*, p. 42.

29 Quoted in John Demos (1996) *The Unredeemed Captive: A Family Story from Early America* (Papermac, London) p. 152.

30 Translated in Evan Haefeli and Kevin Sweeney (2003) *Captors and Captives: The 1704 French and Indian Raid on Deerfield* (University of Massachusetts Press, Amherst and Boston) p. 152.

31 Quotations from Demos, *The Unredeemed Captive*, pp. 105 and 107.

32 Quoted ibid., p. 232.

4 | East meets West: the English East India Company in India

In contrast to their encounter with the 'New World', the people of northern Europe had no moment that they could call a 'discovery' of Asia. Ideas, goods and people had always travelled back and forth across the landmass, and life in each part of Eurasia had been shaped by these relationships of trade and warfare. Indeed, it needs to be remembered that 'the East' was so important to the Spanish and the Portuguese in the late fifteenth century that the voyage that brought Columbus to the Americas had set off in search of an ocean route westwards to China, the land of the Great Khan and the source of spices, silks and other riches (see chapter 2). This long-standing connection did not mean that there were no historical changes in the ways in which people from different parts of Europe and Asia encountered each other. The Portuguese, while demonstrating that Asia was accessible by sea around the Cape of Good Hope, built an empire in the Indian Ocean that changed their fortunes but had little impact either on the flows of goods in Asia or on the overall volume of exports to Europe. They were more content to try and profit from their naval superiority by charging protection money to vessels sailing between Asian ports. More dramatic change, at least as far as the Europeans were concerned, came at the end of the sixteenth century. At that point combinations of north European merchants and financiers organised themselves into new sorts of companies to take advantage of the route pioneered by the Portuguese. The aim of these East India companies was to provide by sea large volumes of Asian goods – first spices, but then mainly cloth – at lower prices on the European markets than those who acquired them by land. As a result their attention first concentrated on the spice islands of the Indonesian archipelago – Ternate, Tidore, Amboina and the Banda Islands – which were the world's only sources of cloves, nutmegs, mace and pepper. These were flavours and preservatives for which northern Europeans were willing to pay high prices, and for which merchants were willing to take substantial risks.

The English East India Company was established in 1600 as a joint stock company with a monopoly on trade with the East Indies that was guaranteed by the monarch. This shared the risk among those willing to put in their money and expertise, and provided a guaranteed market for their goods. It also caused the Company problems. The Company was, from the beginning, closely tied to the monarchy, who saw it as a good source of 'presents' and loans, and to the state, which saw it as a political entity as much as an economic one. This political role was evident in the competition between different European nations in the seventeenth century. The Dutch and the English shared an interest in breaking the monopoly of the Portuguese, but they were also competing against one another for valuable cargoes, for the political alliances with local powers that would deliver them and for control over the markets in Europe that would produce profits for their shareholders and taxes for their governments. The Dutch East India Company had much more capital and many more ships and personnel in Asia than the English. As a result, by the middle of the seventeenth century they effectively controlled trade in the Indonesian archipelago. By the 1670s the English East India Company had been forced to concentrate on trade between Europe and Asia, and they primarily concerned themselves with exchanging gold and silver bullion for Indian textiles.

All of this, however, meant very little to most people in Asia. There were a few small trading states that benefited, or suffered, from the attentions of the European companies. There were some Asian merchants who found ways of profiting from European demand or the availability of Company shipping. However, the vast majority of people lived their lives within the great land-based empires of Asia – the Mughal empire, the Ottoman empire and the Chinese empire – and were unaffected by the Europeans rounding the Cape and competing for a slice of the spice trade. Equally, the political elites of these empires also judged the Europeans to be an insignificant presence, just one more set of merchants with whom it might be useful to deal but who were not a major force in shaping their worlds.

The presence and significance of large-scale and well-organised empires, and smaller-scale competitive and flexible coastal and island states, meant that the European companies could get nothing from trade in and with Asia without the collaboration and co-operation of Asian intermediaries. This established important and changing relationships of dependence between Europeans and Asians. This chapter explores two phases in those relationships to demonstrate their basis and the patterns of dependence that existed and to show how these patterns changed over time. It first examines the relationships forged between the English East India Company's employees (or 'servants') and Indian traders as they both sought to profit from the explosive boom in trade on the Coromandel coast of southeastern India in the 1670s. It does so by exploring the lives of two merchants – Kasi Viranna and Streynsham Master. The second part of the chapter attends to

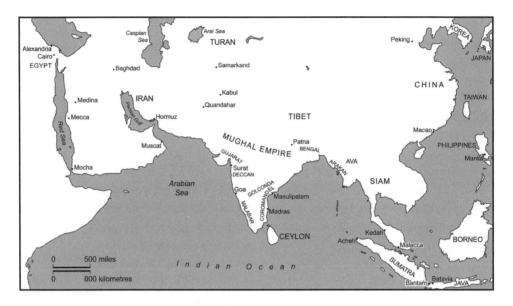

Figure 4.1 Major ports and trading places of the Indian Ocean in the seventeenth century. The Indian subcontinent was connected into an extensive network of ocean-going trades from the Red Sea to Japan, and a series of land-based caravan routes running both east–west and north–south.

a different period and a different place: Bengal (in northeast India) in the 1780s. By this time the English East India Company was no longer simply a trading operation; it had become the ruler of a large territory. This altered the basis on which relationships were built between the British and their Indian subjects as the Company sought to develop appropriate ways of governing an Asian empire. Again the complex and changing relationships of dependence and independence are explored through two lives. In this case it is two men deeply interested in the law: Sir William Jones and Radhakanta Tarkavagisa.

The world of Kasi Viranna

By 1650 the Coromandel coast had long been bound into a vibrant network of oceanic trade (figure 4.1). In the early fifteenth century the rise of the sultanates of Gujarat and Malacca, several thousand miles apart at either end of the Indian Ocean, and the Chinese decision to stop sending their huge fleets of junks west to trade opened up a new set of opportunities for Bengali, Tamil and Gujarati merchants to traffic in spices, rice, sugar, cloth,

Persian horses and Thai (Siamese) elephants to all points between the Red Sea and the Indonesian archipelago. Indian and Armenian traders also took advantage of land routes north, via Quandahar by camel, into Iran, Turan and Russia, where there was, by the seventeenth century, an established settlement of Mughal-Indian merchants at Astrakhan on the Caspian Sea with connections as far north as Moscow. (Perhaps even more surprisingly there were Armenian settlers farming silkworms in Virginia by 1655.) On the ocean, west Indian merchants, many operating from Surat, some of whom were also pilgrims to the holy cities of Mecca and Medina, traded mainly with Mocha on the Red Sea, Muscat in southern Arabia and Hormuz in the Persian Gulf. In these places they exchanged textiles, sugar, southeast Asian tin and spices, and precious stones and steel from the Deccan for cotton yarn, gold and silver. Both Hindu and Muslim merchants from Gujarat also traded with East Africa, and to Kedah, Acheh and Bantam in southeast Asia where the exchange of textiles, wheat and rice for spices, pepper, tin, elephants and gold was facilitated by networks of Indian merchants who had taken up influential political positions within these small states. On a smaller scale, a coastal trade in higher-bulk and lower-value commodities linked Surat to Malabar, Coromandel and Golconda.

This link between Gujarat and Coromandel was a strong one. Surat was increasingly tied to Masulipatnam – the key southeast coast port which served the kingdom of Golconda – through the Muslim merchants who had moved there to trade Coromandel goods to southern Arabia and the Persian and Ottoman empires back through their former home. It was Coromandel's woven textiles that were most in demand and that formed a key part of the whole Indian Ocean trading network. This demand produced a sophisticated regional economy with some areas specialising in cloth production and others producing the food for the cloth workers, the links being made by the ubiquitous local merchants. These export goods might be made in a location twenty days' travel from the port from which they were shipped. Although Coromandel's speciality was dyeing, printing and painting cloth in bright colours (what became known as 'chintz'), different areas produced different textiles. The villages around Kalingapatnam and Vizakhapatnam produced coarse long cloth (what the Dutch called 'negro cloth' because of its use in the slave trade; see chapter 8), gunnies, twine and thread. In the district of Elluru, a dozen villages produced high-grade cloth (sallampores, percallen, bethiles) for export. Other villages specialised in washing, bleaching, dyeing or painting cloth. Production and sale were well organised. Merchants loaned capital to independent weavers who owned their own looms and raw materials and maintained the right to sell their cloth to whomever they wished, as long as they could pay back their debts. Weaving villages collectively organised to sell their cloth and pay their taxes. These different varieties of cloth found different markets in the Burmese kingdoms of Arakan and Ava, where they were exchanged for rice and slaves; in the Thai kingdoms, where they brought in elephants, Chinese goods and Japanese copper; and in the sultanates of the Malay peninsula, Sumatra, Java and the Moluccas, where they were traded for spices, pepper, opium, indigo, steel, tin, gold and yet more elephants. Indeed, it is possible to talk of an export boom on the seventeenth-century Coromandel coast which took its cloth, in all its diversity of colours, patterns and textures, out across the Asian trading world.

Much of this Indian Ocean trade was undertaken by small merchants. There were thirty thousand merchants in seventeenth-century Surat, many of whom shipped a bundle or two of coarse cloth at a time. However, there were also merchants who can be seen as the Asian equivalents of the great European trading families with extensive and varied mercantile operations: Virji Vohra in Surat; the Jagat Seths and Khwaja Wazid in early eighteenth-century Bengal; Mir Jumla in the kingdom of Golconda; Omickand, who was master of the Mint at Patna; and Abdul Ghafur, Surat's grandest merchant who owned seventeen sea-going vessels in 1700 (ten more than the Mughal emperor himself), traded everywhere from Mocha to Manila, and died in 1718 worth eight and a half million rupees.

Kasi Viranna was another of these great merchants. Operating from Madras, he was very much a part of the plural mercantile community of seventeenth-century Coromandel. Telugu Hindus dominated all areas of trade and finance. Yet there were also Persian Muslims, and a mix of Arabs, Turks and Pathans, who involved themselves in the overseas and coastal trades. They also maintained strong ties to the Golcanda kingdom's administrative nobility and royalty, facilitated their trading interests and gathered (or, as it was known, 'farmed') their taxes, both for a profit and to gain leverage over the cloth- and food-producing districts. Viranna was part of this world to the extent that no one knew for sure if he was a Hindu or a Muslim: he sometimes also used the name Hasan Khan and was reported to have founded a mosque at Madras. Some even said he had been enslaved in his youth and converted to Christianity. Viranna also had commercial interests everywhere. He had investments in shipping and overseas trade. He financed cloth production for export. He was rentier of almost all of the coastal territories north of Madras as far as Arumugam, and had a lease on the port of Cottapatnam. He farmed taxes for the Golconda kingdom and had negotiated with them to pay only half the usual customs duty on moving his goods. Running all this at a profit required both the hard-headed individualism and the business partnerships based on personal and familial relationships and secured by customary law that characterised this commercial world. Viranna was an adventurer, a well-connected and pushy operator, and he became a very powerful and rich man. Part of this, but only part, was due to his relationship with the English East India Company, and its servants in Madras, men such as Streynsham Master.

The world of Streynsham Master

The English, Dutch, Danes and French played their part in fuelling the trade boom on the Coromandel coast in the seventeenth century. However, they did not significantly reshape the patterns of production or oceanic trade (let alone trade on the land routes), and they certainly could not dominate them. Only about 10 per cent of Coromandel cloth production was for export, and little of that went to Europe. Cloth producers could easily accommodate the new demand, and they showed themselves to be less concerned with the European fixation on size and shape than with the concentration on pattern, colour and quality that animated their Eastern export markets. In most instances the Europeans simply took their place alongside the Asian merchants, often acting in concert with them to supply traditional markets. In these circumstances the Asian merchants, with their lower overheads and better knowledge of the commodities and markets, were more than able to compete. In some trades – in Thai elephants and Burmese rubies for example – the Europeans could simply find no way to make a profit. It was only in those few situations where the Europeans could use armed force, such as the Dutch in the Moluccas in the early seventeenth century, that they had any real advantage.

Yet there were differences between the Indian Ocean trading world and the world of the East India companies. During the seventeenth century, the English East India Company recognised that it could not compete with the Dutch Company in the spice trade and increasingly fell back on trade in cloth from India. This was traded eastwards, alongside merchants from the Coromandel coast and elsewhere, but it was also shipped directly to England. By 1661 the Company had resolved that this trade to Europe, one on which they claimed a monopoly, was to be the prime business of the few hundred Englishmen that worked for them in India. The 'country trade' with the rest of Asia was, therefore, to be left to private merchants unattached to the Company, and to the private trade of their own employees. The Company's crucial problem was how to organise the direct trade between Europe and India as a single successful commercial operation.

In 1657 the Company had been reorganised in London as a permanent joint stock company which would undertake regular voyages to particular Asian ports, where established 'factories' (or trading stations) staffed with permanent agents (factors) would provide a predictable supply of goods. The Company would pay dividends to shareholders rather than dividing up the proceeds of each voyage. So, every year, in about December or January, a fleet of ships would be loaded with cargo for the Coromandel trade. Over three-quarters of this was bullion gathered in European markets; the rest was predominantly English woollen cloth. The voyage round the Cape to India would take about eight months, and the cargo would be distributed according to the directors' orders among the various factories along the coast and in the Bay of Bengal. The bullion was coined into local currencies and used to trade for cloth (both cottons and silks), but also saltpetre, sugar, turmeric and cinnamon. To catch the winds the ships had to be dispatched home in December or January. On arrival in London, some months after the next fleet had sailed east, the Indian goods were sold at quarterly sales at East India House. This trade was worth an average of over £300,000 per year in the 1670s and 1680s, and it required co-ordinated action in many places up and down the coast, as well as between India and England, to make it work effectively. This was a prodigious feat of administration, but in the early 1670s the Company's infrastructure in India was a shambles and its factory at Fort St George (Madras) had been riven with conflict. The man who was sent to sort this out was a former Company servant and accounting expert called Streynsham Master (figure 4.2).

Master was born into a landed family in Kent in 1640. As the thirteenth child of twenty his future lay not on the family estate but in seeking his fortune in India. He arrived in Surat aged sixteen under the care of his uncle and godfather George Oxenden. He supervised a number of private voyages down the coast and to Mocha and the Persian Gulf, surviving several bouts of serious illness that might easily have killed him. In 1660 Master was appointed as a Company factor and, after employment at Ahmedabad, was promoted in 1668 to the council that ran the Company's business at Surat. It was there that he earned the directors' praise by devising a new system of bookkeeping, organising the Company's factories at Karwar and Calicut, and defending the Company's house and customs money against an armed attack by the Maratha leader Shivaji. He returned to London in 1672, married the daughter of a baronet and bought an estate near Dover. However, in 1675, with his wife now dead, he was commissioned by the

Figure 4.2 Streynsham Master. This portrait was painted in the early eighteenth century when Master was in England. It shows the former defender of the English East India Company's factory at Surat and chief agent of Fort St George (Madras) in an imperious pose, in full armour, and set against the backdrop of Company fortifications in India.

Company to return to India, 'for the Regulating and new Methodiseing their Factorys and Accounts upon the Coast and Bay'.[1]

Streynsham Master was to be a new broom. He was also someone who believed that a combination of accountancy and Christianity could solve everything. His first task was to inspect the smaller factories subordinate to Fort St George and put them to rights. In order to place them more firmly under the control of the fort, and ultimately London, he examined their accounts; gave orders for the institution of new systems of bookkeeping, decision making, and letter writing; investigated the endemic disputes among the handful of Company servants that staffed each outpost; and sought to enforce the Company's rules on morality and sobriety. When he assumed control of Fort St George in January 1678 he issued orders to regulate and rationalise the work of the council. Everything that moved was to be accounted for. He wanted records kept of money, goods, ships dispatched, letters sent and received, gold, ammunition and stores, slaves, land, customs, rent and revenues, wills, births, marriages and deaths. There was also to be a new moral order regulating personal behaviour by a system of fines for such things as swearing, drunkenness, missing prayers and staying out late. Master's control also extended over the town of Madras. He instituted a court of judicature to judge its inhabitants by English law, a land tax, systems of licences for both drinking houses and Catholic priests, and rules on who could carry swords and symbols of status such as parasols. The Company certainly appreciated Master's efforts to impose order on their trade.

However, like all the Company's servants in India, Streynsham Master's intention was to build a private fortune and return to England with enough capital to live a comfortable life as a landed gentleman. The route to this was private trade. This might involve the 'country trade', or trading to England in commodities not monopolised by the Company. Most lucrative of all was being a commissioner for the diamond trade, and it was this that provided Streynsham Master with his fortune (as well as generating the funds which Elihu Yale, a later governor of Fort St George, gave to found a university in New England). On the one hand, these private interests provoked conflict with the directors in London. As Master observed, 'our Company are very ungrateful and cruel to a man that has got an estate in their service, although he has done them a hundred times more service'.[2] On the other hand, such deals provided the circuitry through which the Company operated. Master's posting to India and his continuance as governor was not simply based on his accountancy or management skills. It was also a matter of how long the coterie of business partners and family members tied to him by private profit and personal preferment could keep him in favour with the Company's directors.

Master, like the agents and governors before and after him, had to strike a difficult balance. He had to do what he could to ensure that the Company's business ran smoothly. Indeed, more than others, he was concerned with regulating the infrastructure of factors and factories, books and bullion, cloth and currency. He had to ensure that the local political rulers made concessions on customs and let trade flow freely (a matter of diplomatic negotiations and well-placed presents and bribes), that there were goods to load on to the ships, that money was available to buy cloth before the ships arrived, that the bullion was coined at a good exchange rate and that the Company's servants were not cheating their masters or each other too outrageously. All the wheels of commerce had to be aligned and oiled. Master also had to ensure his own future. The Coromandel coast in the middle of the seventeenth century was potentially a very lucrative place to be. Master had to find the capital to trade on his own account; he had to be careful to ensure his own profit margins on the private trade he was allowed; he also had to judge what he could get away with in terms of trades, deals and negotiations that were semi-legal or even illegal as far as the Company or his partners were concerned. Agents lasted only as long as it took for the Company to become suspicious enough about their conduct to seek a successor. Since there were many temptations and little that the directors could do, suspicion was rife.

In all of these activities, and in striking the right balance between them, both Master and the Company needed Indian intermediaries. In the Company's trade it was not possible to make agreements with local rulers, to gather sufficient goods of the right types and quality, to coin bullion and to have cash in hand before the ships arrived without recourse to Indian brokers, interpreters, agents, attorneys, writers, money-changers, cashiers and subcontracting merchants. Indeed, this was even more evident in private trade where Indians lent money to the English, arranged deals for them, negotiated for diamonds, owned joint shares in shipping and paid for freight to be carried. In the Company's trade, and also in private trade, recourse was often made to the largest merchants who, if given appropriate incentives, would contract for all the exports and imports (even the English broadcloth that was so hard to sell in India) and ensure that the organisation ran smoothly, albeit at a price. On the Coromandel coast these relationships were crucial in shaping the geography of Madras and, as we shall see, the merchant who was most prominent was none other than Kasi Viranna.

Making Madras

The English East India Company had traded on the Coromandel coast through various factories since the early seventeenth century. However, the first territory acquired by them came when the raja of Chandragiri, eager to attract European trade, granted them rights over the small village of Channapatnam in 1639. By 1641, the Company had constructed Fort St George nearby, and the town that grew up around it became known as Madras. It took its place among the European outposts on the coast. The Dutch were nearby at Puleacat, and later at Masulipatnam, where the

English also had a factory. The Portuguese held on to Nagapatnam, and San Thomé changed hands between them, the Dutch and the French. There were good and bad things about the location of Madras. It was one of the worst harbours in the region, and had a river blocked by sandbars for most of the year. Goods and passengers had to be unloaded from ships at sea and delivered through the surf on small masoola boats, making for many wet arrivals and substantial losses. More positively, the weakness of the raja meant that he was willing to grant the Company substantial tax cuts when it came to customs on imports and exports, the right to build a fort and to establish a mint, and the power to administer the land granted to them and the people living on it as they saw fit. The natural disadvantages were matched by political and economic advantages. These advantages had, however, to be continually fought for and negotiated over after the Hindu Vijanayar empire fell to the Muslim kingdom of Golconda in the 1650s. Successive rulers tried to squeeze more from the English in taxes and presents, sometimes blockading the town and preventing trade, and sought to reduce the Company's independence.

It was in this context that the town grew as the focus of trading relationships between English merchants and Indian producers, brokers and rulers, and its geography bore the stamp of those connections (see figure 4.3). At its heart was the fort, completed in 1666, with an area of just over a hundred square yards. With Bombay and St Helena (and later Bengkulu on Sumatra) this was one of the few fortified trading places the English Company had. While the directors in London griped over the cost of building its mudbrick and laterite walls and bastions, it provided a necessary safe place for people, goods, guns and paperwork. At the centre of the fort was the governor's house. Inside this were the rooms where the factory's governor and council met to do business and to eat at a common table, the living quarters for the senior Company servants and, by 1665, a library of religious books, a hospital and a wooden chapel that also doubled as a courtroom. This chapel had, as one Dutch visitor reported, an 'inside so beautiful that it is a pleasure to peep into it'.[3] Outside the fort was what became known as the 'White Town' or 'Christian Town'. By the 1670s this was also surrounded by walls high enough to be an effective enclosure but too thin to offer much defensive protection. Within these walls lived the English inhabitants, whether attached to the Company or not, and many of the Portuguese residents, who also had their church there. Beyond the walls to the north was the 'Black Town', a densely populated suburb, some of its streets carefully divided between caste groups, which was occupied by the merchants, weavers, cloth painters, carpenters, stonemasons, boatmen and

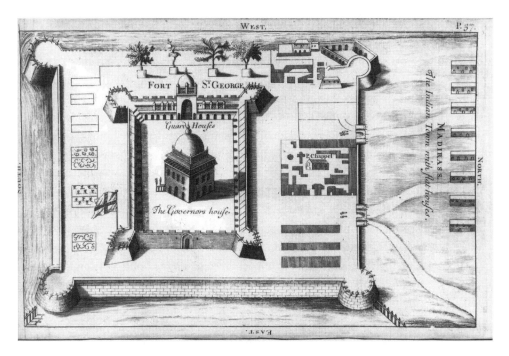

Figure 4.3 Fort St George in the late seventeenth century. This depiction of the English factory of Fort St George (Madras) offers a schematic view of the centre of English power on the Coromandel coast. It overemphasises the East India Company's fortifications and the separation of the Company's domain from 'the Indian Town'. The reality was much more complex.

labourers who made a living from the Company's trade. Beyond the houses were gardens where Company officers grew guavas, mangoes and jasmine; garden houses where they relaxed and entertained visitors; and, to the west, agricultural land dotted with tiny villages.

The town was the Company's power base. Governors, including Streynsham Master, renewed the fortifications, added buildings (Master founded the first Anglican church – St Mary's), governed the Indian and European populations through a mixture of English statutes and Indian customary law, and sought to extend control over neighbouring villages and avoid exorbitant taxes through diplomacy at the Golconda court. The town grew as the Company's trade, and the freedom of other trade that it allowed, attracted those Indians and Europeans who felt they could profit from it too. These were merchants, weavers and builders, but also 'idlers', thieves and punch-house keepers. In the ten years to 1678 the settlement doubled in size to number 50,000 people.

Yet there were also other powers in the town. As one Company servant put it in a letter to London complaining about Master's predecessor as agent, 'Sir William [Langhorne] governs within the Fort and Verrona without.'[4] Kasi Viranna was rentier of almost all the revenue-producing land and hamlets in Madras, and tax-farmed the village of Triplicane when it was added to the settlement in 1676. This gave him great power in the native government of the town, including being a judge in the Choultry court that administered the native population. Abbé Carré, a French visitor, reported Viranna's symbolic domination of the Black Town, 'in the centre [of which] is a magnificent pagoda or Hindu church, called Virena's pagoda – he is the richest and most powerful Brahman merchant in the country'. Viranna also owned substantial property in Madras, including in the White Town, and was continually building houses and warehouses to profit from the settlement's expansion. He himself lived in a large house on the outer edge of the city that was lavishly decorated with 'rich carpets and satin cushions, richly embroidered with gold'.[5] Viranna had a hand in shaping the city's geography and used it to manage his relationships to the Company. He was able to use his power to confuse any simple geographical distinctions between Indians and Europeans, by owning property in the White Town and exercising political authority over the Portuguese residents of the Black Town. He was able to intervene on the side of the English in negotiations with local rulers, helping to end Lingappa's blockade of Madras in 1676, and being rewarded by both sides. Viranna also exerted his power over the Company's highest officials, keeping William Langhorne cooling his heels on those plush carpets. As Streynsham Master put it, 'he hath had ye boldnes to make Sr W. L. stay a considerable time at his house when he hath called in there (as he would often doe) at his going abroad to take ye air, before he would be dress'd to come down to him'.[6] Yet Master himself was unable to avoid becoming entangled with Viranna.

Master and merchant

Indian merchants such as Kasi Viranna, Europeans in India such as Streynsham Master and the English East India Company itself all sought to make profits from the boom years of the Coromandel coast in the middle of the seventeenth century. In some ways their interests converged, and in other ways they came into conflict. Kasi Viranna had many strings to his mercantile bow. Yet he clearly saw the European companies, and their servants' private trade, as an opportunity that should not be passed up or passed over to others. First in partnership with another substantial trader, Beri

Timanna, and later on his own, Viranna occupied the role of chief merchant throughout the 1660s and 1670s. This meant heading the group of merchants who had a monopoly of supply of export goods to the Company, first call on imports, and a share of its fiscal privileges. Such conglomerates were not new in India. However, under the European companies they did bring together bodies of merchants that were novel in both their diversity and the opportunities for leadership and wealth they gave to men of lower castes, men such as Viranna who would not have risen so far and so fast under other conditions. Since the European companies had no direct access to the weaving areas, and required a regular supply of local currency and finished cloth of good quality, Viranna's expertise was essential. He employed eighteen servants, each with responsibility for a different district, to oversee the weavers. Since he was contracted to make good any default by the weavers this supervision was clearly in his own interests. It was also in his interest to drive as hard a bargain as he could over prices, and over the acceptance (or 'sorting') of the textiles he delivered to the Company. Managed correctly, the returns could be huge. Since Indian merchants did not depend upon the trade of the competing European companies, they had a strong say in setting the terms of trade. Where their knowledge of the trade was unrivalled they might profit from the 'rawness' of inexperienced Europeans through high prices or bad goods.[7] Both sides tried to squeeze their profits out of each other.

The same Indian merchants and Company servants were also linked in a network of other transactions. Private trade drew them together. Kasi Viranna is alleged to have entered private trade with Edward Winter, the agent at Fort St George from 1662 to 1665. He suffered a setback when Winter was dismissed for corruption, but bounced back under William Langhorne to whom he gave 'presents' of twenty thousand pagodas a year, which he more than recouped by extorting funds from Madras's Indian population with the governor's connivance. The next governor, Streynsham Master, certainly had a half-share in a voyage of Viranna's ship *Tandore*, and probably much more. Like most Company servants Master realised that if he was to make a private fortune it needed to be through collaboration with this powerful man. In turn, it was clear to Kasi Viranna that cultivating personal relationships with individual Company servants could, if he played his cards right, yield benefits in other areas of his portfolio.

The directors of the English East India Company in London were certainly suspicious that these relationships worked to their detriment. Thomas Chambers, agent from 1659 to 1662, was reported to take advice only from Beri Timanna. Winter, his successor, was accused of acting in concert with Timanna and Viranna to monopolise food supplies at Madras and drive up prices. They were also suspected of conniving to charge the Company artificially high prices for textiles, splitting the difference between them. Under Langhorne and Master the constant refrain in the Company's letters to Fort St George was that Viranna had too much power, and that they should 'prudently contrive soe to manage o^r affaires as not wholly to rely (as now yo^u doe) upon Verona only, or upon any one or two merch^{ts} or Brokers for the doing of all business'.[8] What was in the interests of those in India, either in terms of the predictability of the trade or lining their own pockets, was not necessarily in the interests of the East India Company in London.

It is clear, therefore, that Streynsham Master, in both his private and corporate roles, needed the merchant Kasi Viranna more than Viranna needed him. For Viranna, trading with the English was only one activity among many. He dealt with the other European companies (especially the French), he tax-farmed for the kingdom of Golconda and he engaged enthusiastically in overseas and coastal trade through commercial networks the English factors were never even aware of. When the East India Company sought to end his monopoly he responded by reminding them that 'the country [is] wide'.[9] Yet from the middle of the seventeenth century there were forces drawing Indian merchants closer to the English and reducing their independence. The increased trade of all the European companies made them a more attractive proposition, and Dutch attempts to enforce their 'protection' of ships sailing from the Coromandel coast led merchants to side either with them or their rivals. Also, the desire of the new Muslim states of Golconda and Bijapur to increase taxation on trade made the freedoms available to merchants under the English at Madras more attractive, even if those merchants did not trade exclusively with the East India Company. However, it was the fall of these kingdoms to the Mughal empire in the 1680s that further hastened the decline in mercantile independence. Where they involved themselves in the minting of money and the raising of taxes, Mughal governors' interventions destabilised the currency and disrupted the connections between the coast and the hinterland. This prevented merchants from operating in both areas and cut the throat of the port of Masulipatnam. More generally, the Mughal empire's inattention to an area on the periphery of their concerns allowed more leeway to the European companies than the kingdoms it replaced had permitted.

An element of Indian mercantile autonomy ended when Kasi Viranna died suddenly in 1680. The English reactions were indicative. To commemorate his passing the council at Fort St George ordered that a thirty-gun salute be fired in recognition of his importance. Yet Streynsham Master's first impulse was to imprison Viranna's less powerful partners and extort as much money from them as possible. While Viranna was succeeded by his younger brothers Pedda Venkatadri and Chinna Venkatadri, it became possible with his death, as it had not been before, for the English to impose conditions on the merchants at Madras which were more in the Company's favour. These agreements over imports and exports were possible only where Indian merchants could not resist, as they were able to do to the north, in Bengal, due to their strong organisation and abundant alternative sources of wealth. The Company's determination to prevent the extortion that Master had practised, by enforcing the payment of debts to Indians and by recognising Indian oaths in the Company's courts, could not conceal the merchants' loss of autonomy.

Streynsham Master did not remain in power long either. His refusal to conform to Company orders (including those over Viranna), his unwillingness to show due respect to the directors in London and his numerous dubious activities led to his dismissal in 1681. He returned to England a wealthy man, remarried and divided his time between a new country estate in Derbyshire and a townhouse in Red Lion Square, Holborn. Having won a lawsuit against the Company, he also took up the cudgels against it as chairman of the rival New East India Company, and was knighted by King William III in 1698. He died in 1724.

The worlds of Kasi Viranna and Streynsham Master were in many ways quite different. Yet it was also in the interests of each to understand what the other did as well as possible, so that they could both find common cause *and* make profits at their rival's expense. This phase of the relationship between Europe and India has been called the 'age of partnership', yet it was a much more tense and competitive relationship than this suggests. While Master, like the other Europeans, started from a position of dependence upon Indian intermediaries such as Viranna, the relationship developed in unexpected ways. Through their interaction, but also through political and economic circumstances beyond their control, such as the changes in the Mughal empire, the relationships of dependence shifted, bringing with them a new set of geographies, new concerns and new forms of negotiation. It is with those in mind that we turn to the later eighteenth century.

From trade to territory

Between 1675 and 1765 there was a dramatic change in the East India Company's relationship to India. The Company and its servants went from being mere merchants to becoming imperial rulers. That transformation reshaped the ways in which the Company worked. In particular, it altered relationships that were forged between the British in India and the indigenous intermediaries that they still depended upon.

Increasingly the Company's attention shifted from Madras to Bengal. By attracting Indian migrants, Calcutta, the northern province's largest Company settlement, grew to perhaps a hundred thousand inhabitants by the middle of the eighteenth century. This growth, along with the ever-extending activities of private traders, began to challenge the power of the local ruler. The subsequent conflict between the nawab of Bengal and the Company, which included British deaths in Calcutta's infamous 'Black Hole' when the city was taken by Bengali forces in 1756, and the subsequent defeat of the nawab at the battle of Plassey, needs to be set within the broader context of the waning of the Mughal empire. Across the subcontinent the shell of declining Mughal power was being filled, destroyed and replaced by smaller, more dynamic states such as the Maratha confederacy in the north or Mysore in the south. The East India Company actively sought advantages within this changing political scene. The Company's military victories over some Indian rulers, and diplomatic negotiations with others, led to it becoming the diwan of Bengal, Bihar and Orissa in 1765. This Mughal title effectively made the Company the ruler of twenty million people, and put it in charge of a complicated taxation system generating revenues worth £3 million a year, and of the elaborate legal infrastructure which supported it. The Company's elevation to the status of a significant territorial power (see figure 4.4) was both part of a series of long-running Indian political processes and a dramatic departure for a company of European merchants.

Company rule of Bengal began badly. Company officials and their Indian associates plundered the province's treasury, established restrictive monopolies on foods and textiles (which broke the power of the weavers and Indian merchants, beginning their decline) and channelled a flow of gold back to Europe that reversed the pattern of hundreds of years. The result was a famine that killed ten million people in three years and, along with charges of corruption and abuses of power, brought the nature of Company rule in India into question both in Asia and in Britain.

The problem the Company faced was how to govern a distant land taken by conquest which contained large numbers of people who claimed no British origins, who were not enslaved, but who were ruled without political representation. This problem had not been faced in either the North American colonies or in the Caribbean, and provoked an intense debate. The key outcome in the late eighteenth century was that the East

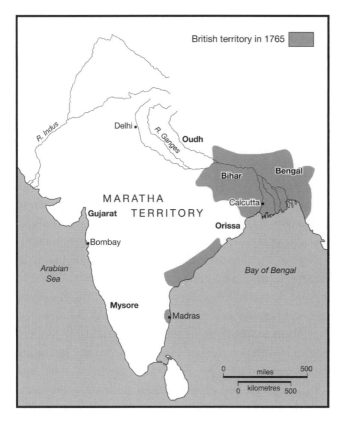

Figure 4.4 The political geography of late eighteenth-century
India. The East India Company, with its territories in northern and
eastern India, was one of several successor states which competed to
benefit from the decline of the Mughal empire. In the late
eighteenth and early nineteenth centuries the Company fought a
series of wars against the Marathas and the Kingdom of Mysore.

India Company should continue to govern the Indian possessions, the state
having neither the expertise nor the will to enter into imperial rule on such
a scale. The Company should also continue to concentrate on commerce,
using the revenue from Bengal's land taxes as capital to buy commodities to trade (increasingly this meant tea from China bought with Indian
opium). Finally, it was assumed that the only way to govern legitimately in
India was through the administrative mechanisms and symbolic forms long
established under Mughal rule. Indeed, this need to justify the power of
rulers through a Mughal political language, and via control over an increasingly frail Mughal emperor, was shared by the militarily powerful states,

particularly the Maratha confederacy, with which the Company was in a tense balance of power until the early nineteenth century.

Yet the Company was not simply a regional Indian state. It may have been a player in complex post-Mughal diplomacy, but its priorities were shaped, at least in part, by the Company's directors in London and by the British state, both of which understood how much depended upon the India trade. It may also have ruled through a series of Indian intermediaries with Mughal titles, but its administrative system also had to conform to British notions of justice, discipline, order and deference. The result was a hybrid. In the early 1770s, Warren Hastings, a Company servant who had been in India since he arrived in 1750 aged eighteen, was made governor general, with increased power over the other presidencies, and was charged with organising the civil administration of Bengal on a more systematic basis. To prevent continued corruption, this involved substantial salaries for the British officials, restrictions on private trade and the establishment of a Supreme Court in Calcutta with judges appointed by the crown to administer English law where necessary. However, the primary mode of government for the indigenous population was to be 'Orientalist'. Rather than imposing European forms of rule on Indian subjects, the intention was that the revenue system and the legal system would, where this did not conflict with British law, be based on ancient Indian modes of governance and on Hindu and Muslim legal principles. It was on this revolutionary basis that the British Empire began in earnest in India. Its implications can be seen in the ways in which the geography of 'British India' was reshaped, both in terms of changes on the ground and in the way these overseas possessions were understood.

This new Indian empire was built from Calcutta, and that city was rebuilt in the process. Hastings effectively centralised the legal, monetary and fiscal state apparatus when he moved the Supreme Court and the Khalsa (the Mughal term for exchequer) from Murshidabad to Calcutta, and replaced five provincial Revenue Councils with one in the city. This produced a set of fine new public buildings which were both the sites and symbols of British power. There was a new fort, the Writer's Building, Government House, the Council House, the Accountant General's Office, St John's Church and the New Court House (see figure 4.5). As the artist Thomas Daniell put it, 'The splendour of British arms produced sudden change in [the city's] aspects; the bamboo roof suddenly vanished, the marble column took the place of brick walls; princely mansions were erected by private individuals.'[10] Wealthy residential areas such as Garden Reach became filled with large

Figure 4.5 The New Court House and Chandpal Ghaut, Calcutta, by William Daniell, 1787. As Calcutta was remade as the capital of British Bengal it became a city that included the imposing neo-classical architecture of the Company's administrative and legal infrastructure, Indian pageantry and display, and the social lives of newly rich Europeans. Daniell tried to capture the sort of juxtaposition that would have been familiar to William Jones and Radhakanta Tarkavagisa.

houses which combined European neo-classical architecture with Indian design features such as flat roofs, blinds and white plaster to temper the climate. They were set within gardens that mixed extensive lawns with luxuriant tropical foliage. Calcutta was, with its new architecture and lively social life, as one visitor had it, 'not only the handsomest town in Asia, but one of the finest in the world'.[11]

Company rule in Bengal also required knowledge of the territory that it ruled. It necessitated a command over geographical information that had not been needed to trade for cloth with Indian merchants. This was evident in increasingly institutionalised interest in the languages, botany, history, archaeology and geology of India. However, it was clearest in the new desire for accurate maps of the territory. James Rennell's *Map of Hindoostan*

(1782) provided a detailed cartographic survey of British possessions in India before there was any similarly unified and comprehensive mapping of the British Isles. This new cartography was an imperial project that aimed to define frontiers, facilitate revenue collection and provide the information necessary for military engagements. However, it was also a product of the Company's distinctive form of rule. While utilising a regional survey undertaken between 1765 and 1771 (primarily employing Company soldiers, many of whom were south Asian sepoys, to measure distances marched along the province's roads) and the accounts of European travellers, it was also based on Indian sources such as the *Ain-i Akbari*, a Mughal manual on imperial government. This governmental ethos was captured in the map's cartouche (figure 4.6). Here learned and high-caste Brahmins were shown passing sacred manuscripts (the *sastra*s, Hindu religious and legal texts) to Britannia, 'in Allusion', as Rennell noted, 'to the humane Interposition of the British Legislature in Favor of the Natives of Bengal in the Year 1781'.[12] This testified to the British Parliament's decision to have the Calcutta Supreme Court, the highest court in the land, recognise the customs and usages of Hindus and Muslims in matters of inheritance and contracts. Hereafter, this court's British judges would administer Hindu and Muslim law.

However, what Rennell presented as a charitable act was really a set of difficult problems. Warren Hastings' attempts to keep the courts which administered English and Indian law separate had broken down under a torrent of litigation, as Indians sought to gain what advantage they could from their new rulers. The Supreme Court had also been accused of exceeding its powers and oppressing the people. Finally, the British judges in India, unable to read Sanskrit and untutored in Hindu law, could not decipher or understand the *sastra*s themselves. They remained dependent on the interpretation of these texts given by those pandits – professors of the *sastra*s, and the source of the term 'pundit' for someone who gives an opinion – that Rennell had shown deferentially handing them over. In response, Hastings had attempted to provide a definitive book of Hindu laws on property and its transmission, matters vital to the taxation system. The *Vivadarnava-setu* ('Bridge across the ocean of litigation') was compiled under his orders in 1775 by eleven pandits, and was translated (via Persian) into English in 1777 as *The Code of Gentoo Laws*. However, the pandits could not be compelled to use it in the courts and it became just one of the many sources from which they compiled their opinions. The legal system's dependence upon Indian intermediaries remained. One person who sought to resolve this problem of imperial governance was the judge, linguist and Orientalist scholar, William Jones.

Figure 4.6 Britannia and the Brahmins. From James Rennell's map of *Hindoostan*, 1782. This allegorical cartouche shows Britannia receiving the *sastra*s from their Brahmin keepers. The backdrop to this transaction shows the glories of past, present and future Hindoostan. There is an ancient Indian temple; two Indian Company soldiers beside a monument topped by Britain's imperial lion and showing their military victories; an East India Company ship being loaded with goods; and an Indian ploughman cultivating the rich soil.

The world of William Jones

William Jones (figure 4.7) had a talent for languages and a phenomenal memory. Although from a relatively modest family background, he had attended Harrow school where he once memorised Shakespeare's *The Tempest* to amuse his classmates. He excelled at Latin and Greek at Oxford, and began to learn Persian and Arabic, employing as his tutor a Syrian called Mirza whom he had met in London. He also had a taste for gentility. As tutor to the children of the hugely wealthy and politically influential Spencer family, one of whom was to become Georgiana Duchess of Devonshire, he participated in the Grand Tour and in fashionable London life. At the same time he gained a wider reputation as a scholar of Oriental languages in the early 1770s by translating a history of the Persian king Nader Shah, writing a Persian grammar and publishing a set of 'Asiatick' poems. This brought him membership of Samuel Johnson's literary club and elevated him into circles where he mixed with the painter Joshua Reynolds, the historian Edward Gibbon and the controversial politician John Wilkes.

But despite his celebrity Jones could not make his talent pay, and it did not provide him with the independence he sought to develop his political views and enter Parliament. It was with this in mind that he decided to become a lawyer, studying at the Middle Temple and acting as a barrister in London and a circuit judge in Oxford and Wales between 1774 and 1783. He also continued to be active in politics. However, his support for the American revolutionaries (and friendship with Benjamin Franklin), authorship of a radical pamphlet arguing for parliamentary reform (which got his future brother-in-law tried for publishing a seditious libel) and a failed attempt to be elected as MP for Oxford University all meant that his political ambitions were thwarted. So, in the late 1770s he decided that his language skills and his legal training could be turned to good account by his becoming a judge in the Bengal Supreme Court. On the one hand, he had become interested in the problems of administering law in India, publishing a work on *The Mohammadan Law of Succession* (1782) and being consulted on the 1781 reorganisation of the work of the Bengal Supreme Court. On the other, he judged that by spending five or six years in India he could return to England with a fortune of £30,000, enough to guarantee his independence and to enter politics.

After concerted lobbying, Jones was appointed to a judgeship in the Supreme Court of Judicature. He was knighted and got married to Anne Marie Shipley; they sailed for Calcutta on the *Crocodile* on 12 April 1783. Living in a large house in the elegant and wealthy Garden Reach, spending

Figure 4.7 William Jones. This portrait from 1793 by Arthur Devis shows the great Orientalist Jones as an austere and scholarly figure late in life. The imposing classical background, and the books and manuscripts on his desk in front of a statue of the Hindu god of learning, Ganesh, show the nature of his influences and interests.

other parts of the year at Alipur or Krishnagar, and working at the New Court House, Jones threw himself into both the law and scholarship. He tried cases and delivered charges to the Calcutta Grand Jury, and in 1784 he and a group of like-minded Company servants founded the Asiatick Society of Bengal, which also met in the Grand Jury Room, to further the study of Asian society, culture and natural history.

Yet aspects of his work as a judge troubled Sir William Jones. As a result of Warren Hastings's Orientalist philosophy of imperial government the British judges were, as we have seen, responsible for adjudicating cases on the basis of Hindu and Muslim law. Moreover, their decisions would be binding as precedent. They were assisted in their work by the Brahmin pandits and their Muslim equivalents, the maulevis, attached to the courts who, in response to written questions from the judges, produced learned opinions based on their knowledge of the *sastras* or Islamic law. But how could judges such as Jones – fearing that these intermediaries might be open to corrupt influences – know whether to trust them? For Jones the linguist there was one obvious solution. As he wrote to Hastings's private secretary in 1785, 'I am proceeding slowly, but surely ... in the study of Sanscrit; for I can no longer bear to be at the mercy of our pandits, who deal out Hindu law as they please, and make it at reasonable rates, when they cannot find it ready made'.[13] With this began a process whereby Jones sought to ensure that 'the Hindus may be convinced, that we decide on their law from the best information we can procure'.[14] This meant finding someone who would teach him Sanskrit, and Jones eventually brought the Vaidya scholar Ramalocana back to Calcutta from the celebrated centre of Hindu learning at Nadiya. He would then spend time each day at home with his teachers learning Sanskrit and Arabic. It also meant finding ways of working out which pandits he and the courts could trust. Here he relied on recommendations from Company servants who had employed Brahmins as language teachers, on those who taught at Nadiya and on the pandits' own written works. Finally, based on Jones's belief that there was a set of ancient Hindu laws written in the *sastras* which could be codified, known and agreed upon as the basis for legal decisions, it meant finding the crucial texts and making them available independently of the pandits themselves. As a result his notebooks were full of the names of Indian scholars, lists of books that he needed to consult and memos to himself about the administration of the law.

William Jones is best known as the founder of comparative linguistics. Learning Sanskrit from Ramalocana he deduced that this ancient language had evolved from the same common language, now disappeared, as Latin and Greek. This was also to raise the value of Sanskrit in European eyes, and Jones and the Asiatick Society promoted a serious and intense engagement with Indian culture and history. Jones was proud of his association with Nadiya and reported that the Brahmins 'consider me as a Pandit'.[15] Yet this was always combined with his suspicion about contemporary Indians, particularly those outside elite circles. Jones argued that it was the British who would restore to the Hindus their ancient laws, but that the Indians 'must be ruled by an absolute power'.[16] He proposed to resolve the courts' problems by using ancient texts to establish written laws that all could understand and agree. This would break the judges' dependence on the pandits. The irony was that in pursuing such a project he was dependent on certain pandits himself.

The world of Radhakanta Tarkavagisa

The pandit who eventually worked most closely with William Jones was Radhakanta Tarkavagisa. Born in the early eighteenth century into a family of modest means he was already an old man with a long life of study behind him when he became involved with Jones. His work had been undertaken as part of a distinguished tradition of learning in Sanskrit, the ancient language of an elite group and unknown to most of the country's inhabitants. This scholarship had long been pursued through the Brahminical universities and centres of learning, such as Nadiya or Benares, and through patronage from Hindu kings and rich men's charitable endowments which meant that the scholars were respected but became neither rich nor independent. The eighteenth century had not produced works in *dharmasastra*, the science of sacred Hindu law, that were as brilliant as those of the seventeenth century. Indeed, attention had shifted to the study of logic (*navyanyaya*). However, there was a continuity of Brahminical learning through the arts of discussion and memory and the popularisation of legal knowledge that had persisted over time.

Radhakanta's father had been acquainted with the great pandit Jagannatha Tarkapancanana, and had taught with him at the request of the raja of Krishnagar. His son had subsequently studied with Jagannatha, produced important Sanskrit manuscripts and received the title of Tarkavagisa from his teacher and, from the Mughal emperor, the title of Panditpradhana. Indeed, this latter title had been procured at the request of the man who became Radhakanta's patron, the Maharaja Navakrsna of Sobha Bazar. Both Radhakanta and Jagannatha were members of his celebrated *sabha* (or association), and received charitable gifts from him. Radhakanta was given 1,200 bighas (about 400 acres) of revenue-free land. These sources of patronage and respect meant that Brahmins were selective about whom they worked for and the conditions under which they worked. They were not necessarily keen to enter service for the British, and the Company's servants, including Jones, had problems encouraging Brahmins to become their teachers. As a result, Jagannatha turned down the request that he work on Hastings's *Vivadarnava-setu*, and Radhakanta, while willing to work for the British in a private capacity, was not prepared to take up an appointment as pandit to the Supreme Court in 1785. Indeed, as Jones reported it in 1787, Radhakanta 'told Mr. Hastings that he would not accept of it, if the salary were doubled; his scruples were probably religious'.[17] Brahmin scholars valued their independence.

However, involvement with the British was not so easily avoided. Radhakanta's Indian patron, known to the British as Nobkissen, had risen to wealth and influence on the basis of his association with the new imperial rulers. He had been Persian tutor to Warren Hastings in the 1750s, had served Robert Clive and had been the only South Asian employed in the negotiations with the Mughal emperor when the *diwani* was granted to the Company. He was richly rewarded for his services, and took full advantage of his new position of power. He was also keen to make careful use of Brahminical learning, charitable giving and religious endowments to consolidate and legitimate his position as a non-Brahmin, and therefore lower-caste, leader of Calcutta's Indian community. His association with the traditions of the ancient Hindu kings helped to obscure his rapid rise to prominence. Also, his strict adherence to the rulings of the authoritative religious books was combined with an active involvement in the Calcutta social scene. He threw lavish parties for socialites such as Emma Wrangham, a fixture in the gossip columns of the city's newspaper. It was presumably through Nobkissen that Radhakanta came into contact with the British.

In 1783 Radhakanta was working privately with John Shore (a later governor general). He then accepted a commission from Hastings to provide a summary of the *puranas*, a set of ancient Hindu texts concerning history and religion, and to oversee its translation into Persian. Radhakanta's *Puranarthaprakasa* ('Puranas explained') celebrated Hastings in a hyperbolic dedication and the author was duly rewarded with a piece of land worth 1,200 rupees a year, a gift made in the Indian tradition of royal patronage. The manuscript quickly became well known among the small group of British Orientalist scholars in India. Hastings sent the Persian version to Shore, who passed it on to Jones, his old schoolmate. Jones, distrusting the translation, was 'only tantalized with a thirst for more accurate information' and persuaded Shore to ask Radhakanta to lend him the original manuscript in Sanskrit.[18] On receiving it Jones proclaimed it 'a treasure', and commented to Shore, 'need I say, that I shall ever be happy in the conversation of so learned a man as Rhadacaunt?'[19] Jones did consult Radhakanta, and used extracts from his work in a paper 'On the Chronology of the Hindus' which was presented to the Asiatick Society.

By the time Radhakanta Tarkavagisa and William Jones met in 1787, the former was about eighty-four years old. Their subsequent discussions covered a variety of topics. Jones consulted Radhakanta on Indian drama, translations of inscriptions, chess, botany and religion. This educational process was not all one way. Jones reported that Radhakanta had 'long been attentive to English manners' and had compared Indian dramas to the English plays that were performed in Calcutta.[20] However, what really drew them together was Radhakanta's financial troubles. As Jones retold it, 'My father (said he) died at the age of an hundred years, and my mother, who was eighty years old, became a *sati*, and burned herself to expiate sins. They left me little besides good principles. Mr. Hastings purchased for me a piece of land, which at first yielded twelve hundred rupees a year; but lately, either through my inattention or through accident it has produced only one thousand. This would be sufficient for me and my family; but the duty of Brahmans is not only to teach the youths of their sect, but to relieve those who are poor. I made many presents to poor scholars and others in distress, and for this purpose I anticipated my income: I was then obliged to borrow for my family expenses, and I now owe about three thousand rupees. This debt is my only cause of uneasiness in the world. I would have mentioned it to Mr. Shore, but I was ashamed.'[21] Jones, rather insensitively, was soon writing to Shore to tell him the story and, perhaps more helpfully, to come up with some assistance for this 'honest man'. Given Radhakanta's previous refusal, a position with the Supreme Court was now out of the question. The endeavour that provided financial independence for Radhakanta was also that which threatened to undermine the collective independence of the pandits. This was William Jones's proposal to codify Indian law.

Laying down the law

Since at least 1785 William Jones had planned the production of a comprehensive book of laws necessary to guide the decisions of British judges. His reading of the Sanskrit and English versions of *The Code of Gentoo Laws*, probably with Radhakanta's help, had convinced him that 'the translation of it has no authority'. In 1788 he put his plan to Lord Cornwallis, then governor general, whose patronage was essential to funding the project:

> If we had a complete Digest of Hindu and Mohammedan laws, after the model of Justinian's inestimable Pandects, compiled by the most learned of the native lawyers, with an accurate verbal translation of it into English; and if copies of the work were reposited in the proper offices of the Sedr Divani' Adalat [the civil court], and of the Supreme Court, that they might occasionally be consulted as a standard of justice, we should rarely be at a loss for principles at least and rules of law applicable to the cases before us, and should never perhaps, be led astray by the Pandits or Maulavi's, who would hardly venture to impose on us, when their impositions might so easily be detected.[22]

The plan was approved by Cornwallis and by the British government, and, on the basis of its necessity and Jones's reputation, it was to be generously funded.

William Jones was able to put together a team of pandits and maulevis to complete the project. Based on reputation and recommendation, including advice from Radhakanta, he engaged six pandits at 'handsome salaries' of two hundred rupees a month (double what Radhakanta had hoped to be able to live on, or what was paid by the courts). Perhaps it was this that enabled Jones to overcome 'their reserve and distrust'.[23] Jones also got the agreement of Jagannatha to lead the project at three hundred rupees a month, and appointed Radhakanta to work on the Bengali material. Indeed, Radhakanta did most of the work. He was appointed first, along with Sarvoru Candra Tripathi who was to work on Bihar, and was last still to be employed even though he was by then 'old and infirm'.[24] He worked closely with Jones for many years on the manuscripts, and was entrusted with them when Jones died. After four years the pandits delivered the Sanskrit text of the *Vivadabhangarnava* ('Ocean of resolutions of disputes'). The text contained material extracted from the *dharmasastras* that covered contract and inheritance law, and was described by Jones as 'a noble legacy from me to three & twenty millions of black British subjects'.[25]

It was not the case that all the problems of imperial governance that the British faced could be resolved by the book which Jones and Radhakanta had put together, or by Henry Colebrooke's translation of it into English as *A Digest of Hindu Law on Contract and Successions* (1798). This was because the British belief that a written code of ancient and accepted laws could be constructed did not quite fit how law was practised in India. While the idea that Hindu law resided in the *dharmasastras* did receive support from the Brahmins, this glossed over the ways in which the pandits' interpretations of the *sastra*s, in court and in the production of legal texts such as the *Vivadabhangarnava*, was an active and creative process, even when they claimed that it was not. In part this came through particular modes of arguing and oral expertise peculiar to the pandits as they sought to reconcile contradictory statements within the *sastra*s using the rules of *mimamsa* philosophy and *nyaya* logic, which pay particular attention to debating the meanings of Sanskrit words in the search for higher truths. Presented in the *Digest*, such arguments were unintelligible to British judges who simply sought 'the right answer'. It also meant that when Jones thought he was getting a definitive distillation of the ancient texts he was actually getting something new, something that went beyond existing Hindu law books. The *Vivadabhangarnava* demonstrated a bias towards interpretations characteristic of the Bengali school of pandits due to the composition of the team that compiled it. It also showed both an active engagement with the issues that most exercised the British (the ownership of land, for example) and clear evidence that its pandit authors had been influenced by someone versed in the English common law in their discussions of issues such as the status of kings and fraudulent litigation. The *sastra*s could not be fixed forever and simply handed over to Britannia intact. It seems that the attempt to recover a timeless ancient Indian wisdom was inevitably shaped by William Jones's conversations with Radhakanta Tarkavagisa in British-ruled Bengal in the late eighteenth century.

Jones died of hepatitis in 1794 after the *Vivadabhangarnava* was finished but four years before its translation appeared. He left a fortune of £50,000 and an intellectual legacy that has been argued over ever since. Radhakanta was, as a result of the *Digest*, appointed, along with Sarvoru, as pandit to the Sadar Diwani Adalat. This was, however, primarily as an interpreter of the text that he had produced and that was intended to take pride of place in determining the law. As the British authorities said, 'they trust they [the pandits] shall be able to render the digest the book of authority for determining legal questions and consequently to attain the desirable object of introducing uniformity in the Decisions of the Courts'.[26] Radhakanta's work as a pandit was increasingly tied to the British rulers. While there were financial rewards, as there had been in producing the *Digest*, these came at the cost of the pandits' independence and the respect for their active tradition of scholarship. Radhakanta never resigned the post and died in British employ on 8 March 1803.

While the knowledge of the law that was produced through an intellectual engagement between Indian and British jurists represented a real interaction between the two traditions, it was the case that in such an asymmetrical situation the independence of Indian law and the pandits who interpreted it inevitably suffered. As a result of the interactions between the two legal systems, and the British attempts to fix Hindu law, it became the case that more rigid notions of the *sastra*s, of Hinduism and of the caste system came to dominate. It was also the case that British notions of precedent came to shape Indian law in ways that were contrary to the more open panditic practice. Indeed, what Jones could never see was that it was the dependence of the pandits that had caused the problems in the first place. The British courts in India had made the pandits into mere officers of the court, dependent on the judges for their jobs and for advancement, rather than independent advisors or advocates who were valued for the opinions they gave. Such a situation of dependence bred a mistrust that could not easily be resolved by making Indian intermediaries even more dependent upon their imperial rulers or on their ideas of what Indian law should be.

The relationships between northern Europeans and Asians were shaped by the balance of power between them. Unlike Europeans in other parts of the world, the merchants and statesmen of the English East India Company had, in the seventeenth and eighteenth centuries, entered a situation that they could not dominate. In large part they had to conform, in both the conduct of trade and the building of a territorial empire, to the ways that such things were done in India. In both 1670s Madras and 1780s Bengal their success depended on their relationships with intermediaries, people such as Kasi Viranna and Radhakanta Tarkavagisa, who had the knowledge, skills and power to shape how East India Company servants such as Streynsham Master or crown-appointed judges such as William Jones dealt with the unfamiliar context in which they had to work. In each case this chapter has shown that these intermediaries had sources of power, influence and status that were independent of the newcomers – either extensive networks of Indian Ocean trade or a long tradition of Brahmin scholarship and patronage – and that they sought to maintain that independence in their new relationships.

However, getting involved with English merchants or British judges meant becoming part of something different, and part of the creation of a new set of conditions in India. Both sections of this chapter have shown that, in various ways, the local and regional geographies of Madras, Calcutta and Bengal were changed in ways that reflected the interactions between the English and their intermediaries. Neither Madras nor Calcutta would have existed without the presence of the East India Company, and in their architecture, layout and social divisions they bore the imprint of a meeting of East and West. The Company played a large part in making these new places and landscapes, but it is also important to stress the active role of indigenous intermediaries in making these geographies, whether it be Kasi Viranna's profit-driven building programme, or the work of Indian sepoys in measuring Bengal for James Rennell's maps.

This was not, however, a situation of simple equality. In each case it is important to assess the balance of power and to see how and why it changed. While Viranna was company merchant in Madras and pulling the strings of the networks of private trade and the political relationships with the Golconda kingdom, the advantage lay with him rather than with Streynsham Master and the East India Company. As long as Sanskrit was the language of a Brahmin elite, the laws remained a matter of the privileged interpretation of the *sastra*s, and the *Digest* was still to be written, the pandits could retain their independence and power. Yet both situations changed. In part this was through interactions between those whose lives have been set out here. It is a matter of Viranna's sudden death and Radhakanta's perilous finances. Yet it is also a matter of the contexts in which all these merchants and lawyers worked. These were changing contexts over which these participants had little control. In the late seventeenth century, the fall of the Golconda kingdom to the Mughal empire disrupted the trading patterns of merchants such as Viranna and gave more leeway to the Company. In the eighteenth century, the decline of that same empire opened the space for the Company to become a territorial power, and for British interests and power to be gradually extended through and over their Indian intermediaries. European interests, lives and geographies in India were powerfully shaped by Indian political processes, but changed them in the process too. By the late eighteenth century a combination of the tax-gathering power of the British, the military strength that it funded and a questioning of Orientalist forms of rule had begun to give the British Empire in India a new and enduring shape. It must be remembered of course that this Asian empire rose just as another British empire was being made and lost on the other side of the globe in the Atlantic world.

Further reading

On the Coromandel coast's trade in the seventeenth century, including material on Kasi Viranna, see Sinnappah Arasaratnam (1986) *Merchants, Companies and Commerce on the Coromandel Coast, 1650–1740* (Oxford

University Press, Delhi). For the East India Company in this period, see Kirti N. Chaudhuri (1978) *The Trading World of Asia and the East India Company, 1660–1760* (Cambridge University Press, Cambridge) and, on Streynsham Master, see Sir Richard Carnac Temple (ed.) (1911) *The Diaries of Streynsham Master, 1675–1680* (John Murray, London). For overviews of the British Empire in India, see the essays by P. J. Marshall, Huw Bowen and Rajat Kanta Ray in P. J. Marshall (ed.) (1998) *The Oxford History of the British Empire*, vol: II, *The Eighteenth Century* (Oxford University Press, Oxford). For the lives of William Jones and Radhakanta Tarkavagisa, see S. N. Mukherjee (1968) *Sir William Jones: A Study in Eighteenth-Century British Attitudes to India* (Cambridge University Press, Cambridge); Garland Cannon (1990) *The Life and Mind of Oriental Jones* (Cambridge University Press, Cambridge); and Rosane Rocher (1989) 'The career of Radhakanta Tarkavagisa: an eighteenth-century pandit in British employ', *Journal of the American Oriental Society*, 109:4 pp. 627–633. For a direct insight, see Garland Cannon (ed.) (1970) *The Letters of Sir William Jones* (Clarendon Press, Oxford).

Notes

1 Quoted in Sir Richard Carnac Temple (ed.) (1911) *The Diaries of Streynsham Master, 1675–1680* (John Murray, London) I p. 192.

2 Quoted in Ian Bruce Watson (1980) *Foundation for Empire: English Private Trade in India, 1659–1760* (Vikas, New Delhi) p. 179.

3 Quoted in Henry Davison Love (1913) *Vestiges of Old Madras: 1640–1800* (John Murray, London) I p. 216.

4 Quoted in Sir Charles G. H. Fawcett (1952) *The English Factories in India: The Eastern Coast and Bengal, 1670–1677* (Clarendon Press, Oxford) p. 124.

5 Quotations from *The Travels of the Abbé Carré in India and the Near East 1672 to 1674* (Hakluyt Society, London, 1947) II pp. 549 and 608.

6 Oriental and India Office Collection (OIOC) European MSS E210/1: *Master Papers* Item 10 f. 30v.

7 OIOC India Office Records (IOR) E/3/88 *Despatch Book 5, 1672–1678* f. 81v (8 January 1675).

8 OIOC IOR E/3/88 f. 74v (23 December 1674).

9 Quoted in Watson, *Foundation for Empire*, p. 251.

10 Quoted in Mildred Archer (1980) *Early Views of India: The Picturesque Journeys of Thomas and William Daniell, 1786–1794* (Thames and Hudson, London) p. 14.

11 Grandpré quoted in H. E. A. Cotton (1980, originally published in 1909) *Calcutta Old and New* (Surajit C. Das, Calcutta) p. 73.

12 Quoted in Matthew H. Edney (1997) *Mapping an Empire: The Geographical Construction of British India, 1765–1843* (University of Chicago Press, Chicago) p. 13.

13 Garland Cannon (ed.) (1970) *The Letters of Sir William Jones* (Clarendon Press, Oxford) 418 (28 September 1785).

14 Ibid., 400 (March 1785).

15 Ibid., 494 (19 September 1788).

16 Ibid., 443 (1 October 1786).

17 Ibid., 465 (16 August 1787).

18 Ibid., 457 (25 March 1787).

19 Ibid., 459 (12 May 1787).

20 Quoted in Rosane Rocher (1989) 'The career of Radhakanta Tarkavagisa: an eighteenth-century pandit in British employ', *Journal of the American Oriental Society*, 109:4 p. 629.

21 Cannon, *Letters of Sir William Jones*, 465 (16 August 1787).

22 Ibid., 485 (19 March 1788).

23 John Shore (1835) *Memoirs of the Life, Writings, and Correspondence of Sir William Jones* (John W. Parker, London) II p. 100.

24 Cannon, *Letters of Sir William Jones*, 592 (1 March 1794).

25 Ibid., 565 (19 October 1791).

26 Quoted in Rocher, 'The career of Radhakanta Tarkavagisa', p. 632.

5 | Into the Atlantic: the triangular trade?

The East India Company's trade to and from India was one part of a series of interconnected changes in Britain's involvement in foreign trade from the early seventeenth century onwards. These changes can be traced via the shifts in the volumes, composition and destinations of imports and exports, which show that the other key element in this new world of trade was the increasing amount of goods moving around the Atlantic Ocean. It is the world of those trading between Europe, Africa and the Americas that this chapter explores. Delving beneath the figures of goods shipped in and out of Britain to see how merchants in London, on the West African coast, in Boston and on the Caribbean Islands worked shows that trade in the Atlantic world both shared similarities with the work of the East India Company's merchants (men such as Streynsham Master) and took on quite different characteristics and structures. This is a complicated story of the interconnections and interdependencies that created a new Atlantic world of trade made up of many thousands of merchants all around that world endeavouring to profit from borrowing money, shipping goods and extending credit.

Britain's foreign trade was growing in the late seventeenth century. Imports increased by a third between 1663 and 1701, and exports by more than a half. Absolute values are difficult to determine, but total imports for 1699–1701 have been estimated at £5,849,000 and exports at £6,419,000. Until the middle of the seventeenth century English exports were dominated by woollen cloth. As late as 1640 this made up 80–90 per cent of exports from London. By 1699–1701 that was reduced to 47 per cent. What now made up 30 per cent of these exports were American and Eastern products – especially tobacco, sugar and cotton cloth – re-exported to other markets in Europe. The volume of re-exports of these three commodities had trebled between 1660 and 1700. This was the really dynamic and revolutionary element of late seventeenth-century trade. Since it was based on goods produced outside the British Isles the profits made were not reinvested in their manufacture. Instead the money went back into commerce – merchants making a profit moving goods from one place to another, and increasingly across the Atlantic. Indeed, if the exports to the Americas and India are

Table 5.1 Exports of miscellaneous manufactures (from London only) (£000)

	1663–1669	1699–1701
West Africa, America and the East	86	259
Europe, etc.	136	161

Source: Ralph Davis (1954) 'English foreign trade, 1660–1700', *Economic History Review* 7:2 p. 154.

taken together with these re-exports, they make up 40 per cent of the total export trade. These exports east and west are interesting too. The majority was still woollen cloth, but the proportion of other manufactures was growing fast, particularly in exports to the Americas. While making up only 8 per cent of total English exports from London in 1699–1701 miscellaneous manufactures – metal goods made of brass, copper and iron; silk and linen; hats and clothes; glass and earthenware; paper and leather goods – were both expanding in value and being increasingly shipped to settlers in the Americas (see table 5.1).

Looking forward across the next century reveals an equally dramatic set of changes. By 1772–1774 total exports and re-exports stood at £15,671,000. This was more than double the value in 1699–1701. Imports had also more than doubled to £12,735,000. Yet this was not a smooth process of expansion. The long wars between 1689 and 1713 severely disrupted trade, as did protectionist policies in Europe, and it was not until mid-century that the expansion in British foreign trade took off again. Overall, however, the trends evident in the previous century were reinforced. Woollen cloth continued to decrease in importance as an English export, particularly to northern Europe (in 1699–1701 this trade made up 24 per cent of all English exports and re-exports by value; by 1772–1774 it was only 6 per cent). In its place the revolution in colonial trade continued. As table 5.2 shows, the proportions of imports and exports going to the East Indies remained relatively stable (the table does not include the large amounts of bullion exported to fund the trade), with an upturn in exports coinciding with the beginnings of territorial rule. It was in trade with the Americas – both the northern colonies and the Caribbean – and Africa where growth occurred. Imports from these areas (primarily the Americas since few slaves – the main export from Africa – came through British ports) increased from 18.9 per cent of total imports in 1699–1701 to 37.4 per cent in 1772–1774. In the same period, exports to these colonies increased from 13.3 per cent of

Table 5.2 Imports to and exports from Britain, 1699–1774

	1699–1701	1722–1724	1752–1754	1772–1774
EXPORTS (£000s)				
East Indies	136	112	748	780
	2.1%	1.4%	6.3%	5.0%
Europe*	5432	5899	8827	9743
	84.6%	76.1%	74.1%	62.2%
Americas†	851	1745	2334	5148
	13.3%	22.5%	19.6%	32.9%
Total	6419	7756	11909	15671
Re-exports	1986	2714	3492	5818
	30.9%	35.0%	29.3%	37.1%
IMPORTS (£000s)				
East Indies	756	966	1086	1929
	12.9%	14.3%	13.2%	15.1%
Europe*	3986	4113	4433	6037
	68.1%	60.9%	54.0%	47.4%
Americas†	1107	1679	2684	4769
	18.9%	24.8%	32.7%	37.4%
Total	5849	6758	8203	12735

*Includes Ireland and the Channel Islands.   †Includes West Africa.
Source: Adapted from Ralph Davis (1962) 'English foreign trade, 1700–1774', *Economic History Review* 15:2 pp. 300–303.

all exports and re-exports to 32.9 per cent. This extraordinarily dynamic sector was made up of a huge volume of everyday manufactured goods, most of which were made in Britain: nails, axes, guns, kettles, clocks, saddles, handkerchiefs, buttons and linen cloth from Scotland and Ireland. Exports from British ports to Europe did remain high throughout the century, but at least a third of this was re-exported colonial produce: American tobacco, sugar, coffee and rice, and cloth from the Indies, which also went to Africa and the Caribbean. The table further exaggerates European exports and imports since they include those from Ireland when its markets were actually tied into the colonial Atlantic economy too. Britain's foreign trade, it is clear, was increasingly an Atlantic trade.

These import and export figures tell only part of the story. First, since they count only those goods that passed through British ports they do not demonstrate the truly pan-Atlantic nature of this pattern of trade. They do not include the fortunes of the Newfoundland fishery, the first of the Atlantic staple trades, which was funded from the West Country but sold its product directly to southern Europe and later to the Caribbean, supplying a taste for salt cod that still endures. They also do not count the profits and ruined lives of the Atlantic slave trade which took its human cargo directly from Africa to the Americas for sale (see chapter 8). Nor do these figures include the trade between the North American colonies and the West Indian islands on which the slaves toiled. Second, these numbers say little about the organisation of the trade. Just as with the trade to the East Indies, the Atlantic trades had begun with a series of royally chartered monopoly companies: the Virginia Company, the Plymouth Company and the Massachusetts Bay Company, which divided up continental North America between them, and a succession of companies, ending with the Royal African Company, given a monopoly over the slave trade. However, only the Hudson Bay Company, which traded manufactures for furs in Canada's frozen north, lasted until the end of the eighteenth century. The others fell by the wayside from the early seventeenth century onwards; those in the slave trade – where the advantages of a centralised network of trading forts and of organised dealings with African polities were most evident – survived the longest. They were gradually replaced by a highly decentralised and competitive structure of many competing merchants, planters and ship-owners, all vying to make a profit from these Atlantic trades in whatever way they could. Thus, these aggregate accounts of imports and exports to and from the Americas and Africa were made up of many ventures and many cargoes coming through many ports. Unlike the East India trade, which was all channelled through London, the Atlantic trade was open to those in Bristol, Liverpool, Glasgow, Hull, Exeter, Tynmouth, Dartmouth and so on. Trading west was quite different from trading east. Almost anyone could join in.

However, the end of the chartered companies did not mean the end of state involvement in the Atlantic trades, and it certainly did not mean an era of free trade. From 1651, in order to keep the Dutch out of the colonial trades which they had the financial muscle and commercial know-how to dominate, Parliament passed a series of Navigation Acts (which also include legislation in 1660, 1663 and 1696). Together these acts stipulated that all trade to and from the colonies was to be carried in English or colonial ships, and that three-quarters of the crew were to be English or colonial sailors. They identified the most valuable and least perishable colonial commodities as 'enumerated goods' (for example, tobacco but not fish) and stipulated that they had to be carried directly to either an English or another colonial port, even if aimed at a foreign market. Finally, they ruled that foreign goods (with some exceptions – slaves, Madeira wine and salt for the fisheries) had to be sent to the colonies via England. This would both raise customs revenue and ensure that England's interests were at the heart of the Atlantic trades. It amounted to a set of protected colonial markets for English goods together with severe restrictions on colonial producers shipping their goods anywhere but England.

While there was plenty of evasion (and smuggling), the import–export figures help show how these regulations worked to shape the pattern of foreign trade. In return, the state protected colonial trade with armed force. An increasingly large British navy protected trade routes across the oceans, manned fortified colonial ports and (with the army) fought wars that, among other things, aimed to secure the benefits of commerce within what was increasingly seen as a distinctively English maritime empire of trade. Indeed, it was after the Seven Years' War (1756–1763) that Britain secured global dominance and the Atlantic trades really took off. Much of the export of manufactured goods to the Americas in the middle of the eighteenth century comprised military supplies paid for by British taxpayers rather than nails and handkerchiefs bought by New England farmers. War and trade were closely entwined in the Atlantic world.

The triangular trade?

The basic underlying structure of this new Atlantic world has been described as 'the triangular trade'. It evolved a pattern that involved three crucial transfers from the points of a triangle made up of Africa, Europe and the Americas, aided by the general clockwise circulation of winds and currents in the Atlantic basin. Labour power – in the form of enslaved Africans – was shipped to the Americas. There that labour produced a series of tropical and semi-tropical agricultural commodities – sugar, tobacco, rice, coffee – which were sent, often semi-processed, to European markets. In return for both those slaves and the products of their labour, manufactured goods and provisions were shipped from Europe to Africa and the Americas (see chapters 8 and 9). However, it was certainly not the case that all ships engaged in Atlantic trade sailed all legs of this triangular course like some nightmarish and never-ending merry-go-round. Indeed, considering all the movements of goods and people in the Atlantic world means that the basic triangle soon becomes overlain by a more complex pattern of exchanges (figure 5.1). Furs, fish and naval supplies such as masts were exchanged for non-slave labour, provisions and manufactured goods across the high latitudes of the North Atlantic between Britain, Hudson Bay, Newfoundland and New England. Merchants in New England also found a ready market for lumber, cattle and foodstuffs both in Newfoundland and in the Caribbean Islands which were devoting themselves wholeheartedly to producing fish and sugar

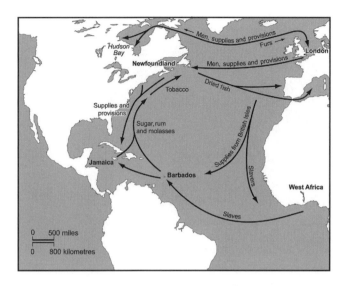

Figure 5.1 Atlantic trade routes, c. 1750. The key trades in people, produce and manufactured goods used the currents and winds of the North Atlantic basin to bind together the economies, societies and cultures of West Africa, the Caribbean, the North American seaboard and Europe.

for European markets. Merchants and ship-owners from Rhode Island were then able to exchange rum (made in New England from Caribbean molasses) for slaves on the West African coast. In all of this merchants aimed to buy something in one place and transport it somewhere else where it could be sold for enough to make a profit.

There were lots of choices to be made about what and where to buy and sell. Treating 'the Americas' as one point of the triangle obscures the fact that the thousands of miles of North Atlantic coastline from Barbados to Baffin Island were being turned into a series of specialist production zones. A new landscape was emerging where those involved in gathering and growing concentrated on producing one thing – furs, fish, sugar, tobacco or rice – for sale, and then supplied their other needs in the marketplace with the money it brought. A whole series of commodities went through dramatic transformations of price and volume. The most astonishing were tobacco and sugar. The tobacco planters who transformed the landscape and prospects of the Chesapeake (see chapter 3) produced just 20,000 pounds (weight) of leaf in 1619 but had increased this to over 1 million pounds by the 1630s. In 1668–1669 9 million pounds of tobacco were exported to London. This rose to 22 million pounds in 1699–1701,

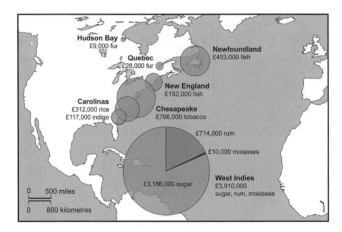

Figure 5.2 Exports to Britain from the staple regions of the
Americas, 1764–1775. The Americas produced a range of animal
and agricultural products for export to Europe. By the middle of
the eighteenth century these were dominated by the sugar and
sugar by-products (rum and molasses) produced on Caribbean
islands such as Barbados and Jamaica.

two-thirds of which was re-exported to Europe. Despite ups and downs,
increases continued through the eighteenth century. In the period 1771–
1775 England imported 278 million pounds of American tobacco (and
re-exported 230 million).

Sugar tells a similar story. In the early 1650s only a few thousand tons of
sugar were exported from the West Indies to England. By 1700 exports had
reached 24,000 tons, and by the 1770s about 88,000 tons per year. Sugar was
by then the most valuable of all Britain's imported goods. Between 1768
and 1772 an average of £3,910,000 worth of sugar, rum and molasses was
exported from the British West Indian islands per year. This was more,
by value, than the combined produce of the North American colonies
(figure 5.2). In each case, increased volume meant a fall in price. Before
1619 tobacco fetched twenty to forty shillings a pound in England; by the
1670s it sold at a shilling or less (with the plantation price at not more
than a penny a pound). The retail price of sugar halved between 1630 and
1680. By the eighteenth century, therefore, the Atlantic world had produced
something else that was new: mass market luxury commodities. The vast
majority of British consumers expected to be able to enjoy a pipe of tobacco
and a cup of tea, coffee or chocolate sweetened with sugar. Millions of
tiny purchases of American goods at rock-bottom prices sent huge volumes
of agricultural produce across the Atlantic world. Fortunes were there to

be made for those who could work between the producers, suppliers and consumers of these goods.

What was significant about the Atlantic trades, in contrast to the traditional trades with Europe and the Company-dominated trade to Asia, was the range of people involved. For example, records from Bristol for 1654–1656 show 423 individuals involved in the importing of colonial tobacco and sugar. Of the 305 men whose occupation is known only 26 per cent were defined as merchants. The rest were, first, a mixture of soap-boilers, grocers, mercers, tailors, shoemakers and metal craftsmen and, second, those in a range of maritime trades: mariners, coopers and shipwrights. There were also thirty women, most of whom were the wives or widows of mariners or shopkeepers who had engaged in the Atlantic trades. Each person invested in a small way. As one commentator put it: 'It is remarkable there that all men that are dealers, even in shop trades, launch into adventures by sea, chiefly to the West India plantations and Spain. A poor shopkeeper, that sells candles, will have a bale of stockings, or a piece of stuff, for Nevis, or Virginia, &c. and, rather than fail, they trade in men.'[1]

At this early stage Atlantic commerce was a speculative venture. Vessels were loaded with a range of merchandise and set off to find a market in Virginia or the West Indies. Planters there, with only one commodity to sell, exchanged their tobacco or sugar directly for indentured servants, stockings or that piece of stuff on the best terms they could. This decentralised and self-organised system operated within the framework of the Navigation Acts on the basis of a shared language, some local or familial connections between planters and merchants, and a common desire for profit. However, one side's profit was the other's loss, and for those working within it the Atlantic world looked less like an orderly triangle than an uncertainly balanced and complex contraption put together by many hands. In the face of this uncertainty it was evident that knowledge, experience and new forms of social and economic organisation were needed to find ways of deciding when and where to invest, and when and where to buy and sell. One of those who made this his business was William Freeman.

The world of William Freeman

Born in 1645 on the Caribbean island of St Christopher (or St Kitts), William Freeman was the son of one of the earliest English planters. He grew up on a 500-acre sugar and indigo plantation in the shadow of Mount Misery on the northwest side of that volcanic island. Displaced by a French invasion in 1666, William moved to the nearby island of Nevis where he worked as a merchant, was a member of the local assembly (the island's elected governing body) and a captain in the militia that was formed to protect the island. In 1670, along with his friend John Bramley, he bought a sugar plantation on the island of Montserrat. By 1673 they owned 23 slaves, at a time when there were only 575 enslaved people on the whole island. Bramley managed the plantation because Freeman had other business interests to attend to. There was his work as a merchant, and there were other investments in other plantations on Montserrat and St Kitts. In partnership with another man Freeman also acted as the agent of the Royal African Company in the Leeward Islands. They were charged with selling the enslaved Africans the Company's ships brought to the port at Morton Bay; feeding the Company information on the state of the market; and making sure that payments (usually on six to nine months' credit for the planters) were eventually made for the slaves sold. The two agents received salaries of six thousand pounds of sugar each year, but most of their money was made from the commissions of a few per cent per deal that they made selling people to other people. William had also got married. His wife, Elizabeth Baxter, brought him many things including the trading connections of her father, uncle and brother in the West Indies, southern Europe and London. Indeed, in late 1674 William and Elizabeth moved to London. He never returned to the Caribbean, but his fortunes remained intimately connected with it for the rest of his life.

The problem that those engaging in commercial and productive investment in the Atlantic world faced were, in many ways, similar to the problems of the English East India Company. In fact, William Freeman's role in the Royal African Company was the same one Streynsham Master performed for the East India Company (see chapter 4). The difference was that Master was a salaried employee who was expected to work for no one else, and Freeman was operating on both salary and commission. However, when it came to the many planters, investors, ship-owners and merchants there was no central company organisation. Freeman, as a planter, and certainly his father in the 1640s, would have felt at the mercy of ships arriving to buy their sugar and indigo, and unsure of where and when they could buy the labour, provisions and equipment that they needed to run their plantations. Such uncertain meetings of supply and demand made prices erratic and long-term planning difficult. Freeman's move to London solved some of these problems. He was then able to co-ordinate by handwritten letter the dispatch to the Caribbean of hundreds of barrels of salt beef (along with butter and candles) from Ireland; staves and hoops for making barrels from southern England; and wine from Madeira. He could also arrange the sale of his own sugar in England, keeping an eye on the market and getting the best price he could. Finally, he could then act more effectively as the London partner for the two Royal African Company agents in the Leeward Islands, and as such effected the transportation of around ten thousand Africans. The problem in being in London was that he was now away from his plantations (production and sale of sugar were separated by four thousand miles of ocean) and needed constant reports from people on the spot to tell him whether his partners and employees were managing them well for him. He had, as he said in his letters, 'a world of buisness to doe'.[2] An important development, however, was that he was also doing this business for others.

What the letters that Freeman recorded in his letterbook show is that his position in London, his many years of experience of plantation slavery in the Caribbean (and his continuing interests there), his contacts with the political establishment of those islands (his sister's brother-in-law was the governor of Montserrat), his extensive trading (and family) connections and his reputation put him in a position where planters still in the Caribbean were keen to do their business through him, and to pay him a 2.5 per cent commission on the deals that were done. Freeman had become what was later called a 'commission agent', but most simply he was getting done in his counting house in the City of London all the things that planters in Nevis, Montserrat, St Kitts and Antigua needed done. By 1680 Freeman and his partner (and brother-in-law) William Baxter were corresponding with fifty Leeward Islands planters and merchants, thirty-four suppliers in Ireland, Scotland, France and Portugal, and eleven sea captains. They sent about eight ships a year to the Caribbean to supply the plantations with goods, and sold a lot of sugar.

Although Freeman's work as a commission agent involved a network of people stretched across the Atlantic Ocean, his relationships with them were very intimate and personal. They had to be. First, he acted for the planters in all matters. He did not just sell their sugar and send them beef. He organised their investments; bought them the clothes, furniture and tableware they wanted from London; looked after their children's education (and dancing lessons); sought out servants; and passed on news and gossip. They had to be able to ask him to do anything. Second, the whole system depended on trust. Planters, suppliers and merchants had to be able to feel that they could trust those working for them away across the ocean. This was particularly the case since the whole system depended upon extending credit. Payments were not received until many months after goods were dispatched. Freeman experienced the gaining of trust and the extension of credit from both sides. He had to stress to those he worked for that, as he put it to General William Stapleton of Montserrat, 'you may assure yourself that what I can sarve you in that peticular or any other shall navor bee wanting'.[3] The basis of these relationships of trust in friendship, extended family or shared experience was crucial, and Freeman emphasised it in his letters. Yet Freeman also had to trust others himself: suppliers, ship-owners and especially those who managed his plantations. Again, friendship and family were crucial, but so was a set of gentlemanly and mercantile values that connected financial credit with trustworthiness. Freeman had to be aware of people's reputations, their personal 'credit'. This was not just a money matter. As he put it to John Bramley, when they finally fell out with each other over the management of the Montserrat plantation, 'I can never be satisfied that my estate should be under the manadgm.t of a p.son whose word is of noe vallew'.[4] It was these fragile networks of credit – financial and personal – through which men such as Freeman integrated the Atlantic world economy from the 1670s. Doing so was good business. When Freeman died in 1707 he had made enough to build himself a small country house at Fawley Court near Henley, furnished with wainscots made of Leeward Islands wood.

What William Freeman had recognised was the differentiated nature of the Atlantic world and the different relationships its parts had with one another. Beyond the obvious geography of production zones, regional specialisation and markets were questions of power. Where did producers, suppliers, buyers or sellers have the advantage over each other? How far did that influence stretch? By moving to London, he increased the control of Caribbean planters over the market for their produce, but reduced his direct influence on production. The rest of this chapter will move around the Atlantic world to explore these questions of power in relation to different Atlantic regions and the merchants within them before returning to the question of integration and the heirs of William Freeman, the London merchants of the middle of the eighteenth century.

Africa in the Atlantic world

Freeman himself sent few ships to Africa; most went straight to the Caribbean planters. However, his work for the Royal African Company meant that he was directly involved in the slave trade with West Africa just at the point when it was undergoing a great expansion based upon increased north European involvement and increased demand from the Americas. The

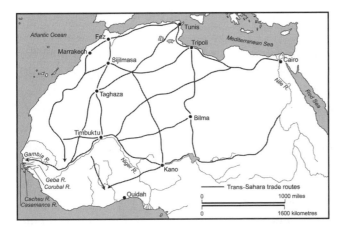

Figure 5.3 West African trade routes, c. 1500. Prior to the
expansion of the transatlantic slave trade West African trade
operated through a series of regional and local trading networks.
These spanned the Sahara desert, and meant that places such as
Timbuktu – which later became the very symbol of remoteness for
Europeans – were thriving centres of commerce.

mechanics of the slave trade itself are primarily dealt with in chapter 8. What
is important here is the role of African traders and merchants in making
and negotiating the position of Africa and Africans in the Atlantic trading
world.

Africans had been involved in extensive trade long before the first Europeans arrived. Networks of markets and the long- and short-distance trade
routes that connected them linked together very different ecological zones,
from forest to desert, and enabled the exchange of natural and manufactured products. Caravan routes across the Sahara, passing through the great
trading centre of Timbuktu, allowed the exchange of gold, slaves, ivory and
kola nuts for horses, cloth, glassware and leather goods. There were also
dense and overlapping regional trading networks. For example, along the
coast and rivers of Senegambia, Banyan-Bak mariners traded salt, dried fish
and dried molluscs, and Biafada-Sapi traders in long, low dugout canoes
capable of carrying more than a hundred people transported kola nuts,
malaguetta pepper and other forest products north into the savannah zone.
At the heads of navigation of the Gambia, Casamance, Cacheu, Geba and
Corubal Rivers, up to a hundred miles inland, these traders exchanged what
they had with Mande traders bringing iron and ironwares from the savanna-
woodland zone, and cotton and other cloth from further north, tying them
into the trans-Sahara trade (figure 5.3). Part of this extensive and intensive

world of African commerce was a widespread and long-standing African slave trade.

When ship-borne Europeans began to arrive off West Africa from the late fifteenth century they sought the same goods that had long been traded there – gold, ivory, beeswax, malaguetta pepper and, increasingly, slaves – and African traders were ready to sell them for what these new merchants brought: textiles, metalware, distilled spirits, tobacco and, increasingly, guns. Trade had different emphases along different stretches of the 1,000-mile West African coast as highlighted in the names the Europeans assigned to them: the Ivory Coast, the Gold Coast, the Slave Coast. It also changed its structure over time. African states engaged and disengaged with European trade as their domestic and foreign policies dictated. For example, in the early sixteenth century the king of Benin withdrew from the slave trade for a time, and the Diola and Balanta of Guinea-Bissau and the Baga of Sierra Leone long excluded both African and European slave-traders from their territories. The Europeans changed too. What began with the Iberians was eventually, as in other areas of the Atlantic world, taken up by northern Europeans (John Hawkins's foray into the Cacheu River in 1568 was an early instance; see chapter 2). By the second half of the seventeenth century the West African coast was dotted with some fifty forts and factories of competing English, Dutch, French, Danish, Swedish and Courlander (a German duchy) monopoly and state-chartered companies (see chapter 8). Each sought preferential trading arrangements with African rulers, and as the tides of war and peace between European states ebbed and flowed across the seventeenth and early eighteenth centuries they also fought each other for access to African trade. Thus, the coastal forts regularly changed hands with the shifting fortunes of war. The English monopoly – the Royal African Company succeeding the Company of Royal Adventurers in 1672 – lasted longer than in the Americas, but not as long as in Asia, and the trade was opened to all merchants in the middle of the eighteenth century.

One reason for the persistence of the European monopolies in this part of the Atlantic trading world was that it was, in an age of mercantilism, a buttress against the considerable power of African consumers, merchants and states when it came to trade in Africa. European merchants had to be sure that they brought what African consumers wanted, since they were bringing nothing that Africans did not already have, or for which there were not ready, and often better, alternatives. Even guns were not a surefire improvement on edged metal weapons and throwing clubs since their slow loading made them less useful against cavalry, their potentially increased range was dramatically decreased in forest conditions, and the tropical humidity

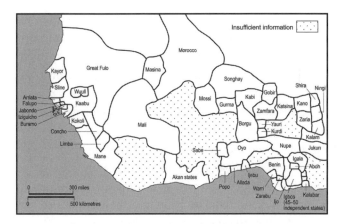

Figure 5.4 West African states, c. 1625. Early seventeenth-century West Africa was a very varied and shifting patchwork of political territories. The relationships between these polities made for complex economic and political dynamics that did not simply reflect the interests of Europeans. It was, however, the case that wars fought to dominate parts of this terrain often involved enslaving those who were defeated and selling them to European merchants.

rendered it uncertain whether they would fire at all. When it came to cloth, with its extensive indigenous production and trade, African consumers were as driven by motivations of fashion and style as consumers in Europe and the Americas. As one European visitor to the Gold Coast put it in 1673, the Akan 'are so vain about what they wear, at one moment they like this new fashion, at another moment that; and whatever appeals to them at a particular time they must have, even if they have to pay twice as much for it. This is why so many goods remain unsold and are sent back to Europe at great loss'.[5] As a result, Europeans had to think hard about the African market, and African merchants were able to drive a hard bargain.

The European market position was further weakened since most West African trade was conducted within the purview of African states able to offset any organisational advantages the companies had. These polities took many different forms, and their political geography was one that shifted, as it did in Europe, through constant warfare and diplomacy, and competition over trade (figure 5.4). Yet they were certainly effective in managing trade. European merchants had to give gifts and pay customs duties to local rulers and officials to open and close the markets for each commodity, and often had to give rulers the first choice of merchandise and preferential prices for their goods (effectively another tax). The extent of African control is indicated by the increased cost of this political economy to European merchants. In 1700 the independent ruler of Ouidah, an important port on the Slave Coast, was able to charge the value of around ten slaves to open the market (a fee known as the *comey*) and a premium price for his own slaves. By 1720 Ouidah was the greatest trading post in West Africa, visited by forty to fifty European ships a year, and the *comey* had doubled to twenty slaves plus privileged buying and selling for the ruler. Overall, it is a clear indication of African rulers' and merchants' power in relation to increased demand from European and American merchants (and plantation-owners in the Americas) that by 1800 they received goods for each slave worth three or four times as much as in 1700. Europeans may have controlled the long-distance trades across the Atlantic, but they did not control trade on the African coast. There African merchants and rulers (who were often also merchants) skilfully negotiated their place in the new Atlantic economy, keeping Europeans confined to their ships and forts. There was no extensive settlement or control of territory by Europeans in Africa. The potential profits and the tense politics of these mercantile exchanges produced a space in which a range of cultural brokers operated and sought to make their fortunes. One such mediator, who frequented the mouth of the Gambia River, was a woman known to the Europeans as La Belinguere.

The world of La Belinguere

Also known as Marie Mar and Maguimar, La Belinguere was a Luso-African woman (of mixed Portuguese and African descent) who was the daughter of a former ruler of Niumi, a small independent state on the northern bank of the mouth of the Gambia River (figure 5.5). Her name was probably derived from 'linger', a Jolof title of respect which denoted powerful women with certain legal powers over women's affairs. La Belinguere was certainly powerful. She was said to be the most influential person in Niumi after the *mansa* (or ruler), and she possessed a fortune worth more than forty thousand livres in gold, slaves and cattle. Much of this she had made by translating for and trading with European traders. She was one of several *nharas* (the Portuguese pidgin (*crioulo*) term derived from *senhora*) who rose to prominence in Senegambia in the second half of the seventeenth century. Like other *nharas*, such as Senhora Catarina and Bibiana Vaz, La Belinguere opened the way for Europeans to engage with Luso-African and African trading networks. She dealt with Europeans both via their companies and, more significantly, through the private trade in which Company servants

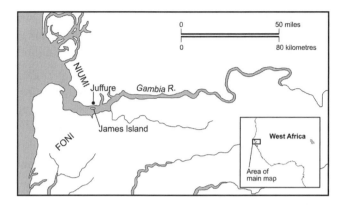

Figure 5.5 The Gambia River in the late seventeenth century.
Trading places such as this involved local polities (Niumi and Foni);
European traders representing various nationalities at places such
as Juffure that already housed African merchants and notables; and
purpose-built European forts, as on James Island. Traders such as
La Belinguere worked within and between these worlds.

(once again, just like Streynsham Master) sought to make their fortunes if
they were not to be part of the majority who died of tropical diseases on
the coast. Women such as La Belinguere, through what were called 'country
marriages' contracted with Europeans, made it possible for these men to
profit from African trade. The women brought their familial connections,
linguistic skills and trading expertise; the European men brought access
to a new set of trade goods. Just like Luso-Africans since the first days of
European trade in the West African trade, these *nhara*s were cultural and
economic brokers of great consequence.

There is a vivid description of La Belinguere from the director of the
French Compagnie de Sénégal Michel Jajolet de La Courbe who visited
Gambia in the summer of 1686 and had dinner with her:

She was garbed in a very elegant man's shirt and a small Portuguese-style corset
which emphasised her figure, and for a skirt she wore a beautiful African cloth …
from Sao Tiago in the Cape Verde Islands. She had a very fine muslin coiled
around her head in the shape of a turban raised a little in front. She had a gracious
manner and a gift for conversation, and spoke Portuguese, French, and English well,
indicative of the extensive commerce she carries on with all nations.[6]

His appreciation of the mixture of cultures that she embodied in her dress
and speech extended to the food that she had had prepared for her guests.
They enjoyed millet bread and rice from West Africa, chillies and pineapples
originally from South America, bananas from South Asia and the brandy

that La Courbe had brought from France as well as Portuguese wines. Significantly, however, the applause of this gallant Frenchman for La Belinguere's
cultural hybridity did not extend to her male counterparts whose dugout
canoes controlled the trade in slaves, ivory and gold on the river. As he put
it, 'They usually wear a hat, shirt, and breeches like Europeans [and prominent crucifixes], and although they are black, they nevertheless assert that
they are white, trying to show that they are Christians like white people.'[7]
Indeed, there were very different meanings of 'white' and 'black' at stake for
different players on the West African coast, ones which signalled religion
and freedom as much as skin tone. There was certainly no agreement on
who was 'black' or 'white'. As Francis Moore, a Royal African Company
employee in the Gambia, noted in 1730 of the Luso-Africans he met, 'they
reckon themselves still as if they were actually White, and nothing angers
them more than to call them *Negroes*, that being a Term they use only for
Slaves, and their not understanding the true Meaning of the Word is the
Reason of their being so very much affronted at it'. However, the fact that
these words' 'true meanings', and the designation of Eurafricans as either
'black' or 'white' could not be fixed in this complex contact zone, is evident
in the resolution of Walter Charles, the Royal African Company's chief factor at Bance Island at around the same time, that he would 'take effectual
care . . . that no white black man shall make any figure here, above what the
meanest natives do'.[8] Such hybridity was a danger too.

La Courbe, evidently quite taken with La Belinguere, did also see her as
dangerous. He described her as the 'reef' on which many Europeans had
been 'shipwrecked', and depicted her as Circe to his Ulysses.[9] This danger was some indication of the power she could potentially deploy. One
incident shows this well. In the spring of 1687, La Belinguere and a group of
other women had gone to a party at the fort on James Island at the entrance
of the Gambia River that the English had built in the early 1660s. A drunken
comment to one of the women sparked a fight in which she was injured.
The knife was wielded by Captain Cornelius Hodges, an English mariner
living at Foni (on the other side of the river from Niumi) who was married
to another *nhara*, and who had undertaken a reconnaissance voyage to the
upper Gambia for the Royal African Company in 1681. Learning of the
incident at Fort James, the *mansa* of Niumi, Jenung Wuleng Sonko, seized
the English factor at Juffure and confiscated all his trade goods in compensation. When Alexander Cleeve, the chief agent on James Island, went to
negotiate he was also held hostage. It was only with the payment of two
hundred iron bars (the trading currency for Europeans in West Africa) and
the intervention of the Banyun ruler of Foni that the English and the *mansa*

of Niumi were reconciled. In the meantime, and with English trade at a halt, La Belinguere and the French agent La Coste combined to recruit a network of Luso-African traders to break the Royal African Company's monopoly on the upper river trade, much to the annoyance of Cleeve and the African notables at Juffure who were thus bypassed. La Belinguere was able to take advantage of her intimate relations with various European traders, and the protection given to Luso-Africans by African states (at a price), to play one side off against the other to her own advantage. In microcosm, this incident signals the broader history of African control over their Atlantic trade and, more particularly, the advantages reaped by African and Luso-African traders from the constant competition and conflicts between Europeans. African rulers and traders may not have extended their control of trade into the Atlantic but neither did they need to.

New England in the Atlantic world

The situation was quite different in parts of the Americas. Newfoundland, the Caribbean Islands and Virginia soon developed their concentrations on fish, sugar and tobacco, fitting them into the Atlantic trading system (see also chapter 9). New England, however, had little by way of natural produce that did not replicate what was already available in England itself. Also, unlike in Africa or Asia there was no existing network of long-distance continental trade in large volumes of spices, textiles and metalwares to tap into. The Plymouth Company which set up trading factories on the New England coast in the early seventeenth century waited in vain for native Americans to arrive with goods to exchange. Neither was this to be another Hudson Bay, supplying furs to Europe. The New England beaver were hunted out by the 1670s, and the monopoly companies chartered to deal with the colonies had themselves already become extinct. New England was, as chapter 3 showed, an agricultural settlement frontier based on the Puritan Great Migration and the desire for land and religious and economic autonomy. Yet, despite having crossed the ocean these settlers could not break free. They could eat well enough on what they and their neighbours produced, but they needed clothes, sheets and blankets; they needed iron pots, pans, nails and farm implements; and they needed little things such as buttons, hats, and pins and needles.

The merchants who came to supply these demands were Puritan settlers themselves. Many of them had been small London tradesmen and shopkeepers. None of them were in the first rank of England's commercial classes that served as London aldermen and heads of City livery companies. The voyage across the Atlantic and the market there for manufactured goods of cloth and metal turned them into merchants. What they had were the connections back to London, through family ties or long-standing friendships, that would enable them to obtain a stock of coveted goods on sufficient credit to cover the time it took to transport and sell them. In doing so they faced two problems: Puritan ethics and mercantile economics. The first meant that all areas of life were subordinated to the Puritan ideal of a new commonwealth built upon godly terms. Commerce, with its debts and inequalities, was particularly suspect, even if merchants were pious men themselves and were supplying the tools to build the Puritan promised land. Puritan exchanges were governed by notions of the just price and by condemnations of usury (money-lending at unjust interest) which shaped the actions of merchants and reined in the market. The second problem involved the brute economics of the Atlantic mercantile world which dictated that without something to offer in return for these manufactured goods, other than the savings of settlers who had sold land in England, the new colony would be in a dangerously subordinate position. The merchants might make money in the short term, but they could not control the trade in the long term.

The solution to the second problem – and it turned out to be the solvent that also gradually dissolved the first – was a simple one: cod. When the English Civil War of the 1640s prevented West Country boats from fishing in New England waters, and supplying Boston with fish as well as taking it back to Europe, local ship-owners and merchants stepped in. At first the Boston merchants took a small and localised role in the trade. In return for manufactured goods from England they were able to supply cargoes of salt cod, often by advancing credit to the captains of fishing vessels, to fill the holds of ships sent by London merchants who had the capital and connections to access the markets in southern Europe and the Wine Islands. From this toehold, secured by access to the fishery and by the kinship and friendship networks that gave them credit and credibility with their London counterparts, the New England merchants sought to expand their role in the trade. Instead of just selling their fish, some were able to use it as capital to take a share of the voyage's profits. Others grouped together and sent voyages to Madeira and the Azores to exchange fish and other foods for wine and salt. Although they could not complete the trade by bringing manufactured goods from England, these merchants gradually developed different forms of independent commerce from the New England seaports. In 1643 five New England vessels set out on ocean routes, and one returned from the

Canary Islands via Barbados where it sold a cargo of slaves. Not only did this open the possibility of slave trading from the North American colonies in North American ships, but opened the eyes of New England merchants to the markets developing in the Caribbean where land that could grow sugar was too valuable to use for anything else.

By 1660 these attempts by New England merchants to overcome their subordination within the Atlantic trading system by extending control over trade into and around the Atlantic world had created a pattern that, in its basic shape, endured until the American Revolution. Within the framework created by the Navigation Acts, and increasingly based upon the sort of commission merchandising familiar to men such as William Freeman, New England merchants shipped provisions, lumber and horses to the British West Indies in exchange for sugar, molasses and rum. The salt cod which made up a large part of this trade came both from Newfoundland (which New England merchants now supplied with all those goods that had once come from England) and from an outer banks fishery developed from New England which, because of longer periods at sea, produced a cheaper, more heavily salted product that found a better market among the slave-owners of the Caribbean than with the diners of Portugal and Spain. These trades provided bills of exchange that were used to buy manufactured goods from Britain. They also stimulated a trade in rum to Africa and a trade in naval stores – masts, lumber, rope, tar and turpentine – that, along with ships themselves, began to form a major export to Britain. By 1775 of the seven thousand vessels on the register of Lloyds of London, 32 per cent had been built in the American colonies. Rooted in huge state investment in naval power, and the British desire to have sources of supply more secure than those of the Baltic, these industries formed a pillar of the New England economy.

New England merchants were never entirely autonomous or independent. They operated within the mercantile and military framework of Britain's Atlantic empire. They did, however, forge a distinctive place within that world by extending their control over oceanic trades and, in the process, building new trading ports along the coast. Some Puritans grew rich from this Atlantic trade. Others grew angry at the way in which the dream of the autonomous commonwealth had been realised only by binding it ever more tightly into a world of trade and extending ever further the domain of commerce. Increasingly, however, both the Puritan merchants and the religious leaders with whom they had come into conflict were succeeded by new migrants from England who saw Massachusetts as a place of potential profit and not of promised religious purity. Cod had meant that mercantile

economics won out over Puritan ethics. This was the unintended consequence of the work done by pious Puritan merchants such as Robert
Keayne.

The world of Robert Keayne

Born a butcher's son in Windsor in 1595, Robert Keayne noted as he composed his last will and testament in 1653 that he had received 'no portion
from my parents or friends to begin the world withal'. This self-made man
and devout Puritan had become a successful merchant tailor in Birchin
Lane, London, and heeded the call to migrate to Massachusetts in 1635
at the height of the Great Migration taking with him his family and 'two
or 3,000 lb. in good estate' to trade with. Once there he used his London
connections to import goods needed by the new colonists. At the heart of
Boston's growing commercial district, Keayne and other new merchants just
like him established a New World facsimile of what they had left behind.
They called the port's main street Cornhill, in imitation of the thoroughfare at the heart of the City of London, and set up the shops and counting
houses where they might deal in all the commodities the colony had to buy
and sell. Keayne was among those who expanded his interests by trading
with the West Indies. This was, however, by no means an easy business.
Long-distance trade was a volatile and risky enterprise and Keayne suffered
and survived financial setbacks 'sufficient to have broken the back of any
one man in the country'.[10]

There were other setbacks too. In November 1639 Robert Keayne was
charged by the civil authorities of the colony in their General Court with
'taking above six-pence in the shilling profit; in some above eight pence; and
in small things, above two for one'. Customers who had bought bags of nails,
buttons, a bridle and a skein of thread queued up to denounce what they saw
as Keayne's unchristian exploitation of his advantageous position. Unable
to understand how the abundance of land combined with the undersupply
of labour and goods was fuelling rampant inflation they fell back upon
old ideas of the gouging middleman and his unjust prices. The court fined
Keayne £200, although there were those who argued that he should pay five
times that.[11] Neither were his trials then over. This pious Puritan was forced
to admit his sins under threat of excommunication and was given a severe
dressing down 'in the name of the Church for selling his wares at excessive
Rates, to the Dishonor of God's name, the Offence of the General Cort, and
the Publique scandal of the Cuntry'.[12] As he wrote his will fourteen years

later it was these difficulties with reconciling God and Mammon, and other accusations against him for sharp practice and drunkenness, that drove Keayne to compose a 50,000-word apologia justifying his life's work.

He had certainly sought to be both a Puritan and a merchant. He attended as closely to the books of Scripture as he did to his account books. Indeed, he calculated his balance of profit and loss in both registers, also noting that he 'had good credit and good esteem and respect' wherever he had lived. He spent his evenings in Bible study and stated that he would not part with the four works of spiritual exegesis that he had written for himself even if offered £100. He obeyed the Calvinist injunction to avoid 'an idle, lazy, or dronish life' and applied himself to work.[13] Indeed, he judged that the sign of God's favour for his diligence lay in the success of his business, as well as the trials it had put him through. Like his fellow merchants he invested the wealth he made in land, and sought to make himself a gentleman. Unlike those who returned to England, he did so in New England, building himself a fine house at Rumney Marsh.

As well as passing on this hard-earned wealth to his son, who had acted as his agent in London, in the tangible form of fields, forests and buildings, he also wanted to give something back to the community of which he was a part. Keayne's will made provision for the construction of a two-storey townhouse at the centre of the market and meetinghouse square in Boston where he had had his shop. This would be a major public building, providing rooms from which the General Court could govern the colony, a 'room for a library and a gallery or some other handsome room for the elders to meet in and confer together', and an armoury for the Artillery Company. It also served crucial economic purposes, acting as the point where the colony's rural economy met the merchants' long-distance trade by offering both a shelter 'for the country people that come with their provisions . . . to sit dry in and warm both in cold, rain and dirty weather' and, in the open space beneath the building, a place that would 'serve for merchants, masters of ships and strangers as well as the town to meet in at all times to confer about their business and occasions'.[14] Keayne's townhouse was where the connections that bound the colony into the Atlantic world were to be realised. It was the place from which the commercial power of New England might be articulated on an oceanic scale. He saw this as both a matter of private property and civic benefit. His aim was to invest in New England, both privately and publicly, and not to let the wealth created find its way back to London. This was the creation of something new and forward-looking in North America, yet it was a quite different vision for the colony from John Winthrop's religious utopia, the 'City on the Hill'.

When he died in 1656, the rest of Keayne's wealth passed into the densely intermarried society of Massachusetts merchants. There it found new forms of investment and sought new profits. One major beneficiary, Keayne's granddaughter Anna, eventually married the newly arrived English merchant Nicholas Paige. Unlike Keayne, a careful and worried Puritan, Paige was an Anglican, a royalist and a commercial imperialist. Unconcerned by theological doctrine, new men such as Paige, many of whom married the daughters and granddaughters of the first generation of Puritan merchants, set out to build upon the Atlantic trading system their in-laws had developed. They reaped the benefits of the hard-won control over oceanic trade, and no longer felt the need to exert strict moral controls over their own commercial activities. With them we leave Keayne's world behind and begin to enter the age of integration in the eighteenth-century Atlantic.

Integrating the eighteenth-century Atlantic world

The work of seventeenth-century merchants such as William Freeman, La Belinguere and Robert Keayne did much to establish the basic framework of Britain's Atlantic trade. Other merchants were constructing French and Dutch networks, or maintaining those of the Spanish and Portuguese. Over the course of the eighteenth century these structures were filled out and elaborated. The substantial changes in the volume, composition and geography of imports and exports have already been outlined. The Americas became more and more important to Britain's trade, and much more of this commerce passed through the Atlantic outports, especially Liverpool and Bristol, than ever before. This trade was also increasingly concentrated in fewer hands, which each handled larger amounts of goods. For example, there were 573 tobacco importers in London in 1676, but only 56 in 1775. The value handled by the average firm had increased fortyfold. There were no significant transformations in sailing times across the ocean to facilitate this, but there were many more ships plying the routes back and forth with cargoes of people and goods. The tonnage of ships leaving British ports for the Caribbean, North America and Asia rose from 82,000 tons in 1686 to 182,000 tons in 1771–1772, and 467,000 tons by 1815. These connections also produced, and were then supported by, substantial transatlantic migrations, both forced and voluntary. British slave ships took over three million Africans to the American plantations between 1662 and 1807 (see chapter 8). By 1815 around 877,000 people lived in the British Caribbean, of whom 743,000 were enslaved. An estimated 217,000 people from England, Wales, Scotland and Ireland emigrated to the North American colonies between 1700 and 1775, helping to increase their population from 265,000 to 2.3 million in 1770. In all of these places substantial investment and hard labour had created farmsteads, plantations, towns and cities. The Atlantic world looked quite different at the end of the eighteenth century than it had a hundred years before.

One set of key agents of this transformation were merchants engaged in long-distance trade. Atlantic merchants in London arranged for the shipping and sale of American agricultural produce, just as William Freeman had done. They did this for others on a commission basis, and they did it for themselves as they gathered the necessary capital, credit and connections together. Unlike the late seventeenth-century merchants, their commercial interests increasingly spanned all areas of activity in Britain's new global trading network. They shipped provisions to the Caribbean, sent manufactured goods to the North American colonies, engaged in the slave trade after the end of monopoly control, invested in plantations in the Americas and speculated in the new markets in government securities and company stocks. Their business interests and the Atlantic world became integrated at one and the same time. They formed temporary partnerships with each other which could engage in complex exchanges of goods and people around the Atlantic and beyond – Indian, German and British cloth and metalwares bartered for slaves, who were then sold for Caribbean sugar or Virginian tobacco, which was then re-exported to France. Their aim was to control the whole circuit of exchange. Doing so involved lengthy work in a wide range of different markets. This required the construction of complex networks of credit and trust which could facilitate purchases and sales, and ensure a profitable outcome. These merchants worked hard to secure these networks, using relatives, friends, friends of friends and trusted former employees to do business for them in far-flung places. Their counting houses became clearing houses for information from across the world and control centres for managing the many ventures that had to be integrated together to work the exchanges of the Atlantic world (figure 5.6).

The framework within which these merchants worked was still that established by the seventeenth-century Navigation Acts that channelled and protected trade within the geography of Britain's Atlantic empire. There was little doubt in the minds of either merchants or politicians that trade and military power were inseparably connected in what was called Britain's 'Empire of the Seas'. The overall volume of international commerce was seen as more or less fixed, so gains were mainly to be made at the expense

Figure 5.6 'A London Merchant's Office', by Thomas Rowlandson, 1789. This lively late eighteenth-century caricature shows merchants' clerks, old and young, hard at work at their office desks. They are surrounded by the ledgers, papers and information they needed in order to effect their global business transactions. Many prosperous merchants learned their business by starting their working lives in offices like this.

of international rivals: the older, weaker powers of Spain and Portugal, whose empires were ripe for the taking, and the newer competition with the Netherlands and, increasingly, France. Once taken, these gains – as colonies, trading posts or ocean routes – had to be held by military power. In turn, merchant shipping provided a 'nursery' (or training ground) for seamen and taxation revenue to pay and provision the army and navy. Nevertheless, as had been the case for Elizabeth I (see chapter 2), the diplomatic, military and dynastic interests of British rulers were more fixed on Europe than they were on the rest of the world for most of the eighteenth century. The wars of 1688–1697 and 1701–1713 were fought in the Americas primarily by colonial troops and their Amerindian allies (see chapter 3). Even though the war of 1739–1748 started as a conflict over Caribbean trade – as the War of Jenkins' Ear it flared up when an English captain had his ear cut off by the Spanish coastguard assigned to prevent smuggling in the

Americas – it soon, as the War of the Austrian Succession, shifted to a European focus. Even the Seven Years' War (1756–1763), which expanded the theatre of operations in Africa, India and the Americas, saw the majority of the British navy staying in home waters or the Mediterranean.

Yet it was this security in Europe that allowed expansion abroad. By 1763, albeit in fits and starts, Britain had substantially expanded its empire by force of arms. The Treaty of Utrecht (1713) had brought into the empire Gibraltar, Minorca, Hudson Bay, Nova Scotia, Newfoundland, the French half of St Kitts, and the Asiento grant to transport slaves to Spanish America. Later, the Treaty of Aix-la-Chapelle (1748) delivered a return to an uneasy status quo between Britain and France – Madras being returned to the British and Louisburg to the French – but it was the Seven Years' War that cemented British military dominance. After a slow start there were significant naval victories at the battles of Lagos (off the Portuguese coast) and Quiberon Bay (off France), which secured the Atlantic. British forces also captured Havana, Guadaloupe, Martinique, Grenada, Dominica, Tobago and St Vincent in the Caribbean (the last four islands being ceded to Britain in the Treaty of Paris in 1763); Quebec and Montreal, leading to the surrender of New France, and the creation of a British colony in Canada; and Senegal and Gorée in West Africa. Using a substantial army in the Americas for the first time, Britain also gained control of territories in East Florida and over the land between the Appalachian Mountains and the Mississippi River. To these were added the new territories controlled in India after 1765. The Seven Years' War made Britain a global superpower and effectively forced France out of contention in the Atlantic. Within this new imperial geography some merchants were able to thrive.

The world of Richard Oswald

Richard Oswald ended his life a very rich man. When he died on his country estate at Auchincruive in Ayrshire in November 1784 his personal property – in land, money due on bonds and mortgages, claims on the government, bank accounts, and stocks and annuities – was assessed at £500,000 (the equivalent of over £28 million now). Although he had also been born and brought up in Scotland he had travelled far and come a long way. Born in around 1705 in Caithness, he had joined the Glasgow tobacco merchant firm run by his cousins when his father, a Presbyterian minister, died in 1725. Richard first worked as a clerk, writing letters and tallying accounts. His cousins trained him well and rewarded his diligence by promoting him to work as a supercargo (travelling with the merchandise) on voyages to Virginia, the Carolinas and Jamaica. During the late 1730s he lived mainly in the Chesapeake buying tobacco and chasing debts. Made a partner in 1741 he returned to Glasgow where he ran the counting house, expanded the firm's interests into the Caribbean trade and began to venture capital on his own account on transatlantic voyages. He moved to London in 1746, leased a counting house at 17 Philpot Lane and began to develop trading, shipping, planting and slaving ventures around the Atlantic with a set of like-minded merchants, many of whom shared his provincial background, American experience and boundless energy.

Oswald and his associates began their London careers as factors or agents for others. Just like William Freeman their business was shipping and trading in merchandise from around the Atlantic world. By 1747 Oswald was already the ninth-largest metropolitan tobacco trader, but he also traded in the whole variety of Atlantic goods for himself and others. He did so through an international network of contacts: his partners in London; his cousins in Glasgow; the mercantile and planting connections in Jamaica and London which came (along with more capital) from his marriage to Mary Ramsey in 1750; and the friends, relatives, fellow Scotsmen and former employees that he assiduously cultivated in Europe, the Caribbean and North America. Oswald's aim in mobilising this network was to keep the holds of his ships full, and to keep those vessels under way from place to place around the ocean. Unlike Freeman, who began as a planter and became a merchant, Oswald became a planter – in the Windward Islands, South Carolina and East Florida – because he was a merchant. It enabled him to further integrate his business interests. He could supply his own plantations and also fill his own ships with their produce. This process also led Oswald into the slave trade. In 1748, as part of a consortium of merchants, he bought the slave-trading 'castle' of Bance Island at the mouth of the Sierra Leone River which they refurbished, refortified and restaffed ready to do a wholesale trade in enslaved labour bought with cloth, metalware, tobacco and sugar that they shipped from Europe, India and the Americas. Over the next thirty-six years they sold 12,929 slaves, supplying their own plantations with labour, fulfilling contracts with a variety of clients, undertaking speculative voyages to slave markets in the New World and selling to ships which sailed from European ports to the African coast. The 6 per cent profit that Oswald averaged selling people across the Atlantic to work on sugar plantations enabled him to return to Scotland as a rich and successful land-owner, and allowed him to experiment with growing sugarcane in his own elaborately designed Ayrshire hothouses.

Yet this is not simply a story of mercantile success in a new global marketplace. Richard Oswald's world was an imperial one too. The patterns of his shipping, trading and planting interests were set by the geography of empire. Imperial victories opened up new avenues of opportunity and new places for profit. The Seven Years' War was the great watershed for Oswald as well as for the empire. Victory opened up possibilities for planting and trading in East Florida and the Ceded Islands, even if his indigo plantation south of St Augustine came to little. It also made a success of the Bance Island slave factory when previous merchants had failed to turn a profit there. The war decimated the French slave trade and disrupted France's plantation economies in the Caribbean. After 1763, with the Atlantic under British control, new plantations to supply in new imperial territories and the demand from French planters to meet too, Grant, Oswald & Co.'s business boomed. Indeed, 37 per cent of their sales up to 1784 were to French trading companies such as the Société pour la Rivière de Sierralionne.

The war was also crucial for Oswald because it was the key to his most profitable enterprise. Using all his skills of co-ordination, management and careful accounting Oswald became one of the largest government contractors supplying bread to the British, Hanoverian and Prussian troops fighting in Germany. By the end of the war there were more than 101,000 soldiers in Europe, and another 70,000 at sea or in the Americas. They all had to be fed. Oswald managed a third of the fifty-five bread magazines (storehouses) serving the army in Germany, taking responsibility for the baking, storage and distribution of ninety tons of bread a day to forty-three British battalions spread across 66,000 square miles. In four and a half years his field ovens baked more than five million loaves. This work was so important that Oswald supervised it himself, travelling with his wife from magazine to magazine inspecting his staff and facilities. He was richly rewarded for what he did, earning £112,000 for his troubles (around £8.5 million today). Unsurprisingly, it was after the Seven Years' War that Oswald began investing in government securities and the stock market, buying land in Britain and the Americas, and building the country estate, art collection, library and garden that would allow him to die a gentleman. He had helped make Britain's 'Empire of the Seas', and it in turn had made him rich.

Britain's Atlantic empire did not last very long in the form established by the Treaty of Paris. The cost of the army stationed in North America, and the controls on the colonial merchants, planters and farmers exerted by Britain, lay behind the successful American Revolution of 1776. Yet as Richard Oswald sat across the table from Benjamin Franklin in Paris in

1782 negotiating the peace treaty that would end the Revolutionary War (he was chosen because he was a merchant who 'had seen at once America & an army', because he was 'devoid of the pride of aristocracy, without being suspected of democracy', and because he was 'a man old in experience yet, with a versatility of mind and temper, capable of entering new affairs').[15] He sought to ensure that the commercial integration of Britain and America was preserved even as the former colonies split from the empire. The ties of trade lasted beyond the bonds of empire.

Each of these ties of trade was, as this chapter has shown, part of a complex and differentiated whole which shifted and changed in kaleidoscopic patterns that rarely resolved into a simple triangle. Different parts of the Atlantic world were integrated into this emerging whole in different ways, with different degrees of control and with different outcomes. It was the strength of the African hold over their coastal trade which meant that African rulers and merchants – adaptable and strong traders that they were – did not need to extend their control over the more difficult oceanic trades. In contrast, it was the weakness of New England's producers and merchants – with their Puritan concerns and uncertain place in the market – which meant that they had to find ways to push out into the Atlantic world. In each case, and with the work of those such as William Freeman and Richard Oswald, who tied people, places and forms of exchange together, trade relied upon the hard work of managing networks of people who could be trusted at a distance. The Atlantic trading world was based on the extension of credit across the ocean.

There is, however, more to this than the world and work of the merchants. There were others at work here too, and it was upon the labour of sailors and slaves that mercantile profits depended. It is, therefore, at this point that the book splits to explore two different but connected paths. The first (chapters 6 and 7) explores the world of the sailors (and their counterparts beyond the law, the pirates) whose labour on ships and in ports made real the material transfers of cargoes agreed upon in merchants' letters and tallied in their account books. The second (chapters 8, 9 and 10) explores the labour of enslaved Africans that underpinned the Atlantic world. Most of what moved around the Atlantic was either intended to buy slaves, or to provision slaves on plantations and farms, or was the product of slave labour.

Further reading

For overviews that concentrate on the Americas, see Bernard Bailyn (2005) *Atlantic History: Concept and Contours* (Harvard University Press,

Cambridge, Mass.) and Donald W. Meinig (1986) *The Shaping of America*, vol. I, *Atlantic America, 1492–1800* (Yale University Press, New Haven). Changes in imports and exports are covered in Ralph Davis (1954) 'English foreign trade, 1660–1700', *Economic History Review*, 7:2 pp. 150–166 and Ralph Davis (1962) 'English foreign trade, 1700–1774', *Economic History Review*, 15:2 pp. 285–303. A concise overview of the Atlantic economy is offered in Nuala Zahedieh (2002) 'Economy', in David Armitage and Michael J. Braddick (eds.) *The British Atlantic World, 1500–1800* (Palgrave Macmillan, Basingstoke) pp. 51–68. Its various parts are differentiated in Stephen J. Hornsby (2005) *British Atlantic, American Frontier: Spaces of Power in Early Modern British America* (University Press of New England, Hanover). For William Freeman, see David Hancock (2000) '"A world of business to do": William Freeman and the foundations of England's commercial empire, 1645–1707', *William and Mary Quarterly*, 57:1 pp. 3–34 and David Hancock (ed.) (2002) *The Letters of William Freeman, 1678–1685* (London Record Society, London). On 'credit', see Nuala Zahedieh (1998) 'Credit, risk and reputation in late seventeenth-century colonial trade', in O. U. Janzen (ed.) *Merchant Organization and Maritime Trade in the North Atlantic, 1660–1815* (International Maritime Economic History Association, St John's, Newfoundland) pp. 53–74. For African trade, see John Thornton (1998) *Africa and Africans in the Making of the Atlantic World, 1400–1800*, 2nd edn (Cambridge University Press, Cambridge) and David Northrup (2002) *Africa's Discovery of Europe, 1450–1850* (Oxford University Press, Oxford). The few snippets of information available about La Belinguere from European sources are presented in George E. Brooks (2003) *Eurafricans in Western Africa: Commerce, Social Status, Gender, and Religious Observance from the Sixteenth to the Eighteenth Century* (Ohio University Press, Athens) along with much valuable material on the details of Senegambian trade. For New England's merchants, including Robert Keayne, see Bernard Bailyn (1979) *The New England Merchants in the Seventeenth Century*, 2nd edn (Harvard University Press, Cambridge, Mass.), Bernard Bailyn (1950) 'The apologia of Robert Keayne', *William and Mary Quarterly*, 7:4 pp. 568–587 and Bernard Bailyn (ed.) (1964) *The Apologia of Robert Keayne: The Self-Portrait of a Puritan Merchant* (Harper & Row, New York). For Britain's eighteenth-century Atlantic empire see P. J. Marshall (ed.) (1998) *Oxford History of the British Empire*, vol. II, *The Eighteenth Century* (Oxford University Press, Oxford), particularly the chapters by Patrick O'Brien, Jacob Price, Bruce Lenman and N. A. M. Rodger, and, for Richard Oswald and London's Atlantic merchants, David Hancock (1995) *Citizens of the World: London Merchants and the Integration of the British Atlantic Community, 1735–1785* (Cambridge University Press, Cambridge) and Jacob M. Price (1989) 'What did merchants do? Reflections on British overseas trade, 1660–1700', *Journal of Economic History*, 49:2 pp. 267–284.

Notes

1 Roger North quoted in David Harris Sacks (1991) *The Widening Gate: Bristol and the Atlantic Economy, 1450–1700* (University of California Press, Berkeley) p. 263. The trade in men refers to the sending of indentured servants to the Americas; see chapter 9.

2 David Hancock (ed.) (2002) *The Letters of William Freeman, 1678–1685* (London Record Society, London) p. 6.

3 Ibid., p. 9.

4 Ibid., p. 34.

5 Wilhelm Johann Müller quoted in John Thornton (1998) *Africa and Africans in the Making of the Atlantic World, 1400–1800*, 2nd edn (Cambridge University Press, Cambridge) pp. 51–53.

6 Quoted in George E. Brooks (2003) *Eurafricans in Western Africa: Commerce, Social Status, Gender, and Religious Observance from the Sixteenth to the Eighteenth Century* (Ohio University Press, Athens) p. 151.

7 Quoted ibid., p. 153.

8 Quotes from ibid., pp. 228 and 243.

9 Quoted ibid., p. 150.

10 Quotations from Bernard Bailyn (ed.) (1964) *The Apologia of Robert Keayne: The Self-Portrait of a Puritan Merchant* (Harper & Row, New York) pp. 27 and 82.

11 In fact, the fine was reduced to £80 in May 1640.

12 Quotations from Bernard Bailyn (1979) *The New England Merchants in the Seventeenth Century*, 2nd edn (Harvard University Press, Cambridge, Mass.) pp. 41–42.

13 Quotations from Bailyn, *The Apologia of Robert Keayne*, pp. 73 and 82.

14 Quotations from ibid., pp. 6–7.

15 Quoted in David Hancock (1995) *Citizens of the World: London Merchants and the Integration of the British Atlantic Community, 1735–1785* (Cambridge University Press, Cambridge) p. 390.

6 | Maritime labour: sailors and the seafaring world

The increased movement of goods around the world detailed in the two pre-vious chapters, and the use of the navy to protect merchant shipping, meant a dramatic increase in the number of ships and sailors in the seventeenth and eighteenth centuries, particularly those sailing into and out of British ports. In the middle of the sixteenth century, when John Hawkins went to sea, there were only about 3,000 to 5,000 English mariners. It is estimated that by 1703 there were more than 12,000 seafaring Londoners who worked in the international trades, and several thousand more who undertook coastal voyages. By 1750 there were more than 16,000 British sailors. These ebbed and flowed between the merchant fleet and the Royal Navy with the peri-ods of war and peace across the seventeenth and eighteenth centuries. The number of merchant ships saw significant expansions from 1660 to 1688 as the Atlantic trades took off (and before the cycle of global wars began) and after 1748 as British merchant shipping became dominant under the wing of the Royal Navy. Following the reforms of the period after 1660, the navy itself had become a government-controlled military force, rather than the public–private partnership of Hawkins's day (see chapter 2). Indeed, it was not only the most money-hungry and demanding part of the eighteenth-century British state, but by far the largest industrial organisation in the Western world. The Royal Navy's fleet increased from around 270 ships in 1700 to about 500 in 1793, and around 950 in 1805. During peacetime in the eighteenth century the number of serving seamen required fluctuated from 12,000 to 20,000, but during wartime the demand massively expanded. Around 40,000 seamen fought in the war of 1739–1748, there were nearly 82,000 men on board ship in 1762 (during the Seven Years' War) and more than 150,000 in the Napoleonic Wars at the turn of the century. Naval dock-yards, commercial quaysides and all the facilities needed by sailors on shore also developed to service the comings and goings of these vessels and men around the seven seas.

These overall figures conceal the variety of ships, and the different con-ditions of life and work that they offered to seafarers. The largest first-rate ships of the line, the navy's premier fighting vessels, were vast, complex constructions (figure 6.1). Each one used the wood of sixty mature oak

Figure 6.1 Ships of the line. This painting by John Cleveley was completed in 1757 and shows two Royal Navy ships on the River Thames at Deptford: the *Cambridge* (80 guns), being floated out of the dry-dock, and the *Royal George* (100 guns) fully rigged and on the river. They are shown surrounded by a variety of other craft as part of a scene that presents an imagined display of naval power rather than the depiction of actual events.

trees, as well as elm and pine for keels and masts, a hundred tons of wrought iron and thousands of feet of rope. They housed from 600 to 800 men in cramped conditions along with all the food and water needed to supply them, albeit with no extravagance, for six months. They carried up to a hundred guns, ready to deliver broadsides of heavy shot against the enemy from their serried ranks of gunports one on top of the other along the sides of the ship. However, navies required many sorts of vessel from these great ships down to fourteen-gun sloops and ten-gun yachts, with crews to match. With the exception of the East India Company's fleet, merchant vessels were generally on the smaller side. The Company, sailing long distances to India and later to China, and unable to depend upon naval protection beyond the Cape of Good Hope, needed vessels that could fight as well as carry their valuable cargoes. In the Atlantic Ocean the demands were different. Looking at this from the point of view of William Freeman or Richard Oswald (see chapter 5), we can appreciate that large ships had the advantage of reducing running costs per ton of cargo, but they ran the risk of having to sail with their holds only partly full while still paying the wages of the increased number of seamen required to handle them. Smaller ships were more reliably profitable. Although the increase in the predictability of supply and demand brought by the integration of the Atlantic, and indeed global, economy across the eighteenth century meant that the average size of ships did increase, in 1788 it was still the case that 83 per cent of the ships registered as English-owned were under two hundred tons. These were typically three-masted brigs or snows which could operate on the deep oceans and in coastal waters, and could be handled by relatively small crews.

Indeed, the main problem that faced both the navy and the merchant fleets was manpower. In the navy the crucial issue was having enough men to work the guns, which required about six men each. This did not change significantly over time, and the navy needed to force experienced men to serve during wartime. However, as the merchant vessels increasingly received their protection from these warships they were able to dispense with the specialist gunners and the larger crews needed to man these weapons that had been common in the late seventeenth and early eighteenth centuries. As a result of this, of the pressure to increase profitability by decreasing the wage bill as far as possible, and of a number of technological changes to merchant ships which meant that fewer hands were required to transport the same weight of cargo, the crew sizes of Atlantic shipping vessels fell across the eighteenth century. This was slower in some trades – slave ships, for example, requiring larger crews to deal with problems of disease and disorder (see chapter 8). However, ships trading to Virginia were manned at an average rate of about ten tons of cargo per man at the beginning of the eighteenth century, thirteen tons in 1748 and sixteen tons in 1775. Over the century, therefore, the average crew of a 200-ton ship bringing tobacco to Britain fell from twenty-one to about thirteen. This increase in productivity for the merchant put increased pressure on the bodies of the working men who loaded the hold, turned the capstan to raise the anchor, unfurled the sails and hauled the ropes.

It is this world of maritime labour that this chapter considers in more detail, moving the focus from the merchants to the workforce whose muscle power moved goods around the world. Through the lives of both sailors and those on shore it explores the nature of maritime work, the society on board ship through which that work was done, the degree of choice and constraint placed on seafarers in undertaking this work, and the inequalities of getting by on ship and shore. It starts by looking more closely at what was required to get moving around this maritime world.

Maritime labour

Maritime labour was hard physical work, whether on merchant ships or in the navy. Much of what sailors did required sheer bodily strength in order to harness the power of the wind to move these huge ships and their cargoes and guns across vast distances. Merchant ships needed to be loaded, often from smaller vessels, with cargoes of bales, boxes and casks swung into the hold using cranes, ropes and pulleys. They also needed to be unloaded. Anchors needed to be weighed by the collective effort of all hands straining to turn the capstan. Sails needed to be unfurled, reefed or gathered in, both by men on deck and high up in the rigging, depending on the direction and strength of the wind and the course that the captain or master had decided to take. Sailors had to take their turns aloft, watching out for other ships, land, or changes in the weather, perched high up the mast being pitched and tossed as the ship ploughed through the waves. They also had to man the pumps which, through the hard labour of those working their handles, kept the water that constantly seeped through the wooden walls to a safe level. Even when there was plain sailing there was the continual work of attending to the wear and tear on wood, canvas and ropes, all of which could crack, tear or fray under the strain of pushing through the seas. On the navy's ships of the line, fighting at sea was added to the work of sailing. Gun crews were drilled to be able to fire their guns in unison as rapidly as possible. This meant running heavy cannon back and forth on their carriages to repeatedly load and fire in the confined spaces of the gun decks.

This labour could not, however, be simply a matter of brute force and ignorance. Any sailor knew that effort misapplied on a ship was effort wasted against the force of winds and currents. What was required was agility and dexterity as well as strength. Work also had to be organised to be effective. In part that was a matter of labour being collective: pulling or pushing in unison, perhaps given rhythm by a song or chant. In part it was a matter of specialisation. Ships were hierarchical. Captains or masters undertook navigation and decided, with their mates, on how to set the sails, directing the physical labour of others to make the maximum use of the wind, or to keep the ship safe in high seas. Other workers on board had their own specialist skills, mixing mental and manual labour: the carpenter looked after the hull, masts and yards; the gunner took care of the guns; the boatswain took charge of the rigging, sails and anchors; the purser provided the provisions; and the surgeon and the cook (whose skills were often in short supply) saw that men were mended and fed, and ready for work. The largest naval ships included all these and more: complex ranks of officers and men, a chaplain, sailmakers, a schoolmaster and a whole collection of boys being bred up to the sea life as 'servants' of the officers. On every ship, regardless of size, the crew was divided into two watches: the starboard watch and the larboard watch. These alternated on four-hour watches starting at 8 p.m., with a pair of two-hour dog watches from 4 p.m. to 8 p.m. to ensure that each watch alternated ten- or fourteen-hour days, and undertook different duties in each cycle. On the larger naval ships the higher-ranking officers were not part of the watches and there were more 'idlers', who worked by day and slept by night, such as the carpenter, purser, surgeon and sailmaker.

Despite the idea that there was a strict division between those who commanded and those who bent their backs to do the work, this could never entirely be the case. The ships of the eighteenth century were the most complex machines of their age. Cargoes had to be packed carefully to properly distribute their weight and to prevent the goods shifting around when at sea. More importantly, each rope, spar and sail had its own name and function, and each had a set of procedures for handling it correctly. The work required to sail a ship could not be learned except by doing it. The cost of doing it badly was potentially disastrous, with the boundless oceans ready to swallow up ships that set sail unprepared, or whose crews could not cope with what nature threw at them. In these conditions seafaring knowledge was won by hard experience, whether that was gained by those who stayed as common seamen or by those who rose to be in command on the quarterdeck. Sailors valued their skills and despised those, regardless of rank, who put them in danger by bad decisions or inept actions. Mariners of all sorts had respect for the experience of those who 'knew the ropes', and no ship could afford not to mix young and old in its crew, even though seafaring was predominantly a young man's occupation. This was certainly the case on the large fighting ships, and even the small merchant ships would typically include ten common seamen (divided between able seamen who knew their trade and the ordinary seamen who were still learning) with one or two each in their late teens and in their forties and fifties, and two or three each in their early twenties, late twenties and thirties. Seamen learned how to be seamen by working with each other in fair weather and foul. As they learned, their clothes, their bodies and their ways of speaking marked them out as men of the sea.

The world of Edward Barlow

When Edward Barlow left the sea in 1703 at the age of sixty-one he certainly had some tales to tell. Since going to sea in his teenage years he had served on over twenty-five ships of all shapes and sizes. He had been on the ship that brought King Charles II back to England, and he had fought in sea battles against the Dutch in the 1660s. He had sailed to the Mediterranean to challenge the Barbary pirates, and also to trade pickled herrings for wine. He had made voyages on merchantmen to Brazil, Barbados and Jamaica, and had been to India and China and back several times on East India Company vessels. He had been nearly shipwrecked near Mauritius; he had caught the bloody flux and been imprisoned by the Dutch in the East Indies; he had watched the rigging freeze solid in the North Sea; and he had exchanged fire with Captain Kidd in the Indian Ocean (see chapter 7). As a boy he had grown up near Manchester, some distance from the sea, but had dreamed of 'some strange things which I always had a desire to see, and to travel from one place to another'.[1] By the time he hung up his tarpaulin jacket for the last time, he had seen many curious things: the king of Portugal at a bullfight, the brothels of Calicut, Chinamen's beards, the smoke from Mount Etna and all manner of alligators, jackals, sharks and brightly coloured parrots. Yet there was a price to pay, and Edward Barlow bore the marks of it on his body. His head was scarred from his first day on board ship. Hit by the capstan's handle as it leapt forward, he had been knocked down a hatch into the hold fracturing his skull. He limped from the injury to his leg sustained when an 'unlucky shot' from a Dutch ship pierced the side of the vessel just where he was standing.[2] His skin was weather-beaten from days and nights on deck and in the rigging, and his joints ached from a life of hard work.

Just how hard and dangerous the work was is best told by Barlow himself:

[A]t night when we went to take our rest, we were not to lie still above four hours; and many times when it blew hard were not sure to lie one hour, yea, often [we] were called up before we had slept half an hour and forced to go up into the maintop or foretop to take in our topsails, half awake and half asleep, with one shoe on and the other off, not having time to put it on: always sleeping in our clothes for readiness; and in stormy weather, when the ship rolled and tumbled as though some great millstone were rolling up one hill and down another, we had much ado to hold ourselves fast by the small ropes from falling by the board; and being gotten up into the tops, there we must haul and pull to make fast the sail, seeing nothing but air above us and water beneath us, and that so raging as though every wave would make a grave for us: and many times in nights so dark that we could not see one another, and blowing so hard that we could not hear one another speak, being close to one another; and thundering and lightening as though Heaven and earth would come together.[3]

This was, he said, no life for an old man, and he pitied anyone who had to be at sea after they had turned forty, 'little better than a slave, being always in need, and enduring all manner of misery and hardship, going with many a hungry belly and wet back'.[4]

Barlow's complaints were the complaints of many seamen: harsh discipline, uncertain wages, poor food and many injustices. They were forced to live under 'commanders and masters [who] are grown up with pride and tyranny' with 'all the men in the ship except the master being little better than slaves, being under command'.[5] Barlow had seen slaves in South America and the West Indies and he knew the 'torture and hardship' they endured.[6] He had been forced into the navy, and had been denied the chance of seeing his family or collecting his wages as he was shipped off to fight. He also resented the ways in which merchants safeguarded their profits at the expense of the hard-working seamen. He had had his wages stopped 'for goods that had been damnified and spoilt in the ship, which they said the men . . . were in the fault of, for not stowing them better and not taking enough care of them'.[7] The merchants, denying that the fault lay with old and leaky ships, bad weather or holds that were crammed too full, used the mariners' wages to make good their own losses. Too many times he had felt in his guts the penny-pinching of merchants and ship-owners keen to make a profit. He complained that they only put on board enough food and drink for 'so many days, and if they have to be a little longer in their passage and meet with cross winds, then the poor men's bellies must be pinched for it'.[8] Indeed, as someone who rarely had enough to eat he constantly thought about food. He commented on the poor rations the men were forced to eat, while the officers dined in style. One Christmas dinner was 'nothing but a little bit of Irish beef for four men, which had lain in pickle two or three years and was as rusty as the Devil, with a little stinking oil or butter, which was all colours of the rainbow, many men in England greasing their cartwheels with better'.[9] He took advantage of whatever other food he could find by any means necessary: dining on plantains, yams, cassava, mangoes, turtle meat, bonito and albacore when he could. He knew well that the seaman's labour was vital to both international trade and to safeguarding England's shores, and he was well aware of the rights that this should confer. Yet he knew the realities of life on board ship, and that 'a poor man dare not speak for that which is his right . . . many times poor men's lives being taken away for speaking for what is their due'.[10] Like other seamen, he took the knowledge that he had accumulated at sea and used it to get the best work that he could, choosing between the better food available in the navy or the higher wages but harder work of merchant ships. He fought his corner over food, wages and conditions, and although he said that he 'could wish no young man to betake himself to this calling', he was evidently proud of counting himself among the 'poor true-hearted seamen'.[11]

The wooden world: society at sea

The social structure of the ship within which men such as Barlow lived and worked was a complex matter. It differed between the smaller merchant ships where the master stood apart from the men, and the larger naval vessels where the cross-cutting divisions of officers on the quarterdeck and men on the lower deck, seamen and idlers, topmen (who worked high above the deck) and waisters, old hands and greenhands each subdivided the ship's company in different ways. Yet it is possible to broadly identify ways in which the wooden world was different in its organisation of the social relations of class and of race from landed societies. Overall, ships were more fully the domain of wage labour than the societies they sailed from; and they generally offered more equality and liberty to those whose skin colour marked them out for oppression and enslavement on land.

When Barlow went to sea he did so as an apprentice to a chief master's mate in the Royal Navy. This was certainly common on land in the seventeenth century. Boys would be apprenticed for seven years to learn a trade. Indeed, Barlow had already tried out apprenticeships to a cloth bleacher and an innkeeper to see if he liked the work (unsurprisingly, he didn't). The apprentices would live in their master's house, eat at his table and learn his skills. If they were lucky they might marry his daughter and take over the tools of his trade and the running of his workshop. Apprenticeship was based upon a set of paternalistic values, specialist skills (and the tools needed to deploy them) and forms of payment within which wage labour played only a small part. As Barlow soon noticed, going to sea was different. As he put it later, 'if I had known then as much as I know since, and what it was to serve apprenticeship seven years to sea, I would have gone and learned as much in two or three voyages as a hired servant, as many do by the voyage or the year'.[12] Seafaring was something that was to be learned on the job, but it was a job that once learned was part of a labour market in which seamen sold their labour for a wage to a succession of ship's masters or to the state.

Despite what many captains said about being like fathers to their crews, the sea was not like the land: there were fewer social bonds tying sailors to their masters (who were the direct representatives of the merchants); seamen owned no tools except their own bodies; their work was done only with others, not on their own; and they worked primarily for a money wage. The medieval world of sailors who all had shares in the voyage persisted only in the limited spheres of fishing, whaling, privateering and piracy (for the latter, see chapter 7). Most sailors worked for a wage agreed by contract before the voyage. This stipulated what they would be paid (on merchant ships in the early eighteenth century this was usually between 22 and 35 shillings per month in peacetime and 35 to 55 shillings per month in wartime; masters earned £5–£6 per month), and set out the length and nature of the voyage for which they were engaged. Merchant ships, without any of the institutions of family, religion and law to mediate the relationship between master and men, were defined by the social structures of waged work. This meant that economic disputes over the nature of the work (including changes to the voyage), the provision of food (part of the sailor's social wage, but also eating into the merchants' profits) and the eventual payment of wages were unmediated by other social relationships. It is unsurprising that it was said of sailors like Barlow that 'They were peculiarly sensitive and selfish as to what they required as their rights.'[13]

Ships' crews were remarkably mixed. British sailors of all sorts laboured with other men from the Netherlands, France and Spain; from Africa, North America and the Caribbean; and from parts of Asia. Despite the Navigation Acts' stipulations that three-quarters of crews should be English, merchant ships were more mixed by nationality, ethnicity and race. It is very difficult to put figures to this diversity, and it is also apparent that the composition of crews in both merchant ships and the navy was shaped by different and changing circumstances at different times and places. For example, the reluctance of planters in the Caribbean to allow slaves to be on board naval ships in the 1740s meant that crews there were less mixed than the crews on merchant ships which had sailed to Jamaica from Bermuda or from North American ports, some of which were 30 per cent black.

To take just these black seafarers, it is apparent that the maritime life offered them opportunities unavailable on shore. Slave sailors in the West

Indies – fishermen, canoe-handlers (using craft which combined African, American and European hulls, rigging and skills), coastal traders or those shipping out with their master's goods to more distant ports – had a degree of freedom unknown to those on the plantation (see chapter 9). Like other sailors, once they had learned the ropes they were part of a group of workers within which their skills and experience might be valued for what they were. More than on shore, their working lives could be shaped by what they could do and what they knew, and not on the basis of the colour of their skin. Ships might also be a place of safety for free blacks who risked enslavement in the Caribbean Islands if they were found without work. Yet the society on board was not without prejudice. Edward Barlow's identification of sailors with slaves could be both a statement of solidarity and also an affirmation that the white sailor's oppressed condition should not be tolerated. Black sailors often found themselves the victim of their white counterparts' assertions of superiority, and many were consigned to particular roles upon the ship: as musicians, servants or cooks. While the ship may have offered a freer space than the plantation, it was not one without the antagonisms of race.

The worlds of Briton Hammon and John Jea

One indication of the freedoms the seafaring life offered to African-American men was that seamen wrote the first six autobiographies of black people published in English before 1800. These were men who were defining themselves in new ways in relation to a transatlantic world within which they moved in patterns unfamiliar to other black people. They did, however, feel both the freedoms and the constraints that this maritime world presented.

Briton Hammon, 'a Negro Man' from New England, was to spend much time in captivity yearning to be free, but he began his narrative of thirteen difficult years with a striking declaration of his own will: 'On Monday, 25th Day of *December*, 1747, with the leave of my Master, I went from *Marshfield*, with an Intention to go a Voyage to Sea, and . . . immediately ship'd myself on board of a Sloop, Capt. *John Howland*, Master, bound to *Jamaica* and the Bay.' Among the crew was at least one other man of colour, 'Moses Newmock, Molatto'.[14] Hammon's tale, perhaps a yarn he had told many times in the foc'sle, was then one of many 'Uncommon Sufferings'. He was captured by Amerindians on the South Florida coast after the ship, heavily laden with logwood, had run aground. These 'barbarous and inhuman Savages' eventually sold him to the governor of Havana, having killed most of his shipmates. Since Hammon refused to serve on the king of Spain's ships he was kept confined in a dungeon for four and a half years. Following his release from this close confinement he took a year trying to escape from the island. Finally successful, he sailed for Jamaica, then London, and after serving on a series of Royal Navy ships he was wounded in the head in a sea battle with a French vessel, and then in the arm seriously enough to end his career as an able seaman. He finally re-encountered his master, General Winslow, in London and returned with him to New England.

Hammon's negotiations of these sufferings show him to be deeply, and usefully, embedded in a maritime world which offered him certain resources. The captain who helped him escape from the Florida Indians (although they soon caught up with him again) was someone Hammon had previously met in Jamaica. It was also a sympathetic Bostonian ship captain who got him released from the governor's Havana dungeon. Later, although one English captain who found Hammon on board his ship had turned him back over to the governor, another, from the *Beaver*, had refused saying 'he could not answer it, to deliver up any *Englishmen* under *English* Colours'. As well as extending him the rights of a true-born Englishman, no doubt he also found Hammon a useful addition to his crew. This experienced sailor certainly had no trouble serving on merchantmen and fighting ships, and as a cook when he lost the use of his arm (there were many one-armed cooks at sea). He was also part of the world of sailors' talk about ships and captains. He had just negotiated work on a ship sailing to the Guinea coast when he heard 'in a publick House one Evening' of a ship sailing to New England on which he was determined to go, and in which his master was, by chance, sailing as a passenger.[15] Hammon's world was one in which being a sailor and being black led him both into and out of captivity, and took him around the Atlantic.

John Jea had none of Briton Hammon's seafaring skills. Born in Old Calabar on the Slave Coast of Africa in 1773 (see chapter 8), his first oceanic voyage had been in the hold of a slave ship, before being sold to a cruel master in New York. Finding God at fifteen, and finding the usefulness of God as a master to whom all masters had to answer, he got himself freed by convincing the city's ministers and magistrates that he had been taught to read St John's Gospel in one night by an angel. They said 'that I should have my liberty, for they believed I was of God, for they were persuaded that no man could read in such a manner, unless he was taught of God'.[16] Preaching to increasing numbers around New York and Boston, Jea brought many souls to redemption. However, he could not save the troubled soul of the woman that he married, who killed their baby daughter and swore that she would kill him too. Eventually, as he wrote, 'it pleased God to put it into my mind to cross the Atlantic main'. He found himself a ship and signed up as cook, a position familiar to black men at sea.

Jea, unlike Hammon, found himself an outsider on board. The captain set him the dirtiest and lowest work on the ship, cleaning the filthy coppers in which the men's food was made. The crew laughed at him for thinking that he could go back ashore after a day if he didn't like it. They mocked him for thinking that the helmsman made the ship roll from side to side on purpose. When the deck moved beneath his feet and he took a tumble 'all the men sung out, "Hollo, there is a horse down."' They poked fun at his faith: 'When they saw me praying to God, they called me by way of derision, a Jonah, because I prayed to God to calm the tempestuous weather.' And they beat him. As he said, 'they used to flog, beat, and kick me about, the same as if I had been a dog; they also rubbed grease and dirt over my face and eyes; oftentimes they swore they would beat me till they made me jump overboard'.[17] Jea took comfort in his religion, and took particular comfort when the crew's defiance of the Lord's power led, as he saw it, to a lightning strike that killed two of them and endangered the ship. John Jea was a black man at sea, but it offered him few freedoms. As a greenhand he was out of place in the maritime world, and perhaps as a black man he was more open to abuse. He was pleased when his first voyage was done, but his ability to take ship around the Atlantic world to preach was too valuable and he later travelled as a ship's cook to Amsterdam, New Orleans, the West Indies and back to Britain and Ireland. While he never reconciled himself to the irreligion of sailors, he came to know the life of the sea well.

The press and the cat: constraint and freedom in the maritime world

For different reasons, Edward Barlow, Briton Hammon and John Jea were all keen to go to sea. Once on board they realised the pains as well as the pleasures of maritime life, and the variety of ships and voyages that a sailor might take. To some degree picking a ship was their own choice. Hammon negotiated his way out of a slaving voyage to join one to New England. Barlow's journal is full of his deliberations over where to go next, in the hope of profit or just to see another part of the world. But there were other forces at work here too. Merchant seamen had to find a living, and the ups and downs of international trade with the fortunes of war and peace, as well as with the seasons, dictated what ships were available.

More significantly, the expansion of the navy's demand for labour during wartime meant stiff competition for seamen and a range of measures for getting them on board the monarch's ships. Manning – the provision of men to sail the ships – was the navy's most acute problem, and attempts to resolve it took a variety of forms. Many men volunteered, and received the financial reward (the bounty) that brought. Landsmen going to sea for the first time were often recruited to serve captains whose families owned land in their counties, or by personal connections with serving men. The social bonds of land, locality and family were put to work at sea. Others enlisted for patriotism or the thought of a share in the prize money gained from captured ships. Landsmen were actively recruited by the Impress Service which sent sailors in their blue jackets, white trousers and red waistcoats to market towns to dazzle the country boys and sign them up for the Sea Service.

However, no ship's company could be made up only of landsmen, and the Impress Service had to use other means to ensure a supply of experienced seamen. Most notorious was the press gang. The Admiralty had the right to compel the recruitment – to 'press' – all 'seamen, seafaring men and persons whose occupations or callings are to work in vessels and boats upon rivers', and who did not have 'protections' granted by Parliament or the Admiralty for those in necessary maritime occupations (seamen on outgoing merchant ships, dockyard workers and so on).[18] This required careful organisation and planning. Local magistrates would not allow any but experienced tars to be taken, or private premises to be entered, and sailors would fight back with whatever weapons came to hand. Pressing in the streets was ineffective and liable to provoke local opposition. Most effective were press gangs' swoops on taverns known to be full of sailors or pressing at sea, from incoming British merchantships near to shore. Both offered up a rich harvest of able, if not immediately willing, tars, and both kept the workings of the press away from all but the maritime community. The attentions of the press gang were an occupational hazard for sailors, and reveal the compulsions necessary to man the navy in wartime.

If ships were manned by both consent and compulsion, they were also governed that way too. The press gang's violence sat alongside the volunteer's enthusiasm just as the crew's loyalty for an officer worked alongside corporal punishment for those who stepped out of line or neglected their duties. The overwhelming punishment for those on the lower deck, who were inevitably those most likely to be punished, was to be flogged. Confinement, fines and hard labour had little meaning as punishments on board ship so lashes across the back were the currency of discipline. These floggings were with the cat-o'-nine-tails, a many stranded knotted rope. They were administered to men tied by the wrists and ankles to an upright grating set against the quarterdeck or the mast. They were done before the ship's assembled company, often after divine service on a Sunday, and with some degree of theatre. Captains were authorised to punish only with a dozen lashes, although many simply ordered more, often by multiplying the offences or separating the beatings. Courts martial for more serious offences, or when demanded by the accused, could award punishments which far exceeded that: six hundred lashes for defying the authority of an officer, two hundred for knocking down a midshipman, five hundred for theft. Sailors might be flogged around the fleet, being beaten on each ship before each ship's company, in cases where a particular example was to be made. It is estimated that just over one in five of all crewmen on British ships in the Pacific between 1767 and 1795 were flogged (on one ship it was nearly half), a third for insubordination and disorderliness and a third for failing in their duties. The captain's orders were backed by the threat of the cat.

This was also true on merchant vessels. However, with crews of fifteen to twenty men rather than stretching into the hundreds, and with merchants' profits at stake rather than the security of the state, the dynamics of discipline were rather different. Ships' masters had a startling array of powers over their crews and they enforced them in the end in ways that could only be personal and violent. The Admiralty courts heard stories of murder, cracked heads, beatings and intimidation as masters put their men to work. Sailors choosing ships in either the merchant service or the navy (and the volunteer chose his ship when the pressed man did not) did well to listen to stories about how a captain or master ran his command. Those who found themselves on ships that were not to their liking had to consider what degree of freedom they had, and what they might do about it. Sailors complained to the Admiralty and through the courts. They used mutinies and strikes to challenge illegitimate authority (see chapter 7). Seamen also found many ways and means of running from ships and captains that did not suit them. For those who dared to do it, it was another way of making a choice.

The world of William Spavens

William Spavens knew all about choice and compulsion. As he reached sixty years of age, back in Louth in Lincolnshire near where he had been born in 1735, he reflected on what he had seen and done, and how he had moved around the world between, as he put it, 60° N and 40° S and from 107° 57' E to 90° W. By that time moving was more difficult. He may have rubbed the stump of his amputated leg, crushed when loading water casks at Batavia for a voyage to Madras, as he contemplated 'the vicissitudes of human life, particularly among the sons of Neptune and Mars!!!'[19]

Spavens had worked on both merchant ships and naval vessels. He had begun, as befits a boy from Lincolnshire, carrying cargoes of flax, metal and wood to Hull from Russia, Sweden and France. He had later found himself rounding the Cape of Good Hope bound for Sumatra as part of the crew of an East Indiaman. Yet most of his working life was in the navy. During the Seven Years' War his skill and muscle power was part of what secured Britain's Atlantic hegemony. He was on ships cruising the Channel and the Bay of Biscay, and he fought at the crucial battle of Quiberon Bay in 1759 (see chapter 5). He escorted merchant ships and chased French privateers in the Caribbean. He brought the new queen Charlotte from Hamburg to Harwich when the old king died, and he was among the English forces at the siege of Quebec (figure 6.2). He had seen enough by the time he sat down to write his life story to provide a description of the Royal Navy, an account of the countries and peoples that he had seen, and an introduction to Geography, 'that useful science'.[20]

Like all sailors, Spavens often had little choice as to where and when he moved between ships. He was pressed out of the merchant ship *Elizabeth and Mary* as it approached Hull from Le Havre, and kept under armed guard before being moved into the seventy-gun HMS *Buckingham* to begin his naval career. He was then moved between different navy ships as required by the demands of the service, such as being ordered to serve as gunner's mate on a tender that was part of a fleet escorting three hundred merchant ships back across the Atlantic from Jamaica. Changes also came when ships were declared unfit for further service and their crews were redeployed. One such deployment came when Spavens was moved from HMS *Blandford* to the *Vengeance* (a 28-gun frigate recently captured as a prize from the French), and sent to Ireland 'to procure men for the service'. Enforcing the press in the Irish Sea, he was to be involved in compelling others to serve. There was certainly resistance to this compulsion. The crew of the *Dublin*, returning from New York, had to be taken by force. As Spavens recalled, the press gang boarded the ship and 'finding the men had taken close quarters, we scuttled their decks with axes, and fired down amongst them, while they kept firing up at us where they saw the light appear. After having shot one of our men through the head, and another through both his thighs, they submitted, and we got 16 brave fellows.' At Liverpool, attempting to press on shore, Spavens's gang was escorting seventeen seamen back to the ships when they

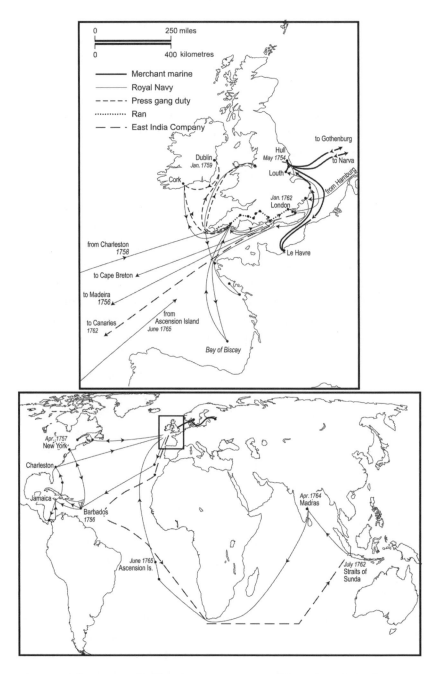

Figure 6.2 The voyages of William Spavens, 1754–1766. Through service in the merchant marine, the Royal Navy and the East India Company this mariner sailed the seven seas. He did so through both compulsion and choice, including two episodes when he ran from his ship, and a spell working on a press gang. His patterns of movement were shaped by Britain's maritime trade, the wars that were fought to defend and extend it, and the navy's need for manpower.

were attacked by several hundred 'old men, women, and boys' throwing stones and brickbats. The press gang had to fire their muskets over the heads of the crowd who had followed them down to the waterline. Spavens expressed concern about the press, calling it 'shocking to the feelings of humanity' that sailors should be taken away from family and friends in this way. He concluded that 'it is hardship which nothing but absolute necessity can reconcile to our boasted freedoms'.[21]

William Spavens's shipboard life also showed this play of necessity and freedom. His description of the navy included a long section on the punishments that might be imposed by captains: flogging, of course, but also running the gauntlet and a variety of public humiliations. He had the misfortune to serve under one of the three naval captains who were dismissed from the service during the Seven Years' War for cruel treatment of their crew, Penhallow Cuming of the *Blandford*. Spavens called Cuming 'an excellent seaman' but noted his readiness to resort to the cat on the least provocation, and his willingness to withhold the men's grog.[22] Freedoms might, however, be carved out from this unpromising situation by the sailors themselves. Spavens was part of a riotous mob of seamen intent on being paid their overdue prize money at Antigua. Along with others, he also convinced their drunken captain that they had accidentally lost sight of a Dutch ship they were escorting through the Caribbean when they had purposefully sailed away from it in the night while the captain was asleep. The captain had thought that they could have the ship declared a prize at Rhode Island; the crew were less certain and did not want to take the risk.

There was also some choice to be had between ships, if one was daring. When Spavens found himself taken out of HMS *Winchester* at Plymouth, and put into the *Flora*, the officers picking man by man alternately, he thought himself ill favoured. The ship had too few men to sail her and newly appointed petty officers 'who I was confident were neither so good seamen, nor of so long duration in the service as myself'. He took his land clothes aboard and, at the first opportunity, ran from the ship and made his way by horseback, foot and coach to London disguised (although perhaps not very effectively) as a 'rustic countryman'.[23] There he first signed up for a ship to Guadaloupe, but left her the next day for the better prospect of the *Elizabeth*, sailing to the East Indies. Before the ship got underway Spavens narrowly avoided lieutenants looking for deserters, and escaped the press gang when an officer he had served with on the *Vengeance* failed to recognise him as they stood side by side at a Tower Hill bookstall. Perhaps Lieutenant Thomas did not expect to see a sailor buying books. When Spavens next went on board a Royal Navy ship it was in Batavia harbour. By then he had run again. Pursuing his shipmate's promise of the riches to be had working on the ships in the country trade (see chapter 4) they had left the *Elizabeth* only to be imprisoned by the Dutch on a small island in Batavia harbour. Necessity and freedom, compulsion and choice certainly marked out the vicissitudes of the sailor's life.

Port life

Maritime life is, however, not only about the sea. It is about how the sea meets the land. Royal Navy ships in the Seven Years' War were, on average, at sea less than half their time. The rest was spent in port – or, more accurately, moored offshore to avoid the difficult business of negotiating narrow harbour mouths – with sailors passing back and forth between the wooden world and dry land. On shore, sailors had what they called their 'liberty'. Released from the confinements of the ship they were able to spend their money and relish their temporary freedoms. For some this meant finding a place among the transient residents of lodging houses, taverns and houses of ill repute. For others, a return to the shore was a return to family life. For Edward Barlow, anchoring in the Thames first meant being badgered and put to work by the innkeeping wife of the man to whom he was apprenticed. He could not wait to set sail again. Later, after he had married Mary Symans, leaving for foreign shores and ocean storms was more of a wrench for them both. Many of the women who lived along the quaysides and wharves may never have gone to sea – although there were certainly many women on ships both as officers' wives and as seamen in disguise – but they had to work out how to make a living from it. As they became tied into the oceanic economy of maritime labour they managed their lives in ways that reveal both hardships and the resourcefulness with which they were met.

The maritime economy produced a distinctive society. The New England port towns of Boston, Salem, Newport and Portsmouth had many more women than men. In 1764–1765 Boston had 122 women for every 100 men; in 1773 Portsmouth (New Hampshire) had 129 women for every 100 men. As a result, by the late eighteenth century around one-fifth of households in these towns were headed by women, compared to the 1–3 per cent of households headed by women in the inland towns of Rochester and Concord. Many of these women were never married, many were widows (5–7 per cent of these seaboard towns' populations) and many were the wives of husbands who were away at sea for long periods. Most of these households were financially insecure, trying to stay afloat amidst the storms of a fluctuating economy. They did not know when or even if sailors would return, or when or if the money the men earned would be paid. These women had to find ways to live, so they sought various forms of work. They plied their needles to make clothes, they produced and sold food and they worked in the homes of other families – as servants or wet-nurses – or provided food and lodgings for those who had no families themselves. Women in New England ports were a crucial part of the economy: they made goods for export, they made sails and fishing nets, they made bread for slaving voyages, they fed and clothed sailors, returning them to the sea. Yet earnings were both small and irregular in this economy of makeshifts. Families tied to the maritime economy by the wages sailors earned through prolonged periods of absence, and the uncertainties of final payment, found themselves plunged into the cold waters of poverty. They relied upon mutual support to get by, and where that failed had to apply for poor relief to authorities whose ideas of respectability, prudence and responsibility had little room for the maritime poor, even when they actually acknowledged their own responsibilities for this mobile population. Port life meant trying to keep body and soul together where the sea met the land.

Doing so meant not only the drudgery of paid and unpaid domestic labour, the scant rewards of the needle trades and the condescension of the overseers of the poor. It also meant an active knowledge of the working of the maritime economy and the legal and military institutions that regulated life at sea. Women were central to the flows of information, coursing through taverns and lodging houses, that helped men to find good ships and avoid bad ones. As boarding-house keepers, men and women organised sailors' lives on shore. Along with food and lodgings they gave credit, signed bonds for surety when men were suing for wages, and put up bail money. In a world that depended upon paying wages in arrears, particularly in the Royal Navy where a six-month wait was the least a sailor might expect, women were essential in closing the gap between work and its rewards. To do so they needed, and were given, significant authority. Through the widespread practice of granting mothers or wives power of attorney before they set off on a new voyage, sailors gave them the right to collect their wages from ship-owners or the Navy Board, and to conduct necessary legal and financial business in their husband's or son's name.

Many women became adept at managing this system of 'tickets' – the promises of the Navy Board to pay wages in the future – to realise the money and credit needed to live. Some bought and sold the tickets (at discounted prices) and lent money. Others were active in pursuing their claims, to men's wages and prize money, through the courts and state offices. These women's encounters with the hazard of financial wreckage and with the strange customs of bureaucrats and lawyers meant that they became enmeshed in both the global maritime economy and the workings of the state that protected and extended it. Theirs were global lives too. As an eighteenth-century broadside that made a claim for restitution put it, the wives and children of naval officers, as much as their husbands were 'always willing to hazard their lives in the Service of their King and Country'.[24] Whether the womenfolk of the men of the lower deck were willing to suffer or not is hard to determine. It is certain, however, that they did hazard their lives, and also that like the men at sea they were unwilling to go down without a fight.

The world of Essa Morrison

They saw him coming. Rolling up Nightingale Lane from the River Thames full of drink and trying to lose his sea legs, he looked a likely one. Just paid off from one of His Majesty's ships in Deptford yard, James Glass had had a good night. Essa Morrison and Barbara Waller sat at the mouth of Bright's Alley, across from the Red Lion, and watched him as he made his unsteady progress towards them. They could see from his rig that he was a sailor. Maybe they could even hear the coins chinking in his pocket.

The three met on a summer night in 1765 in the heart of maritime London. They were just east of the Tower where the river was lined with docks, wharves and stairs giving access to the water, and letting goods and people get ashore. They would have known the names of Brown's wharf, Alderman Parsons's stairs, Hermitage dock – where Nightingale Lane began – Wapping Old Stairs and the Gun Dock (figure 6.3). Ships of all shapes and sizes rode at anchor in the river. The skyline visible above the buildings at the water's edge was a forest of masts swaying as the wind and tides moved the vessels. There was constant activity on the water. Small barges and lighters shuttled between the ships and the shore unloading sailors, casks, bales and barrels (figure 6.4). The sounds of the river were never far away. The smell was all around. This part of the city was given over to the sea. It was where London met the oceans. Close by the Tower were the Navy Office and the Victualling Office, which supplied men for ships and food for those men. There were numerous merchants' warehouses and damp cellars for storage. There were timber yards ready with lumber for building and repairing vessels. There were the long narrow rope-walks

Figure 6.3 London's docklands, c. 1750. East of the Tower of London, on both sides of the river, was a landscape of wharves, rope-walks, shipyards and sailors' lodging-houses and taverns. It also included major state institutions such as the Victualling Office. Nightingale Lane, where James Glass met Essa Morrison, is at the heart of this map, weaving its way south towards the river from East Smithfield.

The IMPORTS of GREAT BRITAIN from FRANCE.

Figure 6.4 London's quayside, c. 1750. This satirical print depicts the teeming quayside west of the Tower of London as a ship arrives and unloads. It shows a varied crowd, mounds of goods and a forest of ships' masts. Its purpose was to question British dependence on luxuries imported from France.

needed to twist fathom upon fathom of cable, shrouds and sheets. South of Ratcliff Highway there was a mass of lanes, alleyways and dark corners full of taverns and lodging houses – places where men such as James Glass might find another drink, a bed for the night or more.

As he told it later it happened this way. The two women asked him to buy them a drink. He said it was too late. They took his arms, although he said he could manage by himself. He felt their hands about him. He thought they were feeling for his money. There were enough pickpockets about off the Highway to be wary. They took him to a room in a private house which was lit by a single candle. He asked Essa Morrison what it would cost to stay all night. Her price was a shilling for herself and a shilling for Waller, the landlady, to pay for the bed. He paid. He then tied the seven and a half guineas and six shillings in silver that he had left into the corner of his handkerchief, and lay down with it beneath his head. He didn't think that she lay down too. He had to sleep. 'I was pretty far gone in liquor; I heard my money fall off the bed, and I believe she heard it too; but I thought it was safe.' When he woke at a quarter to four, with a dry mouth and a thumping headache, he was alone. His handkerchief was there but the money and Essa Morrison were gone. He went downstairs, woke Barbara Waller and told her that he had been robbed. She dressed and went out in the early dawn light to search for Morrison. After an hour or so she returned to tell him that she had followed reports that had taken her over London Bridge to the White Hart in Borough. She said that Essa Morrison was gone to Portsmouth. Glass would not give up his money that easily. Asking around he discovered that she had not run nearly so far as the south coast. He and a constable apprehended her in the Ship in East Smithfield. She had only gone to the other end of Nightingale Lane. Barbara Waller was later arrested, having had 25 shillings of the money from Morrison.

Essa Morrison and Barbara Waller told it differently. For Morrison, it was all Glass's doing: 'This man pick'd me up, and went to a public-house; he went home with me, and gave me a shilling for supper, and gave this woman a shilling: he pull'd his money out of his handkerchief, and said, I'll give you this money if you'll live along with me. He made me a present of 4 guineas and 5 s. and desired me to make the best advantage of it: he said he was going to sell his ticket, and would bring me more. I had lain with him before that.' As she told it, this was to be a temporary union, something like a marriage for the time he was on shore. There were many working women and sailors who spliced themselves together in this fashion in Wapping and Shadwell. She would look after him in return for her looking after his money, including what was to come when his ticket was sold. Barbara Waller also set a domestic scene: 'When they came in, she told me he was her husband; they gave me a shilling to get supper: I fetch'd in a twopenny-loaf and a pot of beer: she told me he had made her a present of the money to live along with him.' The women had shared the money he had given to Essa Morrison: landlady and lodger making a sailor at home.

Which sort of dockside making-do was it? Prostitution and theft, or a temporary union in which both Essa Morrison and James Glass might get some value from the Navy Office's ticket. Which sort of co-operation among women without men was it? Waller and Morrison rolling a drunk, and then lying and splitting the proceeds; or lodger and landlady finding a means to pay the rent and make a living? Either way speaks of both hardship and resourcefulness. The court took the sailor's side. Barbara Waller was acquitted of receiving stolen goods, but remanded to prison for keeping a disorderly house. Morrison was found guilty of stealing. If she had not yet been aboard a ship, felt the swell of the ocean, and seen faraway places she would do now. Essa Morrison was sentenced to transportation to the American colonies.

This chapter is about lives of hard physical work. The global economy that knitted Britain into a new world of trade through voyages across the oceans was made possible by the labour of the men and women of the maritime trades. On merchant ships and on naval vessels, at sea but also on land, on the gun deck, aloft in the crow's nest or in the boarding house or poor house, men and women worked in the maritime economy. Their work moved goods, bodies and ships around the world as much as the work of merchants with account books, maps and quill pens. These lives were hard ones, as Edward Barlow, Briton Hammon, John Jea, William Spavens and Essa Morrison would all testify. They all suffered in different ways from the constant effort to survive, the grinding poverty of maritime labour and the violence of its unequal relations between masters and men, black and white, and men and women. Yet their lives all speak of the ways in which difficulties were endured, skills were learned, useful knowledge was accumulated, and advantage was taken where and when it could be found. Freedoms were to be found by these people too: Edward Barlow and William Spavens both found room to challenge the seamanship of those put above them, and to leave ships they did not like. Briton Hammon and John Jea used the sea in ways that took them beyond the pain and confinements of the plantation economy, even if they were hurt and held by other means as a result. Essa Morrison did what she could to get by. She took a chance when it came. As Edward Barlow put it, the sailor's cry was 'A merry life and a short one. The longest liver take all.' The ever more global geography of maritime labour may have been increasingly organised for the merchant's accumulation of capital, but for these oceanic workers their global lives were, where the demands and pains of work allowed it, for the living.

Of course the many ways of living afloat are not exhausted by the worlds of merchant shipping and the navy. The next chapter considers the ways in which privatised violence could be used both for and against the state, and in the service of the seaman's own notions of life, by outlining the global lives of the pirates.

Further reading

Overall discussions of the maritime world are presented, from quite different perspectives, and concentrating respectively on the navy and the merchant marine, in N. A. M. Rodger (1988) *The Wooden World: An Anatomy of the Georgian Navy* (Fontana, London), Marcus Rediker (1987) *Between the Devil and the Deep Blue Sea: Merchant Seamen, Pirates, and the Anglo-American Maritime World, 1700–1750* (Cambridge University Press, Cambridge) and Ralph Davis (1962) *The Rise of the English Shipping Industry in the Seventeenth and Eighteenth Centuries* (Macmillan, London). A shorter overview is provided by J. H. Parry (1974) *Trade and Dominion: European Overseas Empires in the Eighteenth Century* (Cardinal, London) chap. 11, 'Ships and sailors'. The life of Edward Barlow is recounted in Basil Lubbock (ed.) (1934) *Barlow's Journal of His Life at Sea in King's Ships, East and West Indiamen & Other Ships from 1659 to 1703* (Hurst & Blackett, London). The world of black seafarers is set out in W. Jeffrey Bolster (1997) *Black Jacks: African American Seamen in the Age of Sail* (Harvard University Press, Cambridge, Mass.). The narratives of Briton Hammon and John Jea are available in full at www.docsouth.unc.edu/neh/hammon/hammon.html and www.docsouth.unc.edu/neh/jeajohn/jeajohn.html. There is a useful discussion of shipboard discipline in Greg Dening (1992) *Mr Bligh's Bad Language: Passion, Power and Theatre on the Bounty* (Cambridge University Press, Cambridge) pp. 113–156. William Spavens gives his own account in *The Narrative of William Spavens, a Chatham Pensioner: Written by Himself* (Chatham Publishing, London, 1998). On women and port life, see Elaine Forman Crane (1998) *Ebb Tide in New England: Women, Seaports, and Social Change, 1630–1800* (Northeastern University Press, Boston), Margaret Creighton and Lisa Norling (eds.) (1996) *Iron Men, Wooden Women: Gender and Seafaring in the Atlantic World, 1700–1920* (Johns Hopkins University Press, Baltimore) and Margaret Hunt (2004) 'Women and the fiscal-military state in the late seventeenth and early eighteenth centuries', in Kathleen Wilson (ed.) *A New Imperial History: Culture, Identity, and Modernity in Britain and the Empire, 1660–1840* (Cambridge University Press, Cambridge) pp. 29–47. The trial of Essa Morrison and Barbara Waller (10 July 1765) can be found in *The Proceedings of the Old Bailey, London 1674 to 1834* at www.oldbaileyonline.org (ref: t17650710-27).

Notes

1 Basil Lubbock (ed.) (1934) *Barlow's Journal of His Life at Sea in King's Ships, East and West Indiamen & Other Ships from 1659 to 1703* (Hurst & Blackett, London) p. 15.

2 Ibid., p. 118.

3 Ibid., p. 162.

5 Ibid., pp. 553 and 339.

6 Ibid., p. 314.

7 Ibid., p. 89.

8 Ibid., p. 83.

9 Ibid., p. 68.

10 Ibid., p. 162.

11 Ibid., pp. 128 and 134.

12 Ibid., p. 29.

13 Quoted in Greg Dening (1992) *Mr Bligh's Bad Language: Passion, Power and Theatre on the Bounty* (Cambridge University Press, Cambridge) pp. 73–74.

14 *A Narrative of the Uncommon Sufferings, and Surprizing Deliverance of Briton Hammon, A Negro Man* (Boston, 1760) pp. 3–4 and 6.

15 Ibid.

16 *The Life, History, and Unparalleled Sufferings of John Jea, the African Preacher* (Portsea, 1811) p. 38.

17 Ibid., pp. 50, 51 and 55.

18 Quoted in N. A. M. Rodger (1988) *The Wooden World: An Anatomy of the Georgian Navy* (Fontana, London) p. 150.

19 *The Narrative of William Spavens, a Chatham Pensioner: Written by Himself* (Chatham Publishing, London, 1998) p. 172.

20 Ibid., p. 77.

21 Ibid., pp. 19–21.

22 Ibid., p. 11.

23 Ibid., pp. 35–36.

24 Quoted in Margaret Hunt (2004) 'Women and the fiscal-military state in the late seventeenth and early eighteenth centuries', in Kathleen Wilson (ed.) *A New Imperial History: Culture, Identity, and Modernity in Britain and the Empire, 1660–1840* (Cambridge University Press, Cambridge) pp. 46–47.

7 | Maritime violence: buccaneers, privateers and pirates

Pirates are often understood in terms of fantasy, romance and the thrill of dangers now safely confined to the past. The stories of piratical deeds in films and novels seem as real – or unreal – as the histories of pirates' lives. Fact and fiction merge in the tales of Long John Silver and Blackbeard. While it is important to remember that piracy today remains a real and violent threat to shipping in parts of the world's oceans, it is also necessary to situate history's pirates within the discussions of imperial politics, New World settlement, global trade and maritime society and culture that have been discussed in the previous chapters. As those chapters have shown, and as the subsequent chapters will also demonstrate, the use of violence was a crucial element in making the early modern world. Moreover, it was a world in which European states – the official armies and navies of nations and empires – were not equipped until at least the second half of the eighteenth century to effectively wage wars or to protect ships, merchants and settlers in Asia, Africa and the Americas. This had certain implications. First, these states had to find ways to deploy violence against their enemies which were more economical than large permanent armies and navies. This led to settlers taking up arms to defend themselves; it led to trading companies such as the East India Company, the Virginia Company and the Royal African Company building fortifications on foreign shores, employing their own soldiers and equipping their ships with cannon; and it led to 'privateering': the fitting out of ships to fight wars as a business enterprise. Second, it meant that there were plenty of gaps and opportunities within the oceanic world of overextended imperial rivals, poorly defended merchant ships and badly provisioned settlers from which a good living might be made, at least until the authorities caught up and tried to close the gap.

There are, therefore, political, economic and social dimensions to the history of piracy which need to be explored. In each case the issue is the way in which those engaged in the violent appropriation of ships and goods at sea (we might, like the pirates, call it 'treasure' or 'booty') are, from different perspectives, defined as engaged in legitimate or illegitimate political and economic activities ordered according to valued or denigrated forms of social organisation. Piracy is to a great extent in the eye of the beholder. For example, England's great sea-going hero of the Elizabethan era, Sir Francis Drake, was from the Spanish perspective a mere pirate. The same could be said of his friend John Hawkins in light of the latter's trading activities in Africa and the Caribbean (see chapter 2). Drake allied himself with French privateers, escaped slaves and indigenous peoples in his attempts to capture the gold that the Spanish were transporting from the Americas to Europe. For his English supporters, including the queen, who greatly benefited when he succeeded, he was a sea-going courtier and knight engaged in a just war against a Catholic empire, and he deserved the riches that he took from it. To his Spanish enemies he was no better than a common pirate who was hungry for gold and willing to use any means, often vicious and despicable, to get it.

Pirates have long been defined as *hostis humani generis*: the enemies of all humanity. They are seen as marauders from the sea who recognise none of the laws of the land. However, the power to make that definition stick and to bring a person to justice for piratical acts, is just that: a matter of power. Since the oceans are beyond national law, and there has never been an effective body of international law, or any agency that could enforce it, it was a matter of nations and empires deploying such definitions in their own interests. In doing so, prosecutions were issues of politics and economics. In a world where the violent commerce of empires was little different from acts of piracy, and might even be carried out by those that others called pirates, the story that St Augustine told in the middle ages about the pirate and the emperor still had resonance. The emperor Alexander asked a pirate how he dared molest the seas. The pirate replied, caring little for the emperor's status, 'How darest thou molest the whole world? But because I do it with a little ship only, I am called a thief: thou doing it with a great navy, art called an emperor.'[1]

This intimate connection between pirates and political and economic power means that there were many different sorts of pirates across the maritime world in the period covered in this book. The Indian Ocean and the South China Seas were periodically plagued by pirates. Notorious pinch points such as the Straits of Malacca, which merchant ships had to negotiate, became the favourite haunt of pirate crews. Indeed, the Chinese and Mughal empires were involved in their own battles with pirates over the control of the seas. There were also the pirates of the Mediterranean and the Atlantic coast of North Africa. Armed vessels operating from islands such as Malta and the Barbary corsairs of Morocco, Libya, Tunisia and Algeria were a significant force acting against European shipping. In the early seventeenth century, backed by the political powers of the region, they were able to kidnap English men, women and children from the coasts of Devon and Cornwall. They were estimated to have held at least 20,000 British and Irish prisoners as slaves between 1600 and 1750. The ransoms for these captives proved a profitable business for the corsairs' political masters. Many attempts were made to curb their power. For example, Edward Barlow (see chapter 6) sailed south in a campaign against the corsairs of Algiers in the early 1660s. When periodic warfare proved ineffective, treaties were signed to protect British shipping. Yet it was not until France imposed imperial sovereignty on Algiers in 1830 that their activities were finally brought to an end.

This chapter, however, will concentrate on the pirates whose main arena of operations was the Caribbean, but who, as we shall see, at times extended their activities to the coasts and islands of North America, Africa, the Indian Ocean and the Pacific. In tracing the history of piracy over the seventeenth and eighteenth centuries there are two basic processes at work. First, pirates are gradually pushed towards the margins of political and economic life by the processes of empire building and oceanic mercantile integration that have been traced in the previous chapters. Second, as a result of that marginalisation, there is a shift in the social status of pirates: sea-going noblemen in the sixteenth century, they became mercantile buccaneers in the seventeenth century, and merely common sailors helping themselves to booty in the early eighteenth century. Using the lives of William Dampier, Captain Kidd, Bartholomew Roberts and Anne Bonny, this chapter will trace how they were part of building both alternative worlds and the now familiar early modern geography of empires and markets. We start in the frontier zone of the Caribbean in the middle of the seventeenth century.

Privateers and buccaneers

The Caribbean was, as outlined in chapter 2, at the centre of a struggle between Spain's attempts to retain control over the flows of goods and treasure into and out of its extensive American empire and the efforts of the rising imperial powers of the Netherlands, France and England to take as much from the Spanish as they could. It has been described as a 'cockpit' – conjuring up the furious and chaotic blood-spilling of the cock fight – but it was actually more like a bearpit, with the strong but slow bear of Spain being hounded by the terrible energy of the pit bull terriers which were its north European rivals. Indeed, when these dogs of war started fighting amongst themselves in the Spanish region west of the boundary agreed at the Treaty of Tordesillas (see chapter 2), it really became clear that there was, as the saying went, 'no peace beyond the line'. However, despite what the flags on the ships might have led observers to believe, those doing the fighting under French, Dutch and English colours in the early seventeenth century were a more mixed bunch. First, they were often privateers hiring themselves out to do the job on the promise of financial reward. Second, these privateers were often buccaneers whose national origins and social organisation were a long way from the single identities and hierarchical societies one might expect of representatives of imperialist states. Privateering buccaneers were a product of weak and nascent empires attempting to exert their strength in the Caribbean wild west.

As the discussion of John Hawkins and the Elizabethan navy in chapter 2 argued, the organisation of maritime violence in the early modern era was a public–private partnership. The state hired or required merchant vessels to become ships of war, giving them commissions to fight the enemy and to share in the 'prizes' that they captured: the enemy ship and its cargo. Since the assault on the enemy's merchant shipping was a vital part of waging war this could be achieved without engaging in set-piece sea battles, and could be done by ships converted from commercial to more military uses. Although as the seventeenth century wore on the Royal Navy became less reliant on these commissions to sustain its basic fighting force, it remained a way in which naval power could be rapidly expanded upon declaration of war without dramatically increasing state expenditure on ships and men. For those who took up the challenge it was a business opportunity. For the investors the costs of fitting out a ship, manning it and supplying the cannon, balls and powder necessary to fight were undertaken in anticipation of the prize money that would be the reward of a successful cruise. Those who manned these ships did so without the contract for regular wages that a merchant seaman or naval rating would expect (see chapter 6). They also gambled on hitting the jackpot: a Spanish treasure ship, or a French merchantman loaded with cloth, sugar or slaves. Articles were drawn up detailing how the shares would be divided. In Britain the convention was half to the owners and half to the crew (in the seventeenth century this was after a bounty had been paid to the crown). Each half would then be divided unequally: the owners' half on the basis of the capital invested, and the crew's half on the basis of rank and position. The weighting changed over time, and varied between ships, but for the seventeenth century it was of the order of ten shares to the captain, seven to the master, five each to the gunner, mate and carpenter, four to the quartermaster and one or less to the ordinary seamen.

The vital element that made legitimate this form of waging violence at sea for private profit was authorisation from a government that the privateer was acting in its name. Ships were issued with letters of marque that commissioned them to act in wartime to attack enemy shipping. Doing so without such a document was judged an act of piracy. Yet recognising such documents and the rights of, for example, colonial authorities to issue them in the name of the European power made the distinction between piracy and privateering a contested one. This was further complicated by European governments' tacit approval of the actions of privateers even when they strayed beyond their remit, but their ability to disown them as pirates when it was convenient to do so. Things were not made any easier by those they employed to do this work for them in the Caribbean: the buccaneers.

Buccaneers take their name from the *boucan* – a sort of barbeque adopted from the Taíno people of the Caribbean Islands – on which they roasted the meat of the wild cattle they hunted for food. These were people of the margins. Forced off the rich lands of the sugar islands by the rise of the plantation economy in the early seventeenth century (see chapter 9), they sought a freer life hunting and gathering on smaller islands in egalitarian bands which mixed French, Dutch, English, Irish and Scottish with indigenous Amerindians and runaway slaves, or cutting logwood in the Bay of Campeche, north of the Yucatan peninsula and beyond the reach of formal imperial control. Gradually, their sharp-shooting, wood-working and island-hopping skills meant that they graduated to the ship-borne plundering of passing Spanish treasure convoys. It was these buccaneers that became a significant part of the fighting force used by the English in their new colony of Jamaica (taken in 1655) to attack Spanish cities, ships and mule trains for the treasure that underpinned and developed the island's whole economy. Under commissions issued by successive Jamaican governors, bands of buccaneers terrorised Spanish settlers and ship captains. Henry Morgan led the sackings of the cities of Portobello in 1668, netting between £70,000 and £100,000, and Panama in 1670, torturing its citizens to discover hidden gold and silver.

Buccaneers were both serving as an imperial fighting force, and living beyond the reach of imperial control. They fought the Spanish in the name of the English monarch and the empire, but governed themselves according to principles of liberty, equality and fraternity known as the 'Jamaica rules' or the 'Custom of the Coast', voting for their leaders, dividing their booty so that no one received more than two shares, compensating the injured and rewarding the brave. Once unleashed these forces proved hard to control. Captain Morgan, the buccaneer who led the assaults on Panama and

Portobello, was later both to become the governor of Jamaica and to be imprisoned in the Tower (although not tried) for his actions against the Spanish. By the 1680s the English were enforcing laws against the buccaneers who had once served them but now saw no reason not to rob the empire under the colours of other nations. In all of this, the definitions and accusations of piracy and privateering were being deployed and contested to deadly effect.

The world of William Dampier

William Dampier sailed right round the world three times in his life chasing after Spanish treasure and wondering at the curious plants, peoples and animals which he recorded in his famous journal (figure 7.1). This son of Somerset farmers, who went to sea from Weymouth at eighteen and had seen the East and West Indies by the time he was twenty-three, eventually fell in with a buccaneer fleet determined to repeat the earlier successes of Captain Morgan by attacking Portobello and Panama with the help of the Miskito Indians. Failure on the American isthmus in 1680, and in a subsequent cruise up the Pacific coast of South America in 1684, led the buccaneers of the *Cygnet*, captained by Charles Swan and navigated by Dampier, to undertake the 6,000 mile voyage across the Pacific from Mexico to Guam in search of the huge prize of the Spanish galleon which set sail each year from Manila to Acapulco. They did not find it and failed to capture anything but small merchant vessels. Dampier had to content himself with recording strange plants, describing the indigenous people, and speculating on opportunities for English commerce in the South Seas. He did not, however, lose his taste for new experiences and the promise of riches. Subsequent voyages took him back to Australia, and on two privateering expeditions during the War of the Spanish Succession. The first was a failure, dragging a mutinous crew around the Pacific in vain attempts to gather Spanish gold. The second, under Woodes Rogers, finally took a Manila galleon, allowing Dampier to retire to London where his writings had already given him some fame.

After 1670 the English and the Spanish were meant to be at peace, regulated by the Treaty of Madrid. While there was often quiet official toleration for buccaneers such as Dampier who worked to erode Spain's monopoly position in the Americas they could not be given English commissions or letters of marque, and the Jamaica Act of 1683 allowed for their execution for piracy. They needed, therefore, some legitimate authority to avoid this charge. One option was for the English privateer captains under whom

Figure 7.1 William Dampier. The late seventeenth-century buccaneer and naturalist is shown here later in life with a copy of his *New Voyage Around the World* (1697). The book, and perhaps this portrait, did much to cement his reputation as a natural philosopher rather than as a pirate.

Dampier sailed in the early 1680s to take up commissions offered by the French. As Dampier noted, 'It has been usual for many Years for the Governor of Petit Guavres [on the French colony of Saint Domingue (later Haiti)] to send blank Commissions to Sea by many of his Captains, with Orders to dispose of them to whom they saw convenient. By this means, those of Petit Guavres make themselves the Sanctuary and Asylum of all People of desperate Fortunes, and increase their own Wealth, and the Strength and Reputation of their Party thereby.' Captain Davis took one, 'having before only an old Commission which fell to him by Inheritance at the decease of Captain Cook'. Captain Swan, however, refused, 'saying he had an Order from the Duke of York [the future English king James II], neither to give Offence to the Spaniards nor to receive any affront from them; and that he had been injured by them at Baldivia, where they had killed some of his Men ... so that he thought he had a lawful Commission of his own right to himself'. Each piece of paper was contestable. Could commissions be passed from one captain to another? Did the French commissions cover more than 'a Liberty to Fish, Fowl and Hunt'? Was the Spanish affront to Captain Swan enough to justify his later actions? Yet each provided enough authority for these captains to argue that they were privateers, not pirates, and these documents might keep Dampier from being hanged as a pirate if it came to that.[2] The buccaneers he sailed with later sought a commission from the prince of Mindanao to plunder the Spanish in the Philippines.

The other concerns Dampier had about authority were on the buccaneers' ships themselves. The crews – men who valued their liberty and were adventuring for shares and not wages – demanded a say in the running of the ship and the conduct of the voyage: 'For Privateers are not obliged to any Ship, but free to go ashore where they please, or go into any other Ship that will entertain them, only paying for their Provision.'[3] Dampier's journal is full of crews changing ships and deposing captains in favour of quartermasters, who were second in command 'according to the Law of Privateers'. So, 'at the Isle of John Fernando, Captain Sharp was, by general Consent, displaced from being Commander, the Company being not satisfied either with his Courage or Behaviour'.[4] They later divided over who should be captain and voted on it, with the majority taking the ship. Their choices were governed by the search for treasure and the high living it brought. Nothing prompted them to mutiny more quickly than hunger. Nothing pleased them more than plentiful food and drink. They disliked cowardly captains unwilling to take a risk, and they wanted to go where the gold was. The *Cygnet*'s dangerous voyage across the Pacific was prompted by the 'Hope of Gain'. The captain convinced the crew to undertake the perilous trip with tales of the rich Manila galleons, even though he had no intention of being a privateer in the East Indies himself, telling Dampier that 'there is no Prince on Earth that is able to wipe off the Stain of such Actions'. He had to conceal his desire to return home, perhaps after a little illegal country trade, from a crew hungry for plunder. They later got rid of him, and soon 'this mad, fickle Crew were upon new Projects again'.[5] The buccaneers' ways made Dampier worry about his own safety. Rounding Cape Horn he was concerned 'because our Men, being Privateers, and so more wilful and less under Command, would not be so ready to give a watchful Attendance in a Passage so little known'. More disturbingly, having crossed the Pacific, Dampier discovered that when the remaining three days' worth of short rations had been consumed, the crew planned to eat the captain and himself. Although, as he put it, 'I was as lean as the Captain was lusty and fleshy', he did not doubt that the sailors could have made a meal of him.[6]

Dampier's final concern was for his own reputation. The careful and distanced observer of nature's wonders, winds and currents, and of exotic tribes of indigenous people and European buccaneers was not as distant from the action as his *Journal* suggests. His published writing downplayed his involvement in acts of violence, legitimate or otherwise, but his later voyages were followed by his prosecution for assaulting and imprisoning his lieutenant, George Fisher, who considered him nothing more than an old pirate. The boundary between piracy and legalised violence at sea was, by the end of the seventeenth century, becoming an increasingly important one.

Piracy and imperial authority

Taking a broader view means seeing William Dampier's voyage into the Pacific as part of a more general pattern in the late seventeenth century. The English authorities' increasing intolerance of buccaneering in the Caribbean, under legislation which saw many pirates and privateers leave the trade either by being hanged or pardoned, and the hardening up of Spanish targets, experienced by those such as Dampier who tried to replay in the 1680s and 1690s the successes of the 1670s, meant that pirates had to look further afield for shipping to prey upon. Spreading out of their Caribbean hunting grounds, they tried their luck along the North American coast, in the Pacific and Indian Oceans and off the coast of West Africa. Buccaneering had gone global by the 1690s. As these pirates expanded their horizons they sought on a grander scale the conditions that had existed in the Caribbean before the new imperial powers tried to replace the buccaneers' political economy of terror and plunder – supplying markets and providing development capital via stolen goods – with the more routine and regulated economic and political relationships of a plantation economy based on long-distance trade (see chapters 5 and 9). They sought well-loaded and badly protected merchant ships plying predictable routes. They spied out poorly supplied markets that would be eager for goods and free-spending sailors without asking too many questions. They looked for weak imperial authorities, with little control over the oceans and a tendency to license private suppliers of maritime violence. And they pored over their maps to find out-of-the-way places where they could repair their ships, divide their treasure and prepare for the next raid.

The pirates found all of these by making new connections between places as far apart as New York, the Red Sea and Madagascar. In the 1690s the French privateering war in the Atlantic (another dimension of King William's War of 1689–1697) badly damaged English shipping and drove the economies of the North American seaports into depression. Merchants could find no outlet for their capital, and were irregularly supplied with commodities for which there was a demand. In ports such as New York, then a marginal place in the North Atlantic economy, these gaps were filled by the pirates. They brought slaves, sugar, cloth, spices and logwood to market; and they needed the city's merchants to enable them to refit and provision their ships. New York in the 1690s was a pirate town. The governor, Samuel Fletcher, and his council were all deeply involved in the business and, for a fee, provided the pirates with safe-conduct passes under the guise of attempting to make these brigands into law-abiding citizens. Meanwhile, pirate gold flowed through both the city's taverns and the purses of its elite.

Increasingly, this gold came from taking ships in the Indian Ocean. Generally avoiding tangling with the well-defended ships of the European East India Companies, the pirates hunted Asian-owned merchant ships trading along long-established routes across and around the Indian Ocean (see chapter 4). The strength of Asia's land-based empires was not replicated at sea, and such ships were poorly protected. They also carried great wealth. For example, the annual pilgrim fleet, from Surat to Mocha (in the Red Sea) where the pilgrims disembarked for Mecca, was also a trading opportunity for wealthy Indian merchants. It returned heavily laden with gold and jewels that were the payment for Indian cloth and spices. Pirates looking to tap this rich vein needed an Indian Ocean base. They created it on the small island of Saint Mary's off the northeast coast of Madagascar (figure 7.2). It offered favourable winds for raiding the routes between India and Arabia, as well as a return to the Atlantic. It provided a sheltered and easily defended port, and they were tolerated by local political authorities on the mainland who welcomed both their goods and their martial expertise. The pirates created a haven for themselves at Saint Mary's which became known as 'Libertalia' – the pirate republic – supposedly governed by the democratic codes of liberty, equality and fraternity that the buccaneers lived by. Yet this was no isolated desert island where pirates buried their treasure chests. From 1691 the successful New York merchant Frederick Philipse established an agent, Adam Baldridge (with his apprentice John King), on the island to manage a trade between New York and Saint Mary's that he had been carrying out for some years by sending ships to supply the pirates with clothing, drink, naval supplies and weapons in exchange for their plundered

Figure 7.2 The pirate rendezvous: Saint Mary's Island, Madagascar. This pirate stronghold off the southeastern coast of Africa provided an ideal base for raiding the treasure, merchant and pilgrim ships of the Indian Ocean while maintaining a market in and supply links with the North American colonies. It was used by notorious pirates such as Henry Avery and Captain Kidd.

goods, which he sold, contravening the Navigation Acts, in ports such as Hamburg. Like any agent (see chapters 4 and 5), Baldridge's efforts would make the long-distance trade more efficient, matching supply and demand and decreasing the turnaround time of the ships. The arrangement also offered any pirate who wanted to leave the life and return home a berth back to New York for a hundred pieces of eight plus provisions. New York–the Red Sea–Madagascar–New York marked out a global pirate geography.

This geography did not go unchallenged. New York's trade with the pirates, both up the Hudson River and at Saint Mary's Island, was illegal, although without changes in both law and administration there was little that the authorities in London could do about it. The English East India Company also complained bitterly about the pirates in the Indian Ocean. The buccaneers may have only taken a few Company ships, but every time a significant Indian trading vessel was attacked the Indian merchants, well-connected men such as Abdul Ghafur, complained to the Mughal emperor who then held the Company responsible. The Indian authorities refused to believe that not all pirates were English, and that not all of the English were in it together. They knew that the Company depended upon the emperor to permit them to trade. They knew that the English factories at Surat and Bombay and along the coast were vulnerable. So when the pirates took a ship – such as Henry Avery's capture of Ghafur's *Fath Mahmamadi* (with a £50,000 cargo) or that of the imperial ship *Ganj-i-Sawai* in 1695 – the factories were blockaded and the factors were imprisoned and threatened with death. Few lives were lost, but the Company's profits suffered considerably. There were also political concerns that the pirates would establish an enduring, and dangerously democratic, settlement on Saint Mary's Island that was beyond imperial control and would interfere with the workings of global trade. In 1697, the secretary of state, James Vernon, pointed to the need to prevent them from creating what he called 'a formed Government of Robbers there' complete with a fort and reproduced by pirate liaisons with local women.[7] The global stage was set for a momentous clash between the pirates and the empire. At the heart of all this was Captain William Kidd.

The world of Captain Kidd

Captain Kidd, one of the best-known pirates, had an intriguingly complicated life that was lived on both sides of the law. It began simply enough. Kidd was born in Scotland in about 1645, perhaps the son of a Church of Scotland minister. By 1689 he was a Caribbean buccaneer, a pirate signed up by the governor of the Leeward Islands, Christopher Codrington, to fight the French in King William's War. However, his pirate crew disliked the constraints of serving as privateers, stole his ship (the *Blessed William*), and headed for New York to sell their cargo. Kidd followed, determined to get revenge, but once in the American seaport he found other fish to fry. He got involved in the fractious political scene. He made new friends among the city's merchants and land-owners. He married the twice-widowed Sarah Oort on 16th May 1691. And, with the influential Robert Livingston, he devised a plan that would send him back to sea again in search of an even more substantial prize. The plan, which the two men travelled to London to put into action, was to sail to the Indian Ocean to capture the pirates themselves and take their treasure from them. Kidd would bring them, their ships and their plunder back to London or Boston for trial of the miscreants and plentiful profit for the investors. Kidd would be a private pirate hunter, pirating the pirates, and he and Livingston found backers for the scheme among the most powerful men in the land. Fronted by Richard Coote, earl of Bellomont – the newly appointed governor of New York and Massachusetts – the capital was provided by a group of hidden partners who were the key figures in England's Whig government. The king himself was even cut in for 10 per cent for providing a warrant for the voyage. With this powerful patronage, and the subsequent investment capital, Kidd fitted out a ship – the *Adventure Galley* – and recruited a crew of 152 in London and New York, enough to sail the 287-ton vessel halfway around the world and to fire broadsides of the thirty-four guns when they got there. They sailed out of New York in September 1696 in search of pirate gold.

Things did not, however, turn out quite as planned. Perhaps once he had rounded the Cape of Good Hope, or sighted Madagascar, Kidd realised that the odds were stacked against him. Instead of sailing to Saint Mary's Island he headed for the busy shipping lanes between western India and the Red Sea. He might have been seeking pirates. That was certainly where they could be found, looking to prey on the pilgrim fleet returning from Mocha. More likely, he thought he might take an Indian ship, return to London or Boston, and claim that the treasure had come from a captured pirate vessel. What he did not count on was that the pilgrim fleet would be well protected. The Mughal emperor's insistence that the English East India Company do something about piracy had, eventually, meant that the *Sceptre*, an East Indiaman, was assigned to sail with the fleet. In charge, the original captain having died, was Edward Barlow (see chapter 6), the hardened old tar determined to prove to his powerful employers that he was as able a commander as any gentleman. Kidd backed off as Barlow further surprised him by putting out his boats to haul the *Sceptre*, guns blazing and the crew cursing Kidd's men from the rigging, after the *Adventure Galley*.

Kidd's crew were now that most damned thing: failed pirates. They had crossed the line, but had no treasure to show for it. If Kidd was still keen to try and square plunder in the Indian Ocean with legitimacy at home – avoiding Company ships and examining his victims' documentation – his men were not so careful, particularly if it meant sticking to the original contract which gave Kidd thirty-five shares in any prize, and most of the crew only one. The troubled ship, which Kidd increasingly ruled through murderous violence, eventually took six ships off the Indian coast. These included the *Quedah Merchant* from Surat which carried a cargo worth 400,000 rupees, much of which belonged to a secretary of state of the Mughal court. They took their prizes to Saint Mary's Island. By April 1698 Captain Kidd had certainly joined the pirates that he had originally set sail to fight.

Kidd was determined to return to New York and claim that he had been forced to do what he did by his mutinous crew: the only two ships he would admit to taking were, he later insisted, legal prizes sailing under French passes (which he had brought back with him as proof). The majority of his crew, however, were determined that if they were to be pirates they might as well be rich ones, and they left Kidd's ship to sail with Robert Culliford (who, fittingly, had been one of the men who had stolen away with the *Blessed William* all those years before). Meanwhile, in London, the Whig rulers who had supported Kidd were slipping from power. At the same time the East India Company, under pressure from the Mughal emperor and the courtiers and merchants who had backed the *Quedah Merchant*, were insisting that something had to be done, and that Kidd had to be captured and prosecuted. Concerted effort was applied on many fronts as the 1690s came to an end in the construction of an administrative and legal framework that could tackle the problem of piracy by pressuring colonial authorities to stop supporting pirates and start hanging them. When Kidd and what remained of his crew sailed the *Quedah Merchant* (now renamed the *Adventure Prize*) back across the Atlantic to the Caribbean they were sailing into dangerous waters. Off-loading their cargo in remote Caribbean inlets and swapping the distinctive Indian ship for a vessel that was less associated with piratical deeds, Kidd and his men returned to New York. Kidd was unable to persuade Bellomont that he should still support him. The earl's political and financial calculations put Kidd firmly on the debit side of the balance sheet, and the pirate captain was sent to London for trial. Unable to produce the French passes which he claimed would clear his name, and unwilling to please the Whigs' Tory rivals by selling out his patrons, Kidd was sentenced to death. His trial was witnessed by Coji Babba, an Armenian supercargo from the *Quedah Merchant* who had suffered at his hands, and was brought to London by the East India Company to see justice done. Captain William Kidd was hanged at execution dock in Wapping on 23 May 1701, abandoned by his powerful patrons and an example to all those who might defy the empire by crossing the line and turning pirate.

Under the black flag

The attempts to wage a war on piracy as the seventeenth century ended and the eighteenth century began, and which saw off Captain Kidd, were less effective at shifting the balance of maritime violence from illegitimate to legitimate forms than was the onset of the War of the Spanish Succession in 1701. Large numbers of privateers, including William Dampier, were given letters of marque by the British crown, and set off to reap the rewards of fighting the French and the Spanish. Piracy could once again be undertaken for national purposes and private gain in time of war. Transatlantic trade was severely disrupted, and many ships were taken, renamed and turned back against those flying their former flag. The end of the war in 1713 saw a dramatic decrease in the size of the navy and the end of the privateering commissions. For a few years this surplus maritime labour power was employed in the post-war mercantile boom that moved all the goods that had been waiting on docksides around the oceans, and resupplied colonies and plantations that had been cut off by enemy shipping. Yet this could not last. By 1716 the final, and perhaps greatest, wave of piracy had begun across the Atlantic world. If the sixteenth-century pirates had been noblemen seeking glory, and the seventeenth-century pirates had been supported by colonial merchants seeking profits, then the eighteenth-century pirates were often the working men of the ocean searching, as Edward Barlow had put it, for 'a merry life and a short one'. Much about the social organisation and terror tactics of those who sailed beneath the black flag between 1716 and 1726 can be explained by understanding them in terms of the world of the common sailor (see chapter 6).

It has been estimated that about 1,500 to 2,000 pirates sailed between 1716 and 1718, and up to 2,400 between 1719 and 1722, followed by a decline to 1,000 in 1723 and 500 in 1724. Compared with a peacetime navy of 13,000 this was a substantial force. Sailing fast, easily manoeuvrable ships, they were certainly a match for the small crews of heavily loaded merchant vessels and not easily captured by the state. Admiral Edward Vernon compared chasing a pirate ship in a man of war to sending 'a Cow after a Hare'.[8] As a result they did substantial damage. It is always hard to separate fact from fiction, both in the history of piracy and in merchants' claims about their losses, but these pirates have been calculated to have captured and plundered more than 2,000 ships between 1716 and 1726, perhaps more than were taken by the French and Spanish in the previous thirteen years of warfare. These pirate crews were a destructive force within the changing Atlantic economy, described in chapter 5, which was beginning to knit together Europe, West Africa and the Americas with regular shipping. Their prey were not the vast treasure ships of the Spanish and Asian empires, but often the routine shipping of the Atlantic world. They took what they could sell or consume, and destroyed the rest. Indeed, they often destroyed the ships themselves. Their black flag was the opposite of the merchant's account book. When it appeared on the horizon it signalled an end to accumulation and profit.

Pirates knew their prey. Pirate crews were formed and increased through mutinies on merchant ships, and especially when pirates captured a likely vessel. The sailors on board the captured ship would be given the choice to join the pirates or fend for themselves. They had to make a careful calculation of what sort of choice this was, and what the implications were of choosing either way. Which would lead to an easier life, which to death? Pirates also knew each other. Pirate crews frequently divided, just as the seventeenth-century buccaneers had, taking a new ship and a new captain when the old one no longer promised what was wanted. Pirates, therefore, knew very well the world of hard maritime labour that they had left and they set about constructing a different world that was more or less shared between the different pirate ships' crews. If merchant crews were small, pirate crews were large. They had to be to both sail and fight, but they were even larger than that required. The sort of early eighteenth-century merchant ship that had around sixteen hands would carry eighty or ninety pirates. This meant that there was less work for each member of the crew, and more time for gambling and drinking.

These early eighteenth-century pirates also followed the democratic traditions of the buccaneers. Crews voted on all things, including who should be their captain. They reorganised the hierarchy of the typical merchantman or privateer to elevate the quartermaster to unprecedented prominence as a sort of 'civil magistrate', regulating the affairs of the ship according to its traditions, mediating conflicts and overseeing the division of treasure.[9] This division was also strikingly egalitarian in comparison to naval practice, and even compared to the privateers. Nothing was to be kept back from the commonwealth, and the captain and quartermaster received a maximum of two shares to the common pirate's one. Booty was also set aside for a welfare scheme that compensated crew members who lost limbs and eyes. While the crew agreed to obey the captain's orders in the chase or the fight, none would stand for him having undue privileges, ordering unjust punishments or keeping them from their share of the food or drink. They had not turned pirate to live as they had under the captains and masters of merchant vessels.

While in some ways pirates turned the maritime world upside down, they also lived lives shaped by its relationships of power. Pirate crews were certainly as multi-national and multi-racial as those of any other ship, maybe even more so. Perhaps up to a third of pirates were black. Sam Bellamy's crew on the *Whydah Galley* was 'a Mix't Multitude of all Country's' including Europeans of all sorts, Amerindians, African-Americans, and twenty-five Africans liberated from a slave ship.[10] In 1718, five of Blackbeard's eighteen-man crew were men of colour, as were half of Captain Lewis's eighty-man crew. All shared equally in the dangers and the spoils. Yet pirates are also said to have taken violent dislikes to the Irish, French or Spanish, and to have abused, killed or sold enslaved Africans rather than incorporating them into their crews. There are no records of black pirate captains, although they were quartermasters. The ambiguities of race and nation aboard ship in the eighteenth century remained even when the class hierarchy had been rejected.

Other ambiguities surrounded pirates' terror tactics. In part they worked effectively to prevent violence. Faced with a pirate ship with all guns manned and the rigging full of heavily armed men shouting terrible threats – the very tactic Barlow had turned against Kidd – few merchant seamen would fight to defend their employers' cargo or ships. Most gave up without a fight. Yet the pirates' success also depended upon terror and on their willingness to use spectacular and horrific violence against those who defied them. They tortured ship captains to get them to reveal treasure, and they sometimes killed in cold blood. The terror they spread was also turned back upon them. The stories of pirate barbarity were used to justify the campaign of pirate hunting and the many executions that followed across the Atlantic world. By the early eighteenth century the states and empires that confronted piracy increasingly did so by separating pirates from any claims to legitimacy. The rules on privateering were redefined to make piracy a more obvious act. The once blurred boundary was clarified. Legislation was also passed to more easily enable a range of authorities across the Atlantic world to prosecute those accused of being pirates. If pirates themselves increasingly rejected national affiliations and claimed that they 'came from the sea', the authorities also used this to enforce the definition of them as *hostis humani generis* and to argue for the violent eradication and extermination of these enemies of all settled and civilised people. Thus, terror bred terror as the decreasing number of pirates in the 1720s used increasing violence to gather crews, take ships and evade capture, and the authorities increasingly executed those they caught, hanging their bodies in chains around the Atlantic coasts until they rotted away.

Perhaps the combination of equity and terror that shaped the pirate world as these ships roamed the Atlantic Ocean and tried to establish in the Bahamas a new Madagascar, a new pirate haven and republic, is best captured by the pirate flag. What is now thought of as the 'Jolly Roger' – a white skull and cross-bones on a black background – was part of a range of symbols the pirates devised for themselves. Others showed the whole skeleton, or 'anatomy', sometimes bearing a weapon or an hour-glass. The pirates had rejected the flags of the imperial powers for something more universal and even more steeped in terror. They knew that their lives were shadowed by death: the deaths that they brought to others, and the deaths that would be brought down upon them in turn. Few pirates lasted in the life longer than two years, and many died on the gallows as the authorities battled to prevent them disrupting trade and capital accumulation. The pirates recognised the equality of all in the face of death, and used it both to shape a social order in which they might live and to bring terror to their enemies. In the pirate's creed the one who lived the longest was welcome to whatever remained.

The world of Bartholomew Roberts

The pirate captain Bartholomew Roberts devised his own flags (figure 7.3). Furious at the attempts of the English governor of Barbados and the French governor of Martinique to capture his ship, he had his black silk jack decorated with his own figure, flaming sword in hand, standing on two skulls under which were stitched the letters ABH and AMH: A Barbadian's Head and A Martinican's Head. This he flew with a St George's ensign (a sign of the English king that Roberts called 'the Turnip-man'), and a flag 'with a Death in it, with an hour-glass in one hand and cross-bones in the other, a dart by it, and underneath a heart dropping three drops of blood'.[11] Yet this fearsome figure had begun a reluctant pirate. When the slave ship *Princess*, on which he had sailed from London as second mate, was taken by the pirate Howel Davis off the Guinea Coast port of Anoumabu in 1720, Roberts was said to have been 'very averse to this sort of life, and would certainly have

Captain Bartho. Roberts *with two Ships, Viz. the* Royal Fortune *and* Ranger, *takes it Said in* Whydah *Road on the Coast of* Guiney, *January 11ᵗʰ 172¼.*

Figure 7.3 Bartholomew Roberts. The Welsh pirate captain is shown in all his finery, complete with sword and four pistols, on the West African coast where he had his greatest successes and where he was finally killed and his ships captured. Behind him his two vessels fly the flags that he had made for them, depicting trampled skulls, skeletons and hourglasses, as they bear down on the slaveships moored off Ouidah.

escaped from them, had a fair opportunity presented itself'. But when Davis was killed shortly after, Roberts – judged 'one who by his counsel and bravery seems best able to defend this commonwealth, and ward us from the dangers and tempests of an unstable element, and the fatal consequences of anarchy' – was voted his successor by the crew.[12] Thus began his reign of terror on all sides of the Atlantic.

Roberts's crew is said to have taken four hundred ships in the two years that he captained them. They terrorised the coast of Portuguese Brazil, the banks of Newfoundland, the British and French islands in the Caribbean, the Slave Coast of Guinea and the merchant ships of all nations. They found safe havens where rogue governors and traders would buy their plunder: at Saint Bartholomew in the Caribbean, and with the interlopers on the Royal African Company's privileges near Bance Island in the Sierra Leone River. They set fire to twenty ships in a Newfoundland harbour, and another twenty at Martinique. They burned a ship holding eighty chained African slaves off the Guinea coast. They sank many of the ships they robbed, and turned others into pirate vessels. They spread terror. On the *Samuel,* the passengers 'were used very roughly in order to make them discover their money, threatening them every moment with death if they did not resign everything up to them. They tore up the hatches and entered the holds like a parcel of Furies, and with axes and cutlasses cut and broke open all the bales, cases, and boxes they could lay their hands on; and when any goods came upon deck that they did not like to carry aboard ... [they] threw them overboard into the sea. All this was done with incessant cursing and swearing, more like fiends than men ... that if they should be overpowered, they would set fire to the powder with a pistol, and go all merrily to Hell together.'[13] As they took ship after ship the crew grew. As it grew it spawned other pirate crews.

Early on they took a Portuguese ship laden with sugar, hides, tobacco and gold (including a diamond cross intended for the king of Portugal), and chased a Rhode Island brigantine carrying provisions (food was as useful as treasure since, as one pirate maxim had it, there were 'No adventures to be made without Belly-timber'). They found themselves a safe retreat on, appropriately enough, Devil's Island in the Surinam River where they might trade their plunder with the Dutch governor, and enjoy 'all the pleasures that luxury and wantonness could bestow'.[14] There they are also said to have sworn allegiance to a set of articles 'for the better conservation of their society and doing justice to one another.' There were rules to safeguard the ship. To avoid fires, lights and candles were to be out at 8 p.m. and drinking after that was to be done on open deck. Each man's weapons were also to be kept clean and ready. There were rules on government and punishment. Each man had a vote and equal access to provisions and strong drink. Any pirate holding back treasure or deserting the ship in battle would be marooned (left on an uninhabited island) or suffer death. Those crippled in the service would get $800. There were rules to prevent disputes among the crew: no gambling with cards or dice; 'No boy or woman to be allowed amongst them'; and all arguments to be settled by duels on shore.[15] There were rules on the division of the spoils. Captain and quartermaster – the military commander and the civil magistrate – would receive two shares of the plunder; the master, boatswain and gunner, one and a half; and the other officers one and a quarter. Finally, the musicians would be required to play six days and nights a week, but would get Sundays off, and the whole company resolved to stay together until each man had £1000 in his sea-chest. Yet despite these egalitarian and democratic articles Roberts is also said to have ruled his own men by terror, threatening and even killing those who defied him.

On 10 February 1722 Roberts's *Royal Fortune* – with 40 guns and 157 men, of whom 45 were black – was finally trapped in a Guinea coast bay by the Royal Navy ship *Swallow* commanded by Captain Chaloner Ogle. It was do or die. Roberts resolved to pass close to the *Swallow* with all sails set, and to receive their broadside before returning fire. If the pirate ship sailed clear they would get away. If they were disabled they would beach the ship 'and everyone to shift for himself among the negroes'.[16] If they were caught they would blow themselves up and take the *Swallow* down with them. Roberts stood on the quarterdeck resplendent in a crimson damask waistcoat and breeches, sword in hand, pistols on silk ribbons over his shoulders, a red feather in his hat, and a diamond cross on a gold chain around his neck (perhaps the same one that had been intended for the king of Portugal). His flags flew proudly above him. If this son of Pembrokeshire was going down he was going down fighting. As he is reported to have said to the pirates who joined him, 'In an honest service there is thin commons, low wages, and hard labour. In this, plenty and satiety, pleasure and ease, liberty and power; and who would not balance creditor on this side, when all the hazard that is run for it, at worst, is only a sour look or two at choking.' He had made his choice, and it was 'D—n to him who ever lived to wear a halter.'[17] As the ships engaged Roberts took a shot in the throat and was killed instantly. His men, observing his last wishes, threw him and his fine clothes and weapons over board. They tried to do the same with his flags 'that they might not rise in judgement nor be displayed in triumph over them'.[18]

The world of Anne Bonny

In this world turned upside down women might turn pirate too, confounding the expectations of those on dry land and seeking another kind of freedom. It is said that Anne Bonny was born in Cork in 1698, the illegitimate daughter of the lawyer William Cormac and his maidservant. The subsequent scandal drove Cormac – with the maid and baby Anne (perhaps dressed as a boy) in tow – to South Carolina where he found success as a merchant and plantation-owner. When she was twenty Anne caused her own scandal by defying her father's attempts to make a match for her and marrying a poor sailor called James Bonny. Her father closed his door to her and the couple moved to New Providence in the Bahamas looking for work. In this notorious nest of pirates, diversion was never hard to find and Bonny found herself subject to the amorous attentions of Captain John Rackham, who was then taking advantage of the royal pardon for pirates that had been extended to try and stop them using the islands to attack merchant ships. Calico Jack, as he was known on account of his fancy clothes, must have looked the better bet for riches and a wild life. He persuaded Bonny to go to sea with him and, after giving birth to his child on Cuba, she took a full part in their attacks on Caribbean shipping until they were captured off Negril Point, Jamaica, by Captain Jonathan Barnet's privateering vessel.

As the story goes, Anne Bonny developed an affection for another sailor on board, and 'not being so reserved in point of chastity' made her feelings quite plain, revealing to him that she was a woman.[19] However, he was also a she, an Englishwoman named Mary Read who had first dressed as a man to enter the army in pursuit of her lover. After his death, and having been on board a ship bound for the West Indies which was taken by pirates, Read had ended up in New Providence too. Sailing as a privateer, she had been part of a crew who had risen up against their commanders and turned pirate. Her adventures had brought her on to Rackham's ship and into company with Anne Bonny, two women pirates together. However, this story of gender hidden and secrets revealed may be just that, a story, all the better to scare and thrill the people of the land with the strange ways of the pirates. Before the capture of Rackham's ship, the governor of the Bahamas, Woodes Rogers (the former privateer with whom Dampier had sailed), had issued a proclamation on 5 September 1720 announcing quite plainly that Calico Jack and twelve others 'including two women, by name Anne Fulford alias Bonny, & Mary Read' had stolen a six-gun, twelve-ton sloop, the *William* and committed acts of robbery at sea.[20]

The two women certainly did not seek to hide themselves on board, putting themselves forward for the most dangerous duties. Witnesses at their trial testified that 'they were both very profligate, cursing and swearing much and ready and willing to do any thing on board'.[21] Others said that they only wore men's clothes to fight (figure 7.4). These women could certainly hold their own on a pirate ship, and the rest of the crew seemed to respect them for it. Indeed, a later report of the engagement in which they were captured noted that 'when they were at close quarters none kept the deck except Mary Read and Anne Bonny and one more; upon which she, Mary Read, called to those under deck to come up and fight like men'.[22] When they continued to cower below Read fired her pistol down into the hold, killing one and wounding others. Bonny was similarly forthright in her treatment of those she saw as cowards who could not live up to the demands of the pirate life. On the day that John Rackham was to be executed he was allowed to see her. She gave him cold comfort, saying 'That she was sorry

F.º 221.

Anne Bonny op Jamaica Gevangen.

Figure 7.4 Anne Bonny. Armed with pistol, sword and hatchet, and not afraid to use them, this woman pirate is shown dressed in men's clothing, but with her breast bared. At once a threatening and a romantic figure she captures the transgressions associated with piracy.

to see him there, but if he had fought like a man, he need not have been hanged like a dog.'[23] Anne Bonny and Mary Read understood the value all common seamen, and pirates in particular, placed on courage, and used it as a weapon against the men who might have exercised power over them.

All of Rackham's crew of twelve were hanged with their captain except Bonny and Read. Both 'pleaded their bellies', claiming they were pregnant in order to escape the gallows. Mary Read died in prison shortly after of a violent fever. Anne Bonny was let free. Her gender and her connections allowed her to escape the noose. Perhaps it was the baby. Some said it was her father's name and his reputation among the great planters of Jamaica before whom she stood trial. Class privilege may have saved her life. She certainly made it back to Charleston, South Carolina, where she had Rackham's baby, married a local man and lived to the age of eighty-four. She died a respectable woman and mother of eight children, but one who had once fought like a man against the forces of law and order.

The end of the early eighteenth-century 'golden age' of Atlantic piracy was brought by a wave of prosecutions and executions. It has been estimated that over 450 pirates were hanged between 1716 and 1726, more than one in ten of those who terrorised the high seas. They were executed on gallows – or 'turned off' – in North America, Europe, the Caribbean and Africa under the eyes of a range of imperial and colonial authorities implementing new laws designed to halt their disruption of the new mercantile empires of settlement and trade (figure 7.5). Bartholomew Roberts's men, those with him in the *Royal Fortune* and those sailing alongside in the *Ranger* – were tried at Cape Coast Castle, a Royal African Company slave-trading factory on the Guinea coast, by a court of Company officials, naval officers and merchants. Of 267 men on both ships, 32 had died in the battle or before trial, 17 were sent to London for imprisonment, 20 were sentenced to seven years' indentured servitude for the African Company (a death sentence for many; see chapter 8), 74 were acquitted (usually on the basis that they had come from ships very recently taken by Roberts's crew and could not yet be held individually accountable for the actions of the whole) and 52 were executed. Some went to their deaths penitent, others were defiant. They had been living closely with death since they turned pirate and now faced it head on.

The executions of Roberts's men were the end point of the two processes shaping the changes in piracy from the sixteenth to the eighteenth centuries, and transforming the organisation of maritime violence. Across this period the merchant empires of the European powers had become more established, more routine and more regular. Their power and profits depended increasingly on the regular armed forces – the armies and navies – of the imperial state on the one hand, and the predictable profits of the plantation economy and transatlantic shipping on the other. The sea-rovers, buccaneers, freebooters and pirates who had been the agents extending empires and markets in their earlier, violent and unpredictable phases had

Fol: 86.

Majoor Stede Bonnet Gehangen

Figure 7.5 The hanging of the pirate Stede Bonnet at Charleston. Many pirates met their fate at the end of the hangman's rope in a theatre of punishment orchestrated around the Atlantic world by imperial and colonial authorities. Here on the dockside in South Carolina in 1718 the cart pulls away to send the Barbadian pirate captain who had sailed with Blackbeard to his death in front of the watching crowd.

later become the problematic symbols and agents of just that violence and unpredictability. They had gone from being a key part of the mercantile and imperial transformation of the Caribbean to a barrier to its further development for profit and power.

These agents of devolved violence had previously inhabited and exploited the marginal areas where empires and merchants were weak: finding markets that were poorly supplied, treasure that was badly defended, and islands and coasts that were sparsely settled by Europeans. When the integration of imperial and mercantile spaces meant that there were no more margins they had to move, and when there was nowhere to move to they had to be eradicated. This also went hand in hand with piracy's slide down the social scale. Its value changed over time as those involved changed. Francis Drake's aristocratic search for martial glory against the Spanish on the high seas was replaced with Captain Kidd's cabals of merchants and politicians, and then with Bartholomew Roberts's plea for a life of plenty and liberty, freeing the working man from the halter of exploitation at the hands of ships' captains. There were many reasons for the forces of imperial and mercantile order to declare the early eighteenth-century pirates the enemies of all mankind, and call for their violent destruction. Piracy by that time had been made separate from privateering – now governed by financial bonds which would be forfeited for going beyond the commission, and sets of rules which defined appropriate actions – and therefore from the legitimate use of violence at sea. It had also been made separate from mercantile accumulation. Pirates gloried in destroying and wasting merchants' goods. It was often a merry life but it was a short one.

The accounting of the trial of Roberts's crew set out above leaves out one large group. Of the 267 men on both ships, 70 were 'Negroes', a quarter of the pirates captured by the *Swallow*. We know little about them. Some may have sailed with Roberts for some time, others were certainly recently enslaved Africans taken from slave ships by the pirates. The Cape Coast Castle authorities lumped them all together and decided that they should share a single fate: instead of execution or acquittal they were sold into slavery and shipped off for the New World. They were not the only ones.

Further reading

For overviews of piracy and privateering, see the excellent essays collected in C. R. Pennell (ed.) (2001) *Bandits at Sea: A Pirates Reader* (New York University Press, New York), Kris E. Lane (1998) *Pillaging the Empire: Piracy in* the Americas, 1500–1750 (M. E. Sharpe, London) and Janice E. Thompson (1994) *Mercenaries, Pirates, and Sovereigns: State-Building and Extraterritorial Violence in Early Modern Europe* (Princeton University Press, Princeton). Barbary corsairs are discussed in Linda Colley (2002) *Captives: Britain, Empire and the World, 1600–1850* (Jonathan Cape, London) Part I. I have used William Dampier (1998) *A New Voyage Round the World: The Journal of an English Buccaneer* (Hummingbird Press, London), but there are many other editions available. The stories of Captain Kidd and the pirates of Madagascar are told in different ways in Robert C. Ritchie (1986) *Captain Kidd and the War Against the Pirates* (Harvard University Press, Cambridge, Mass.) and Jan Rogoziński (2000) *Honour Among Thieves: Captain Kidd, Henry Every, and the Story of Pirate Island* (Conway Maritime Press, London). The pirates of the early eighteenth century are interpreted in Marcus Rediker (2004) *Villains of All Nations: Atlantic Pirates in the Golden Age* (Verso, London) which reworks material previously presented in Marcus Rediker (1981) '"Under the banner of King Death": the social world of Anglo-American pirates, 1716–1726', *William and Mary Quarterly* 38:2 pp. 203–27; Marcus Rediker (1987) *Between the Devil and the Deep Blue Sea: Merchant Seamen, Pirates, and the Anglo-American Maritime World, 1700–1750* (Cambridge University Press, Cambridge), chap. 6, 'The seaman as pirate: plunder and social banditry at sea'; and Peter Linebaugh and Marcus Rediker (2000) *The Many-Headed Hydra: Sailors, Slaves, Commoners, and the Hidden History of the Revolutionary Atlantic* (Beacon Press, Boston), chap. 5, 'Hydrarchy: sailors, pirates, and the maritime state'. The stories of Bartholomew Roberts and Anne Bonny are among those in Captain Charles Johnson (1724) *A General History of the Pyrates* (London). I have used the reprint *Pirates* (Creation Books, London: 1999). There are many editions. Dampier, Kidd, Roberts and Bonny all have entries in the *Oxford Dictionary of National Biography*.

Notes

1 Quoted in Anne Pérotin-Dumon (2001) 'The pirate and the emperor: power and the law on the seas, 1450–1850', in C. R. Pennell (ed.) *Bandits at Sea: A Pirates Reader* (New York University Press, New York) p. 25.
2 William Dampier (1998) *A New Voyage Round the World: The Journal of an English Buccaneer* (Hummingbird Press, London) pp. 101–102.
3 Ibid., p. 27.
4 Ibid., p. 5.
5 Ibid., pp. 132, 170 and 243.

6 Ibid., pp. 49 and 134.

7 Quoted in Robert C. Ritchie (1986) *Captain Kidd and the War Against the Pirates* (Harvard University Press, Cambridge, Mass.) p. 158.

8 Quoted in Marcus Rediker (2004) *Villains of All Nations: Atlantic Pirates in the Golden Age* (Verso, London) p. 29.

9 Captain Charles Johnson (1999, originally published in 1724) *A General History of the Pyrates* (Creation Books, London) p. 185.

10 Quoted in Rediker, *Villains of All Nations*, p. 53.

11 Johnson, *A General History of the Pyrates*, p. 202.

12 Ibid., pp. 167–168.

13 Ibid., p. 188.

14 Ibid., p. 177.

15 Ibid., pp. 182–183.

16 Ibid., p. 211.

17 Ibid., p. 212.

18 Ibid., p. 208.

19 Ibid., p. 133.

20 Quoted in the *Oxford Dictionary of National Biography* entry for Anne Bonny.

21 Quoted ibid.

22 Johnson, *A General History of the Pyrates*, p. 133.

23 Ibid., p. 141.

The goods that sailors shifted as merchant seamen and protected as naval ratings, and that the pirates sought as plunder, were often intimately connected with slavery. Most of the cargoes moving around the Atlantic Ocean were either goods used to purchase slaves, food and equipment for slaves on plantations and farms, or the end product of slave labour itself (see chapter 5). And, of course, the enslaved themselves were transported across the oceans as valuable cargo too. This trade was vast. Over 11 million men, women and children departed from Africa on ships bound for the Americas during the 350 years of the transatlantic slave trade. As is evident from table 8.1, this trade really expanded in the late seventeenth century as the Atlantic economy became an integrated network of trade routes and markets worked by merchants in Europe, Africa and the Americas. Between 1676 and 1800 over 6.5 million enslaved Africans were packed on ships to cross the ocean to the plantations and mines of the European empires in the New World (see chapter 9). Slave ships came from many European nations to trade on the West African coast, but the majority of this oceanic trade was in the hands of those from Portugal, Britain and France. The Portuguese dominated the earlier and later periods, carrying 75 per cent of slaves between 1519 and 1675 and 66 per cent after 1801. British shipping, which had started with John Hawkins's opportunistic voyages in the 1560s (see chapter 2), had the prime share of the trade in the boom years, carrying 41 per cent of slaves between 1676 and 1800. At the height of British involvement in the trade a large slave ship left England every other day for the African coast. Overall, nine out of every ten enslaved people who were carried to the Americas were packed into Portuguese, British and French vessels. However, it must also be remembered that of those who embarked from Africa at least 1.4 million of them did not reach their destination. They died during the Middle Passage and their bodies were thrown into the ocean.

This was the largest forced migration in history. The ocean voyage from Africa to the Americas was only one part of the world of Atlantic slavery: an interconnected set of trades in a range of goods, a variety of forms of labour exploitation and commodity production, and an array of modes of

Table 8.1 Volume of the transatlantic slave trade by nationality of carrier (in thousands)

	Britain	France	Netherlands	Spain	United States and British Caribbean	Denmark	Portugal	All nations
1519–1600	2						264.1	266.1
1601–1650	23		41				439.5	503.5
1651–1675	115.2	5.9	64.8			0.2	53.7	239.8
1676–1700	243.3	34.1	56.1			15.4	161.1	510.0
1701–1725	380.9	106.3	65.5		11	16.7	378.3	958.7
1726–1750	490.5	253.9	109.2		44.5	7.6	405.6	1311.3
1751–1775	859.1	321.5	148	1	89.1	13.4	472.9	1905.0
1776–1800	741.3	419.5	40.8	8.6	54.3	30.4	626.2	1921.1
1801–1825	257	217.9	2.3	204.8	81.1	10.5	871.6	1645.2
1826–1850		94.1		279.2			1247.7	1621.0
1851–1867		3.2		23.4			154.2	180.8
All Years	3112.3	1456.4	527.7	517	280	94.2	5074.9	11,062.5
Share of Trade	28.1%	13.2%	4.8%	4.7%	2.5%	0.9%	45.9%	

Source: David Eltis (2001) 'The volume and structure of the slave trade: a reassessment', *William and Mary Quarterly* 58:1 p. 43.

warfare and other types of violence at least as complex as in any other part of the early modern world. These involved the economics and politics of the American plantations (see chapter 9) and those of the African states and merchants that traded with the Europeans and waged war with each other. As shown in chapter 5, African traders and rulers exercised tight control over their trading relationships with Europeans, determining the terms of trade. European traders had to be well aware of the nature and structure of supply and demand in order to profit from a trade that was, up until the point of embarkation, largely in African hands. The process of enslavement began far inland from the coast, and long before European involvement. People were taken into slavery via capture in warfare, through the violent raiding of other societies, and as punishments for crimes such as adultery, murder and sorcery. These people, already defined as enemies, aliens and criminals, then began what was often a very long walk to the coast, becoming separated from places where they were known and relationships that might have saved them. Uncounted millions died on the way.

Slavery also has a long history. Just as in Europe and Asia, forms of slave labour existed in African societies back into antiquity, but they were rarely central to the economies of which they were a part. Since, unlike in Europe, land could not be owned, it was the people who performed work who were the major form of property that could be accumulated and transferred. Various forms of dependent labour – extended families, women taken as wives, 'pawns' held to guarantee the payment of debts and slaves bought and sold as property – were a key part of African societies' forms of wealth. This meant that there was an active slave trade both within Africa, and between sub-Saharan Africa and other parts of the world before and during the time of the Atlantic slave trade. It is estimated that 2.4 million enslaved Africans were transported east out of Africa via the Red Sea coast and East African coast slave-trading routes between 800 AD and 1600 AD, and over 4.8 million were taken north by the trans-Saharan slave trade between 650 AD and 1600 AD. During the seventeenth and eighteenth centuries these routes continued to transport substantial numbers of slaves, even as the transatlantic trade rose to prominence (table 8.2).

Although all these forms of slavery were based on the idea that one person could own another there were great differences between them. Slavery in Africa and the Islamic world was not based on racial difference, as it was in the Americas. Africans held as slaves other Africans they saw as ene-mies, aliens and criminals, and the slaves held on the Barbary coast were both African and European, including those snatched from the beaches of Devon and Cornwall (see chapter 7). African slavery and Islamic slavery

Table 8.2 Estimated numbers of enslaved people exported from Africa (in thousands)

	1500–1599	%	1600–1699	%	1700–1799	%	Total	%
Red Sea	100	9.3	100	4.4	200	2.7	400	3.7
Sahara	550	51.0	700	31.1	700	9.5	1950	18.2
East Africa	100	9.3	100	4.4	400	5.4	600	5.6
Atlantic	328	30.4	1348	60.0	6090	82.4	7766	72.5
Total	1078		2248		7390		10716	

Source: Paul E. Lovejoy (2000) *Transformations in Slavery: A History of Slavery in Africa,* 2nd edn (Cambridge University Press, Cambridge) p. 47.

also involved a greater range of forms of work than in the Americas. In the New World slaves were forced to do the heavy agricultural and mining labour that other workers would not perform (see chapter 9), and such labour was absolutely central to the economy and society. In Africa and the Islamic world slaves did agricultural and extractive work, and worked in their owners' houses, but they also did service in the rulers' armies and the state bureaucracy. Slaves in those parts of the world could rise to positions of authority as officials and generals. More broadly, the children of slave mothers and free fathers often became free, unlike in the Americas, and second-generation slaves acquired some rights and privileges. Finally, there were differences in gender. Slave-holders in the Americas preferred strong, young male slaves as field hands and miners. On average they transported two men for every woman. The trades across the Sahara, Red Sea and Indian Oceans reversed that ratio. Here the demand was for women and children who could be employed in domestic service. Transatlantic slavery was, therefore, both part of wider patterns of enslavement in Africa and shaped by European mercantile organisation and American demand.

In the face of the scale of exploitation and suffering represented by the transatlantic slave trade it is both difficult and necessary to concentrate on the broad structures of the trade and on how individuals operated within it. This chapter will attempt to set out how the processes of enslavement and transportation were organised – by both Africans and Europeans – and the responses to those processes (see also chapter 10). This will involve consideration of the lives of merchants and traders actively involved in buying and selling slaves on the West African coast. The chapter will detail the worlds of Archibald Dalzel and Walter Prideaux, who each sailed this way from Britain at least once. It will also tell the stories of Little Ephraim Robin John and Ancona Robin Robin John in order to trace the lives of Africans who were both slave-traders and slaves. Finally, although the chapter cannot do justice to the millions of lives that were shattered and lost in the slave trade, it tries to recover some of the forms of resistance to enslavement used by Africans in Africa and on the slave ships. This involves the story of a late eighteenth-century slave insurrection on the American ship *Felicity*, whose participants left some record by their actions even if we cannot know their names. We begin, however, with the European merchants looking out for profits in the Atlantic world and hoping to find them by trading in people.

Trading in people

The slave trade was both a routine part of Atlantic trade and an exceptional enterprise in that it involved transporting a human cargo. Chapter 5 demonstrated the involvement of merchants such as Robert Freeman, La Belinguere and Richard Oswald in buying and selling slaves, and showed how they integrated this set of exchanges into their other activities. For Oswald and his associates in particular there was an attempt to supply labour for their own plantations, as well as to profit from selling enslaved Africans to others. In their activities on Bance Island in the Sierra Leone River, and in the dispatch of ships to and from it, these associates were keen to follow the rules that made them profits elsewhere: timely and integrated shipments of goods to the markets where they were in demand. The logic they applied to supplying cloth or metalwares for African markets, or sugar and rice to European ones, was also applied to the supply of enslaved labour for the Americas. Yet there were also differences. Merchants had to respond to the fact that they were carrying, and buying and selling, a forcibly enslaved cargo of human beings.

For the European merchants the West African trade sat, both organisationally and geographically, somewhere between the trade with the American colonies and the trade with the East Indies (see chapters 4 and 5). It became part of the Atlantic world of routine and regular shipping following the huge clockwise pattern of currents and winds in the ocean basin. It was not too difficult to sail to West Africa and on to the Americas or back to Europe. However, as in Asia, the terms of trade were controlled by the well-organised indigenous polities and merchants the Europeans encountered from Senegambia to Angola. As with all long-distance trades the initial response in Britain was to form a chartered monopoly company with royal patronage that would control the trade and have the exclusive rights to develop it. There was a succession of such companies. The Company of Adventurers of London Trading to the Ports of Africa (better known as

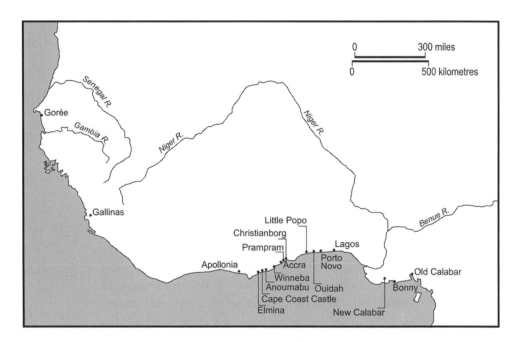

Figure 8.1 Major European factories on the West African coast. With the permission of local rulers, the English, French, Dutch, Danish and other European slave-traders established a series of bases on the Slave Coast in order to facilitate their trade in human cargo. These factories and forts often changed hands between European powers, and their influence rose and fell with the economic and political fortunes of the localities and regions in which they were based.

the Guinea Company) was given a monopoly of trade 'for ever hereafter' by King James I in 1618, but was replaced by the Company of Merchants Trading to Guinea in 1631.[1] In turn this was succeeded in the early 1660s by the Company of Royal Adventurers of England Trading into Africa (commonly called the Royal African Company), set up by Prince Rupert and James, Duke of York. Their 1,000-year charter actually lasted only twelve years, and a new Royal African Company, formed in 1672, was dominated by merchants rather than courtiers.

Until the 1670s all of these companies were more interested in African gold (and in redwood for dyeing) than in slaves. Like the East India Company in the Indian Ocean, and like the other European companies in West Africa, they established a series of forts and factories along the coast to facilitate their activities (figure 8.1). However, these groups of English merchants faced strong competition from the other Europeans (particularly the Dutch West India Company) and from interloping English merchants who did not pay the costs of fixed establishments on the coast. Part of the problem was that the African rulers with whom they dealt, both to buy goods and to establish factories, liked things this way. They sought to maintain the competition and conflict between Europeans and to keep them as dependent as possible. This manifested itself in higher prices for African goods and, in the seventeenth century, in a merry-go-round of forts changing hands between Dutch, Swedish, Danish and English companies as their mercantile and military fortunes rose and fell. In each case these forts were built on land leased from African rulers, and existed only because the latter allowed them to. Their guns were directed against other European traders rather than against their African trading partners.

The other supporters of competition were the European merchants left outside these exclusive companies. In Britain they quickly succeeded in eroding the Royal African Company's monopoly. From 1698 anyone was allowed to enter the trade on payment of a 10 per cent duty on goods exported. After the abolition of this tax in 1712, the trade was still full of interlopers. By 1750 the Royal African Company was reduced to running its forts and factories to facilitate the slaving voyages of other merchants by providing diplomatic, financial and warehousing services.[2] By the eighteenth century, therefore, the slave trade was part of the Atlantic world of many merchants with many vessels organising many voyages and trying to make them turn a profit. These merchants organised the trade from a range of British ports, and it was increasingly Liverpool that came to dominate the trade in the late eighteenth century, Bristol and London having sent more ships in the first half of the century (see table 8.3).

In fitting out ships, planning voyages and finding markets these merchants faced conditions particular to the slave trade. They needed cargoes that would find buyers in the selective and differentiated regional markets of West Africa (see chapter 5). They needed ships that could be fitted out to carry enslaved people. Although most merchant ships could be turned to this purpose, it did involve hiring well-paid carpenters to build platforms of Baltic timber on which the slaves could lie below decks, and wooden bulkheads to separate groups of slaves from each other. Merchants also had to invest in chains, shackles, collars and other restraints, often made in the foundries of the West Midlands, and they needed force-feeding equipment and surgeons to preserve the value of their cargo. For the same reason, slave ships were supplied with nets strung out around the vessel like a skirt to prevent the enslaved Africans brought on board from throwing themselves into the sea. For the Middle Passage the ships had to be provided with huge casks of fresh water, needing coopers to provide and mend them, and sufficient food for those onboard. Merchants bought beans from England,

Table 8.3 Departures of slave ships from British and British colonial ports, 1699–1807

	London	Bristol	Liverpool	Newport, Rhode Island	Other	Total
1699–1709	545	60	2	1	77	685
1710–1719	450	194	75	2	70	791
1720–1729	600	332	96	9	70	1107
1730–1739	282	405	231	72	70	1060
1740–1749	81	239	322	46	64	752
1750–1759	164	215	521	102	170	1172
1760–1769	335	256	725	152	197	1665
1770–1779	370	153	703	104	89	1419
1780–1789	166	111	646		87	1010
1790–1799	173	123	1011		64	1371
1800–1807	185	17	867		2	1071
All years	3351	2105	5199	488	960	12103
	27.69%	17.39%	42.96%	4.03%	7.93%	

Source: David Richardson (1998) 'The British Empire and the Atlantic slave trade, 1660–1807', in Peter J. Marshall (ed.) *The Oxford History of the British Empire*, vol. II, *The Eighteenth Century* (Oxford University Press, Oxford) p. 446.

rice from the Carolinas and cod from Newfoundland; and, while gathering slaves, they bought African rice, maize and yams, depending on the region. Ships sailing from the slave ports of Bonny and Old and New Calabar left Africa with 10,000 to 50,000 yams on board each vessel, about a hundred for each enslaved African carried.

Slave ships were also different in that they were manned by crews of about twice the size of comparable merchant vessels. On average, a captain would expect to command a crew of thirty to carry three hundred slaves. The additional men were needed to secure those forcibly held on board, and also because about one in five of these sailors could be expected to die of disease on the voyage, a much higher proportion than on ships carrying other cargoes. Merchants tried to make sure that they used captains who had prior experience of the tropics, and preferably of West Africa. These men would be both hardened to disease and experienced in the ways of the trade.

Merchants investing in slaving voyages did it to make money. The profits that might be expected were, on average, comparable with other Atlantic trades, at about 10 per cent. The business was also comparably risky. Success as a slave-trader was best guaranteed by careful attention to supply and demand in the many markets in which they were involved, all of which had both seasonal and more long-term fluctuations. These were markets for ships, timber, labour (carpenters, captains and seamen), food and all sorts of trade goods, as well as the markets for people in both Africa and the Americas. Merchants aimed to move their ships smoothly and profitably between these markets, avoiding the delays that would mean missing the best prices at any port of call and minimising deaths and insurrections of slaves, which ate into their profits. For most of the history of the transatlantic slave trade, and for most slave-trading merchants, the difference that carrying a human cargo meant was understood less as a moral problem than as an accounting problem. Yet the human capacities of thought and will that even slave labour depended upon also meant that the people carried as goods might always rise up against their captors or might prefer death to enslavement. This also had to be taken into account, if only in the costs of nets, chains and extra sailors. Trading people was not simply like trading sugar, and men such as Archibald Dalzel knew it.

The world of Archibald Dalzel (formerly Dalziel)

Archibald Dalziel knew that he could not get what he needed from being a doctor, so he became a slave-trader. Born in Kirkliston, Linlithgowshire, Scotland, in 1740 as the eldest of five children, he trained as a doctor in Edinburgh. He then saw service in the Seven Years' War as a surgeon's mate, and was present at the taking of Newfoundland. Yet this career path would not do. With his father dead, Archibald had taken on the responsibility of providing for his mother and his siblings, Andrew, William, Jack and Elizabeth. Only Andrew had gainful employment, as lecturer (and later professor) in classics at the University of Edinburgh, but the advantages of this were more than offset by William's ability to run up huge debts without any way to pay them off. Archibald was also dissatisfied with medical practice. He did not like it and thought he would never be very good at it. But in 1762 he did not know what to do instead. As he told Andrew, 'I scarce know how to dispose of myself till I have made a tryal at London. I am determined not to go home to live till I have got something to support me which I shall (work) hard for if I go to the utmost corner of the globe.' Without the capital for a West Indian plantation, he finally resolved that 'Guinea is the only place that I have a probability of raising myself in.'[3] He accepted employment as a surgeon for the Company of Merchants Trading to Africa, the body that managed the British forts on the West African coast. As surgeon he would look after the Company's employees in this white man's graveyard. He was also one of those responsible for ensuring that

Figure 8.2 The Royal African Company's slave fort at Anoumabu. This purpose-built factory on the West African coast was designed using the principles of European military fortification, built with British materials, and tailored to the needs of the trade in enslaved people. It contained within its walls cells where many hundreds of Africans died while the slave-traders awaited ships to transport them to the Americas.

British merchants did not buy old or sickly slaves, and for keeping them in good health while they were in the Company's hands.

In August 1763, Archibald Dalziel arrived in Africa, where he was stationed at Anoumabu on the Gold Coast. This was where Bartholomew Roberts had first become a pirate over forty years earlier. By the middle of the eighteenth century it was the only fort specifically designed and built by the British for conducting the slave trade, rather than being inherited and adapted from other uses and other users (figure 8.2). It was planned in the mid-1750s by the military engineer John Appleby and built with around two million bricks and 25,000 tiles brought from England, and many tons of Portland lime. It had high defensive walls, apartments for the Company's employees and a brick vaulted 'slave hole' lit and ventilated by overhead gratings which was built into the northeast bastion. Dalziel would have known this small fort inside out. Like all Company servants, the surgeons were not, however, officially permitted to engage in slave-trading. These forts were intended to supply the slave ships, not to compete with them. However, Dalziel, like most Company employees, flouted the rules and began to supplement his salary in this way. He did not do this lightly. There was a moral barrier to overcome before this could be treated like any other trade. As Archibald wrote to his brother Andrew, 'I have at last come a little into the spirit of the slave trade and must own (perhaps it ought to be my shame) that I can now traffick in that way without remorse.' The pull of riches was evidently strong. This would be his family's way out of financial difficulty and his way out of Africa. As Archibald continued, 'I have already gained a trifle by it and shall make all the haste I can to revisit my native clime.'[4] By 1767 he had become the director of the British fort along the coast at Ouidah in the Kingdom of Dahomey, and he continued to trade illegally and profitably with the Dutch and Portuguese. In 1770 he decided that he could retire to England 'to spend the remainder of life in ease if not in affluence which I do not aspire to'.[5] He returned via the West Indies, selling a cargo of slaves on the way.

Unfortunately for him, Archibald Dalziel did not manage the markets well. He had failed to buy sufficient slaves, securing only 104 when he had planned to ship 210. He also sold them to indebted planters who were unable to pay him in full. After seven years away Dalziel returned to London with only £2,000 in promissory notes in his pocket. This proved insufficient. William's debts had eaten all of that up by 1773. The price of Archibald's lack of success in the slave trade was having to re-enter that trade. This time he used his experience to make and finance a series of slaving voyages during the 1770s. He eventually accumulated enough cash and credit to buy three ships for the purpose – the *Hannah*, the *Nancy* and *Little Archie*, personal and childlike names for ships trading in human misery. He also bought land for a plantation in Florida, and began planning for one in Jamaica. Again, he prospered right up until the point, in 1778, when he lost everything he had after his ships were taken by American privateers during the War of Independence. His creditors came after him for their money.

Having been declared bankrupt, Dalziel changed his name to Dalzel and began again. He tried piracy and book-selling, sought a civil service post and dabbled in the Spanish wine trade, all with little success. He fared better doing what he knew best, captaining slave ships for London and Liverpool merchants on at least five African voyages in as many different ships between 1783 and 1791. Eventually he returned to the African forts full-time. In 1791 he was appointed governor of Cape Coast Castle, the Company's headquarters on the Gold Coast. Once there he continued to trade in slaves. He was probably an investor in the London ship *Governor Dalzel* which made several voyages stopping at the Castle. Indeed, Dalzel continued to trade in slaves as long as he could. After his return to England in 1802 he became the owner of the *Thames* and the *Chalmers*, at least one of which made a slaving voyage every year between 1805 and 1808 even though the trade had been abolished in 1807.

Archibald Dalzel was both an active slave-trader and, having overcome his scruples early on, a strong supporter of the trade. He testified to its good regulation before the Privy Council in 1788, and his *History of Dahomey* (1793) justified enslavement by arguing that it had saved many from human sacrifice and warfare in Africa. He knew the workings of both the Company forts and the slave ships. He had made money running both. Yet unlike Richard Oswald and so many others, he could not, across a whole lifetime of slave-trading, make trading in the lives of others the basis of a lasting fortune. He died, bankrupt once more, in 1811.

Slaving on the coast

During the seventeenth and eighteenth centuries the majority of enslaved Africans embarked from the 3,000 miles of West African coast from the edge of the Sahara desert in the north to the beginning of the Namib desert in the south. European traders understood this coastline as divided up into a series of slave-trading regions which demanded particular sorts of trade goods in exchange for particular sorts of slave labour (figure 8.3). Most metalwares went to Senegambia and the Bight of Biafra, while most New England rum and Brazilian tobacco went to the Bight of Benin (also known as the Slave Coast). Textiles that were in demand in one region could not find a market in others (see chapter 5). In exchange these merchants might try to fulfil Caribbean planters' expressed preferences for, for example, so-called Coromantee men from the Gold Coast whom the owner of one large plantation called 'the best and most faithful of our slaves'.[6]

As table 8.4 shows, most of the enslaved were brought from West Central Africa (Loango and Angola). It was the first region to be pulled into the trade as the Portuguese began shipping Africans to Brazil and the Spanish Americas. It continued to provide large numbers of slaves into the early nineteenth century as the area from which they were drawn was expanded back into its extensive hinterland. The other regions followed a different pattern. At different times they each experienced an initial upswing in numbers of people sold, a plateau of sustained activity and then a decline from the late eighteenth century onwards. In each case there were regionally specific reasons for the initial expansion: reorientations in trade as gold

Table 8.4 African origins of slave cargoes

	Slaves	%	Expansion of trade
Senegambia	497,500	4.5	after 1750
Sierra Leone	411,700	3.7	after 1750
Windward Coast	180,000	1.6	after 1750
Gold Coast	1,035,200	9.4	after 1700
Bight of Benin	2,030,600	18.4	after 1675
Bight of Biafra	1,515,900	13.7	after 1725
West Central Africa	4,880,500	44.2	after 1575
Southeast Africa	484,500	4.4	after 1775
Total	11,035,900		

Source: Adapted from Johannes Postma (2003) *The Atlantic Slave Trade* (University Press of Florida, Gainesville) p. 40.

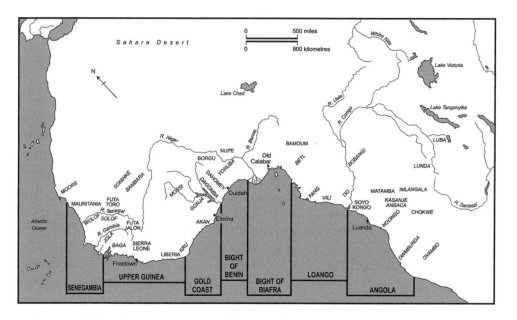

Figure 8.3 The slave-trading regions of West Africa. European traders and plantation-owners understood the Slave Coast as divided into different regions. They had to understand the characteristics of each region to trade effectively there. Each of these regions entered the trade at different times, bringing different sorts of people into the transatlantic slave trade.

reserves were exhausted, the development of African merchant networks, or the emergence of new polities. Regions took time to reorient existing slave-trading routes and markets towards this new demand and to construct the political and economic infrastructures which could supply the large numbers of people required by the Atlantic slave trade. These were matters for African merchants and rulers. The Europeans stayed close to the coast, waited for the enslaved people to be brought to them, and sought as much information as they could on supply and demand.

Most European slave ships traded in only one region on a voyage. Many merchants sent their ships back to the same regions to deal with the same African traders. The European merchants and captains aimed to fill their ships as quickly as possible with slaves bought at the best prices they could get. They could either order larger numbers of slaves in advance, contracting with those in the forts to supply what was needed, or they could engage in the 'ship trade'. This meant moving along the coast filling the ship by buying one or two slaves at a time. Indeed, this was how most slaves were bought, either by the forts or the ships. At each point there was careful bargaining over how many guns, bolts of cloth or barrels of rum might be exchanged for a human being, and careful attention to the additional costs of the necessary customs duties, fees and presents. African merchants and rulers set the terms of trade and ships' captains had always to be aware of their employers' profits. They made continual calculations which saw human lives as items of account. For example, would staying longer on the coast enable them to gather more slaves or would it mean that more of those they already had on board would die? Would it be better to buy some cheaper slaves now with the intention of selling them at a premium to a ship keen to leave, or would it be more profitable to wait for better slaves that would realise higher prices in the Americas?

Europeans could not conduct this trade without relying upon African rulers, merchants and workers for the supply and delivery of slaves. Enslavement was an African matter. As in Europe, warfare between small and belligerent West African states was widespread. Rulers waged wars for reasons of state, but they knew that they could profit from enslaving their prisoners either through using their labour power or by selling it to others. Political elites also sought to dominate other states in order to control slave-trading routes and ports. For example, from the second half of the seventeenth century the Slave Coast was shaken by a series of wars between the kingdoms of Allada, Ouidah, Dahomey and Oyo. At stake, and falling to the Dahomean victors, were regional dominance and the control of European commerce through the ports of Jakin and Ouidah. These wars, like the conflicts between the Akan states of the Gold Coast that accompanied the rise of the Asante, provided thousands of slaves for British ships. However, this was not only about the expansion of the slave trade. Rulers could, if they chose, restrict supply from their regions too.

Operating within this political context were the African merchants. Like their European counterparts they sought to use political influence and economic know-how to operate profitably in a trade with high initial costs and significant expenses. They had to organize porters; gather goods for buying the slaves they would later sell; allow for fees, duties and presents; pay for guards and shackles to prevent escape or attack; and mobilise their contacts to move groups of slaves over long distances to the coast. The relationship between political rulers and merchants was worked out differently in different regions, as each sought to control the trade. For example, the Kingdom of Dahomey's invasion of Hueda and Allada in the 1720s was an attempt to bring inland merchants to heel. In contrast, the Aro merchants who dominated the slave trade to Bonny and Old Calabar on the Bight of Biafra operated in the absence of any strong centralised state in the interior. They used their powerful oracle (Ibinukpabi) at Aro Chukwu to both enslave wrongdoers and to enforce contracts. Finally, the slave trade also depended upon the labour of free Africans. All along the coast it was African canoemen who carried captains and surgeons, and their trade goods, across the dangerous surf to the beaches, and then carried shackled slaves back over the breakers to the ships. These skilled boatmen were either contracted to the ships, and paid in trade goods, or paid by the trip. Without their compliance and labour nothing could be done, and they would strike over pay or if any of their number were taken as slaves. As a result of all this the slaves that were brought to the coast had already had a long journey through many African hands. Most were enslaved further inland through warfare or slave raiding, or as punishments for crimes. Their purchase by merchants and transportation away from their home areas had increased their value by separating them from the social ties that might have limited their uses. Sold several times, they would find themselves carrying merchandise along the slave-trade routes. Some were driven across the Sahara or east to the Red Sea and Indian Ocean. Others were forced down to the Atlantic coast. It was only then that many first saw the Europeans and their ships.

Slave ships varied in size and therefore capacity. Some carried fewer than a hundred enslaved Africans, others took more than five hundred. Over time, however, this diversity decreased, and an optimum type of vessel seems to have emerged by the 1780s. These were between 150 and 250 tons and carried 350 to 450 slaves per voyage. With a roughly estimated price per slave of £15 6s in 1783–1787, a cargo of four hundred slaves would have cost £6120 in trade goods in Africa (something like half a million pounds in today's terms) and could have been sold in the Caribbean for at least twice that. Inside the ship most of the enslaved were arranged side by side on wooden platforms

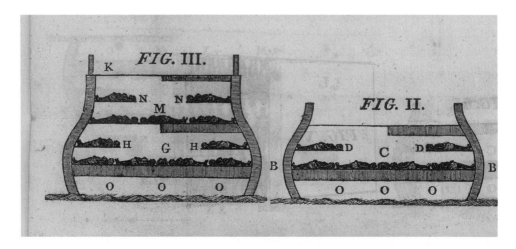

Figure 8.4 Human cargo. This early nineteenth-century abolitionist image attempts to depict the conditions aboard ships engaged in the transatlantic slave trade. The enslaved had to lie chained together side by side on platforms only a few feet high. Such images emphasise the ways in which human beings were treated as commodities, but do little to show the more visceral and emotional horrors of the Middle Passage.

below deck, men separated from women and children by the carpenters' partitions. Others were then packed in to fill the available space. Each had, on average, six to seven square feet to sit or lie in, and rarely more than two or three feet of head space (see figure 8.4 and figure 10.3). The starkness of these numbers and images capture some aspects of the terrible world of the slave ship, particularly its grounding in the logic of mercantile profits. However, it is the location of slavery in the constant labour of trading and oceanic shipping that stands out in a vivid description by the botanist Henry Smeathman. He toured West Africa in the 1770s gathering plant and insect specimens and knew the slave trade well. He visited Bance Island when it was owned by Richard Oswald's company and, like many European men, he made a temporary marriage with a Eurafrican wife whose family's slave-trading connections could assist him in his work. He offered the following in a letter to England:

Alas! What a scene of misery and distress is a full slaved ship in the rains. The clanking of chains, the groans of the sick and the stench of the whole is scarce supportable. When I was on board the *Africa*, Captain Wilding at the Isle de Los, there was Mr Berlin sick; a Captain too, both in the cabin, delirious; two or three slaves thrown over board every day dying of fever, flux, measles, worms all together. All the day the chains rattling or the sound of the armourer riveting some poor devil just arrived in galling heavy irons. The women slaves in one part beating rice in wooden mortars to cleanse it for cooking. Here the Doctor dresses sores, wounds and ulcers, or cramming the men with medicines and another standing over them with a cat to make them swallow. Here they are hoisting casks, boxes and bales; the tackles creaking and the carpenter and coopers hammering and opening. There an armourer rasping and filing and cleaning arms. Here the taylor takes a yard square for his shop board, and there the tonsor has got a fellow by the nose. The mates are hanging goods backward and forward or seeing the slaves eat their rice, which is brought in little tubs, called crews and resemble a firkin cut in two, round one of these six or 8 squat (ten are a mess) and take up with their hands like Monkeys. Sentinels stand at the door of a large barricado, which separates the main deck from the quarterdeck 10 or 12 foot high. The gangway is crowded with black and white sailors – belonging to boats and canoes along side. Here is fire and smoke, chopping, killing, skinning, scalding, boiling, roasting, broiling, frying and scolding. On one side of the quarterdeck a little aft of the main chains, is a gallery for necessary operations, where in the open day indispensable offerings are dropped, while 2 or 3 women are splashing and washing dirty dudds. Here is whetting of knives, wiping of crockery, etc. Upon the round house over which is an awning, sits the Captain delivering out goods, and with his steward booking them in amidst ten or dozen traders, eating, drinking, laughing, squabbling or talking defamation, lies or blasphemy. There is a picture for you, done from life.[7]

Here the slave ship is all the worse for being a stinking, noisy, crowded place of death and pain, where the everyday activities of cooking, eating, defecating and washing must continue to take place under conditions which render the enslaved not so much entries in the merchant's ledger as animal-like bodies that are to be kept secured and alive. They must live to work. They must be force-fed and medicated to stop them dying. All the while more are bought and sold under the round-house awning by the laughing and arguing traders to replace those that have just been thrown to the sharks.

The stench of death followed the slave trade through all its branches. On average 12.2 per cent of slaves died on the voyage from Africa to the Americas. Most died from disease. Yet this figure conceals as much as it reveals. First, there was very great variation between different voyages. A prolonged period on the coast, a voyage extended by adverse weather beyond the six to eight weeks expected for the crossing or an epidemic on board could easily triple or quadruple the death rate. Beyond these unforeseen circumstances the main determinant of death rates was that those embarking from some African regions (notably West Central Africa) died in larger numbers. Circumstances in those parts of Africa rather than shipboard conditions seem to be the cause. Second, this average rate fell over time. The merchants and their employees were finding ways to preserve their profits even before regulations such as the Dolben Act of 1788 set minimum space requirements and bonuses paid by the British government to captains and surgeons for every slave delivered alive. Finally, the Middle Passage was only one part of the slave trade in which Africans died. They were killed in great numbers during the process of enslavement, on the journey to the coast, in the forts and barracoons at the coast, and on board ships gathering cargoes. They also died in the Americas, both after arrival but before leaving the ship and in the process of 'seasoning' where they either survived a new disease environment or succumbed to it. The slave trade was measured out in the terrible currency of life and death. For traders such as Walter Prideaux that meant money; for those he bought it meant much more.

The world of Walter Prideaux

In Devon Walter Prideaux was to be responsible for the cargo. He would take charge of the many differently coloured bales of cloth – woollen serges and perpetuannas from the West Country and cotton baffts, niconees and nehallewares from India; the gunpowder, guns and knives; the barrels of French brandy and other spirits; the tallow, lead and iron; the brass and pewterware from continental Europe; and the beads, Indian corals and looking glasses. These were goods that his employers – the Exeter merchants Daniel Ivy and Henry Arthur, and their partner James Gould of Dorchester – had gathered together to fill the holds of their pride and joy, a ship moored at Dartmouth and named the *Daniel and Henry*. This was a gamble. It was a gamble for these tobacco merchants, used to the Virginia and Maryland trades, to pay the 10 per cent duty on their cargo and enter the Atlantic slave trade.[8] It was also a gamble to employ Walter Prideaux as supercargo. The twenty-three-year-old from Ermington in Devon may have come from a merchant family, at least on his dead mother's side, but he had never taken on an ocean voyage before. The partners were late in their careers, old men who knew the ways of Atlantic trade, so they tried to lessen the risks of the venture. They bought goods they expected would find a ready market: 'Guinea stuffs', 'Guinea brasspans' and 'negro knives'.[9] They also had an experienced captain, Roger Mathew, who had traded slaves before. He was allowed to take a substantial private stake in the voyage (a personal cargo worth nearly £200) and, as Prideaux's uncle, was expected to keep an eye on the young man.

The *Daniel and Henry* was a merchant ship of two hundred tons armed with ten guns. For this voyage the usual crew of twenty was more than doubled. It set sail on 24 February 1700 with forty-four hands, including two gunners. Many were from the parishes in and around Dartmouth. Others, including the free black sailor George Yorke, were from further afield. Also aboard were Walter Prideaux, Roger Mathew and his son William, the surgeon Edward Fenner and his assistant William Hunt. The ship had been specially refitted for the voyage, with chains running the length of the hold, a huge Dutch kettle for boiling up the pottage which would feed the slaves, and over three hundred water casks.

Prideaux was also responsible for filling the ship with slaves. The *Daniel and Henry* arrived on the Guinea coast towards the end of March, and Walter soon found out how difficult trading would be. The first contacts with the canoes that crossed the waves to meet them came to little. Without brokers or interpreters nothing could be achieved. They moved slowly along the shoreline. It was not until they reached the Gold Coast that, on 11 April 1700, they loaded their first slave, 'bought for 3 Perpetuanna, 4 sheets & 2 knives'.[10] Trade was also slow for other reasons. The Dutch governor at Sekondi prevented them trading there. The Royal African Company officers at Cape Coast Castle and Anoumabu were, as ever, willing to go against Company orders and trade, but the competition from other ships was too stiff. Indeed, Prideaux soon discovered that his employers had rated their goods too dear. Everyone else was selling the same wares for 25 per cent less than him. After two months of trading there were only eighty-six slaves on board, so they decided to go to the far eastern end of the Gold Coast to try their luck at Poinyon, Prampram and Ningro. Here they finally found a regular supply, perhaps generated by the wars taking place between the Akan states as they resisted the rise of the Asante kingdom.

Roger Mathew traded on board the ship. Prideaux took the longboat and traded on shore. Both bought slaves in small lots of between one and five persons. Between 14 June and 22 July 1700, Prideaux bought 102 slaves (26 men, 67 women, 3 boys and 6 girls). They were inspected by the surgeon, branded with the letters D and H and sent to the ship. Out of these thirty-nine days he recorded trades on twenty-one days, and there were never more than three consecutive days on which no trading was recorded. He averaged just over three trades a day on those days when he traded, and never recorded more than nine trades in any one day. It took him ninety-three trades to buy the 102 slaves, and only one trade, the first, was for as many as three slaves: a man and two women bought on 14 June for '1 Barrel gunpowder & 7 firkins ditto, 10 × 1lb basins, 4 tapseils'.[11] All the trades were like this. Deals

Table 8.5 Walter Prideaux's trading account for 25 June 1700

			Men	Women	Boys
25 [June]	To:	3 whole & 2 half cases of spirits, 3 × 4lb & 2 × 3lb basins		1	
	To:	5 nickanees & 2A in money	1		
	To:	6 carbines		1	
	To:	2 carbines, 2 × 2lb basins & 1 ackey in money			1
	To:	5 carbines & 1 × 3lb basin		1	
	To:	6 tankards & 24 sheets	1		
	To:	2 bluebaffts, 2 Nehallaware, 3 sall. Powders & 3 × 2lb basins		2	
	To:	5 looking glasses given away			

Source: Nigel Tattersfield (1991) *The Forgotten Trade: Comprising the Log of the Daniel and Henry of 1700 and Accounts of the Slave Trade from the Minor Ports of England, 1698–1725* (Pimlico, London) p. 135. Nickanees (niconees), baffts, sall. (sallampores) and Nehallaware (nehallewares) are all types of cloth. Carbines are small firearms. An *ackey* (A) was a local unit of currency, the equivalent of a sixteenth of an ounce of gold (worth 4s 9d); it was divided into 12 tackeys (from the Akan word *taku*, a seed or pea).

were individually negotiated with particular packages of goods and money being exchanged for one or two slaves (see table 8.5). Occasionally the way was smoothed by a present, including those to the king of Prampram's son.

By 15 August they 'came off with 452 slaves, mostly women & girls, men being very scarce'.[12] Walter Prideaux and Roger Mathew had taken four months to fill the ship. But in order to get the ship 'slaved' they had bought the wrong sort of slaves, and probably paid too much for them. They then had to meet the further expense of preparing for the Middle Passage at the island of São Tomé which provided, at high prices, 'water, wood, corn, plantains, coconuts, [and] yams'.[13] Somewhere along the way it is likely that they made a little profit selling a number of the water casks that had not been registered as trade goods.

Prideaux was now responsible for the ship's human cargo. The *Daniel and Henry* set sail for Jamaica on 6 September 1700 and Prideaux watched as the Africans died. By 28 September he recorded that 'We have now 142 slaves dead & many queasy'. On 6 October he noted that 'We have now thrown overboard 153 slaves'. A month later, by the time they should have reached their destination, things were even worse: 'We have now at this day noon 183 slaves dead and many more very bad. I wish [we] may escape with 200 dead, the doctor not knowing what to do with them'.[14] Walter was not to get his wish. On 16 November they sighted Jamaica, after a voyage of about ten weeks, and the final tally was 206 dead and 246 to be sold. The death rate for enslaved Africans on the *Daniel and Henry* was 45.6 per cent. Nearly half of those taken on board had died of disease and dehydration.

If Roger Mathew and Walter Prideaux had gambled on there being enough rain to replenish the casks that they had not sold, the gamble had not paid off.

The remainder of the cargo found a bad market. Two other slave ships were in port which drove the price for slaves down and the demand for sugar up. Prideaux was unable to secure much of a return cargo. Arriving back in Dartmouth on 23 July 1701, nearly a year and a half after he had left, the final reckoning was an unpromising one for those seeking to profit from slavery. Daniel Ivy had died before their return. Henry Arthur was in serious debt. He was later forced to flee the country to escape his creditors. Of the crew only twenty-four returned. Ten had died, five had run from the ship and three (including Yorke) had been pressed by the Royal Navy in the West Indies. None of the three – James Gould, Roger Mathew or Walter Prideaux – took part in the slave trade again. By 1728 Prideaux was making a living onshore as a maltster. He was, however, still alive, unlike so many of the enslaved Africans he had been responsible for.

The world of Little Ephraim Robin John and Ancona Robin Robin John

There is even less in Walter Prideaux's log book about the Africans that he traded with than there is about those that he bought from them. Yet the slave trade depended upon these African rulers and merchants, and upon the relationships that the Europeans and Americans who controlled the transatlantic shipping of human cargoes developed with them. What was important in these relationships were ways of making the trade reliable, profitable and safe for both the Europeans and the Africans who dealt in slaves, even while both sides collaborated to make the world very unsafe for their victims. Two Africans who were slave-traders but also found themselves among the enslaved were Little Ephraim Robin John and Ancona Robin Robin John of the slave-trading port of Old Calabar in the Bight of Biafra.

The slave trade at Old Calabar expanded rapidly in the second half of the eighteenth century and was largely conducted by merchants from Liverpool and Bristol who traded with the ruling families of three competing trading centres on the Cross River: Old Town, Creek Town, and the latter's offshoot at Duke Town (also known as New Town) (figure 8.5). The Robin Johns were members of the ruling family of Old Town. Its leader, known to the British as Grandy King George (or Ephraim Robin John), was Little Ephraim's

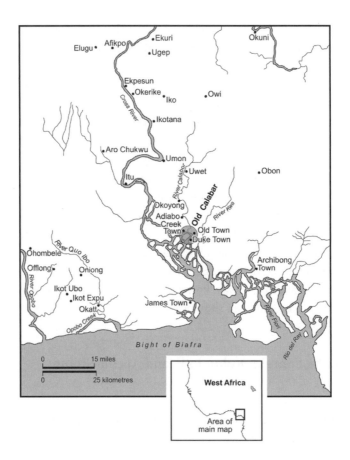

Figure 8.5 Old Calabar, c. 1760. At the heart of the slave-trading region of the Bight of Biafra, at the mouth of the Cross River, the trading centre of Old Calabar was made up of series of settlements, each dominated by competing African slave-trading families. Slaves were brought down the river and sold to the European traders at the coast. The Robin Johns were members of the ruling family of Old Town.

brother and Ancona's uncle. Like their rivals at New Town, the Duke family (an anglicised form of Orok), the Robin Johns were Efik people, traders who controlled the flow of goods up and down the Cross River. They were in a good position to switch to providing slaves, Ibibio and Igbo peoples of the interior bought from Aro merchant networks, to meet the demand from the Atlantic slave trade. As elsewhere, the trade became a regular one and the merchants of Bristol and Liverpool sent their ships, and often the same captains, back time and again to gather slaves from Old Calabar. The African merchants there did not hold large numbers of slaves ready to supply these ships. Instead they were given trade goods on credit by the British captains and contracted to supply a certain number of slaves. They then sent these goods in fleets of canoes up river and returned with enslaved men, women and children.

There was a range of mechanisms to ensure that these contracts were fulfilled. British and African merchants sought to develop personal relationships with their counterparts. They did this through letters exchanged between them in a shared trading language of pidgin English, arranging business, sorting out disagreements and passing on greetings between family members (one Liverpool merchant wrote to Duke Abashy of Old Calabar that 'my Wife is well & sends you her Love'). This was furthered by what Liverpool merchants reported in 1788 as 'the Practice of Merchants and Commanders of Ships trading to Africa, to encourage the Natives to send their Children to England, as it not only conciliates their Friendship and softens their Manners, but adds greatly to the Security of the Trader'.[15] There were about fifty such African children being educated in and around that English port in the late 1780s. Back in Old Calabar there were other measures to guarantee the trade. While African merchants' children were learning English manners, slave-trading captains were compelled to comply with, if not participate in making, the rules of the *ekpe* (or leopard) secret society that regulated trading relations in Old Calabar and its hinterland. This enforced contracts between Africans and could, if European captains broke the rules, also shut them out of the trade. For their part the European captains took pawns – usually members of African merchant families – who were sent on board the slave ships. If the bargain was not fulfilled the pawn would not be released. That was how Little Ephraim Robin John and Ancona Robin Robin John came to be on board the *Duke of York* under Captain James Bivins in the Cross River in June 1767.

Even though they were Africans on a slave ship the Robin Johns would have been confident that they would not be made slaves. They understood themselves as 'free men', quite different from those being brought on board in shackles and confined below. They relied upon the British ship's captain and crew recognising that distinction (and their common bonds as traders) as being necessary for the trade to continue peacefully. Indeed, even if the bargains were not fulfilled it was unlikely that they would be taken away. British captains were wary of enslaving pawns and would seek to exchange them for slaves with ships not yet ready to depart. In June 1767 there were seven British ships anchored in the river. Little Ephraim and Ancona Robin must have felt safe enough. However, this did not take account of the shifting politics of Old Calabar. The long-standing competition and conflict between the Old Town and the New Town over who was to control the slave trade broke out into horrific violence. As the Robin Johns watched from the *Duke of York*, the war canoes of the New Town led by Eyo Nsa attacked the Old Town traders. Worse still, all but two of the British ships opened fire in support of the attackers and sent their longboats out to join the African canoemen in the slaughter. Four hundred men from the Old Town were killed on the river. Their blood flowed down to the ocean.

The bonds of trust had been broken between the British and the Old Town, and forged in blood and fire with the New. The Robin Johns were no longer safe. Fortunately for them Captain Bivins saw more benefit in retaining his Old Town pawns and captives as slaves rather than in handing them over, as he had promised, to Eyo Nsa to be executed. They were taken across the Atlantic to the island of Dominica and sold along with the rest of the cargo.

The slavers had become the enslaved. Yet the Robin Johns knew that there were Africans taken into slavery who had been returned to Africa when it was in the interests of enough influential people to recognise, as one merchant had put it in a similar case, that 'they are ... Freemen & No Slaves'. Taken first to Virginia and then, in 1773, to Bristol, the Robin Johns were able to contact Thomas Jones, an important slave-trader in the city. He already knew of their plight. He had received a letter from Grandy King George as early as 1769 stating that 'Wee son [Wilson?][,] biven & Lewis ben cary a Way his[,] 1 name Lettle Ephraim & Ancone and am Tom & Archibong tom Robin & young Robin Robin Jno & Archibong Robin Jno son & my Boys he name abash & I hop all you will Lete Me have them again.'[16] Jones, with trading relations at Old Calabar in mind, was keen to let him have them. The Robin Johns were also able to pursue their claim in the courts with the help of those opposed to the slave trade. In front of Lord Justice Mansfield, who the year before had judged that slaves could not be removed from England against their will (see chapter 10), they argued that, according to both Efik and English law, 'when we first went on board Captain Bevan's [sic] ship, we were free people, and no ways subject to the people of New Town; nor had they any right or power over us; nor were we conquered in fight or battle, or taken prisoner by them; nor had they any right to sell us ... we had not done anything to forfeit our liberty'.[17] They played on the African and the European need to claim the legitimacy of enslavement by warfare or judicial process. They also played on the requirement that some Africans, those working as traders, needed to be free (and not subject to enslavement) if the trade was to be a profitable one on both sides. The Robin Johns were eventually able to win their freedom and return to Africa. The price was the continued enslavement of others.

Resisting the slave trade

As the Robin Johns knew, at the heart of the system of slavery was violence. Africans were enslaved unwillingly and violently. Their unwillingness meant they had to be chained, shackled and confined. Resistance to the slave trade can, therefore, be charted at every step from defence against the slave raids of the African interior to revolts aboard the European merchant vessels of the Middle Passage. Such resistance then continued in the Americas and Europe, both on the plantations and through the work of African activists in the abolition movement (see chapters 9 and 10). Resistance to slavery could take individual or collective forms. It could lead to the freedom of the enslaved, their confinement or their death. Its successes and failures have to be carefully considered, since the working of the slave trade meant that resistance could lead to some people or peoples escaping slavery only at the expense of consigning others to it.

African societies reorganised themselves in various ways to save themselves from attack by slave-raiding enemies. They moved out of dangerous areas and they defended themselves as best they could. In Benin people moved into lands that were regularly flooded and built villages on stilts over shallow lakes. Around Lake Chad defence against slave raids by armoured horsemen with muskets involved a retreat into other flooded lands or into the mountains where caverns and caves on cliffs or steep slopes provided shelter. The Balanta of Guinea-Bissau moved into the marshy, mangrove-covered coastal strip, the *terrafe*. Those remaining on the savannah constructed defences of earth and stone, often planted with thorny shrubs or venomous plants, or fortified cities with high mud-brick walls. Distinctive house types were developed. The Musgu of the Logone river began to build dome-shaped structures of clay, dung and grass that would not burn, were arranged in closed circles with few entrances, and had look-out positions atop structures that were as much as nine metres high. Others built homes with single low doors that could be entered only by crawling single file, or tightly packed, labyrinthine fortified villages. In Igboland, threatened by the Abam warriors who gathered slaves for the Aro merchants, villagers used Ikoro martial music to warn of impending raids. They also struck back. Young men were initiated into the cult of the war god Ike-Oha, which would protect them from bullet wounds, and the villagers took up weapons.

The Aro nickname for Ikem Elu village was Ndi Olu Mbe: 'those who throw stones at us'.[18] Attack could be the best form of defence. There were slave revolts in African slave-holding societies, and wars were fought to resist predatory polities as well as to provide captives for the slave trade.

Along with transformations in settlement went shifts in social structures. In Senegambia, for example, two different paths were taken. In one, a differentiated social structure developed through which aristocratic families preserved themselves from slavery by using the lower castes as a protective shield. The other was a turn to Islam, within which safe Muslim villages were set up in which all were protected. These had names that translated as 'the village of free people', 'here where no one can reach them anymore' and 'here where we speak of peace'.[19] More generally, protection can be seen to have come from a variety of different social and political transformations. In some cases the formation of strong, warlike, centralised states operated as a protection for their subjects against enslavement by others. Again, the examples are Benin, Dahomey, Oyo and Asante (see pp. 210–11). Elsewhere, decentralised, kin-based societies were protected by collective defence. In each case, however, safety for some was at the cost of the enslavement of others. The military successes of West African polities led to slavery for their defeated enemies. The decentralised societies of Guinea-Bissau, such as the Balanta, also engaged in small-scale slave raiding of neighbouring peoples. They did so when they needed to trade for the iron required to make the weapons with which they protected themselves from enslavement. The same was true for individuals. The use of pawns (as in the case of the Robin Johns) suggests that there were different categories of Africans, some who were more readily, and legally, enslaved than others. As a result, some enslaved Africans might be redeemed by their families or friends. They were taken back out of slavery and returned home from the slave ship. The price, however, was usually the delivery of two others to take their place. In a situation of high demand from the transatlantic slave trade and in a context where those enslaved were thought of as aliens, enemies and criminals, and not as fellow Africans (see chapter 10), this was a common outcome. Resistance to slavery or freedom from slavery for some led to the enslavement of others.

Most attention has been paid to the ways in which enslaved Africans aboard the ships of the transatlantic slave trade resisted their enslavement. Many tried to kill themselves rather than be kept captive or, as they feared, be eaten by these pale, bearded strangers. The nets strung around the ships sought to prevent the enslaved throwing themselves from the decks. Force-feeding also sought to keep alive those who would have starved themselves to death. However, many succeeded in their attempts, depriving the slavers of their profits; perhaps they hoped to return home via the spirit world and its oceanic conduit. Others took what chances they had to rise up against their captors. Seizing guns, knives and other weapons, slaves attempted to free themselves and kill those who held them. Slave revolts relied upon violence and terror and they were suppressed with extreme force. Many died on both sides fighting for the control of these ships.

Such revolts were a real and constant threat to the slave traders, as were violent attacks on ships and ships' boats organised from the land. It is estimated that one in ten of all voyages may have experienced some kind of violent insurrection. These were most likely to happen when the ships were still off the African coast (although this may have been because this was where ships spent a longer period of time rather than its increasing the hope of success). They were also most likely to happen on ships carrying a higher proportion of women, perhaps because of their role in organising the revolts rather than carrying them out, and on ships from certain parts of the coast – Senegambia, Sierra Leone and the Windward Coast, rather than ports further east. This was perhaps because the rapid expansion of demand in those regions had meant the gathering of slaves from politically unstable areas closer to the coast and from groups who previously would have thought themselves secure from enslavement. These insurrections, like the other forms of resistance, were African responses to the slave trade that must be understood, where possible, in the terms of the enslaved themselves.

The world of a slave in revolt, 1789

Despite their frequency it is, however, very difficult to investigate particular examples of these insurrections in any detail, especially in the sort of biographical detail through which this book is organised. The documentation of these events comes from European or American sources and little can be known about their prior planning, their organisation or even their after-effects. For example, what of the slave who, in the name of liberty, and in 1789 – that year of revolution – killed the captain of the slave ship *Felicity* during an insurrection? The ship was a small one. It had sailed from Salem, Massachusetts, to Sierra Leone, probably loaded with rum. There it had taken on board thirty-five slaves, leaving from Cape Mount on 13 March bound for Cayenne on the north coast of South America. After nearly two weeks at sea the slaves had risen up. It is unknown how far this was planned and whether they thought that this might be their last chance, or if they simply took an opportunity that had presented itself to them: the inattentiveness of a crew member, a loose shackle or perhaps a weapon come fortuitously to hand? Initially circumstances were in their favour, and they took advantage of them. The captain's son, William Fairfield, reported in a letter to his mother that his father (also William) and all but two hands – the helmsman and himself – were forward. As he put it 'three of the Slaves took Possession of the Caben, and two upon the quarter Deck, them in the Caben took Possession of the fier Arms, and them on the quarter Deck with the Ax and Cutlash and other Weapons, them in the Caben, handed up Pistels to them on the quarter Deck'.[20] A small group of Africans had succeeded in taking the deck from which the ship was commanded and the cabin where the weapons were kept. They seemed to be working together as a group. They armed themselves with the ship's weapons and 'One of them fired and killed my honoured Sir.'[21] Thus the son reported to his mother the death of the captain, his father, at the hands of those they had held captive. It was, perhaps, unsurprising that an enslaved African might handle a firearm to such deadly effect. The slave-traders had supplied the African market with hundreds of thousands of such weapons. European guns had become a very familiar part of African warfare and African life by the late eighteenth century. It might also be asked whether this slave in revolt had picked out the captain. Was he seeking to strike at the heart of the ship's authority? Perhaps anyone could have been killed. Others had taken up axes or cutlasses to do the job. When it came to it, face to face on a small slave ship, the liberty of the enslaved could only be secured through terror and violence.

The killing continued as the crew fought back up the ship. Their lives depended upon it too. The captain's son reported that 'We got on the quarter Deck and killed two of them. One that was in the Caben was Comeing out at the Caben Windows in order to get on Deck, and we Discovered him and Knock'd him overbord, two being in the Cabin we confined the Caben Doors, so that they should not kill us.' The armed insurrectionaries were prevented from getting to the open decks where the crew's advantage was less decisive. The revolt also seems to have been prevented from spreading to the rest of the slaves on board. Perhaps not enough of them had been willing or able to join the uprising. We cannot know what bound together those who did fight: were they from the same region, did they speak the same language or did they share some other bond? Perhaps it was simply that those below could not get out of the hold and on to the deck where they might have fought for their lives. The crew were, therefore, able to quash the revolt. There was what must have been a tense stand-off between the crew on deck and the Africans locked in the cabin, but 'their being a Doctor on bord Passenger that Could speak the tongue he sent one of the boys down and Brought up some of the fier arms and Powder And then we Cal'd them up and one Came up and he Cal'd the other and he Came up. We put them in Irons and Chained them.'[22] The revolt was over, having lasted over three hours. The captain was buried 'as decent as he could be at Sea', and the ship continued on its way. The cargo was sold in Surinam. It is likely that the enslaved African who had fought back and turned the slavers' weapons against them had been killed in the revolt.

This violent insurrection ended like so many others: in death and slavery. The average number of enslaved Africans killed in these shipboard insurrections was twenty-five, which might be anything between 5 and 25 per cent of the cargo; the rest of those who survived were sold in the Americas. That seems to have been the case on the *Felicity* too. Taken individually these revolts did little to free those who took part in them. Taken together, however, it can be said that they reduced the extent of slavery. The cost of all the measures necessary against violent insurrection – the wooden barricades in the holds, the chains, nets and weapons, and the wages of the extra crew – significantly raised the cost of a carrying a resistant human cargo. Without these forms of resistance the merchants' investment capital used for preventative measures could have been spent on buying more slaves. It has been estimated that, had this been possible, the number of slaves transported across the Atlantic could have been 9 per cent higher. This amounts to around a million Africans prevented from being shipped to the Americas during the course of the Atlantic slave trade by the costs of resistance. If Africans such as the one who grabbed a gun and shot Captain William Fairfield did not win their own liberty, or that of the men, women and children who had been loaded on the slave ships with them, they did something to contribute to the cause of freedom.

This chapter has attempted to set out both the overall scale of the transatlantic slave trade and to recover some of its human scale by recounting the lives of individuals involved in both buying slaves and being bought as slaves. In doing so the aim has been to describe the human cost, the dynamics of the trade, the social relationships involved and the choices made by individuals. The millions of men, women and children who were transported against their will from Africa to the Americas were crucial to most of the forms of global connection described in this book: the English slave trade began under Elizabeth I (with her blessing and investment) and ended with an abolition movement that spanned the continents; enslaved Africans laboured as part of the settlement of the Americas, and they changed the New World in the process; they were bought with goods from India, and traded and carried by the merchants and ships of the Atlantic world. Even pirates found themselves confronted with the choice of whether these Africans were to be sold as plunder or freed as shipmates. The transatlantic slave trade had a huge transformative impact at a global scale, and the numbers involved bear witness to that. Over eleven million enslaved people left Africa on slave ships between 1519 and 1867.

There are, therefore, millions of stories that should be told. The historical record is silent on the vast majority of enslaved Africans transported. They appear only as numbers rather than names. The lives of European slave-traders are more easily traced. They left the records by which the extent of the trade and their involvement in it can be known. The two lives told here – of Archibald Dalzel and Walter Prideaux – serve to outline the sorts of decisions that slave-traders made, and the sorts of circumstances that they took into consideration in organising their part of the trade. In that sense they stand for the many others who participated in the trade as investors, merchants, captains and crew. It fits them into the structures of the trade in human beings. Their concerns were, for the most part, primarily economic. They were trying to profitably co-ordinate supply and demand. Where there were moral concerns they were soon overcome. Slaves became items of account. The deaths of some had to be discounted against the profits of selling others. Making money could not, however, be guaranteed, as both Dalzel and Prideaux found out.

These European merchants also knew that the trade depended upon the African rulers, merchants and labourers who supplied them with enslaved people at the coast. Those who arrived on the ships knew relatively little of the complex politics and economics of the African slave trade as it was reoriented to serve the transatlantic market. At the coast the necessary mercantile relationships had to be carefully worked out between the parties involved. They involved the payment of duties and preferential prices, and the giving of presents, by the slave-ship captains. Over time they also developed more routine forms. The lives of Little Ephraim Robin John and Ancona Robin Robin John, again told primarily through European voices and from European sources, show how this might be established and how it could break down. These two Africans were certainly among the very few of the enslaved who were freed and returned to Africa, yet their story illuminates both the African involvement in the slave trade and the ways in which enslavement also depended on an idea of freedom. Finally, if the Robin Johns sought their freedom through the courts, and through mobilising their contacts with both slave-traders and anti-slavery activists, other Africans were constantly resisting slavery and seeking freedom through a variety of defensive and offensive means. We cannot know the names and actions of any more than a minority of those who resisted, even where that resistance took such dramatic forms as the insurrection on the *Felicity*. But cumulatively, across their many millions of acts of resistance, they limited the effects of the slave trade. They made sure that merchants knew the difference that transporting a human cargo meant. For those who survived the voyage to the Americas, resistance continued, as did the pain of slavery that prompted it.

Further reading

There are good overall introductions provided by Herbert S. Klein (1999) *The Atlantic Slave Trade* (Cambridge University Press, Cambridge) and Johannes Postma (2003) *The Atlantic Slave Trade* (University Press of Florida, Gainesville). The numbers involved are summarised in David Eltis (2001) 'The volume and structure of the slave trade: a reassessment', *William and Mary Quarterly*, 58:1 pp. 17–46. The forms of slavery, and slave-trading, in Africa and the Islamic world are debated in Paul E. Lovejoy (2000) *Transformations in Slavery: A History of Slavery in Africa*, 2nd edn (Cambridge University Press, Cambridge) and John Thornton (1998) *Africa and Africans in the Making of the Atlantic World, 1500–1800* (Cambridge University Press, Cambridge), chap. 3, 'Slavery and the African social structure', and chap. 4, 'The process of enslavement and the slave trade'. On the process of slave-trading by fort and ship, see William St Clair (2006) *The Grand Slave Emporium: Cape Coast Castle and the British Slave Trade* (Profile Books, London) and Stephen D. Behrendt (2001) 'Markets, transaction cycles, and profits: merchant decision making in the British slave trade', *William and Mary Quarterly*, 58:1 pp. 171–204. For questions of mortality, see Herbert S. Klein, Stanley L. Engerman, Robin Haines and Ralph Shlomowitz (2001) 'Transoceanic mortality: the slave trade in comparative perspective', *William and Mary Quarterly*, 58:1 pp. 93–117. On slave resistance, see Sylviane A. Diouf (ed.) (2003) *Fighting the Slave Trade: West African Strategies* (Ohio University Press, Athens) and David Richardson (2001) 'Shipboard revolts, African authority, and the Atlantic slave trade', *William and Mary Quarterly*, 58:1 pp. 69–92. On Archibald Dalzel, see I. A. Akinjogbin (1966) 'Archibald Dalzel: slave trader and historian of Dahomey', *Journal of African History*, 7:1 pp. 67–78, James A. Rawley (1984) 'Further light on Archibald Dalzel', *International Journal of African Historical Studies*, 17:2 pp. 317–323 and his entry in the *Oxford Dictionary of National Biography*. On Walter Prideaux, see Nigel Tattersfield (1991) *The Forgotten Trade: Comprising the Log of the Daniel and Henry of 1700 and Accounts of the Slave Trade from the Minor Ports of England, 1698–1725* (Pimlico, London). For the Robin Johns, see Randy L. Sparks (2002) 'Two princes of Calabar: an Atlantic odyssey from slavery to freedom', *William and Mary Quarterly*, 59:3 pp. 555–584 and Randy L. Sparks (2004) *The Two Princes of Calabar: An Eighteenth-Century Atlantic Odyssey* (Harvard University Press, Cambridge, Mass.). For the insurrection on the *Felicity*, see Elizabeth Donnan (ed.) (1932) *Documents Illustrative of the Slave Trade to America*, vol. III, *New England and the Middle Colonies* (Carnegie Institution, Washington) pp. 82–83.

Notes

1 Quoted in P. E. H. Hair and Robin Law (1998) 'The English in Western Africa to 1700', in Nicholas Canny (ed.) *The Oxford History of the British Empire*, vol. I, *The Origins of Empire* (Oxford University Press, Oxford) p. 251.
2 It was at this time that Richard Oswald and his associates began to run their Bance Island slave factory on the same basis, but as a private enterprise.
3 Quoted in I. A. Akinjogbin (1966) 'Archibald Dalzel: slave trader and historian of Dahomey', *Journal of African History*, 7:1 p. 68.
4 Quoted ibid., p. 69.
5 Quoted ibid., p. 70.
6 Quoted in J. A. Rawley (1981) *The Transatlantic Slave Trade* (Norton, New York) p. 272.
7 Quoted in Starr Douglas, 'Natural History, Improvement and Colonisation: Henry Smeathman and Sierra Leone in the Late Eighteenth Century', unpublished PhD thesis, University of London, 2004 pp. 97–98.
8 The cargo was valued at £2,251 19s 4d, the equivalent of about a quarter of a million pounds today.
9 Nigel Tattersfield (1991) *The Forgotten Trade: Comprising the Log of the Daniel and Henry of 1700 and Accounts of the Slave Trade from the Minor Ports of England, 1698–1725* (Pimlico, London) pp. 41–43.
10 Ibid., p. 100.
11 Ibid., p. 134.
12 Ibid., p. 115.
13 Ibid., p. 119.
14 Ibid., pp. 166, 168 and 173.
15 Quotations from Paul E. Lovejoy and David Richardson (2001) 'Letters of the Old Calabar slave trade, 1760–1789', in Vincent Carretta and Philip Gould

(eds.) *Genius in Bondage: Literature of the Early Black Atlantic* (University Press of Kentucky, Lexington) pp. 99 and 95.

16 Quotations from ibid., pp. 99 and 103.

17 Quoted in Randy L. Sparks (2004) *The Two Princes of Calabar: An Eighteenth-Century Atlantic Odyssey* (Harvard University Press, Cambridge, Mass.) p. 101.

18 See John N. Oriji (2003) 'Igboland, slavery, and the drums of war and heroism', in Sylviane A. Diouf (ed.) *Fighting the Slave Trade: West African Strategies* (Ohio University Press, Athens) p. 128.

19 See Adama Guèye (2003) 'The impact of the slave trade on Cayor and Baol: mutations in habitat and land occupancy', in Diouf, *Fighting the Slave Trade*, p. 55.

20 Elizabeth Donnan (ed.) (1932) *Documents Illustrative of the Slave Trade to America*, vol. III, *New England and the Middle Colonies* (Carnegie Institution, Washington) p. 83.

21 Ibid., p. 83.

22 Ibid.

9 | Sugar islands: plantation slavery in the Caribbean

Slavery transformed the Americas. The enslaved created a new world. The combination of African labour, American land and European capital established new plantation landscapes where cash crops – tobacco, rice, sugar, indigo, ginger and coffee – were grown for export to Europe. The slave ships took their cargoes where there was the demand for what they had to sell: over 2.1 million people to Brazil before 1800, over 3.65 million to the Caribbean Islands and over 287,000 to mainland North America. There they were put to work. In doing so they underpinned the creation of different economies and societies based on slavery across the Americas. Slaves could be found in the port cities of New England, and on the farms of Rhode Island. Further south, tobacco increasingly dominated the mainland colonies of Virginia and Maryland (see chapter 3), generating a class of wealthy planters that included Thomas Jefferson and George Washington. Southwards, huge rice plantations were established from the 1690s on the low-lying coasts and islands of the Carolinas, creating a new landscape of levees and flooded fields, and generating the flamboyant wealth of the city of Charleston. But furthest south, and the scene of the earliest and most dramatic transformations of all, were the sugar islands of the Caribbean that had either been taken from the Spanish empire by the northern Europeans, or which had been beyond Spanish control in an arc of small islands facing out to the Atlantic: Barbados, Jamaica, St Kitts, Nevis and others in British hands; Saint Domingue, Martinique and Guadeloupe for the French; and St Eustatius and Curaçao for the Dutch (figure 9.1). These islands were given over to growing sugarcane, and this 'sugar revolution' changed everything from their natural environments to how their societies worked.

Barbados was the first island to experience this transformation. First claimed by the English in 1625, Barbados's initial exports were tobacco, ginger and cotton, grown on small farms using the labour of indentured servants from England, Wales, Scotland and Ireland. These were predominantly poor young men who exchanged, on average, six years of their labour for the price of the passage to the Americas and the chance for a new life. Their hope was that at the end of their contract they would be able to set up for themselves on their own land and become independent farmers.

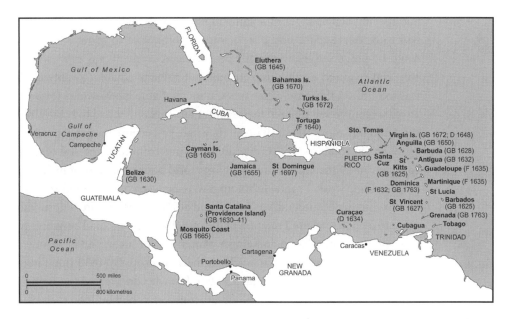

Figure 9.1 European possessions in the Caribbean, c. 1700. From the early seventeenth century onwards the challenge posed by the Dutch, British and French to the Spanish empire in the Americas produced a complex and changing geography of imperial power in the Caribbean. Coastal settlements and islands large and small were first taken from Spain by force, and later fought over by these nascent imperial powers, some changing hands several times.

However, this ambition became a remote one in the 1640s when Barbadian planters began to take advantage of the conflicts between the Dutch and Portuguese in the sugar-growing areas of Brazil which had previously dominated the European market. Using capital from London merchants, and perhaps from the Dutch, planters invested in land, labour and the necessary processing technology – mills and boiling houses – and began to produce sugar. The huge potential profits produced a great demand for land on this tiny island. Land that had not already been cleared of the forests that the settlers had found there in the 1620s was soon stripped bare. The trees were replaced wherever possible with fields of sugarcane. By 1667 80 per cent of the island was planted in sugar, and lumber for building had to be imported from New England (see chapter 5). It was more profitable to grow sugar and import wood than to leave the trees standing. The same went for food, clothing and tools. Slaves lived on a diet of imported salt fish, wore cottons from India and worked with metal tools from Europe. The demand for land also forced the prices up. Land that had sold for ten shillings an acre in 1640 had reached £5 an acre in 1646, a tenfold increase. Sugar also had specific demands when it came to forming plantations. The ripe cane had to be harvested quickly, so it was not profitable to grow more than could be processed. However, the processing equipment was expensive to run, and required a minimum throughput to be profitable. Twenty acres was too little, a thousand acres was too much. Large land-owners found it advantageous to sell some of their land; small ones either had to borrow the capital to buy more land, sell up all they had, or become marginal producers of less profitable crops. Indentured servants coming to the end of their contracts had little chance of buying land, and poor prospects of making a small holding work. Profitable holdings were between one hundred and two hundred acres of cane land, with a mill and boiling house on site. Those who came to own them were a mixture of the initial settlers who had been able to turn their cotton, tobacco and ginger plantations to sugar, and newcomers attracted by the profits to be made in the new crop. By 1650 these men formed a planter elite of around 150 families who dominated the island's economy and its politics from the Great Houses they had built on their new sugar estates.

This white planter elite governed an increasingly polarised society as the small holders who could not join them sold up, and the land was consolidated into plantations. At the other end of the social scale the work on those plantations was increasingly performed by enslaved Africans bought from the slave-traders. These slaves replaced the white indentured servants. In 1640 there were about thirty servants to every slave. By 1680 there were about seventeen slaves to every servant. With less to attract indentured servants to Barbados and more to keep them at home, and an increasing supply of enslaved Africans, it was a matter of responding to the changing price of labour in the context of a continuing high demand for sugar. Due to high slave mortality, planters expected to get about the same amount of work from a black slave before death as from a white servant working for six years. In the 1640s servants were cheaper and in more plentiful supply. By the 1660s slaves were cheaper and more readily available. The island's population changed accordingly, and Barbados became a slave society. In 1645 there were 5,580 slaves on Barbados; by 1698 there were 42,000. They made up over two-thirds of the island's population, a proportion that had increased to 80 per cent by 1710.

This new labour force was controlled by violence enforced by the overseer's whip, the island militia and a slave code which permitted brutal punishment for runaways and rebels (and compensation for the owners whose goods were damaged or destroyed when they were mutilated or executed in public spectacles designed to make an example to others). From 1661 the legal code also drove a wedge based on race – a division of black and white, regardless of economic circumstances – through this slave society. By giving white servants legal protections from their masters that were not afforded to slaves, this code offered the privileges of whiteness to even the poorest former indentured servants. This aimed to separate them from the black majority and to remove the basis for the rebellions and conspiracies of the 1680s and 1690s in which white servants and black slaves had joined together against the rich planters who worked them hard side by side in the cane fields.

Barbados was transformed by sugar. In search of the profits from sweetness the island was deforested, divided into plantations, turned over to one cash crop for export and ruled by a small white elite who governed a huge black slave majority through violence and racism. From Barbados the sugar revolution spread to the other Caribbean islands. Jamaica passed through the same transformation from 1680 onwards. These sugar islands were one slave society among many in the Americas, and enslaved Africans lived and worked within quite different social and economic contexts in different places. By the end of the eighteenth century the tobacco areas of the Chesapeake Bay had a resident planter class, relatively small plantation units and a self-reproducing slave community which made up only 40 per cent of the population. In the Carolinas big plantations were the norm, as were absentee planters, and three in every five people were black. In contrast, with their large sugar plantations and absentee planters, there were five black inhabitants to every white on Barbados and ten to one on Jamaica. It is the implications of the dramatically polarised societies of these islands with their new relationships between land and labour that this chapter explores. It does so by considering the lives of those who profited from slavery, those who did the work, those who mediated between the rich plantation-owners and the slaves and those who rebelled in various ways against the tyranny of slave labour. The context for all this is the crucial new institution of American slavery and its geography: the plantation.

Land and labour: plantation life

Taking its name from the first colonial ventures in Ireland (see chapter 2), the plantation became a new way of organising land and labour. A sugar plantation was part farm, part factory, part prison camp and part country house estate. Its aim was to achieve a profitable exploitation of labour in the growing and processing of sugarcane. The cane (*Saccharum officinarum*) had worked its way westwards over the centuries from the Pacific, through India and Persia and into the Mediterranean, where it was grown extensively in Sicily and North Africa. The Spanish then took it with them as part of their colonisation of the Canary Islands, and it travelled from there with Columbus to the Caribbean on his second voyage in 1493. Once in the Americas, it was the Portuguese that entered most fully into sugar production, developing large areas of cane in Brazil. Yet it was the English who devised the fully fledged plantation system based on slave labour and export markets. The Portuguese had operated what amounted to a feudal system. The grand land-owners presided over large areas of countryside and leased small parcels of their land (ten to fifteen acres) to tenants who grew the cane with small squads of ten or twenty slaves. These *lavradores de cana* then brought the cane to be processed at the land-owner's mill, receiving back for their trouble considerably less than half the sugar produced. The land-owner was known as the *senhor de engenho*: the lord of the mill, a kind of sugar baron. The English plantation, drawing on and developing a tradition of capitalist agriculture, integrated land and mill ownership with the direct control of labour power. All the factors of production were combined in a single unit. The English islands eventually became covered with plantations made up of one hundred to two hundred acres of cane land, a sea of light green fronds organised around a mill and boiling house, with about one black slave per acre in cane, and a staff of white overseers, attorneys and bookkeepers.

This was a matter of making sugar pay. The plantation was a factory on a farm. Sugarcane had to be planted in regularly spaced holes or trenches dug six to eight inches deep. The new plants had to be protected from weeds until they were strong. They then took eighteen months to ripen. When they were cut, by workers with long and sharp curved knives (known as bills) bending low to hack through the thick woody stalks close to the base, the juice had to be extracted as quickly as possible to prevent its sugar content from reducing (figure 9.2). This was done by crushing the canes in a three-roller mill driven by animal, wind or water power (figures 9.3 and 9.4). The sweet raw liquid then had to be processed immediately. It flowed down a gutter into metal receptacles where it was reduced by boiling over fires of burning cane trash (figure 9.5). After passing through seven progressively smaller boilers – from the 300-gallon 'great copper' to the 75-gallon 'tache' – the moment was reached where the sugar was 'struck', crystallising into a semi-solid mass. This was packed into 56-pound earthenware pots and left to drain for several weeks. What drained out was the liquid molasses, which was either sold itself or distilled into rum. What remained was a basic brown

Figure 9.2 Cutting sugarcane. This orderly agricultural scene shows men and women on Antigua harvesting sugarcane with their sharp bills under the orders and gaze of a white overseer. Other enslaved workers, including children, are bundling the cane and loading a horse-drawn cart to feed the windmill visible in the distance.

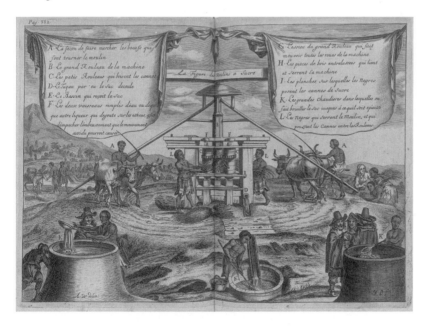

Figure 9.3 Milling sugarcane. This late seventeenth-century French engraving shows the whole sugar-making process. At its heart is the three-roller mill which, driven by four bullocks, crushes the cane that is fed into it. The calm of the scene underplays the danger and relentlessness of the work involved, and the compulsion used to drive it forward.

Figure 9.4 Milling sugarcane by windmill. This Antiguan scene shows the harnessing of wind to mill the sugarcane brought by a row of carts labouring up the hill. The highpoints of the Leeward and Windward Islands were used to capture the strong prevailing winds and turn them to productive use. The mill gear would turn, braced on its extended wheel, as the wind shifted direction.

Figure 9.5 A plantation boiling house. Here a series of boiling vats and basins are used to turn the cane juice into sugar crystals. This orderly image shows the process but does little to represent the hellish conditions created by the constantly burning fires of cane trash, the immense boiling vats of cane juice, and the need to strike each vat at just the right time to create a saleable product.

muscovado sugar, which was usually sent to Europe to be refined into the more highly prized white sugars.

The key to productivity and profit was running the mill and boiling house efficiently. This meant running them as constantly as possible for the harvest period: keeping the rollers moving, the cane juice flowing and the fires beneath the coppers alight. The factory needed to be continually turning stalks into sugar. This meant that the cane lands were divided into 'pieces', which were planted at different times so that they would ripen in succession in the period from January to May when rain was least likely to interrupt the harvest. It meant that all hands were needed at harvest to keep the cane moving quickly from the field to the mill. It meant that the overseers often had to sleep at the mill in the harvest months to ensure that there was no let-up, switching between wind, water and oxen power as the conditions and damage to the milling equipment dictated. It meant that there was no rest in the inferno of the boiling house, lit by the fires below the coppers and constantly filled with smoke and the sickly smell of boiling sugar. Producing sugar was the hardest work, and the most dangerous. Limbs were cut by bills, arms were trapped in mills and hands burned in boiling liquid. The constant labour in the fields wrung out and burned up the slaves' bodies just as the mill and the boiling house squeezed and consumed the cane. One Barbadian slave was reported to have said that 'the devil was in the Englishman that he makes everything work; he makes the negro work, he makes the horse work, the ass work, the wood work, the water work and the wind work'.[1] Like the ship of the line, and with a comparable labour force and level of technology (see chapter 6), the plantation was one of the most complex machines of its age.

Like the ship, the plantation's key moving parts were human bodies, and the organisation of their work was enforced by violence and discipline. The crack of the overseer's whip echoed over the cane fields. Runaways were hunted down and brutally punished. The field slaves were organised into gangs to undertake simple repetitive tasks familiar to those who had known West African hoe-agriculture – holing, planting, hoeing, weeding, cutting, tying, hauling – from sun-up to sun-down six days a week, and three nights as well during harvest. Other slaves had better work, although they would still find themselves in the fields at harvest time or as punishment. Men worked as sugar boilers, carpenters, coopers, stonemasons, fishermen, boatmen, blacksmiths and carters. They also worked as drivers, organising the work of other slaves. Some women worked as laundresses, seamstresses or house servants. However, the larger range of artisanal work that men might do, and their ability to keep it as men's work, meant that most of the field slaves were women. On William Beckford's twelve Jamaican properties in 1780, of the 802 enslaved men 291 (36 per cent) were field workers compared to 444 (57 per cent) of the 778 women. As a result, women bore the burden of the worst and hardest work on the plantation.

Constant work, malnutrition and disease took a heavy toll on all the enslaved. Ill health and physical disability were widespread. Fertility rates were very low, either due to ill health or to women's own preventative measures. In 1780 there were nineteen live births among the 274 women of child-bearing age on William Beckford's Clarendon estate. In the same year thirty-four slaves died. The enslaved died when they arrived – it was estimated that a third of Africans did not survive the first three years – and they died from overwork and poor treatment. Between 2 and 4 per cent of the entire slave population needed to be replaced each year. Until the late eighteenth century the Jamaican plantation-owners judged it more efficient to buy new Africans who, after a period of seasoning, would be ready to work, rather than to support pregnant and nursing mothers and children. Women worked in the fields right up until they gave birth, and returned to the gangs shortly after. Families could be broken up on the decision of the owner or overseer to sell a slave, or send him or her to another plantation. The aim was to run at a profit, and this depended on abstract calculations of the prices of land, labour, equipment and transportation and the selling price of sugar. Using up labour was the same as exhausting land. If the price was right, cane pieces could be manured and reused, rather than left fallow, and more slaves could be bought to replace or augment those who died. This meant that the Caribbean Islands had an insatiable demand for enslaved Africans. Jamaica's slave population doubled between 1700 and 1750 to 120,000, and increased to 300,000 by the end of the century. Even as late as 1800 the majority of the black population of Jamaica was African-born.

With their unprecedented enslaved black majorities, these Caribbean Island slave societies became based on a rigid racial hierarchy which justified and supported exploitation and violence by making both privilege and fear matters of race. As we have seen, legislation increasingly separated 'Negro' and 'white', previous differentiations based on 'Christian' and 'heathen' having run up against the problem of what to do with slaves who converted to Christianity and the Quaker masters who wanted to bring them to church. Skin colour provided an easy shorthand for judgement of who was free and who unfree, and for cross-class white solidarity against the black majority, even if this was complicated by the existence of a small number of free blacks. These categorisations were based on a series of white supremacist ideas about the natural capacities of the different people of the world, the supposed dangers posed by Africans, and religious ideas that identified Africans as the 'sons of Ham', the descendants of the child of Noah who had been cursed and condemned with all his progeny to slavery for seeing his father naked. Such ideas could justify the permanent and hereditary enslavement of other human beings (the children of slave mothers becoming slaves themselves), while still recognising them as human.

Indeed, as well as dehumanising slaves through violence, work gangs and racism, the plantation system did depend upon the human capacities of the enslaved. It depended upon their ability to undertake complex tasks, to engage in co-ordinated labour and to follow orders and even take initiative. It also depended upon the enslaved to feed, clothe and house themselves from the basic materials supplied by the planters. The degree to which slaves grew their own food varied between the American slave societies. For example, on Barbados, where there was little land which had not been turned over to cane, slaves were given a basic and monotonous allowance of salt fish (cod and herring) from the plantation stores, but they grew yams, eddoes, cassava, leafy greens and herbs, and kept pigs and chickens in the small plots attached to their quarters. In Jamaica, the slaves had extensive provision grounds in the mountains, often several miles from the plantations. On these they mimicked the natural vegetation by utilising every level from tubers such as potatoes and yams in the ground, to maize and okra, and on up to mango, breadfruit and palm trees. They also had small gardens near their huts for the crops and animals that needed more careful attention or protection. The enslaved worked on their own plots one or one and a half days a week. In this way, with their own initiative and skills, they reproduced the labour force the master required to work the cane.

The owners of these plantations expected to get returns on their capital of around 20 per cent in the late seventeenth century, about 10 per cent between 1750 and 1775, and 7.5 per cent by 1790. These were promising profit margins, but establishing a plantation was an expensive business. It required a large initial outlay that would not be repaid for some time. In 1690 the start-up cost was put at £5,625; by 1790 it was estimated to be £30,000. Like the Atlantic trading system as a whole, plantations ran on credit (see chapter 5). Merchants gave planters credit to buy slaves, land, machinery and supplies, and to renew them when exhausted. In return they had the produce of sugarcane harvests to come signed over to them, or held mortgages on the land. Whatever their level of debt these plantation-owners were expected to play the part of wealthy, powerful and cultured colonial gentlemen. By 1680, on Barbados, there were nineteen colonists who owned two hundred slaves each, and eighty-nine who owned one hundred each.

They were a mixture of the original planters who had made the transition to sugar, and the agents of European merchants or the younger sons of gentry families. Those who made it were those who had a nose for profit and power, and the connections necessary to succeed. These men dominated society and politics on Barbados, and similar planter elites grew up on the other islands.

Yet, over time, these rich Caribbean planters, unlike those growing tobacco in Virginia and Maryland, increasingly delegated their authority over these large-scale, semi-industrial, quasi-bureaucratic and disciplined productive units to the salaried overseers, attorneys and bookkeepers who ran them. The planters could then remove themselves from the work of the plantation. They might remove themselves to the Great Houses that they built on elevated positions among their cane fields, often in neo-classical or baroque style and set in beautiful gardens. Within their walls, surrounded by imported plate and china, mahogany furniture and silk drapes, and attended by black servants, they might fancy themselves on a displaced version of the English country estate. They might also remove themselves to the social pleasures and political intrigues of the white society of the capital at Spanish Town or Bridgetown, from where they ran island politics and attempted to maintain their influence over parliamentary decisions in the metropolis itself. Indeed, they might even remove themselves to Britain, either temporarily or permanently becoming absentee planters. In the second half of the eighteenth century some 11.1 per cent of land-owners, owning 23 per cent of Jamaican land, and including some of the largest slave-holders, had moved to Britain where the profits of slavery could fund the high life in other country houses or in London society. Some planters, however, travelled the other way.

The world of Sir Charles Price

At the height of his powers Sir Charles Price ruled his world. During the post-Seven Years' War sugar boom on Jamaica, when the island became the world's leading producer, Price was probably the largest land-owner on the island. Between 1738 and 1771 he acquired 21,341 acres of land which, added to what he had inherited from his father, meant that he possessed some 26,000 acres on the island at his death in 1772. He was also Jamaica's largest slave-holder. Between 1741 and 1772 he spent at least £13,730 buying 742 slaves. He acquired slaves when he speculated in land, he bought land to acquire slaves and he bought slaves to work his land. In

1744 he already owned 1,353 black slaves, distributed across at least seven plantations and livestock pens, and this number had increased to 1,800 by the time he died. In addition, Price was a powerful and well-connected politician who had dominated the Jamaican Assembly in his many years as Speaker. Along with his cousins Rose and Stephen Fuller he had crafted the channels by which the 'West India Interest' became the most influential colonial voice in the Houses of Parliament at Westminster. This preserved the preferential place for Jamaican sugar within Britain's Atlantic world. His fellow Jamaican planters called him 'The Patriot', and their cheerleader-in-chief, the historian Edward Long, described him as the perfect gentleman: 'In private life his complacency of manners, accomplished knowledge of books and men, and delicacy of humour, rendered him the polite, instructive and entertaining companion: here he shone the inflexible lover of truth, the firm friend, and the generous patron.'[2] Yet, as well as being built on the beaten backs of enslaved Africans, all this wealth, power and polish was built on shifting sands.

This is a family story. It was Sir Charles's grandfather, Lieutenant Francis Price, who founded a dynasty of Jamaican planters. A veteran of the Cromwellian army that had captured the island from the Spanish in 1655, Francis Price may have come from Barbados or the Leeward Islands to seek his fortune on the new frontier. He was lucky to have survived. Barely 1,500 of the invasion force of 7,000 men were still alive after the diseases of the first two years. Francis started buying land and growing cocoa, indigo and provisions: 175 acres at Guanaboa in St John's parish; 150 acres at Flamingo Savannah in St Catherine's parish in partnership with Nicholas Philpott; and 840 acres in Lluidas Vale in St John's (figure 9.6). It was on the last plot, which he called Worthy Park, that he built his Great House and established his family. When he died in 1689 what he passed on was land. It was his youngest son, Colonel Charles Price, who came into full possession following the deaths of his older brothers and who made the shift to sugar.

Colonel Price lived at Worthy Park all his life. He made it into a sugar plantation, and himself into one of Jamaica's most substantial planters. He was part of the process by which Jamaica turned to sugar just before 1700, equalled the production level of Barbados by 1730 and surpassed it soon after. Price acquired more land and he bought more slaves. Most importantly, he worked through the island's legislature to improve the roads that would allow muscovado and rum to be carried from interior estates such as Worthy Park to the ports. Public works were turned to private profit for planters such as Price. He made a fortune and he continued the dynasty. He and his wife Sarah had thirteen children. For the eight of them that

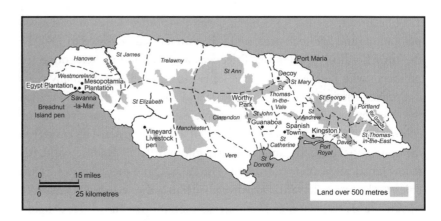

Figure 9.6 Jamaica, c. 1750. The largest of Britain's Caribbean Island possessions and the richest sugar producer by the middle of the eighteenth century was a mountainous island divided into a series of parishes along English lines with its capital at Spanish Town and its main port at Kingston. The Price family operated from the early settled lands at the centre of the island; Tacky's rebellion started in St Mary's parish; and Sarah Affir and Thomas Thistlewood spent their lives in different circumstances in Westmoreland.

died as babies or children their father's wealth was no protection. For those who were still alive when he died in 1730 he made ample provision. Most significantly, he left them money to be educated in Britain and to buy land there if they so chose. Jamaican sugar could be the means to an English end.

So the family story comes back to Sir Charles Price once again: the colonel's eldest son. Sugar money paid for him to be educated at England's finest schools, at Trinity College, Oxford, and on that quintessential educational journey of the eighteenth-century English elite, the European Grand Tour. Sugar money made him a gentleman, and he could have stayed an English gentleman. Yet he returned to Jamaica in 1730 not content to be an absentee planter. A few months later his father died and Charles inherited the earth. He improved the lands bequeathed to him, building roads, windmills and a two-and-a-quarter-mile long aqueduct that brought water to the heart of Worthy Park (figure 9.7). By hard graft and political wheeling and dealing he built the family fortune to unprecedented heights, in land and slaves, and made his name in Jamaican politics. Not only was he long-term Speaker of the Assembly, a position he handed on to his own son, but Custos of St Catherine's (the governor's representative and chief magistrate in the parish), judge of the Supreme Court and major general in the militia. In 1768 he was made a baronet. To display his status, and to consolidate his connections, he built himself a huge town house in Spanish Town for the

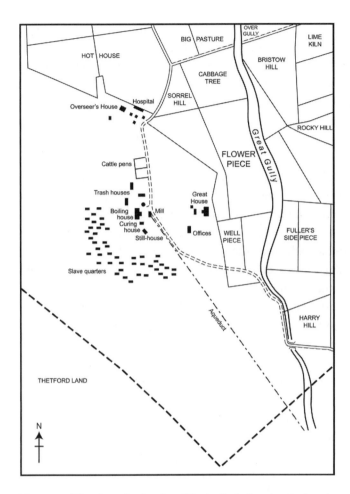

Figure 9.7 The plantation lands at Worthy Park, Jamaica. At the centre of the plantation were the sugar-producing facilities, supplied with water by a purpose-built aqueduct. Arranged around these were the slave quarters, the overseer's house (and the hospital) and the owner's 'Great House' and offices. Around those were the fields and cane 'pieces' which were planted sequentially so that they might be harvested at different times.

November and December season of balls, parties and Assembly and Court sessions, and a new Great House called The Decoy in St Mary's parish. This was an imposing mansion with a number of fine entertainment rooms, including an octagonal saloon decorated with mirrors and carved wood panelling. In front was a lake stocked with waterfowl and a park grazed by imported deer. Behind the house was an elegant garden with vegetables for the kitchen, displays of flowers and walks of coconut, cabbage palms and sand-box trees. One of these walks ended in a triumphal arch affording a prospect over Sir Charles's land: the cane fields and plantain trees of Bagnall's Vale that stretched to the sea. Here Sir Charles Price entertained as a gentleman, a planter and a politician. The house 'was constantly open to the reception of worthy men, whether of the island or strangers: and few gentlemen of rank, whether of the Army or Navy, on service here, quitted the island without having passed some of their time at the Decoy'.[3] Sir Charles Price was in his element.

Yet all this would come crashing down. West Indian fortunes such as that of Sir Charles Price were built on debt. They had to be since the purchase of land, slaves and equipment needed to be funded against profits to come. The island's largest land-owner was, almost inevitably, its largest debtor. By 1753, Sir Charles already owed the London sugar merchant John Serocold £14,000, more than the cost of over seven hundred of his slaves. At first, debts were backed by the security of the next harvest. But as the land-holdings, buildings and enslaved labour forces expanded, and debt piled upon debt, they were backed by the security of the plantations themselves. When Sir Charles Price died in 1772 the estate was disastrously overcommitted. His son, also Sir Charles, was able to continue for some time, borrowing against the debts themselves. When you owe so much it is as least as much of a problem for your creditors. They also stand to lose when you fall. But the coming of American independence hammered the final nail into the coffin. It signalled the end of the colonial system which Sir Charles the elder had done so much to secure, and posed serious problems for Jamaican sugar. The Price family's empire collapsed in 1790 with debts of at least £118,283. Sir Charles's widow, Lydia Ann, was forced to sell The Decoy for a paltry £2,500.

The world of Sarah Affir

Down in the slave quarters they knew the name of Sir Charles Price too. It was said that as well as importing deer for his country park he had also imported a large species of rat to kill the other vermin that were rife since huge areas of the island's complex ecosystem had been replaced by an ocean of sugarcane. A big fat rat was known on the island as a Charles Price rat. Down in the slave quarters they were on intimate terms with hardship, and they knew who caused it too.

When she got to pick her own name she chose Sarah Affir. By then, forty-seven years after she had been born in 1767, she had long been known as

Affy. Sarah was indeed a Christian name. It was chosen when Affy was finally admitted into the Moravian church that her absentee masters, the Barham family, allowed missionaries to run on their Mesopotamia plantation in Westmoreland parish on the far western end of Jamaica. Names mattered. They are one of the few records that remain of some of the thousands of enslaved Africans who lived and died on Jamaica. The Barhams required that their overseers send them an annual inventory of their slaves, and that is how we know of Sarah Affir. Names were also a way in which the slave-owners defined the enslaved. Most slave names seem likely to have been bestowed by the owners as a rite of ownership. Affy lived near Aberdeen, Cambridge, Dundee, Edinburgh and Windsor. She would have talked with Brutus, Cato, Dido, Hercules and Neptune. We don't know what she made of Blackemoor, Christmas, Danger, Goodluck and Trouble. Most of the others, over two-thirds, had standard English and biblical names. Affy was among the one in twelve on Mesopotamia who had African or pseudo-African names. Perhaps her mother picked it. Perhaps the overseer or bookkeeper did. When she could change it she did, at least a bit. After six years of trying to join the Moravians Affy must have known her Bible stories, even if she could not read them herself. Maybe she chose Sarah because that was the name of the Old Testament mother of nations, the one who would bear the kings of peoples. Affir became her surname. She had never had a surname before. She was just Affy, and no mother or father were recorded alongside her birth.

Affy was a rare one. She was a creole, born on Mesopotamia as one of only three babies born in that year from a slave population of 260 men, women and children. She had survived, but she had been born into a world where death outweighed life. Abortion, miscarriage and babies who died shortly after birth were all around but found no place in the plantation records. During her lifetime, death was twice as prevalent as birth on Mesopotamia. New slaves were constantly imported to make up or increase the numbers: 116 from slave ships, 285 from other plantations. Yet, for Affy, birth outweighed death. She had lived, and in her lifetime she had six children. Princess was born in 1785 when Affy was seventeen, Hagar in 1788, Davy in 1790, Robert in 1793, Ann in 1796 and Rodney in 1798. She was the mother of nations. Affy was rare here too. Almost half of the enslaved women on Mesopotamia who survived past thirty had no recorded live births, and those who become mothers had an average of 3.5 births each. Yet each new life came at a cost.

Affy and her children were born to work. The world they knew was the plantation's fields. Affy was put to work at seven years old with the other children on the third, or grass, gang. Thirty of them would take grass to the livestock, carry manure to the cane fields and hoe around the cane stalks to prevent the weeds growing. After six years in the fields she got lucky and moved up to the Great House to work as a domestic servant. This may have been her mother's doing, getting favoured work for her daughter. But it was not to last. After five years Affy was sent back to the cane, and probably back to the grass gang. From there she moved up to the second gang, cleaning the pastures and weeding the cane and, at harvest time, hauling cane trash to be dried for use in the boiling house. By the time she was twenty she was put into the first field gang. This group of around fifty men and women did the hardest work on the plantation: digging a hundred cane holes a day, planting cuttings and harvesting the stalks whose tops waved above their heads. She had five of her children while she worked the cane fields, perhaps getting some respite from the hardest work as her pregnancies neared term and she was shifted to the second gang. But she was always returned to the fields. By 1798, after eleven years of hard toil in the first gang, and eleven years of being described as 'able' or 'healthy', Affy had become 'weak' and was moved back to the second gang. In 1803, she was taken out of the fields and became a washerwoman at the Great House. Twenty-one years of hard labour at the tubs, washboard and mangle followed, broken only by the year (1809) she spent looking after the plantation's small children. She was, from 1810, in a poor state of health and, by 1824, worn out by fifty years of manual labour and disfigured by scrofula, she was recorded as an invalid.

Endless work was the lot of the enslaved. But not all slaves did the same work. Affy's children are testimony to that. Four of them – Princess, Hagar, Davy and Rodney – followed her into the fields. Where they could be made to they were driven down the same hard path from grass gang to second gang to first gang. Sometimes they must have worked the same fields as their mother. This work took the life out of them too, and Affy saw them die or deteriorate. Princess died suddenly in 1811 aged only twenty-six. Hagar committed suicide in 1830 at forty-one. Davy and Rodney were still alive in 1832, but were weak and infirm. The other two children lived different lives. Robert and Ann never worked the fields. Robert, put to work at eleven years of age, became a cooper, a skilled artisan. Ann, sent to work at ten, spent her life as a domestic servant; the future that had been dangled before Affy before she was sent back to the grass gang. The difference was that these two children were half-white. They were 'mulattos'. They were two of the one in ten children born to slave mothers and white fathers on Mesopotamia between 1762 and 1831 who were, according to the logic of a racist society, exempted from field labour. We do not know who Ann's father was. Neither do we know who the father or fathers of Princess, Hagar, Davy and Rodney were. Robert's father is most likely to have been Andrew McAlpin who worked as a bookkeeper on the estate from 1790 to 1796. When Robert got to choose his own name, on conversion by the Moravians at some point between 1818 and 1832, he chose to be Robert McAlpine. He would have known of several mulatto slave children on Mesopotamia freed by their white fathers. But Andrew McAlpin was long gone. Robert, like his mother, was still enslaved.

Most of Sarah Affir's life is closed to us. We don't know how she felt about her work, her children, their fathers or her masters. We don't even know if she survived to see the emancipation of the slaves in 1834. She is last recorded in 1832, a 64-year-old invalid worn out by work and listed in the last inventory her owners received by both her slave name and her new name, the name she had chosen for herself.

Living on the plantation

In many ways men such as Sir Charles Price and women such as Sarah Affir were worlds apart. Yet their lives also intersected in the same place: the plantation. The scale of the sugar plantations of the Caribbean Islands – hundreds of acres and hundreds of workers – and the regimented nature of the labour upon them meant that planters distanced themselves from the world of the slaves. Removed to the Great House, to the towns or to England, they, unlike their Virginian counterparts, did not seek close paternalistic management of the worlds of their slaves. For the enslaved this certainly meant the rule of the whip and of other dehumanising punishments which bridged that distance with the continual threat and use of violence. It also led to slaves often having to provide for themselves in matters of food, clothing and shelter. Yet this distance also meant that the slaves built their own world in order to live on the sugar plantation. They carved out a space for themselves that went beyond their immediate material needs. There was another world on the plantation: one that the slaves made.

Food provides a way into this world. The self-provisioning strategy adopted on Jamaica and on the other mountainous Caribbean Islands has already been presented in the planters' terms as part of the work regime of the plantation. It meant that the slave labour force worked to produce its own food on plots allotted to them by the planters on the steep grounds beyond the cane fields. This meant that slaves could be fed without having to integrate food production into the gang-work of the plantation. However, from the point of view of the enslaved, matters were not so simple. Provision grounds allowed the enslaved a more varied diet, and one over which they had some control, even if they still existed close to starvation. They supplemented the salt fish with yams, cassava, maize and breadfruit, and perhaps a little meat. These grounds may have been up to five to seven miles from the plantation, out beyond the cane fields and the livestock pens that produced the planters' profits. Those who tended them had to spend much time walking to and fro on the days they did not work the cane fields. Yet those journeys, two or maybe three hours on foot each way, also provided opportunities for the slaves to make and consolidate their connections with those enslaved on other plantations. The plantation was not the self-contained, self-sufficient unit that the planters' account books and inventories might suggest. Its daily life was one of interaction with the other plantations and livestock pens around it. Slaves were lent and hired out to other planters, and to labour on public works such as roads and bridges. They were dispatched with messages, assigned to transport goods by road or river, or sent out to fish and hunt. The enslaved also visited each other on their own time, making connections, forming relationships and doing deals that crossed the plantation's boundaries.

The provision grounds also opened out beyond the plantation in another way. They opened the plantation to the market. Each worker decided what to grow. Where they specialised – in plantains, or mangoes, or potatoes – they looked to trade. Where there was a surplus – at harvest, or pig-killing time – they looked to trade. Even on islands such as Barbados where most slaves only had the small plots near their huts there was still enough to trade. In Jamaica, the slave 'higgler' or 'huckster', a small trader taking goods to market, became a familiar figure. Most often women, they sold food crops and craft goods such as baskets or earthenware pots. They sold beads, clothes, ribbons and handkerchiefs. The weekend markets in the towns grew, provisioning not only the slaves but much of the white population too. The enslaved entered in various ways into a money economy. Those working provision grounds sold their produce, and slave artisans – carpenters, masons and bricklayers – sold their skills by working in their own time. In 1774, Edward Long estimated that of the £50,000 in currency in circulation in Jamaica, £10,000 was in the hands of slaves in coins of small denominations. The purchase of some 'fine clothes' or foods to 'gratify his palate' may, as Long thought, have eased the burdens of slavery.[4] But the market also mapped out a range of connections and interactions beyond the purview of white society and beyond the limits of the plantation. Those whites who tried to restrict the slave markets did so against a concerted defence of what the enslaved had come to see as their customary rights over what they grew or made, and their right to sell it and keep the rewards.

These sorts of customary rights also came to govern the notions of property over the provision grounds. As far as the planters were concerned there was no right of ownership granted to their slaves when it came to the 'mountains'. The slaves were themselves property. They could own no property. However, the whites soon found that in practice they could not easily reallocate these provision grounds without offering some compensation to those who were moved. To do otherwise would provoke a storm of protest. Indeed, the enslaved took it to be customary that they would pass on, as an inheritance, the rights to cultivate particular plots of land. This is a family story too. These plots of 'family land' were understood differently from land that might be bought and sold. The notion of family was also a different one. As Sarah Affir's world shows, slavery radically disrupted family life among the enslaved. What they put back together was shaped by the new circumstances. African forms such as polygamy were reordered by the vicissitudes of plantation life and the increased power and choice afforded to women. New forms of kinship also developed. The Jamaican planter Matthew 'Monk' Lewis, a gothic novelist and former absentee slave-owner, asked one of his black servants whether another slave, Old Luke, was a relation of his. The servant replied that he was: 'He and my father were shipmates, massa.'[5] Those who had shared the Middle Passage became kin: 'shipmates'. Those who arrived from Africa and were set to work the provision grounds with those who had been there for some time were kin: 'inmates'. But family went beyond this too. Slavery had also torn asunder the fundamental link between land and ancestors that animated West African life. Family included those who had died as well as those who still lived. Provision grounds and plantation graves worked to restore that link between the spirit world and the material world. Slave funerals, slave 'religions' such as obeah and myalism, the blood oaths sworn among slaves, were rooted in this new American soil and joined the living and the dead. Those whites who saw these rites, or heard of them, were well aware that the slave world was not their own and it was not contained by the plantation. Those whites, such as the plantation-owner Thomas Thistlewood, who lived most closely with the slaves recognised this difference, and reacted with both violence and accommodation.

The world of Thomas Thistlewood

Originally from Lincolnshire, and having not taken to either farming or the East India trade, Thomas Thistlewood arrived in Jamaica in 1750 aged twenty-nine looking to eventually make himself an independent land-owner. He spent the next thirty-six years in the far western parishes of St Elizabeth's and Westmoreland as an overseer and slave-owner on the Vineyard livestock pen, the Egypt sugar plantation (where he spent six-teen years) and finally on his own land at Breadnut Island pen. He never made a fortune, but he lived well and was able to indulge his interests: weather watching and the nascent science of meteorology, gardening and the cultivation of exotic plants, and reading books. Thomas Thistlewood also kept a diary, and it is from this that we know him and those he shared his world with. These were the other white inhabitants of Westmoreland with whom his relations were cordial if not particularly friendly. They were also the slaves he put to work, and bought and sold. About 95 per cent of the population of Westmoreland was black and enslaved, and most of them were African-born. Thistlewood might spend several weeks without white company. His relationships with the black slaves with whom he lived were characterised both by extraordinary violence and by an everyday sociability based on protection and gift-giving.

Violence underpinned the rule of the white minority. Thistlewood learned this lesson early, and in his first year at Vineyard he whipped just under two-thirds of the men and half the women. He continued to wield the whip throughout his career as a routine tool of the overseer's trade, particularly on the Egypt sugar plantation where the work was hardest and the discipline harshest. He was also quickly introduced to even more sadistic punishments. He had watched as the wealthy sugar planter William Dorrill had noses slit, ears cropped and faces cut, and as he had pepper, salt and lime juice rubbed into the wounds of whipped runaways. Thistlewood also saw Dorrill's men cut off the head of a dead runaway, display it on the end of a pole and burn the man's body. Similarly mutilated corpses of runaways and rebels were on display in the towns and countryside across Jamaica. In turn, Thistlewood used these methods and devised his own punishments. He used stocks and yokes, and when a slave named Derby was found to have eaten some of the young canes, the plantation being at the time on short rations, he 'Had Derby well whipped, and made Egypt [another slave] shit in his mouth.'[6] It was a vile punishment Thistlewood used several times.

This violence permeated all his dealings with the slaves. He might have any whipped or punished, so none were safe. It shaped his sexual relationships too. White men such as Thistlewood – and Andrew McAlpin – were expected to sleep with, and even live with, black women. Thistlewood certainly took advantage of this, having sex with 138 women (63 of whom were slaves from other plantations, and only two of whom were white) in his 36 years in Jamaica. He could use force, or make women comply to avoid other punishments, and the threat of violence was always there. He wanted all his slaves to know that he was not to be trifled with, and reported with satisfaction that they called him 'ABBAUMI APPEA i.e. No for Play'.[7] In all this, Thistlewood marked his difference from his black charges with force. They were not part of his moral world. They were different. For him, their race put them outside the compass of humanity.

However, violence was not everything in Thistlewood's relationships with the enslaved. The plantation system could not work that way. It required that whites such as Thistlewood accord some leeway to the enslaved, and even some responsibility and customary rights, even while they openly denied to each other that any of this was happening. It also required that the slaves followed their masters' orders, and even did more than they were told, even if this was done while still chafing against the bonds of slavery. Thomas Thistlewood and the enslaved men and women he oversaw and owned might come to know each other very well. Seventeen of his thirty-four slaves worked for him for over twenty years each. The first slave he bought and named, Lincoln, was with him for over thirty years. The woman who became his long-term slave mistress, Phibbah, did so from 1754 until he died thirty-two years later. Lincoln and Phibbah – and Mulatto John, the son that she bore Thistlewood – were the most long-term and intense personal relationships that he had. They reveal some of the everyday social relationships of the plantation world. Thistlewood relied upon Lincoln to carry messages for him off the plantation. He went out hunting with him, Lincoln carrying a gun alongside his master in contravention of Jamaican law. He gave him favoured work and presents of food and clothing, and Lincoln reciprocated with gifts of food for Thistlewood too. But this slave was also regularly beaten. In turn, Phibbah gradually became Thistlewood's mistress. She suffered for that intimacy, but also gained from it. She gained privileges for herself and others. She was able to intercede with Thistlewood on behalf of other slaves, and she won her freedom in his will. She even wrung from him his only expression of sympathy for a slave – that she was 'in miserable slavery' – when he saw her grief at his leaving Egypt for another job.[8] She may, of course, have been mourning the loss of her limited source of power.

Lincoln and Phibbah did most to blur the hard boundaries of plantation slavery – the owner and the owned, black and white, master and slave – but it was evident in other relationships too. The plantation was bound together by constant interchanges of small gifts and payments, flowing both from and to Thistlewood and among the slaves themselves. His small payments for sex, which increased in frequency as he grew older, replacing his violent sexual opportunism, may not have been much compensation, but they were something. He also gave and accepted money, food and trinkets, and bought and sold guns, horses and other livestock from and to his slaves. He also learned something of their lore about diseases and cures, and probably about plants and animals as well. While he rejected their humanity he was also forced to afford them the recognition that came through everyday interaction.

Overall, the power that Thomas Thistlewood had by virtue of the violence he could wield with the backing of white society and the Jamaican political and legal system, made him both his slaves' worst enemy and their protector too. He was most likely to beat or punish them, but it was him to whom they had to look to protect them from other whites seeking to do them harm, or other slaves from other plantations coming to steal from their provision grounds. Master and slave were bound together on the plantation.

Fighting back: resisting slavery

The nature of life on the plantations meant that resistance to slavery was a complex matter too. Thomas Thistlewood came to understand this well. A few years after arriving in Jamaica he was attacked by a runaway slave known as Congo Sam who, wielding a bill, drove the overseer into a swamp declaring 'I will kill you, I will kill you now'.[9] As they fought for nearly half an hour other slaves stood by, intervening on neither side. Thistlewood was only able to get one of them to go for help when he had restrained Sam himself. He also suspected that there were those among them, including Phibbah, who had known it was going to happen and had kept quiet. They were, perhaps, waiting to see how things turned out. Like Congo Sam, other slaves and indentured servants did fight back, driven by rage and a clear sense of the injustices that their white masters heaped upon them. They did so individually and they did so collectively, with different political ideas in mind (see chapter 10). The pervasive violence of plantation life meant that uprisings broke in great waves across the plantation system from the early seventeenth century to the 1830s. The 1730s and early 1740s, a period of intense activity, saw plots, conspiracies and revolts among slaves and servants on the mainland in Virginia, South Carolina (including the major Stono rebellion), Maryland, New Jersey and Louisiana; and on the islands of Bermuda, Jamaica, St John, the Bahamas, St Kitts, Antigua, St Bartholomew, St Martin's and Guadeloupe, as well as in Dutch Guyana.

Yet none of these overthrew the institution of slavery, and they were put down with an equally savage violence wielded by the planters through their laws, militias and armies. There was a great deal for slaves to lose by joining in violent resistance. As a result, many slaves chose not to take up the bill, the gun or the firebrand against their masters, but that did not mean they did not want to be free. Their resistance might take other forms, all of which involved some necessary accommodation to the plantation system. In the end, the precise dividing lines between resistance, subversion, non-cooperation and grudging acceptance become blurred in the face of the violent opposition slaves faced to their freedom. Understanding any rebellious act, even the most open uprising, always also involves understanding this wide range of different responses.

For some slaves the response was to run away. On islands where there was a mountainous interior, such as Jamaica and St Vincent, long-term independent 'maroon' communities formed. They lived a life shaped by both African cultural origins and American circumstances. On St Vincent this involved alliances with the remaining Amerindians, forming the Black Caribs who long resisted imperial control. On Jamaica the maroons were initially the escaped slaves of the Spanish who were joined by other runaways and put up a determined opposition to British attempts to encroach on their land in the Maroon Wars of the 1730s. Under their leaders, Captain Accompong and Colonel Cudjoe, and expertly using guerrilla tactics, they fought the British to a standstill and negotiated peace treaties in 1739 which preserved their independence. The conditions were, however, that the maroons agreed to return runaway slaves to the plantations, to keep the roads that ran through their areas open and to help the colonial authorities to put down slave insurrections. They had to profess an accommodation with the plantation system in order to preserve their own independence from it. This situation was maintained until the land-hungry plantations began to encroach on the maroons once again in the late eighteenth century, provoking another series of wars which ended with many of the defeated and betrayed maroons being transported to Canada. Those who remained on Jamaica did so in the most inhospitable areas.

Even if they did not form maroon communities, many slaves who ran away from the plantations relied upon the support and help of others. They depended on the connections that they had formed on their own and other plantations to keep them fed and hidden while they remained at large. Most runaways ran away alone and did not stay away for long. They were either easily found again, or they returned to the plantation after a few days. These acts can be seen as ones of non-cooperation which collectively limited the effectiveness of the plantation system and challenged it in the sense that they continually showed that the enslaved did not accept their condition or the exploitation it brought with it. This rarely amounted to outright confrontation. Pilfering from the plantation stores, avoiding work, feigning illness, allowing machines to break, damaging tools, letting animals loose, making errands take all day, passing on gossip about the whites, and keeping or selling the produce of hunting or fishing trips might add up to nothing more than individuals seeking some respite for themselves within a harsh and cruel environment. Or they might be more subversive. Planters, overseers and bookkeepers certainly noted such activities and worried about what they meant. Was it an accidental fire or arson? Had an ox (or even a slave-owner or overseer) died of natural causes or poison? For the slaves themselves these actions certainly operated within an overall rejection of the legitimacy of the relations of property and authority of the plantation system which are well summed up in their justification of theft from the plantation stores: 'For a thief to steal from a thief makes God laugh.'[10]

Many other aspects of slave life were also on the uncertain borders of accommodation, subversion and resistance. As we have seen, the system of self-provisioning was a support to the plantation – providing the food that kept the slaves working in the cane fields – but it also allowed the slaves to have at least a little autonomy, in what they grew and at the market, which demonstrated the limits of the slave-owners' control over their lives and identities. While it subverted slavery by recognising that slaves held some rights of property, it may also have tied them closer to the plantation and given them some stake in it as a place. These bonds formed between slaves and the land, which revealed themselves in funerals moved by dancing and drumming, religious rites and blood oaths sworn between slaves by drinking mixtures of blood, rum, gunpowder and 'grave dirt', could also feed directly into forms of resistance and revolt. The white minority was continually aware that violent rebellion might break out. They were certainly unsure of where the boundaries lay between accommodation, subversion and outright resistance, and they tried to deploy punishment and privilege to keep themselves in control.

The world of Tacky

On Easter Sunday 1760 a group of between fifty and a hundred slaves of Akan origin (or as the planters called them, 'Coromantees'; see chapter 8) from the Trinity, Frontier and Heywood Hall plantations in St Mary's parish,

Jamaica, attacked the fort at Port Maria, killed the storekeeper and got away with forty muskets and four barrels of gunpowder. From there they burned their way across the parish's plantations, gathering other recruits, both men and women, attacking Great Houses and killing whites. These rebels were led by a slave named Tacky who was described by Edward Long in 1774 as 'a young man of good stature, and well made; his countenance handsome, but rather of an effeminate than manly cast'.[11] Almost certainly born in Africa, Tacky came from a region of West Africa whose recent history of warfare and state formation (see chapter 8) had forged a formidable warrior class and a strong sense of Akan collective identity that could be mobilised in the New World.

This uprising was, it seems, intended to be an island-wide revolt which had been carefully planned in the greatest secrecy. The intention seems to have been to create an independent confederation of Akan-ruled states on the island. It would make a Jamaica that was primarily inhabited by Africans into an island that was controlled by them. As Long put it, the intention was 'the entire extirpation of the white inhabitants; the enslaving of all such Negroes as might refuse to join them; and the partition of the island into small principalities in the African mode; to be distributed among their leaders and head men'. It was said that Tacky intended to take 'the lieutenant governor's lady for his concubine'.[12] Long also reported that one rebel had set out the new confederation's economic manifesto: the plantations would continue to produce sugar and rum with slave labour, and the merchants and sailors, who 'care not who is in possession of the country, Black or White, it makes no difference to them . . . will come cap in hand to us (as they do now to the Whites) to trade with us. They'll bring us things from t'other side the sea and be glad to take our goods in payment.'[13] Afro-Jamaica would remain part of the Atlantic world, but on African terms. There is no doubt that these accounts of the revolt speak as much of the fears of the white planters as they do of the aims of the rebels. However, it is clear that Tacky's Revolt became, as it spread westwards – flaring up under different leaders, involving thousands of rebels, and continuing into 1761 – the most significant slave rebellion that the sugar islands had ever faced.

Just as it was a manifestation of African politics in an American setting, so the revolt worked through African-American cultural forms. Tacky's obeahmen oversaw oaths binding their takers to continual revolt. They also concocted a powder to be rubbed into the fighters' bodies that would make them invulnerable. Of Tacky himself it was said that he 'could not possibly be hurt by the white men, for that he caught all the bullets fired at him in his hand, and hurled them back with destruction to his foes'.[14] Other rituals were reported. There was a curious wooden sword with a red parrot feather in the handle being carried as an Akan sign of war, slaves shaving their heads either as a sign that they would join the revolt or in mourning for those who had died pursuing it, and the elevation of Cubah, a female slave, to Queen Mother of the Asante in a ceremony at Kingston with a canopied throne, a robe and a crown. The rebels were mobilising their magic and their power against the white men's weapons. They had some initial success, and proved a match for both the regular military and the militia, especially when fighting in the woods and with military attention diverted by the Seven Years' War. The maroons also initially refused to co-operate fully, particularly without the promise of bounty money. It was only with the gradual co-ordination of these forces, the greater involvement of regular troops and the killing of Tacky by a maroon sharpshooter that the rising was gradually put down. However, sporadic armed resistance continued for many months, particularly in the parish of Westmoreland.

Thomas Thistlewood never faced Tacky himself, but he did face his revolt as it flared up under the leader Apongo (or Wager) in Westmoreland. At the height of the revolt, with other plantations being attacked and their slaves rising, Thistlewood noted in his diary his uncertainty over which way the slaves at Egypt would go. As he put it, 'When the report was of the Old Hope Negroes being rose, perceived a strange alteration in ours. They are certainly very ready if they durst, and [I] am pretty certain they were in the plot.'[15] Several had shaved their heads on the eve of the rebellion, and it turned out later that one called Lewie was well known to Apongo. However, they did not rise against Thistlewood and the other white man on the plantation. Instead, armed with guns from the plantation house, selected and trusted slaves (who were also those most likely to turn to the rebels) stood guard with Thistlewood by night, and by day he maintained the post-harvest regime of work and Sunday tickets for travel off the plantation. We have no way of knowing whether the slaves anticipated that their lives would be no better under Akan masters than under white ones, whether they sought to defend their own grounds and possessions against the rebels' fire or whether they were unwilling to take the chance in the face of Thistlewood's confident front (the other white man, John Groves, certainly panicked) and the increasing evidence of militia, military and maroon patrols.

Those who had risen faced a grisly fate. Sixty whites and as many free coloureds and blacks had been killed by the rebels and the revenge was terrible. Around three or four hundred rebels were killed in the fighting or committed suicide in the woods. One hundred men and women were executed in the most gruesome fashion. They were hanged, or gibbeted alive and burned with slow fire, watching their limbs being consumed before them. Five hundred others were transported, most to the Bay of Honduras. Those who went to watch the executions, including Thistlewood, saw Akan warriors who faced their fate with characteristic discipline. They did not flinch or cry out at the pain, and even laughed at their tormentors. Tacky was not alongside them, but neither were his remains simply in the hands of the white rulers. His killers had decapitated him, and taken his head in triumph to Spanish Town where it was displayed on a pole for all to see. However, it soon disappeared 'stolen, as was supposed, by some of his countrymen, who were unwilling to let it remain exposed in so ignominious a manner'.[16] It was also said that they had sworn an oath to rise again in two years' time.

The new world in the Americas was made by bringing various elements together and shaping them into a new economy, society and culture. If any part of the early modern world was made anew by the forces of global connection it was the cash crop areas of the Caribbean and North America. In part it was a world transformed by the European planters and merchants. They used the force of violence and punishment alongside the power of money to combine American land, African labour and European capital and management into new forms. This made the plantation. It was a place of work discipline, terror and insecurity that squeezed profits out of land and labour out of enslaved bodies just as it squeezed the juice out of sugarcane. The multiplication of plantations created a new environment, a new physical landscape of cane pieces, livestock pens and mountain provision grounds, of slave quarters and Great Houses, that transformed the islands of the Caribbean into a place of production for export. Along with this came a polarised and racially ordered society that depended upon the subordination of the black majority by the white minority through the continued use of terror. The Great House on the hill overlooked the cane fields, the slave quarters and the mill, even when the planters who owned the land were permanently absent. When the mill and boiling house ran for days it did so to fill the pockets of the planters, and to pay the debts they owed to the merchants.

Yet all of this was built on the work of the enslaved. They built the fine houses as well as cutting the cane. They tended the provision grounds as well as making the sugar. In the process the slaves had made this new world too, and made it in their own image. They had fashioned it with agricultural techniques familiar from West Africa. They had also built a culture in the Americas, whose language, songs, dances and foods adapted African traditions to their new circumstances, drawing in new instruments, new sounds and new tastes: the fiddle playing alongside the drum, and cassava being eaten as well as yams. They had carved out what independence and autonomy they could by using their traditions, the land, the market and the connections they forged with each other to make something for themselves. This both prompted and limited the extent of slave revolts against white authority. These uprisings were built within and through the world that the slaves made and, in many cases, drew upon African notions of magic and power to challenge the slave-owners. Yet these revolts were also limited by what the enslaved had to lose in a world where they had succeeded in building something for themselves in the landscape of plantations.

Slaves and slave-owners were tied together on the plantation. There was both the distance that separated men such as Sir Charles Price and women such as Sarah Affir, and the everyday interaction that Phibbah and Lincoln had with their overseer and owner which included both gifts and beatings. When Tacky's Revolt flared up in Westmoreland, Thomas Thistlewood did not know whether the slaves he lived with on the plantation would stand guard, run away or cut out his heart and tongue, as Apongo was said to have done to another white man. He did know that the enslaved wanted their freedom. They wanted slavery abolished.

Further reading

Good general introductions are available in Sidney Mintz (1985) *Sweetness and Power: The Place of Sugar in Modern History* (Viking, New York) especially chap. 2, 'Production'; Robin Blackburn (1997) *The Making of New World Slavery: From the Baroque to the Modern, 1492–1800* (Verso, London); and Verene Shepherd and Hilary McD. Beckles (eds.) (2000) *Caribbean Slavery in the Atlantic World: A Student Reader* (James Currey, Oxford). For the 'sugar revolution', see Richard Dunn (1973) *Sugar and Slaves: The Rise of the Planter Class in the English West Indies, 1624–1713* (Norton Library, New York) and Russell R. Menard (2006) *Sweet Negotiations: Sugar, Slavery, and Plantation Agriculture in Early Barbados* (University of Virginia Press, Charlottesville). For absentee planters, see Trevor Burnard (2004) 'Passengers only: the extent and significance of absenteeism in eighteenth-century Jamaica', *Atlantic Studies*, 1:2 pp. 178–195. On the culture of the enslaved and resistance to slavery, see Michael Mullin (1992) *Africa in America: Slave Acculturation and Resistance in the American South and British Caribbean, 1736–1831* (University of Illinois Press, Urbana) and

Michael Craton (1982) *Testing the Chains: Resistance to Slavery in the British West Indies* (Cornell University Press, Ithaca). For Sir Charles Price, see Michael Craton and James Walvin (1970) *A Jamaican Plantation: The History of Worthy Park, 1670–1970* (W. H. Allen, New York). For Sarah Affir, see Richard S. Dunn (1996) 'The story of two Jamaican slaves: Sarah Affir and Robert McAlpine of Mesopotamia estate', in Roderick A. McDonald (ed.) *West Indies Accounts: Essays on the History of the British Caribbean and the Atlantic Economy in Honour of Richard Sheridan* (University of the West Indies Press, Kingston) pp. 188–210. For Thomas Thistlewood, see Douglas Hall (1999) *In Miserable Slavery: Thomas Thistlewood in Jamaica, 1750–1786* (University of the West Indies Press, Kingston) and Trevor Burnard (2004) *Mastery, Tyranny, and Desire: Thomas Thistlewood and His Slaves in the Anglo-Jamaican World* (University of North Carolina Press, Chapel Hill). For Tacky, see Burnard, *Mastery, Tyranny, and Desire*, pp. 170–174, Craton, *Testing the Chains*, chap. 11, 'Jamaica, 1760: Tacky's revolt', and Mullin, *Africa in America*, chap. 2, 'Africans name themselves'.

Notes

1 Quoted in Robin Blackburn (1997) *The Making of New World Slavery: From the Baroque to the Modern, 1492–1800* (Verso, London) p. 335.

2 Quoted in Michael Craton and James Walvin (1970) *A Jamaican Plantation: The History of Worthy Park, 1670–1970* (W. H. Allen, New York) p. 84.

3 Edward Long quoted ibid., p. 85.

4 Quoted in Sidney Mintz and Douglas Hall (2000) 'The origins of the Jamaican internal marketing system', in Verene Shepherd and Hilary McD. Beckles (eds.) *Caribbean Slavery in the Atlantic World: A Student Reader* (James Currey, Oxford) p. 763.

5 Quoted in Michael Mullin (1992) *Africa in America: Slave Acculturation and Resistance in the American South and British Caribbean, 1736–1831* (University of Illinois Press, Urbana) p. 102.

6 Quoted in Douglas Hall (1999) *In Miserable Slavery: Thomas Thistlewood in Jamaica, 1750–1786* (University of the West Indies Press, Kingston) p. 71.

7 Thomas Thistlewood quoted in Trevor Burnard (2004) *Mastery, Tyranny, and Desire: Thomas Thistlewood and His Slaves in the Anglo-Jamaican World* (University of North Carolina Press, Chapel Hill) p. 30.

8 Quoted in Hall, *In Miserable Slavery*, p. 80.

9 Quoted in Burnard, *Mastery, Tyranny, and Desire*, p. 141.

10 Quoted in Russell R. Menard (2006) *Sweet Negotiations: Sugar, Slavery, and Plantation Agriculture in Early Barbados* (University of Virginia Press, Charlottesville) p. 101.

11 Quoted in Michael Craton (1982) *Testing the Chains: Resistance to Slavery in the British West Indies* (Cornell University Press, Ithaca) p. 136.

12 Quotes from ibid., p. 127 and p. 360 n. 25.

13 Quoted in Robin Blackburn (1988) *The Overthrow of Colonial Slavery, 1776–1848* (Verso, London) p. 56.

14 Edward Long quoted in Craton, *Testing the Chains*, p. 131.

15 Quoted in Hall, *In Miserable Slavery*, p. 99.

16 Edward Long quoted in Craton, *Testing the Chains*, p. 136.

10 | In black and white: fighting against the slave trade

For many in Britain and in Britain's American colonies slavery was, from the early seventeenth century onwards, an unchangeable part of the Atlantic world. The prosperity it brought, and the way it underpinned the circulation of goods around the oceanic triangle, allowed no argument against it. To do so would unravel British power and hand it to their imperial rivals, especially the French (see chapter 5). For the enslaved, slavery's denial of their freedom and its exactions on their bodies meant that it had to be opposed, producing resistance against the slave trade and cycles of revolt against the plantations (see chapters 8 and 9). Between these two poles there were always those who questioned the legitimacy of a political, legal and economic system in which one person could own another as property. These ideas were present in the popular notions of equality espoused by sailors and pirates, in the interpretations of religious texts, and in the finer arguments of philosophers. Yet it was not until the late eighteenth century that the abolition of the slave trade became a political movement within which quite different people – from former slaves in both the Americas and Europe to conservative metropolitan writers – pursued the goal of ending by law what became seen as an unjust and inequitable system. How this happened is a complicated matter. It requires an understanding of the ideas that animated the movement, of the range of political strategies that generated and mobilised those ideas in the push for change, of the global geographies of these ideas and strategies and of the particular characters who put them into action.

The abolition movement in Europe and the Americas was built upon ideas from evangelical Christianity, Enlightenment philosophy and the culture of the enslaved themselves. In their different ways, these ideas provided a basis for abolitionist thought, but they had to be made to do so. Christianity had been one of the pillars upon which the slave system rested. There was plenty of room to argue that the Bible supported the institution of slavery, and plenty of Anglican clergymen willing to do so. Indeed, the Church of England itself owned plantations and slaves in the Caribbean and saw no contradiction in that. It was various non-conformist sects – particularly the Quakers, Methodists and Baptists – and then evangelical

Anglicans who began to argue that enslaving others was incompatible with the personal, moral relationship with God that they put at the heart of their religion. Their appeal to more marginalised people, including slaves themselves, rested on their more democratic and egalitarian notions of religious duty and God's favour.

In turn, increasingly influential Enlightenment philosophies which sought to both judge and change the world according to the demands of reason and the goal of individual liberation from tyranny and tradition could also work for slavery as well as against it. On the one hand, Enlightenment ideas of the stages of human civilisation, and the influence of climate on human development, justified a world in which race could be the basis of political rights and imperial control. On the other, the Abbé Raynal argued in his *Histoire des Deux Indes* (1770) for the end of slavery on the basis of 'the light of reason and the sentiments of nature', and asked where the 'new Spartacus' was who would lead the enslaved 'to vengeance and slaughter' in the name of 'the honour of the human species'.[1] Some Enlightenment thinkers divided humanity up into separate races and others promoted the notion of universal rights. Again, the argument had to be made and won. Finally, slaves sought freedom in different ways according to different ideas. African notions of kingship could animate revolts against racialised plantation slavery, but sometimes this was with the aim of reintroducing a slave society (see chapter 9). Equally, ideas of independent subsistence production founded in the gardens and mountains of plantation societies could both prevent revolt and provide an enduring sense of autonomy and freedom for which the formerly enslaved were willing to fight. None of these ideas was unequivocally anti-slavery. The discussion had to be joined. The case had to be made. Doing so was part of a range of political strategies that anti-slavery activists of all sorts devised and deployed.

An end to the slave trade, and to plantation slavery, was sought in very different ways, and by very different means. The enslaved themselves had long declared their desire for freedom in violent revolts against their owners and overseers, by seeking manumission and by taking whatever opportunities for liberty presented themselves. For others, particularly in Britain, anti-slavery meant a concerted campaign to challenge the rights of slave-owners in the courts and to persuade Parliament to legislate on the limited goal of ending the slave trade (rather than arguing for the end of slavery itself). However, this campaign itself quickly stretched far beyond the narrow confines of the propertied white men who had the vote in eighteenth-century Britain. The abolition movement swiftly broadened political participation in significant ways. Women, former slaves, workers and the provincial middle class became key campaigners, each with their own objectives, deploying new political strategies to put pressure on the establishment. Indeed, abolition could not easily be contained either by its proponents or by its opponents. In this Age of Revolutions – the American Revolution against the British empire from 1776, the French Revolution from 1789 and the revolution of the enslaved in Saint Domingue (later Haiti) from 1791 – the ramifications of new ideas of liberty and rights worked back and forth across the Atlantic world pushing and pulling the abolition movement's many strands in different directions. Abolition was an Atlantic movement in its inception, in its operation and in its effects.

These different ideas and political strategies combined, merged and struck against each other in various ways across the late eighteenth century. The movement for the abolition of the slave trade involved many different people fighting many different battles, sometimes in parallel with each other and sometimes in conflict. Those involved had to seek out their own arguments and strategies, forging new ideas and new political tactics as they went. As this chapter shows, abolitionists could take quite different paths. Thomas Clarkson pursued the route of parliamentary change, but did so by generating extra-parliamentary pressure. This movement was animated by the writings of both the conservative evangelical reformer Hannah More and the former slave Olaudah Equiano whose connections were also with working-class radicals. This movement was, therefore, a political coalition which contained quite different ideas on the relationships between 'black' and 'white', and on the desirability of radical political change. There were quite different responses among abolitionists when the movement was forced to confront the French Revolution and its uses in the active abolitionism of Toussaint L'Ouverture, who led an army of former slaves to victory on Saint Domingue against the imperial armies of both Britain and France.

Empire, law, parliament and the making of a movement

Abolitionism in Britain had many beginnings. Various strands began to emerge in the late 1760s and early 1770s. On the basis of religious principle, the Quakers, mobilising their Anglo-American networks, and then the Methodists, led by John and Charles Wesley, took a strong moral stand. Quaker slave-owners in the Americas freed their slaves, and the Quaker church, known as the Society of Friends, began to publish works arguing against slavery. The Philadelphia Quaker Anthony Benezet's writings on the slave trade as well as Africa found an audience on both sides of the Atlantic. His work influenced John Wesley who, in his *Thoughts Upon Slavery* (1774), argued strongly against the prevailing economic wisdom when stating the moral case that 'It were better that all those [West Indian] Islands should remain uncultivated for ever, yea, it were more desirable that they were all together sunk in the depth of the sea, than that they should be cultivated at so high a price, as the violation of Justice, Mercy and Truth.'[2] However, these were, in many ways, marginal voices speaking from outside the established church and outside the circles of parliamentary and imperial power. They might be dismissed as 'enthusiasts' blinded to the ways of the world by religious fervour.

For others, in contrast, the focus was very much on worldly practicalities and on imperial power. Following the end of the Seven Years' War in 1763, Britain not only controlled the world's oceans but its empire had also gained an unprecedented amount of territory in the Americas and in Asia. The need to establish the basis on which this empire would work exercised many minds (see chapters 1, 4 and 5). As always, a prime concern was the degree of autonomy that the colonies should have in relation to the metropolitan centre. Caribbean Island assemblies' flexing of their muscles in relation to imperial governors (see chapter 9), and North American colonists' disquiet over the relationships between the taxes they paid and the influence they had over legislation (and over where they could sell their goods), quickly demonstrated the tensions involved. One response was a series of schemes to emancipate the slaves in the American colonies. These came from a range of political positions, but shared the goal of increasing metropolitan authority over colonial peoples. Freeing the slaves would rein in the autonomous powers of the slave-holders and subject them to the law. As one proposal put it, 'Every where in every age, the chain of slavery has been fashioned and applied by the hand of liberty.'[3] The liberty of slave-holders would be curbed by extending freedom to their slaves. These emancipated slaves, animated by the rational desire to improve their condition, would then become British subjects cultivating the lands on the frontiers of the British empire. Their right to do so was based on their duty to adhere to a shared and prescriptive Britishness. They would 'talk the same language, read the same books, profess the same religion, and be fashioned by the same laws'.[4] Britain's empire would be peopled by free subjects, whether they be black, brown, red or white, all swearing allegiance to Britain itself.

The American Revolution put paid to such schemes. The loss of the North American colonies ended thoughts of a metropolitan assertion of control. The American revolutionaries also created their new nation without putting an end to slavery. Yet, two of those who had proposed emancipation, Granville Sharp and James Ramsay, also acted against slavery in other ways with lasting effect. Sharp, beginning in the 1760s, had become the defender of London's black poor. In a series of court cases, he challenged the rights of slave-holders over their slaves in England. He sought to use the law in the imperial centre, rather than in the colonies, to curb the liberties of those who claimed they owned other people as property.

The landmark judgment came in 1772 in the case of James Somerset, a slave from Virginia whose owner was seeking to remove him from England. Sharp argued that this was unlawful. Lord Mansfield, unable to get the parties to settle out of court, ruled in Somerset's favour. Although the judgment was strictly limited to the removal of slaves from England, it was interpreted much more broadly by those whom it affected. The bravery of James Somerset in coming before the law was matched by the courage of those who took the judgment to mean that they too might be free in England. By 1774 Virginia slave-owners thought that runaway slaves would try to cross the Atlantic 'where they imagine they will be free (a Notion now prevalent among the Negroes greatly to the vexation and prejudice of their Masters)'. As one slave-holder said of an escaped slave named Bacchus, this was a result of 'the knowledge he has of the late determination of the Somerset case'.[5] Shortly afterwards, the British unleashed this desire for freedom as a weapon against the American revolutionaries, promising freedom for all slaves who left their masters to fight for King George III. Thousands reached for the promise of liberty and ended up on the losing side.

After the loss of the thirteen American colonies James Ramsay revised his arguments for exerting control over the colonists into an attack on slavery and the slave trade, published by the Quaker printer James Phillips in 1784 as an *Essay on the Treatment and Conversion of American Slaves in the British Sugar Colonies*. Ramsay, who had been an Anglican clergyman on St Kitts for fourteen years, and who was a former slave-owner himself, delivered a devastating eye-witness attack on the brutalities of slavery. He repeated his claim that slavery was born of excessive liberty and took the position that the conditions of slavery needed to be improved by legal controls, better treatment, rewarding slaves for their labour and instructing them in Christianity. While arguing only that slavery should be ameliorated he provided page after page of denunciations of the brutality of the slave-owners and the inhumanity of the condition of slavery. He also argued that the slave trade could be ended, and sugar production switched to Africa, with no economic costs to the British Empire. Despite his ameliorationist position, these were effective arguments against slavery as a whole. The apologists for slavery certainly had no doubt about the danger he posed and issued a stream of responses to his ideas and vicious personal attacks on Ramsay himself. Others entered the fray to defend him. The battle of ideas had been joined in public and the strands of the movement had begun to be drawn together. They would be pulled more tightly in by the indefatigable energy of Thomas Clarkson.

The world of Thomas Clarkson

Thomas Clarkson was born at the grammar school at Wisbech in 1760. His mother was from a well-connected Cambridgeshire family of Huguenot descent. His father was a Yorkshireman, a clergyman and headmaster of the school. It was while at St John's College, Cambridge, in training for the church, that Clarkson discovered the cause that would guide his whole life. Having won one Latin essay prize in 1784 he was determined to win another the next year. The title, set by the vice-chancellor, was '"Anne liceat invitos in servitutem dare": is it right to make slaves of others against their will?' With only a few weeks to complete the essay, and starting from scratch, Clarkson drew on the papers of a dead friend who had been in the slave trade, several officers from the Caribbean and, most usefully, Anthony Benezet's *Historical Account of Guinea* (1771). Expecting the pleasures of Latin composition he soon found himself weighed down by the task before him: 'It was but one gloomy subject from morning to night. In the day-time I was uneasy. In the night I had little rest. Sometimes I never closed my eye-lids for grief. It became now not so much a trial for academical reputation, as for the production of a work, which might be useful to injured Africa.' Having won the prize, and having read his essay at the university's Senate House, he still could not shake its subject from his mind as he journeyed back to London in the summer of 1785. Sitting by the roadside at Wades Mill in Hertfordshire, he later recalled that 'a thought came into my mind, that if the contents of the essay were true, it was time some person should see these calamities to their end'.[6]

Looking for a London publisher for the English translation of his essay, Clarkson found James Phillips. This Quaker soon introduced him to others interested in abolition, including Granville Sharp and James Ramsay. On 22 May 1787 twelve men, including Clarkson, Sharp, Phillips and a number of other Quakers, formed the London Committee of the Society for Effecting

Figure 10.1 Thomas Clarkson. In this portrait from 1788, completed just as the campaign for abolition was taking off, the indefatigable anti-slave trade activist is shown penning another pamphlet designed to gain more supporters for the cause. He gazes with the look of a visionary into a dreamed-of future when the traffic in human beings has been ended.

the Abolition of the Slave Trade. They set themselves the task of influencing parliamentary opinion to bring about a change in the law. They chose to focus on the abolition of the slave trade since this, unlike full emancipation, would avoid contravening the private property rights of the planters and raising the question of the power of Parliament over colonial assemblies. Many hoped, however, that ending the slave trade would eventually end slavery itself. Clarkson's translated *Essay on the Slavery and Commerce of the Human Species* had been published in 1786, and it formed a pillar of the subsequent agitation (figure 10.1). It had been instrumental in persuading William Wilberforce, a well-respected independent MP with the ear of the prime minister William Pitt, to represent the cause in Parliament. It was at the heart of a publicity drive aimed at 'distributing Clarkson's *Essay* and such other Publications, as may tend to the Abolition of the Slave Trade'.[7] And it was a model for their other activities. Clarkson's skill lay in gathering and synthesising contemporary information on the slave trade from those involved in it. That was what was new about his essay, and it would also form the basis of the information that the committee wanted to set before Parliament. A few days after it had formed the committee instructed Clarkson to travel to Bristol, Lancaster and Liverpool to collect more evidence. It was to be the beginning of a long journey.

On a series of travels across the length and breadth of the country, Thomas Clarkson covered around 35,000 miles on horseback over the next seven years. He depended upon the support and connections of members of the Society of Friends wherever he went, and impressed them with his energy and commitment. He rose early and stayed up late to write letters. He spent many hours poring over customs house ledgers and ships' muster rolls by candlelight, tracking the movements of vessels and sailors. He engaged others to travel on slave ships to bring back testimony from the belly of the beast. He put himself in danger gathering information at the quaysides of London, Bristol and Liverpool from the sailors and captains of slave ships who would speak to him. Anonymous threats were made against him and those who harboured him. A group of men, finding him alone on the pier-head at Liverpool during a heavy gale, tried to force him over the edge into the sea. Fortunately he broke through their ranks, although 'not without blows, [and] amidst their imprecations and abuse'.[8]

Clarkson's travels served two purposes. The first aim was to attack the slave trade. He did this by gathering the data that would show that the trade was 'impolitick and unjust'.[9] He collected gruesome stories based on eye-witness testimony of the abuse of both sailors and slaves in the trade. For example, he uncovered the tale of the massacre at Old Calabar in which English slave-traders had been involved in the deaths of three hundred Africans and the illegitimate enslavement of Little Ephraim Robin John and Ancona Robin Robin John (see chapter 8). He also drew together the evidence which showed that the pro-slavery lobby's argument that the slave trade was a 'nursery' for seamen was a lie; his research showed it to be their cemetery. Those who manned slave ships from all ports were dying in far greater numbers than those in any other trade. His second aim was to gather support. Armed with a box of 'specimens of African produce', including 'a sample of gum rubber astringents, of cotton from the Gambia, of indigo and musk, of long pepper, or black pepper from Whidàh [Ouidah], of mahogany from Calabar, and of cloths of different colours', he sought to convince those he met that a free trade in African produce could profitably replace the coerced trade in human beings. Where necessary he could also show his collection of 'iron instruments used in this cruel traffic': hand-cuffs, shackles, a thumb-screw, a speculum oris for wrenching open the jaws for force feeding. These would bring the horrors of the trade home to his British audiences.[10] Although Thomas Clarkson was to experience all the highs and lows of the abolition campaign in his long life, he was by the late 1780s instrumental in building it as a popular movement.

Abolition as a popular movement in Britain

Everywhere that Thomas Clarkson went, local abolition committees sprang up. They were formed in every major town and city across the country, and they maintained communication with the central committee in London. These local committees were predominantly made up of members of the provincial middle classes: shopkeepers, professionals, merchants, small manufacturers and their families. Most were non-conformists, members of churches other than the Church of England: Quakers, Methodists, Baptists, Unitarians and Presbyterians. They often lived in places that had been transformed by the economic changes of the eighteenth century – Manchester, Birmingham or Sheffield – but whose new significance found little representation in a parliamentary system based on landed property and traditional privilege. They considered themselves modern and progressive, interested in questions of science and reform. In abolition these people found a cause that spoke to them as enlightened and sympathetic individuals with something to contribute to national politics. Their pursuit of the cause involved devising tactics which drew on the resources they had to build a movement beyond the confines of Westminster politics in order then to bring pressure to bear upon Parliament itself.

One key tactic was the petition. It was a long-standing right, framed within a paternalistic vision of the relationship between the powerful and the people, that those who had a grievance might petition the sovereign or the legislators to request that it be redressed. Petitions usually came from corporate bodies – trades, towns or professions – and related to specific matters of concern. The anti-slave trade movement took the traditional petition and transformed it. They turned it into a tool of mass protest. One abolition petition sent from Manchester in 1788 was signed by 10,000 people, one in five of the city's population. Moreover, the Manchester anti-slavery activists who had gathered those signatures also put notices in the London and provincial newspapers advertising their petition and wrote to the civic leaders of every principal town in Great Britain, and to 'respectable individuals' across the country, urging them to send petitions too.[11] By the end of 1788 Parliament had received 103 petitions arguing for reform or abolition of the slave trade, containing up to 100,000 signatures. There were more petitions than on any other subject. They came from towns large and small, and each one, carried into Parliament and presented to the MPs, signalled the public mood. These petitions were also different from those that had come before in demonstrating a concern that extended beyond their signatories' own immediate interests. As one petition from 769 Sheffield cutlers in 1789 put it: 'Cutlery wares . . . being sent in considerable quantities to the Coast of Africa . . . as the price of Slaves – your petitioners may be supposed to be prejudiced in their interests if the said trade in Slaves should be abolished. But your petitioners having always understood that the natives of Africa have the greatest aversion to foreign Slavery . . . consider the case of the nations of Africa as their own.'[12] New global geographies of sympathy and connection were beginning to form that were based upon more than trade and profit.

There were also novel tactics devised to generate these sympathies and connections, and to broaden the movement even further. The abolitionists took full advantage of the rapid development of the print media in the eighteenth century. Publishers and book-sellers such as James Phillips played a crucial role in producing and distributing anti-slave trade material. There was something for every taste, audience and occasion. There were the closely argued essays of men such as Clarkson, Ramsay and Sharp; volumes of evidence presented before Parliament; the petition advertisements; arguments in the newspapers between pro- and anti-slavery factions; poetry and novels with abolitionist themes; and even children's books which told of the horrors of the slave trade. These works were also distributed in North America and translated into French, Portuguese, Danish, Dutch and Spanish to begin to build an international movement.

Even more dramatic and influential than all these printed words were the visual images that came to define the cause. In 1787 Josiah Wedgwood, the Midlands manufacturer famous for his fine and fashionable tableware, used all his considerable marketing and advertising skills to develop an emblem for the movement. The image of a kneeling, chained slave, looking upwards and asking the viewer 'Am I Not a Man and a Brother?' captured the imagination of the movement (figure 10.2). It appeared in print and also on cups, plates, snuff boxes, brooches and hairpins to be carried and worn by men and women to proclaim their commitments. Benjamin Franklin declared its impact 'equal to that of the best written pamphlet'.[13] It was soon everywhere. Just as widespread and just as dramatic was an image that had first been used by the Plymouth Abolition Committee in December 1788, and was then reworked by the London committee to depict the slave ship *Brookes* (figure 10.3). This showed enslaved Africans packed into the hold

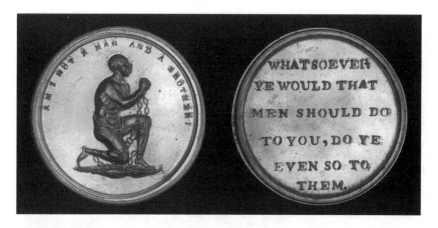

Figure 10.2 'Am I Not a Man and a Brother?' This abolitionist brass medal, cast according to the design of Josiah Wedgwood and bearing his famous slogan and a Christian message of equality, was made to be a symbol of allegiance to the cause. Giving it, or carrying it, meant using the symbolism of a chained and supplicant African rather than entertaining other notions of liberty, equality and fraternity.

of a ship. Without depicting the violence of slavery it showed the inhuman treatment of people as cargo, neatly filling every available space in the ship as if the only thing that mattered was profit. It was, Clarkson said, 'designed to give the spectator an idea of the sufferings of the Africans in the Middle Passage, and this so familiarly, that he might instantaneously pronounce upon the miseries experienced there'. Since 'this print seemed to make an instantaneous impression of horror upon all who saw it', the committee sought the widest possible distribution, printing over 8,000 copies between 1788 and 1789.[14] In Edinburgh it was posted in the streets, and abolitionists had it pinned up at home as an everyday reminder of what they were fighting for.

The home became a battleground for abolition in other ways too. An important aspect of the movement was the involvement of women, and their active role in generating new political strategies. They were unable to vote. They were not meant to sign the petitions (although some did). But they refused to keep quiet on the subject of the slave trade. Women began to take part in the anti-slavery discussions of debating clubs. They produced abolitionist prose and poetry. And they brought the campaign right into the heart of their homes. They did this by wearing Wedgwood's emblem on their clothes or in their hair, and by discussing the anti-slavery poems presented as 'A Subject for Conversation at the Tea-Table'. Most importantly, they did so by making the tea-table itself a political battleground through

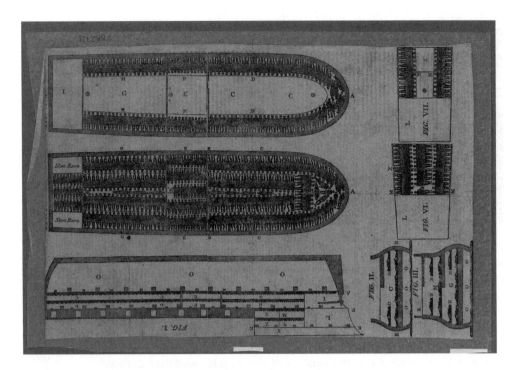

Figure 10.3 The slave ship *Brookes* in abolitionist publicity. One of the most widely circulated and well-known abolitionist images, this diagram of a slave ship was designed to shock those who saw it with the inhumanity of the trade in human beings. Put up in the streets and in abolitionist homes it was both a symbol of the cause and an image that reduced the enslaved to a series of mute silhouettes.

the boycotting of slave-produced sugar. All those British cups of tea with milk and sugar (see chapter 5), all those cakes, biscuits and puddings, were presented as the products of violence and abuse. What had been seen as pure and sweet was turned, through the words of the abolitionists, into something disgusting. As one pamphleteer argued, 'Does it not behove all professors of Christianity well to consider how far they encourage the oppressor, by purchasing their commodities, thus defiled with blood?'[15] To eat Caribbean sugar was to consume slave bodies. This was the first mass consumer boycott, of what was one of the first mass market consumer goods. It was designed to put pressure on the producers to change their ways by hitting them where it hurt: in the account book. It is estimated that in the early 1790s between 300,000 and 400,000 people had stopped using sugar. Women consumers were showing their power.

Overall, therefore, through these different strategies the abolition movement built a broad coalition of men and women from different classes and regions. Within it were those from very different backgrounds who could hold quite different views, men and women as different as Hannah More and Olaudah Equiano.

The world of Hannah More

Hannah More was born a few miles north of the slave-trading port of Bristol in 1745 (figure 10.4). Her mother was from a farming family, and her father was a schoolmaster. Hannah and her four sisters were nurtured in a household that prized intelligence and education. They were encouraged to write and perform. Hannah's talent with the pen, and her drama for schoolgirls, *The Search After Happiness* (1773), soon took her sisters and her on a series of annual visits to London. There her literary talents drew her into the high-flying cultural circles of David Garrick, Elizabeth Montagu, Joshua Reynolds, Samuel Johnson and Edmund Burke, and she made a name for herself with works for the London stage. Yet there was much about this theatrical and literary life, and the fame that it had brought, that did not appeal. Hannah was a strong moralist, with clear views on women's conduct and role. She was also increasingly turning towards evangelical, perhaps even 'Methodistical', versions of Christianity, which stressed the relationship between devotion to God and public action.[16] It was by engaging with these ideas that she would find new uses for her pen.

In the mid-1780s Hannah spent much time at Barham Court in the village of Teston in Kent. This was the home of Elizabeth Bouverie, a model of the godly patronage and beneficence to which Hannah now aspired. As she put it, Teston was 'such an enchanted Country, such Books! Such nightingales! Such Roses! Then within doors such goodness, such Charity, such Piety! I hope it is catching and that I shall bring away some of the odour of sanctity about me.'[17] It certainly seemed that there was something in the air. Elizabeth Bouverie had gathered around her a like-minded group, dedicated to bringing evangelical principles into politics. Lord Charles Middleton, comptroller of the navy and MP for nearby Rochester, and his wife Margaret were central to this. Charles had installed James Ramsay as the local vicar (a far cry from ministering to a parish on St Kitts), and Margaret had encouraged Ramsay to write his anti-slavery pamphlets. It was at Barham Court that Thomas Clarkson, who had come to visit Ramsay, had pledged himself to the cause, and it was also there that William Wilberforce had agreed to act as the public face of the abolition movement in Parliament. More predicted that it was at Teston that 'The great charter of African liberty'

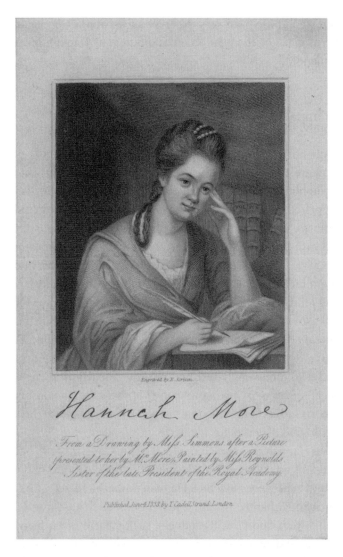

Figure 10.4 Hannah More. This portrait shows the very model of a
woman intellectual: a thinker and writer of classical and refined
sensibility caught in the moment of composition. The caption
shows her to have been part of an influential circle of such women.

would be written. She said this Kentish village would be forever remembered
as the 'Runneymeade of the negroes'.[18] Encouraged, like Wilberforce, by the
former slave-trader turned preacher John Newton – the author of the hymn
Amazing Grace – to exercise her new evangelised moral conscience in public
actions, More looked to play her part in this new politics. She joined Thomas
Clarkson in Bristol, its role as a port for slave ships making this one of the

most difficult parts of his travels, and was shown his gruesome hardware collection. She reported that 'Clarkson desires us to canvass for him from the Member of Parliament down to the common seaman'.[19] She also picked up her pen and set to work.

In 1788, Hannah More published *Slavery: A Poem* as her contribution to the public discussion over the parliamentary debates on the slave trade. Much of the poem reads like Wedgwood's emblem set in verse. It reaffirms the shared humanity of all under God ('Does th'immortal principle within / change with the casual colour of a skin?', lines 63–64); the supplicant appeal of the enslaved; and the sympathetic benevolence that should be mobilised to set them free:

Astonish'd echo tells the vocal shore,
Opression's fall'n, and Slavery is no more!
The dusky myriads crowd the sultry plain,
And hail that mercy long invok'd in vain.
Victorious Pow'r! she bursts their tow-fold bands,
And FAITH and FREEDOM spring from Mercy's hands.
                                        (lines 289–294)

In later editions, 'Mercy' in the poem's last line became 'Britain', reinforcing the poem's message that it was the actions of the British that would spread both God's word and freedom to others. More's conservative Whig politics were loud and clear. The balanced constitution – king and Parliament – and the values of liberty and property enshrined in Britain by the Glorious Revolution exactly a century before had established the founding principles of a political system that was as near perfect as could be.

Yet this did not mean that things should not change. More's poem pointed up the contradiction between English liberty at home and its dependence on slavery in the colonies ('Shall Britain, where the soul of freedom reigns, / Forge chains for others she herself disdains?', lines 251–252). This contradiction was also a sign that Britons, high and low, did not live up to the moral principles of their own political system or to their religious duties. For those who wanted to bring evangelical principles into politics the abolition movement was one part of a broader campaign for the reformation of manners. 'Saint Hannah' was part of this. She and her sisters ran schools in the West Country to educate and give moral instruction to the poor. And, as well as being the year of the publication of *Slavery*, 1788 was also when she wrote, with much advice from her friends at Barham Court, *Thoughts on the Importance of the Manners of the Great*, an anonymous tract devoted to effecting personal moral reform among the elite. Abolition was part of a conservative vision of a remoralised, ordered and deferential society.

Freedom, for More, came at a price. The price was order. Her evocation of the goddess Liberty in the opening stanzas of *Slavery* was not to be taken as an invitation to violent challenge. Not for More her former friend Samuel Johnson's toast to 'the next insurrection of the negroes in the West-Indies'.[20] Instead, as she put it:

Thee only, sober Goddess! I attest,
In smiles chastis'd, and decent graces drest.
Not that unlicens'd monster of the crowd,
Whose roar terrific bursts in peals so loud,
Deaf'ning the ear of Peace; fierce Faction's tool;
Of rash Sedition born, and mad Misrule;
Whose stubborn mouth, rejecting Reason's rein,
No strength can govern, and no skill restrain;
Whose magic cries the frantic vulgar draw
To spurn at Order, and to outrage Law;
To tread on grave Authority and Pow'r,
And shake the work of ages in an hour:
Convuls'd her voice, and pestilent her breath,
She raves of mercy, while she deals out death:
Each blast is fate; she darts from either hand
Red conflagration o'er th'astonished land;
Clamouring for peace, she rends the air with noise,
And to reform a part, the whole destroys.

(lines 19–36)

Change was to come, for Hannah More, not through violence but through the parliamentary process, and the reformation of manners. It was to be led and shaped by conservative Evangelicals. The woman who was later to name her pet cats, of all things, 'Passive Obedience' and 'Non-Resistance', would have much to say about freedom and order when the revolutionary decade of the 1790s rolled around.

The world of Olaudah Equiano

In contrast to More's strong West Country roots, it is uncertain where Olaudah Equiano was born. In the book which made him famous, *The Interesting Narrative of the Life of Olaudah Equiano, or Gustavus Vassa, the*

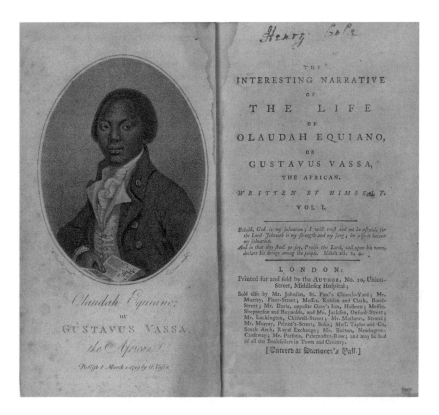

Figure 10.5 Olaudah Equiano. Depicted on the frontispiece of his *Interesting Narrative* (1789), Equiano presents himself as a refined, literate and Christian African. Holding the viewer's gaze he presents to them a life shaped by the Scriptures, guided by his own actions, and related by his own pen. It presented a strong challenge to prevailing images of black people in Britain and its empire, including those in other abolitionist publicity.

African (1789) he told his readers that he was born in West Africa, kidnapped as a child, sold into slavery and carried on a slave ship to the Caribbean (figure 10.5). Other evidence, from baptism records and from the muster books of the ships that Equiano, as Gustavus Vassa (the name of a Swedish liberator king that he was given by one of his owners), sailed on after he had bought his own freedom gives his place of birth as South Carolina. The truth is uncertain. What is certain is that Equiano's story of one African man's enslavement and his fight for freedom captured the imagination of the reading public. He had provided a crucial weapon in the armoury of the abolition movement: an African voice speaking out against slavery.

Equiano made the telling of his life story into his life's work. By the time he wrote it down for others to read he had seen a great deal, and described

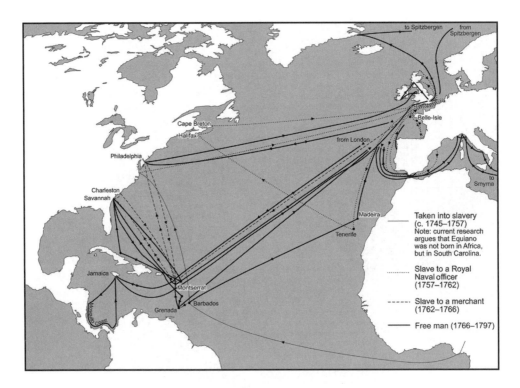

Figure 10.6 The travels of Olaudah Equiano as described in his *Interesting Narrative*, 1789. Shaped by slavery, warfare, trade, exploration and the campaign for abolition, Equiano's travels worked repeatedly back and forth across the North Atlantic world. While he may have started his life's journey in South Carolina rather than West Africa, the extent of his travels is what is most notable.

himself as a 'citizen of the world' (figure 10.6).[21] As a slave in the Americas he had been relatively fortunate. He spent only a short time in the plantation fields, and was sold in 1754 to Michael Henry Pascal, a Royal Navy lieutenant. With Pascal, he saw action in several of the key battles of the Seven Years' War, and learned the ropes of a naval vessel alongside sailors both black and white (see chapter 6). He also came to London and, realising that the freedom of a black man in the Americas would always be in question, began to see it as somewhere he could be at home. Expecting to be granted his freedom in the capital in 1762, he was dismayed and angered when Pascal sold him back into West Indian slavery. However, his new master, Robert King, a Quaker on the island of Montserrat, also realised Equiano's value as more than a field slave. His sailing skills were put to good use, first around the islands and then in voyages – including those carrying slave cargoes – to the North American slave colonies of South Carolina and Georgia, and to the city of Philadelphia. Equiano was able to make these voyages work for his own purposes. Putting ideas of escape out of his mind he emulated other Atlantic merchants, albeit in a small way, buying cheap in one place and selling dear in another.

By July 1766 Equiano had the £70 necessary to hold King to the promise that this slave could buy his own freedom. As soon as he could he returned to London, but it was not long before he was on the move again. Between 1768 and 1786 he sailed from London on ships to the Mediterranean, going as far as Smyrna (now Izmir) in Turkey, and also back to North America and the Caribbean, where he visited Jamaica for the first time and 'saw many cruel punishments inflicted on the slaves in the short time I staid here'. Most dramatically, in 1773 he ventured into the Arctic Ocean, the 'uninhabited extremity of the world', as part of a Royal Navy expedition to navigate towards the North Pole, and investigate the possibility of a northeast passage to India.[22] He also took up an appointment as an overseer on a slave plantation on the Mosquito Coast in the Bay of Honduras (taking pride in his humane treatment of the slaves), although this venture ended in failure, and applied, unsuccessfully, to the bishop of London in 1779 for a position as missionary in West Africa. He had been baptised in 1759, but it was in the mid-1770s that he embraced Methodism and began to understand his life in terms of God's providential plan.

If Equiano was looking for a purpose for his life he found it in the anti-slavery movement. He had met Granville Sharp in 1774 while trying, unsuccessfully as it turned out, despite the Somerset case, to prevent a fellow black man, John Annis, from being taken from London to the West Indies. In 1783, he called on Sharp again to bring to his attention the news reports of the slave ship *Zong*, whose master had thrown 133 enslaved Africans into the sea, alive and still chained together, in order to claim insurance for them as jettisoned cargo. Equiano had also met James Ramsay on St Kitts before the clergyman left in 1781. These connections led, in 1786, to his appointment as the government's commissary for the expedition mounted by the Committee for the Relief of the Black Poor to resettle a group of poor blacks, many of them loyalists from the American War of Independence (along with white family members and poor artisans) in Sierra Leone, West Africa. Equiano, who had his doubts about the venture, clashed with the other organisers, and was dismissed in March 1787 before the fleet had left England. As Gustavus Vassa he defended himself in the press and, if this venture did not take him to Africa, it did bring his name to the attention of the public and connected him to leading figures of the abolition movement right at the moment when they were beginning to come together.

In 1787 and 1788 Olaudah Equiano, as Gustavus Vassa, actively pursued the abolitionist cause. He did so through letters both private and public (especially those published in the *Public Advertiser*), public debates, printed reviews of pro-slavery tracts, and petitions, including one to Queen Charlotte, wife of George III, 'on behalf of my African brethren'.[23] He attended all the deliberations on the matter in the House of Commons and offered to testify before the Privy Council's Board of Trade. They turned him down, so he published his opinions on the benefits of free trade with Africa in the *London Advertiser* instead. In 1789 he made his most important contribution of all, publishing his *Interesting Narrative*. This was something new and proved vital to the cause, not simply another anti-slavery tract, poem, novel or picture, but an account of slavery from one who had 'really been there'.[24] Moreover, the very fact of its having been written, as the title page proclaimed, by an 'African', spoke volumes about universal humanity and the improvement of man through the virtues of religion, civilisation and politeness that late eighteenth-century Britons prided themselves on. Equiano tirelessly promoted his book and its message. In a series of tours around Britain and Ireland between 1789 and 1794 he presented himself to his readers, sold his volumes and gathered subscribers for new editions. Equiano died in 1797, just over a year after the death of his white wife, Susanna Cullen, whom he had met while promoting his book in Cambridgeshire. Having made around £1,000 from his book (the equivalent of about £80,000 today), this former slave was able to leave his surviving daughter a substantial legacy.

The coalition fractures

Despite all this support progress was slow. With popular pressure building in 1788 it was a great disappointment when Wilberforce fell ill before he could raise the issue of the slave trade in Parliament and the debate was postponed. Then King George III fell ill too. His madness paralysed the political process, and it was not until 1789 that an abolition bill could be introduced. In the meantime, the Committee on Trade and Plantations of the Privy Council had been assigned to investigate the trade. The abolitionists, led by Clarkson, used it to present their growing mountain of painstakingly gathered evidence. But the pro-slavery lobby had marshalled their forces too. So, when Parliament considered the matter Wilberforce was unable to convince the House that abolition of the British slave trade would not simply put it in the hands of the French. Despite the 850-page report from the Privy Council, Parliament voted to delay their decision by calling for more hearings. The debate reopened only in April 1791 and, as Clarkson predicted, the motion for abolition was lost by 163 votes to 88. The pro-slavery lobby had bought its way out of trouble.

Undeterred, and backed by the sugar boycott and a massive revitalisation of the petitioning campaign, the abolitionists returned to Parliament in 1792. At this point global political events began to intervene. The French Revolution, which had burst into life in 1789, and a massive slave revolt in 1791 on Saint Domingue, the most profitable French colony in the Caribbean, initially gave force to the argument that the French would not benefit from British abolition. The House of Commons voted to abolish the slave trade. But since Home Secretary Henry Dundas had inserted the word 'gradually' into the bill this was really only another delaying tactic. In the end the bill did not make it past the House of Lords and, by 1793, events in France and in Saint Domingue had begun to have a different effect. The coalition of different interests that the abolition movement had brought together began to fracture.

As well as attracting the provincial middle class, the anti-slavery movement also appealed to working men and women. Popular abolitionism understood slavery as a threat to the rights of the free-born, rights that they also felt were denied to them in Parliament and in the workplace. The fight against the slave trade was broadened into a social and political reform movement. The shoemaker Thomas Hardy, one of the founders of the radical London Corresponding Society in 1792, argued that the Rights of Man 'are not confined to this small island but are extended to the whole human race, black or white, high or low, rich or poor'.[25] This notion of universal human rights led a meeting of thousands of workers in Sheffield in 1794 to call for both 'a reform in the representation of the people' and 'the total and unqualified abolition of negro slavery'.[26] It had also led abolitionists, particularly Thomas Clarkson, to hope that the leaders of the French Revolution would adopt abolition. He spent some months in Paris in 1789 soaking up the atmosphere of a newly minted society and trying to convince the revolutionaries to fully realise the ideas of liberty, equality and fraternity. However, as it became clear that the French were not heading peacefully towards a British-style constitutional monarchy (they cut off Louis XVI's head in January 1793), the more conservative abolitionists began to grow fearful. As Wilberforce put it, 'It is certainly true, and perfectly natural, that these Jacobins are all friendly to Abolition; and it is no less true and natural that this operates to the injury of our cause.'[27]

Hannah More, as might be expected, took up her pen again. In 1792, in response to the success of Thomas Paine's revolutionary tract *Rights of Man*, she published her *Village Politics*. This dialogue between a radical mason and a blacksmith doggedly defending British 'liberties' via the principles of conservative Whiggism was one of the most widely distributed loyalist and anti-revolutionary works. Its message that the working man should 'Study to be quiet, work with your hands and mind your own business', repeated the call to order in the name of liberty of More's abolitionist poetry.[28] Therefore, when war was declared between Britain and France in 1793 the movement was further divided and the possibility of abolition seemed even more remote.

There were also tensions when it came to questions of race. As Olaudah Equiano's life shows, very significant contributions to the movement were made by former slaves living in Britain who spoke and wrote against slavery. Both Quobna Ottobah Cugoano and Equiano contributed to public debates, travelled the country to mobilise support, wrote for newspapers and published extensive works arguing against slavery. In doing so they often argued for more radical measures than their white counterparts were prepared to push for. Cugoano's *Thoughts and Sentiments on the Evil and Wicked Traffic of the Slavery and Commerce of the Human Species* (1787) proposed that 'universal emancipation of the slaves should begin' while the London committee was only lobbying for the abolition of the slave trade.[29] These ex-slaves bore little resemblance to the images used by the abolitionists. Far from the supplicant, dependent negro of Wedgwood's emblem or the silent, suffering bodies depicted packed into the hold of the slave ship *Brookes*, these were men prepared to speak out for themselves. Other ex-slaves were also ready to stand up for their rights. The abolitionists who had planned to find London's black poor (including many of the loyalists from the American Revolution) new homes in Sierra Leone – in a place to be called 'the Land of Freedom' – soon found that those men and women (including Equiano) were prepared to stick up for themselves.[30]

Where the enslaved on the plantations broke out into open, violent revolt in pursuit of their freedom, slaughtering white people rather than looking to them for help, the tensions were even greater. Events in the Caribbean shook the abolitionists. As Wilberforce exclaimed after a debate at Coachmakers' Hall in November 1791, 'People here are all panic-struck with the transactions in St. Domingo'.[31] He meant his people, and once again he saw the parliamentary route to abolition taking an uphill turn. At the heart of this, and at the heart of the story of the revolution on Saint

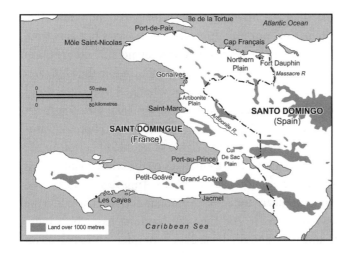

Figure 10.7 Saint Domingue, c. 1790. The western portion of this large mountainous island was the richest colony in the world at the end of the eighteenth century. Its plantation landscape produced sugar and rum for export to France.

Domingue, was an ex-slave who never came to Britain, but whom the British came to know well, as both a villain and a hero.

The world of Toussaint L'Ouverture

Toussaint was born into slavery in the 1740s on the Bréda plantation just outside Cap Français on the north coast of Saint Domingue (figure 10.7). It was said that his father was an African prince, the second son of an Arada chief. Like Equiano, Toussaint was not consigned to the fields, but found a more privileged position, tending the livestock and working as a coachman. It was a position that allowed him to see beyond the plantation itself, travelling around the island's northern plain. Like Equiano, he was also granted his freedom sometime in the 1770s and this freed slave became, at least temporarily, a slave-owner himself and, more permanently, a literate Christian (although in this case a Roman Catholic who was said to have read the abolitionist works of the Abbé Raynal). Saint Domingue was a landscape of slavery. By 1790 its plantations produced more sugar and coffee than anywhere else in the world. In 1789 the colony held 465,000 slaves, 31,000 whites and 28,000 free coloureds (most of whom were of mixed race). Like those of Barbados and Jamaica, this slave society was strictly divided along the lines of race and property (see chapter 9). The *blancs blancs* – literally 'white whites' – who had the privilege of both property and white skin, sought to divide themselves not only from the black slaves but also from the free coloureds who themselves were often slave-owners. As competition increased between recent white migrants and free coloureds in the 1770s and 1780s the latter were barred from the professions, banned from 'affect[ing] the dress, hairstyles, style, or bearing of whites', and denied political rights.[32]

Revolutions changed things. The French Revolution, as Thomas Clarkson had hoped, brought a debate on the rights of people of colour in the colonies, slave and free. In Paris, representatives of the white planters and the free coloureds, and the abolitionist Société des Amis des Noirs, argued over what the Revolution meant for Saint Domingue and its people. On the island, first the Revolution itself, and then the National Assembly's indecision on who should be granted citizenship, prompted a violent revolt of the free coloureds. Their leader Vincent Ogé was said by some to have been given money for arms by Thomas Clarkson. Then, in 1791, the slaves in Saint Domingue's northern province rose in revolt. This was, in part, fuelled by stories that the plantation-owners were refusing to comply with decrees issued by the king and the National Assembly banning the whip and providing slaves with three free days a week rather than two. It certainly used both European and African notions of kingship and freedom against the local rule of the slave-owners. This was a massive, planned and co-ordinated revolt, which wreaked extensive destruction and death across the sugar plantations of the plain. Tens of thousands of slaves joined the rebellion, some marching under a banner proclaiming 'death to all whites!'[33] Others were more circumspect. Although he may have been in contact with the rebels from the beginning, Toussaint initially remained on the plantation where he was a manager, protecting it and the wife of the man who had freed him. After just over a month, he sent her to the safety of Cap Français, packed his own wife and children off to Santo Domingo (the Spanish side of the island), and went to join the rebels. He was forty-five years old, just over five feet tall and already grey-haired. He had no previous military experience, but was to become a formidable leader. In doing so his name changed. The name of those who had owned him was dropped and a new future was imagined. Toussaint Bréda became Toussaint L'Ouverture. He was to be 'the opening' (figure 10.8).

L'Ouverture fought as an officer under the insurgent leader Georges Biassou, in alliance with the Spanish who controlled Santo Domingo. The successes of the revolt brought by leaders such as Toussaint pushed the white and free coloured property-owners into closer alliance under the threat of losing everything. The free coloureds took full advantage. In France

Figure 10.8 Toussaint L'Ouverture. By showing an African leader according to the conventions usually reserved for powerful Europeans, this dramatic image demonstrates the challenge posed by L'Ouverture. He is on horseback, in full uniform and wielding a sword. This 'Chef des Noirs Insurgés' is the very opposite of the supplicant, enslaved African. He threatens to take his freedom by force.

they convinced the government that the only way to stop the revolt, and to save slavery in Saint Domingue, was for there to be equality of political rights between the free, regardless of race. The National Assembly decreed that all non-slaves would be citizens, and radical republican commissioners Léger Félicité Sonthonax and Etienne Polverel were sent, with 6,000 troops, to ensure that the new political order was put into effect. However, stopping the slave revolt was not so easy, especially when things were evidently changing due to the pressure the rebels applied. The insurgents who refused to return to the plantations remained in control of the mountains.

As revolutions change things they change too. In 1793, King Louis XVI was executed, the republic was proclaimed and Britain and Spain declared war on France. This war would be fought in the Caribbean as well as in Europe. The Spanish supported the insurgent slaves. The British sided with the counter-revolutionary planters (many of whom argued that Saint Domingue should simply be handed over to the British king), sending an invasion force of 7,000 men which arrived in the Caribbean in December 1793 and swiftly took several of the island's ports. As the white planters became traitors to the republic, the slaves were able to become its supporters. Coming under increasing pressure, Sonthonax and Polverel declared that slaves who fought for the republic would 'enjoy all the rights attached to the quality of French citizenship'.[34] Born of necessity, as the child of the French Revolution and the slave revolt, this was a dramatic move. It granted not just liberty but full citizenship. The choice appeared clear: fighting for France would bring freedom; the British, on the other hand, were reintroducing slavery in all the territory that they took.

Yet the leaders of the slave revolt, including Toussaint L'Ouverture, were sceptical. He saw an alternative route to liberty and equality through loyalty to the Spanish king and, in particular, the autonomy that this allowed him. He was not ready to throw his lot in with a republic that was weak both in Europe and on the island, and which would immediately demand his subordination. Indeed, it was not even clear that the commissioners' declaration of freedom would be supported in France.

Toussaint L'Ouverture's switch to the republican side on 5 May 1794, bringing 4,000 troops with him, was probably prompted by hearing through unofficial channels that the French National Convention had, in response to the delegation sent from Saint Domingue, abolished slavery throughout its empire on 4 February 1794. This declaration, one of the most revolutionary acts of the whole French Revolution, made all slaves citizens and it made the republic, as it existed on Saint Domingue, something worth fighting for. L'Ouverture, allied with the republican officer Etienne Laveaux, turned his growing military skills, his powerful intellect and political acumen, his feats of endurance and his almost supernatural ability never to be where his enemy expected him to be against the Spanish and the British. He also turned former slaves into a formidable fighting force. The French general Pamphile de Lacroix wrote of this army without uniforms that 'It was remarkable to see these Africans, naked, carrying nothing but a cartridge belt, a saber and a rifle, showing exemplary and severe discipline'.[35] The

Spanish were brought to signing a truce. The British invaders, devastated by disease and harried by ambushes they could never counter, admitted defeat and negotiated their withdrawal with L'Ouverture in 1798, having lost 12,000 men. L'Ouverture had brought freedom to the whole of Saint Domingue. Laveaux called him 'the Spartacus predicted by Raynal, whose destiny was to avenge all the outrages committed against his race.'[36]

In Britain the same actions meant that L'Ouverture had become a demon caricatured in the most racist fashion. Reaction against the French revolution, the Saint Domingue revolt and the notions of universal rights that they brought with them meant that, as Thomas Clarkson put it, 'Many looked upon the abolitionists as monsters.'[37] In the backlash against radical politics, abolitionism suffered too. Thomas Hardy, the founder of the London Corresponding Society and Olaudah Equiano's landlord, was arrested in 1794 and put on trial for treason. Anti-slavery was off the agenda in Britain and its colonies in the face of the revolutionary freedoms that L'Ouverture had brought to Saint Domingue.

Yet this could only be a partial kind of freedom. L'Ouverture simultaneously used all his skills, and eventually his troops (who now numbered 45,000), against his rivals on the island. He became the central political figure in the colony, forcing Sonthonax, the only leader who had as much support among the former slaves, back to France, and fighting a bitter and brutal civil war for territorial control against the 'mulatto' leader in the south, André Rigaud. L'Ouverture's aim was autonomy. He increasingly ran the island like an independent colony, with less and less attention to the authorities in Paris. He even negotiated on his own terms with the British while they were still at war with France, and with the Americans for naval assistance against Rigaud. Yet this autonomy could be preserved, he reasoned, only if the island's shattered economy could be rebuilt to provide the exports for France which would ensure metropolitan support. Beginning during the war, and consolidated by draconian decrees in 1800, L'Ouverture instituted a militarised labour regime that would compel the former slaves to return to the plantations as wage-labourers. This meant respecting the property rights of the white planters, except where this was complicated by the rise of a new plantation-owning class from among the insurgency's own officers, including L'Ouverture himself. It certainly meant no large-scale redistribution of land to the former slaves. Their dream of freedom in the form of control over a small holding, and over their own labour, was denied them (see chapter 9). As L'Ouverture put it 'Work is necessary, it is a virtue, it is for the general good of the state'.[38] Those who did not work would be punished. To those doing the work this kind of freedom looked a lot like slavery. Was Toussaint doing what was necessary to protect liberty and the ideals of the revolution, even if that meant restricting the freedom of some? Or was he becoming an increasingly authoritarian ruler? These were questions that were also raised about another leader who had risen rapidly to power through dazzling military victories, and who wanted to have a say in the future of Saint Domingue: Napoleon Bonaparte.

Bonaparte's new regime in France was markedly less friendly to ideas of racial equality and universal rights than the republicans of 1794 had been. He surrounded himself with advisors on colonial matters who convinced him that the colonies, due to their different environments and climates, each required different laws and forms of government. This racist ideology put the reintroduction of slavery in the French empire back on the agenda, although Napoleon initially reassured those on Saint Domingue that their rights would be respected. Predictably, L'Ouverture recognised the threat and had the island's Assembly ratify a constitution in July 1801 which declared slavery's permanent abolition on the island, and that 'All men within it are born, live, and die free and French'.[39] The constitution also declared that L'Ouverture would be governor for the rest of his life, giving him sweeping powers. His assent was necessary for all laws. He would control all civil and military appointments, and oversee state policy on work and trade. Suppressing any dissent, and requiring that citizens work for the state, L'Ouverture had become a dictator. He had certainly become a threat within Napoleon's empire. Bonaparte soon showed his true colours, taking advantage of peace with Britain to dispatch a fleet of fifty ships, 20,000 sailors and 22,000 soldiers under his brother-in-law Charles Victor Emmanuel Leclerc. This display of military might was, as Napoleon put it, to enable Leclerc to 'Rid us of these gilded Africans', either through their submission or by force.[40]

In the end Napoleon was to send more than 80,000 men and the expedition was to lead only to failure and death. L'Ouverture and many of his followers refused to comply with the demands from Paris and were soon at war again. Fighting for their very freedom, L'Ouverture ordered his commanders to destroy everything so that 'those who have come to put us back into slavery will always find in front of them the image of the hell they deserve'.[41] Roads were torn up, crops burned in the fields and corpses thrown into springs to pollute the water. Despite this Leclerc gained the upper hand and L'Ouverture began to negotiate a surrender, agreeing to settle peacefully on his own plantation. This did not, however, end the hostilities and Leclerc began to doubt L'Ouverture's sincerity and to see his very presence on the island as a threat. The black leader was tricked into attending a meeting and, along with his wife and sons, was arrested and sent to France. Incarcerated high in the Jura mountains in an icy dungeon of the Fort-de-Joux, but with no charges brought against him, L'Ouverture was a danger to the French government, but not one who could be easily dealt with. His captors cut back his food and fuel, reduced his medical care and ushered him towards death. He died on 7 April 1803, having now become a hero in Britain for his defiance of the great enemy, Napoleon. Celebrated in verse by Samuel Taylor Coleridge and William Wordsworth, he was voted man of the year for 1803 by the *Annual Register*.

L'Ouverture had gone, but free Saint Domingue was not yet done for. The mask was off the French intention to reintroduce slavery, and the men and women whom they sought to enslave fought back tooth and nail. L'Ouverture's successor Jean-Jacques Dessalines tore the white heart from the French tricolour and, sewing the blue and red back together, responded in kind to Napoleon and Leclerc's declaration of a 'war to the death'.[42] There were horrendous massacres on both sides and, in the end, the French could do no better than the British. The punishing terrain, unfamiliar guerrilla tactics, the resumption of hostilities with Britain and the diseases that swept through the European ranks all took their toll. Fifty thousand French soldiers died as the former slaves of Saint Domingue fought off another empire. On 1 January 1804 the victors established the Republic of Haiti, taking for themselves the name the original Taíno inhabitants had given the island. Its subsequent troubled history has been one which graphically illustrates the problems of freedom in an unequal world. Yet it remains a testimony to liberty – the most successful slave revolt, a declaration of universal rights, a monument to the abolition of slavery by self-liberation. It, like Toussaint L'Ouverture, was an opening.

The slave revolt on Saint Domingue and the establishment of the Republic of Haiti fractured the abolitionist movement, but, paradoxically, in the end it also made the abolition of the slave trade more likely. With the loss of France's prime sugar colony, the unilateral end of the slave trade by the British could no longer be seen as simply handing the economic advantage to its great rival. Indeed, the long revolutionary and Napoleonic wars, from the execution of Louis XVI in 1793 to the defeat of Napoleon at Waterloo in 1815, changed the relationship between slavery and empire for the British. What was being fought in these years was not simply the ideological battle of republicanism against monarchism in Europe. For the first time since the end of the Seven Years' War in 1763, what was at stake was global imperial control. Fronts were opened in the Americas, in

India and in Africa. Napoleon's invasion of Egypt was intended to cut off Britain's passage to India, and the British feared that Bonaparte's agents were encouraging republicanism amongst their Indian enemies too. On the other side of the world, when Britain faced France in the Caribbean in the early nineteenth century it no longer did so simply as the defender of white planters and their slave regime against republican freedom for all. Instead, it faced a Napoleonic France intent on restoring slavery. Gradually, the anti-slavery cause became associated with the battle against Bonaparte. It became a matter of British liberties against French tyranny. It allowed the pursuit of empire to be clothed in the language of virtue, and it allowed Britain's aristocratic government to introduce a measure of reform dear to the middle classes without fundamentally disturbing the structures of power at home.

The anti-slave trade movement revived after 1803, and Thomas Clarkson and the Anglican evangelicals began to orchestrate a primarily parliamentary campaign. Drawing on the fears evoked by the Saint Domingue revolt, they stressed the need to end the slave trade, but not slavery itself, in order to encourage plantation-owners to create stable slave societies on Britain's sugar islands. Also, drawing deeply on the reserves of patriotism, they got through Parliament the Foreign Slave Trade Bill (1806) which outlawed the involvement of British subjects with the slave traders of France and its allies. No one could, or did, object to a measure which supported the war effort and damaged the French imperial economy. But since many of the nominally 'American' ships in the slave trade, flying the flag of France's republican ally, the United States, were actually British-owned, it dealt a severe blow to the slave-traders of Liverpool, Bristol and London. Following the death of Prime Minister Pitt, Nelson's victories at the Nile and Trafalgar which put Britain in control of the oceans, and the growing desire for some degree of reform, the bill to abolish the slave trade was passed in 1807.

As Clarkson said of the twenty-year battle to abolish the slave trade, 'Of the immense advantages of this contest I know not how to speak . . . Never was the heart of man so expanded; never were its generous sympathies so generally and so perseveringly excited. These sympathies, thus called into existence, have been useful in the preservation of a national virtue.'[43] The movement, and its success, was already on the way to becoming celebrated as a distinctively British moral crusade revealing particularly British virtues. Once the law passed, the Royal Navy was entrusted with enforcing it, stopping slave ships and returning their cargoes to Sierra Leone. Britain sought, from a position of power, to control a new global economy of free labour and free trade. Yet there were paradoxes here too. Britain's wars against

France, wars in the name of liberty and against tyranny, had been fought in the Caribbean using increasing numbers of slave troops. Between 1795 and 1808 the West India Regiment had been manned with over 13,000 slaves purchased from slave traders for around £1,000,000. Indeed, the government delayed the implementation of abolition to enable one final and substantial deal to be set up to send another batch of 'ship Negro[es]' to fight for British freedoms against the French.[44]

The aim in abolishing the slave trade was nothing less than an attempt to remake Britain's place in the world. Of course, without emancipation on the plantations this was a very partial gesture, and slavery in British colonies would continue for another generation. But at the end of the eighteenth century there were already signs of what imperial Britain thought it should be or could become. When, in 1788, Hannah More wanted to present what Britain's empire might be without slavery, rather than what it was with it, she invoked one of the country's best-known dead heroes:

Had those advent'rous spirits who explore
Thro' ocean's trackless wastes, the far-sought shore;
Whether of wealth insatiate, or of pow'r,
Conquerors who waste, or ruffians who devour:
Had these possess'd O COOK! thy gentle mind,
Thy love of arts, thy love of humankind;
Had these pursued thy mild and liberal plan,
DISCOVERERS had not been a curse to man!
                    (lines 231–238)

The memory of Captain James Cook, it seemed, meant that Britain's empire could be different.

Further reading

For a good narrative account of the abolition movement, see Adam Hochschild (2006) *Bury the Chains: The British Struggle to Abolish Slavery* (Pan Books, London). For more analytical perspectives on its rise and fall as a political movement, see Roger Anstey (1975) *The Atlantic Slave Trade and British Abolition, 1760–1810* (Macmillan, London), J. R. Oldfield (1995) *Popular Politics and British Anti-Slavery: The Mobilisation of Public Opinion Against the Slave Trade* (Manchester University Press, Manchester), Christopher Leslie Brown (2006) *Moral Capital: Foundations of British Abolitionism* (University of North Carolina Press, Chapel Hill) and Robin Blackburn

(1988) *The Overthrow of Colonial Slavery, 1776–1848* (Verso, London), especially chap. 2, 'Hanoverian Britain: slavery and empire', and chap. 4, 'British abolition and the backlash of the 1790s'. There are biographies of Thomas Clarkson, Hannah More and Olaudah Equiano in the *Oxford Dictionary of National Biography*. For Clarkson's own account of his role, see Thomas Clarkson (2006, originally published in 1808) *The History of the Rise, Progress and Accomplishment of the Abolition of the Slave-Trade by the British Parliament* (Echo Library, Teddington). For Hannah More, see Anne Stott (2003) *Hannah More: The First Victorian* (Oxford University Press, Oxford) and Brown, *Moral Capital*, chap. 6, 'British evangelicals and Caribbean slavery after the American war'. More's poem *Slavery* is available with much other abolitionist literature at www.brycchancarey. com/slavery/morepoems. For Equiano, see Olaudah Equiano (1995) *The Interesting Narrative, and Other Writings*, edited by Vincent Carretta (Penguin, Harmondsworth), Vincent Carretta (2005) *Equiano, the African: Biography of a Self-Made Man* (University of Georgia Press, Athens) and James Walvin (1998) *An African's Life: The Life and Times of Olaudah Equiano, 1745–1797* (Continuum, London). For Toussaint L'Ouverture and the Haitian Revolution, see the excellent account in Laurent Dubois (2005) *Avengers of the New World: The Story of the Haitian Revolution* (Belknap Press of Harvard University Press, Cambridge, Mass.) and the classic C. L. R. James (1980, originally published in 1938) *The Black Jacobins: Toussaint L'Ouverture and the San Domingo Revolution* (Allison & Busby, London).

Notes

1 Quoted in Roger Anstey (1975) *The Atlantic Slave Trade and British Abolition, 1760–1810* (Macmillan, London) p. 122 and Robin Blackburn (1988) *The Overthrow of Colonial Slavery, 1776–1848* (Verso, London) p. 54.
2 Quoted in Vincent Carretta (2005) *Equiano, the African: Biography of a Self-Made Man* (University of Georgia Press, Athens) p. 170.
3 James Ramsay quoted in Christopher L. Brown (1999) 'Empire without slaves: British concepts of emancipation in the age of the American Revolution', *William and Mary Quarterly*, 56:2 p. 300.
4 Maurice Morgann quoted ibid., p. 280.
5 Quoted in Simon Schama (2005) *Rough Crossings: Britain, the Slaves and the American Revolution* (BBC Books, London) p. 25.
6 Thomas Clarkson (2006, originally published in 1808) *The History of the Rise, Progress, and Accomplishment of the Abolition of the Slave-Trade by the British Parliament* (Echo Library, Teddington) p. 92.

7 Society for Effecting the Abolition of the Slave Trade quoted in Carretta, *Equiano, the African*, p. 251.

8 Clarkson, *History*, p. 163.

9 Society for Effecting the Abolition of the Slave Trade quoted in Carretta, *Equiano, the African*, p. 251.

10 Clarkson, *History*, pp. 150–151.

11 Quoted in Adam Hochschild (2005) *Bury the Chains: The British Struggle to Abolish Slavery* (Pan, London) p. 130.

12 Quoted ibid., p. 5.

13 Quoted ibid., p. 129.

14 Clarkson, *History*, p. 256.

15 Quoted in Charlotte Sussman (2000) *Consuming Anxieties: Consumer Protest, Gender and British Slavery, 1713–1833* (Stanford University Press, Stanford) pp. 117–118.

16 Quoted in Christopher Leslie Brown (2006) *Moral Capital: Foundations of British Abolitionism* (University of North Carolina Press, Chapel Hill) p. 382.

17 Quoted ibid., p. 344.

18 Quoted ibid., p. 342.

19 Quoted in Anne Stott (2003) *Hannah More: The First Victorian* (Oxford University Press, Oxford) p. 90.

20 Quoted in Hochschild, *Bury the Chains*, p. 86.

21 Quoted in Carretta, *Equiano, the African*, p. xiii.

22 Olaudah Equiano (1995) *The Interesting Narrative, and Other Writings*, edited by Vincent Carretta (Penguin, Harmondsworth) pp. 171 and 176.

23 Quoted in Carretta, *Equiano, the African*, p. 263.

24 Thomas Clarkson quoted ibid., p. 320.

25 Quoted in Blackburn, *The Overthrow of Colonial Slavery*, p. 147.

26 Quoted in Hochschild, *Bury the Chains*, p. 245.

27 Quoted in Blackburn, *The Overthrow of Colonial Slavery*, p. 147.

28 Quoted in Stott, *Hannah More*, p. 143.

29 Quoted in Hochschild, *Bury the Chains*, p. 136.

30 Jonas Hanway quoted in Schama, *Rough Crossings*, p. 188.

31 Quoted in Peter Linebaugh and Marcus Rediker (2000) *The Many-Headed Hydra: Sailors, Slaves, Commoners, and the Hidden History of the Revolutionary Atlantic* (Beacon Press, Boston) p. 340.

32 Quoted in Laurent Dubois (2004) *Avengers of the New World: The Story of the Haitian Revolution* (Belknap Press of Harvard University Press, Cambridge, Mass.) p. 62.

33 Quoted ibid., p. 116.

34 Quoted ibid., p. 163.

35 Quoted ibid., p. 184.

36 Quoted ibid., p. 203.

37 Quoted in Carretta, *Equiano, the African*, p. 343.

38 Quoted in C. L. R. James (1980, originally published in 1938) *The Black Jacobins: Toussaint L'Ouverture and the San Domingo Revolution* (Allison & Busby, London) pp. 155–156.

39 Quoted in Dubois, *Avengers of the New World*, p. 243.

40 Quoted in Hochschild, *Bury the Chains*, p. 291.

41 Quoted in Dubois, *Avengers of the New World*, p. 266.

42 Quoted in James, *The Black Jacobins*, p. 293.

43 Clarkson, *History*, pp. 414–415.

44 Quoted in William St Clair (2006) *The Grand Slave Emporium: Cape Coast Castle and the British Slave Trade* (Profile Books, London) p. 239.

11 | Navigation and discovery: voyagers of the Pacific

By the second half of the eighteenth century Europeans were paying increasing attention to the Pacific Ocean. Long regarded as the 'Spanish lake', it had been regularly traversed by ships travelling between Manila and Peru. The southern and far northern reaches of the ocean were, however, poorly charted, and there was much speculation in Britain, the Netherlands and France, as well as in Spain, over what islands it contained, where exactly they were and what lands lay to the south. Looking from far away there were what seemed to Europeans to be blank spaces on the map waiting to be filled in. The idea of a Great Southern Continent, a landmass that would balance the continents in the northern hemisphere, was one that engaged many geographers in their studies and map rooms. This was said to be a rich and fertile land, ripe for settlement and trade, a place that would richly reward its discoverers. Increasingly there were other motivations and other rewards for voyages. Such forms of exploration and 'discovery' promised an increase in knowledge of the world, for profit, but for its own sake too. Voyages into the Pacific aimed to further knowledge of astronomy, of geography, of new plants and animals and of the peoples that inhabited these far-off lands and their ways of life. Journeying to the Pacific promised insights into the human condition and the natural world. Driven by the dual desires of empire and the search for Enlightenment, Europeans set out to navigate and discover the new worlds of the Pacific. In doing so they encountered other people who were also skilled at navigating their way around this ocean, and who became engaged in learning about the new voyagers who had sailed into view, discovering their worlds too.

Britain's involvement with the Pacific was decidedly sporadic until well into the eighteenth century. Francis Drake had trodden on Spanish toes throughout his circumnavigation of the globe in the 1570s but left no lasting legacy. In 1699 William Dampier had seen both Australia's west coast and New Guinea before heading back to the Indian Ocean (see chapter 7). George Anson had crossed the Pacific north of the equator in a dramatic voyage around the world on which he lost four ships and over a thousand men, but had returned to tell the tale in print and become First Lord of the Admiralty. Matters changed in the 1760s, making for a different sort of voyaging. In 1766 the Royal Society, Britain's pre-eminent scientific institution, convinced King George III that he should fund an expedition to the Pacific. The occasion was an astronomical event: the transit of the planet Venus across the face of the sun. Measurements of the time the planet took to make the transit made from different observatories around the world would enable precise calculations of the distance of the sun from the earth and from Venus. At stake were both calculations of the size of the universe and more practical considerations such as the accurate determination of longitude, an enduring problem for European navigators.

This was Enlightenment science at its most expansive: a universal problem with practical applications which was to be solved by the international collaboration of European men of science deploying the latest technology at sites dotted around the globe. However, their activities had themselves to be precisely timed and located. This conjunction of the heavens occurs on a cycle in which such subsequent transits occur either only eight years apart or are separated by more than a century. The transit in 1761 had been a missed opportunity. One hundred and twenty scientists (although only eighteen from Britain) had set out across the world to make their observations, but the results had been inconclusive. The Royal Society was determined that Britain would play a part in making measurement of the second transit in 1769 a success. They sent an appeal to the king announcing that 'The British Nation have been justly celebrated in the learned world, for their knowledge of Astronomy, in which they are inferior to no Nation upon Earth, Ancient or Modern; and it would cast dishonour upon them should they neglect to have correct observations made of this important phenomenon.'[1] The king agreed. He granted the Society £4,000 towards the venture and ordered the Admiralty to provide a ship. The question was where in the Pacific to send it. However, just as preparations for the voyage were beginning, Captain Samuel Wallis and the crew of the *Dolphin* returned from the southern oceans to report that they had 'discovered' and claimed for the British king the Pacific island of Tahiti (renaming it King George's Land in the process). Fortuitously, it lay right in the zone where the Transit of Venus could best be observed. Even more promisingly, Wallis and his men reported that they thought they had seen, on the horizon to the south of Tahiti, the cloud-shrouded mountains of the Great Southern Continent. There was, therefore, every reason in the world to go.

The vessel chosen by the Admiralty for the voyage was, on first glance, an unlikely one. The *Earl of Pembroke*, renamed the *Endeavour* when bought

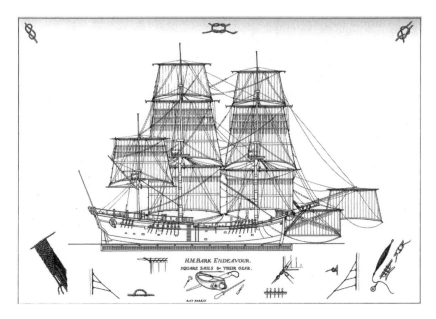

Figure 11.1 The *Endeavour*. The HM Bark *Endeavour* was a Whitby collier purchased by the Royal Navy, renamed and fitted out for Captain Cook's first voyage to the Pacific. This type of vessel's flattened bottom enabled surveying work close inshore and easy beaching for repairs. This was also the type of ship in which James Cook had first put to sea as a boy.

by the Navy Board, had been built in the Yorkshire port of Whitby to carry coal in the trade between the pits of northeast England and the great market in London. Known as a 'cat', the ship was some 97 feet long and 29 feet wide at its widest part, with a capacity of 368 tons (figure 11.1). On closer inspection, however, it offered certain advantages for such a voyage. It had the strength to withstand the high seas around Cape Horn; ample room for stores (there and back); and a flat bottom to allow it to navigate close to shore for surveying work and to enable it to be beached upright for running repairs.

The ship's commander was also a man who knew such vessels well. Lieutenant James Cook had been apprenticed to the Whitby Quaker ship owner John Walker, and had learned his first lessons in navigation in the coal trade. The Admiralty had refused to countenance the Royal Society's suggestion that the expedition should be led by someone from outside the Royal Navy. First in line had been the geographer Alexander Dalrymple, who had made the discovery of the Great Southern Continent (or *Terra Australis*) something of a personal quest, not to say an obsession. Attention then turned to Cook, who had experience surveying coastlines along the

Saint Lawrence River in Canada, but who was then back in London. He would, however, command a ship's company unlike any other the Royal Navy had sent on to the oceans before.

The company was made up of ninety-four men. First, there was a large crew, necessary to deal with the length and rigours of the voyage. It included both seamen and a company of marines, soldiers working on board ship to provide military muscle where need be. The *Endeavour* also carried men of science. The astronomer Charles Green was one of the two observers of the transit nominated by the Royal Society, the other being Cook himself. Yet the scientific ambitions of the voyage were not limited to astronomy. At his own personal expense, a rich young member of the Royal Society, Joseph Banks, had signed on for the voyage. His explorations were to be, primarily, of the animal and plant kingdoms. Yet his interests ranged much more widely. In part this was a matter of the voyage being an extension of his own personal education and experience. On being asked whether he, like many young aristocrats, would journey to Europe he had replied 'Every blockhead does that; my Grand Tour shall be one around the whole globe!'[2] Like any gentlemen would, he also took with him two footmen and two black servants, Richmond and George Dorlton.

Another reason for Banks's wide range of interests was because Enlightenment science in the middle of the eighteenth century, and the universalising forms of reason that underpinned it, did not admit of narrow specialisms. Consequently, Banks's group included the naturalists Daniel Solander and Herman Diedrich Spöring, and the artists Sydney Parkinson, who had experience as a botanical draughtsman, and Alexander Buchan, a landscape painter. Together they would collect, classify and record their new discoveries. This meant loading the ship with equipment. There were the specialist quadrants and sextants necessary for the astronomical observations, and the equipment required for making accurate maps of land and sea. Banks spared no expense. As one Royal Society fellow noted: 'No people ever went to sea better fitted out for the purpose of Natural History. They have got a fine library of Natural History: they have all sorts of machines for catching and preserving insects; all kinds of nets, trawls, drags and hooks for coral fishing, they even have a curious contrivance of a telescope, by which, put into water, you can see the bottom to a great depth, where it is clear. They have many cases of bottles with ground stoppers, of several sizes, to preserve animals in spirits.'[3] He was sure that the expedition would cost Banks as much as £10,000. Part naval venture, part state-sponsored scientific research, and part a private enterprise which mixed knowledge and aristocratic pleasure, the voyage of the *Endeavour* got underway from Plymouth on 26 August 1768.

Cook and the *Endeavour* carried dual instructions for the voyage shaped by the different forces that had come together to propel them towards Tahiti. They carried a set of instructions from the earl of Morton, president of the Royal Society, which set out 'Hints' for how they should treat those they encountered:

To exercise the utmost patience and forbearance with respect to the Natives of the several Lands where the Ship may touch.

To check the petulance of the Sailors, and restrain the wanton use of Fire Arms.

To have it still in view that sheding the blood of those people is a crime of the highest nature: – They are human creatures, the work of the same omnipotent Author, equally under his care with the most polished European; perhaps being less offensive, more entitled to his favor.

They are the natural, and in the strictest sense of the word, the legal possessors of the several Regions they inhabit.

No European Nation has the right to occupy any part of their country, or settle among them without their voluntary consent.

Conquest over such people can give no just title; because they could never be the Agressors . . .

Upon the whole, there can be no doubt that the most savage and brutal Nations are more easily gained by mild, than by rough treatment.[4]

All the principles of Enlightenment humanitarianism are here (see also chapter 10): human beings are part of one universal group, the product of the same God. They have natural rights over their own lands and their own security (see chapter 3). Yet the peoples of the world are also differentiated by their 'stage' of civilisation. Travelling the world also meant travelling across time, back to the past of Europeans to see men in their savage or barbarous states before they had transformed their lands through settled agriculture and then trade.

Yet this civilisation was a two-edged sword. It brought the sorts of progress that made Europeans – at least those beyond the working classes – superior, not least in their possession of weapons of destruction. Yet this 'polish' also meant that Europeans were further from nature, able to restrain their passions, but perhaps less entitled to the favour of their creator. They had, as a result, a duty to restrain the use of violence against 'the Natives'. This, however, all had to be balanced against the secret instructions that Cook carried from the Admiralty. These, following the reports of Wallis and his crew, instructed Cook to proceed southwards from Tahiti in search of the

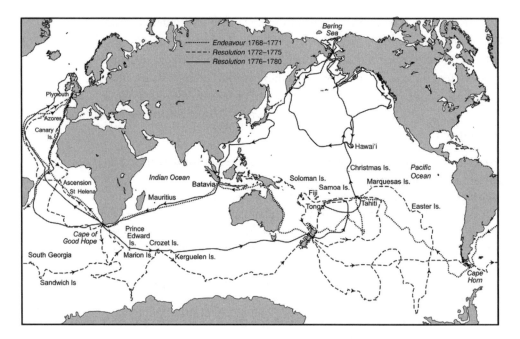

Figure 11.2 James Cook's three Pacific voyages. Captain Cook's voyages into the Pacific criss-crossed the world's largest ocean and took him to its far south and north in search of the Great Southern Continent and the northwest passage. As well as finding himself in places few Europeans had been before, he also revisited a number of places several times, particularly New Zealand and Tahiti, seeing the effects of encounter.

Great Southern Continent. In his explorations he was to provide descriptions of any lands discovered, including the 'Genius, Temper, Disposition and Number' of their inhabitants, and, with their consent, to take possession of any conveniently situated territories for the British king. Although the relationships between them were never fully worked out, and their aims could hardly be said to be coherent, 'Enlightenment' and 'Empire' certainly travelled together on the *Endeavour*.

In the end, Cook's first voyage observed the transit of Venus at Tahiti, albeit inconclusively due to adverse weather conditions. The *Endeavour* then headed south in a fruitless search for land (figure 11.2). Turning westwards they mapped the coast of New Zealand, fixing it as an island and not the beginnings of a new continent, as Banks and many others on board believed. Navigating up the eastern coast of Australia the *Endeavour* was grounded on the Great Barrier Reef and nearly lost. After repairs they passed through the Torres Straits – establishing the difference between Australia and New Guinea – to Batavia in the Dutch East Indies, and home. They arrived back in London to celebrity for Banks and his discoveries, and promotion for

Cook. The encounters with the peoples and places of the southern Pacific soon prompted another voyage. Banks wanted to return to the islands. The Admiralty wanted to know what lay in the vast portions of the southern oceans as yet untraversed. Banks did not get his way. He had planned an even more extensive scientific party. His alterations to one of the ships chosen for the voyage, the *Resolution*, in order to carry his natural philosophers, artists, servants and their equipment, had rendered it unseaworthy. In a huff, he withdrew and travelled to Iceland instead.

The second voyage went ahead without Joseph Banks. Other scientists and artists were engaged for the voyage. The Admiralty did get their questions answered, but no land was discovered. Cook made a series of forays south, crossed into the Antarctic circle three times, and found only ice. He returned to New Zealand and to Tahiti on several occasions, and made new landfalls and encountered new peoples across the islands of Polynesia, from Easter Island in the east to the New Hebrides in the west. Returning home once more, Cook was promoted again and elected to the Royal Society. But it was not long before a third voyage was planned to do what was still left undone. This sought a northwest passage that would connect Europe with Asia, removing the need to travel round either Cape Horn or the Cape of Good Hope. After revisiting New Zealand, Tonga and Tahiti, the *Resolution* and the *Discovery* headed north, came upon the Hawai'ian islands, mapped the coast of the Pacific northwest, and entered the Bering Sea. Once again, however, they were faced with an impenetrable wall of ice. Heading south – the northwest passage rendered another geographical fantasy – they landed again at Hawai'i. Here, on 14 February 1779, having tried to take a chief hostage to ensure the return of a stolen boat, Captain Cook was killed by the islanders as violence flared on the beach at Kealakekua Bay.

These three voyages were, undoubtedly, great feats of navigation and discovery. Cook had sailed further south and further north in the Pacific than anyone was known to have done before. He had destroyed long-standing geographical myths and fixed a new European map of the islands and coastlines of the Pacific. He and the scientists and artists who travelled with him made a series of striking discoveries of things they had not known before: bringing knowledge, and representations and specimens of plants, animals, landscapes and peoples back to Europe. They had, in many ways, fulfilled the promise of Enlightenment reason's will to know. They could not, however, claim that they had fulfilled the Enlightenment's humanitarian promise too. The three voyages had been tense affairs, characterised by violence, murder, theft and disease. These travels had changed the lives of the peoples of the Pacific, and it was hard for Europeans to claim that they had done so purely for the better. Captain James Cook was certainly well aware of the dark side of Enlightenment exploration, and found himself caught within its contradictory forces as he navigated his way across the world.

The world of Captain James Cook

Like many mariners, James Cook was a country boy who felt the lure of the sea. Born the son of a farm labourer in Marton, North Yorkshire, in 1728, he went to work at seventeen in a shop in the small fishing village of Staithes, and was then apprenticed to John Walker of Whitby. He learned valuable lessons about navigating the difficult waters of the North Sea, and, presumably about handling a ship's crew (see chapter 6). Yet when he was offered the command of one of Walker's ships in 1755 he turned it down to join the Royal Navy. Service in the Seven Years' War took him to Canada where, as well as seeing active service, he completed a series of hydrographic surveys, charting the coasts, shoals and channels of the Bay of Gaspé, the Saint Lawrence River and the north and west coasts of Newfoundland. This work made him a suitable candidate to command the *Endeavour* to Tahiti for the transit of Venus, and in search of the Great Southern Continent. In all of his three voyages Cook demonstrated great skill in navigation, and great devotion to the project of accurately mapping the coasts and islands of the Pacific and recording in his journals an account of his discoveries. For many this meant that he became the symbol of a form of rationality associated with careful observation and documentation that could bring truth to the world. It was said of him by James Boswell, the biographer of Samuel Johnson and Georgian London's man-about-town, that he was 'a plain, sensible man with an uncommon attention to veracity. My metaphor was that he had a balance in his mind for truth as nice as scales for weighing a guinea.'[5] His plainness and his biography – his down-to-earth background and promotion on merit rather than connections – seemed to guarantee that what he said was right (figure 11.3).

Yet Cook's problem in the Pacific was that he was facing new situations where it was not quite clear what the right thing to do and say was. There were certainly different versions of how to act. This was most evident in the encounters between Cook and his crews and the indigenous peoples of the islands and coasts. These were extraordinarily varied encounters. They differed depending on what the attitudes of Pacific peoples were to these new arrivals: to incorporate them into their political alliances as on

Capt: James Cook
of the Endeavour.

Figure 11.3 *James Cook*, by William Hodges, c. 1775. This portrait
of Cook was painted by Hodges probably in London after they had
both returned from the second voyage. Quite different from the
official portraits which show Cook in dress uniform with the
paraphernalia of maps and globes, it is an intimate and informal
study of the character of the navigator and explorer by an artist
who knew him well. The painting carefully uses light and shade to
show Cook as a plain, sombre and thoughtful man.

Tahiti; to ignore them and wish them gone as on the Australian coast; or
to challenge them with violence if necessary as on New Zealand. These
meetings also differed depending on what the European strangers made of
what they saw, and the extent to which new peoples could be interpreted for
them by intermediaries. They differed depending on whether those ships
or others had been that way before, and what had happened then. They
differed depending on how the give-and-take of the encounter worked out
on both sides as it unfolded over hours, days or weeks. These encounters
involved both friendship and violence, trust and distrust, understanding
and misunderstanding. The truth was hard to determine as these different
peoples met.

Yet Cook knew, because of the instructions that he had received from the Royal Society, that his actions would be scrutinised in Europe as well as on the beaches of the Pacific. This was particularly the case if violence was used. He seems to have judged it best to demonstrate his willingness to use force, firing with small shot or over the heads of indigenous peoples, reasoning that 'the Natives' would rightly assume they were being invaded until they could be persuaded otherwise. He was also willing to punish thefts by islanders with floggings and other mutilations. Yet no use of weapons or punishments could be uncontroversial; some participants or observers would always feel that undue force had been used, others that undue leniency had been exercised. The truth could not easily be weighed in the balance.

Cook spent more years in the Pacific between 1768 and 1779 than he did in England. Things were different for him there. He was in command of his own wooden world, whereas in England he was in a subordinate position in the naval hierarchy. In the Pacific he was encountering, and being fêted by, Polynesian chiefs who treated him as another chief. They brought him into a new world of rituals; they exchanged names with him and in the process sought to exchange some of their power and prestige for his. In England, he was far outside the structures of power based on land and family which would have brought him similar status and political influence.

Cook was changed in many ways by being in the Pacific, yet the precise dimensions and directions of those changes are hard to chart and navigate. On the one hand, he seems to have become more sympathetic to indigenous peoples and regretful of the changes these European voyages had forced on them. He was increasingly confronted with the evidence of the diseases – particularly venereal diseases – that his men had brought to the islands, and was frustrated by his powerlessness to prevent their spread. He also showed an unwillingness to take action against those Maori he knew to have killed and eaten some of his companion ship's crew on the second voyage. His judgement that this was done from custom angered many of his ship's company – European and Polynesian – who wanted to see revenge against these 'savages'. On the other hand, he was willing to exert increasingly severe physical punishments on islanders who stole from his ships, and to destroy their canoes, and take their chiefs hostage over what at other times had been treated as minor incidents. What perhaps can be said is that Cook's voyages necessitated an interaction with the peoples of the Pacific that left both sides changed. This was evident from the earliest encounters. Encounter was a many-sided process. It explains elements of both Cook's life and his death, but it also involved many lives other than just Captain Cook's. It wasn't all about him.

Navigating the sea of islands

It was not only the Europeans who explored the land and launched voyages of discovery in the Pacific. People had reached Australia by 50,000 BC when lower sea levels meant that it was all but connected to the Asian landmass. Some five thousand years before Cook and his crew arrived in the Pacific a series of waves of voyaging and settling had begun, probably from Taiwan, which had populated the islands to the east, reaching Tonga and Samoa by around 4,000 BC. From there voyages were launched to explore further east: what later became called the Cook Islands, the Society Islands (including Tahiti), the Tuamotu Islands and the Marquesas. From there great voyages of discovery were set forth around two thousand years ago, when Europe was in its Iron Age, which reached Hawai'i to the north and Easter Island to the east. These journeys of over two thousand miles, and the shorter voyages that linked islands together in patterns of trade and ceremony, were undertaken in large double canoes, using a series of carefully learned navigational techniques. These navigators studied the sky at night to memorise the stars which rose and set at particular points on the horizon and over their island destinations, mapping out familiar 'sea-paths'. They felt the ocean beneath them to discern the presence of islands in the patterns made by swells as they deflected off the land. They watched the sky during the day for the movements of the sun, for land reflected in the clouds and for the presence of island-roosting birds at dawn or dusk. They examined the sea for floating vegetation that could only come from land, for patterns of luminescence and for changes in the patterns of waves made by the shadows of islands over the horizon. When they did not know where they were going they made sure they knew how to get back.

These voyages were conducted with the stars in a spiritual sense too. Long-distance navigation was a specialised craft bound up with ritual and religion. For the Tahitians, beyond sea and sky was Te Po, the region of cosmic darkness where the gods dwelt, and from which the ancestors had sailed out in canoes across the sky creating the stars. Voyages on the ocean, following these stars, also followed the journeys of these star ancestors. Like the constellations, the gods also have their risings and their settings. When the British arrived in Polynesia it was the time of 'Oro, a fearsome god of war. 'Oro's temple was at Taputapuatea, on the island of Ra'iatea. For many this was a place of origins. It was known as Havai'i – the homeland – the island from which the other Society Islands had been settled, and which had been at the heart of a far-flung network of inter-island voyaging. Just as those ancestral navigators had voyaged from Ra'iatea, so the cult of 'Oro was carried to other islands from the Taputapuatea *marae*, or temple, on the beach, where the land met the sea and the world of darkness (Te Po) opened into the world of light. It was carried by the *arioi*, an exclusive aristocratic society of travelling priest performers, both men and women, who performed sexually explicit and satirical musical dramas and expected lavish entertainment from their island hosts. *Arioi* spectacle was a theatre of sex and violence. It spoke of the dangerous sacredness, the *tapu*, that all humans were born with as they emerged from the space of darkness into the space of light. It controlled it with laughter and ritual, but also, for the *arioi*, with the tattoos and bark-cloth that both served in their different ways to wrap and seal the body to protect it, and to protect others from it. These protections were also sealed by death. The *arioi* practised infanticide amongst themselves, and their god 'Oro demanded that human sacrifices be made at the *marae*.

Just as navigation was religion, so religion was politics. The British found it hard to understand Polynesian political structures. They looked to find kings and queens, island chiefs for whom property, authority and religious pre-eminence matched up and were stable and hereditary, just as the British liked to think they were at home. They struggled with fluid structures where high rank did not mean political power, or where children were more sacred than their parents, and therefore outranked them. They certainly struggled with the divisions of authority on Tahiti, and with its changing fortunes. Samuel Wallis, arriving in the *Dolphin* at Matavai Bay on the north coast of Tahiti-nui, the larger part of the island, had tried to understand the whole island from the place where he stood (figure 11.4). He was quick to denote Purea, an influential woman and wife of Amo, chief of Papara on the south side of the island, as 'Oberea, Queen of Tahiti'. She may have been pleased with this. She was certainly making a bid for a new kind of political power. Following the invasion of Ra'iatea by warriors from Borabora, sacred relics from Taputapuatea – a red feather girdle and an image of 'Oro – had been brought to Papara. There, at Maha'iatea, Purea and Amo were building a new *marae* for 'Oro. It was intended to be the ruling *marae* of the island and to underpin a new politics. Human sacrifices had been buried in its foundations, and stone was being piled upon stone to prepare for the investiture of Purea and Amo's son Te Ri'i rere as chief. This was a local power struggle, provoking opposition from Purea's sister-in-law and among the leaders of Tahiti-iti such as Vehiatua. It was part of

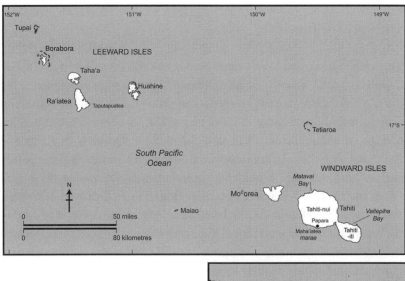

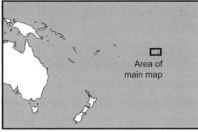

Figure 11.4 The Society Islands, c. 1770. These islands were crucial to the European encounter with the Pacific. European voyagers returned again and again to Tahiti, and places such as Matavai Bay and Vaitepiha Bay became important sites where newcomers and islanders became entangled in each other's politics and intrigued by each other's culture. Tupaia and Mai were both from Ra'iatea, but also travelled to Tahiti.

an inter-island politics, with representatives coming to the investiture from Mo'orea, Borabora, Maupiti and Ra'iatea. It also involved the Europeans too. Purea sought an intimate alliance with Wallis to secure her bid for power. It might have been helpful for her to be thought to be the queen. The visitors were being woven into local politics, just as the red pennant (the sacred colour of 'Oro) with which Wallis had claimed the island for King George was later woven into the feather girdle carried from Taputapuatea to Tahiti. Navigation, religion and politics flowed together around Tahiti, and all those who sailed there were moved by these currents. It was these motions that brought together Captain Cook and Tupaia, a Polynesian navigator, priest and political strategist.

The world of Tupaia

The feather girdle and 'Oro's image had been brought to Tahiti by Tupaia: a navigator from a family of navigators, a high priest and member of the *arioi*. When the Boraborans invaded Ra'iatea they took his family's land, and drove Tupaia from the island. Arriving in Tahiti in about 1760 he became high priest of the district of Papara, forming an alliance with Purea and Amo, and with them built the *marae* at Maha'iatea and the bid for power. Samuel Wallis thought Purea and her lover Tupaia controlled the island. When the *Dolphin* left Purea's enemies from Tahiti-iti proved otherwise. Warriors led by Vehiatua attacked the *marae* in December 1768. The sand of the beach was soaked with blood. Tupaia's body was pierced right through by a spear fashioned from a sting-ray's tail. He fled to the mountains with Purea and her family as their houses, canoes and trees were destroyed by fire.

Cook's arrival four months later in April 1769 seemed to signal some much-needed good fortune for Purea, Amo and Tupaia. Vehiatua was forced to postpone an attack that would have finished them off. Their British allies were back, and Tupaia made sure that he was in the vanguard of trying to weave them back into his side of Tahitian politics. Tupaia also shared with Cook, and especially with Banks, a knowledge of navigation and an ethnographic and geographical curiosity about the world. As Cook put it, 'This man had been with us for the most part of the time we had been upon the Island which gave us an oppertunity to know some thing of him: we found him to be a very intelligent person and to know more of the Geography of the Islands situated in these seas, their produce and the religion laws and customs of the inhabitants than any one we had met with'.[6] When the *Endeavour* prepared to leave, Tupaia asked to go with them. Perhaps he wanted to see where he could go and what he could learn, perhaps it was to serve his own political ends. Cook could not take him as a passenger, because there would be no official support for that expense, so Banks's private wealth secured it. He knew the value of the knowledge that Tupaia would bring, but he also joked to himself in his journal about what it would mean to bring home so exotic a specimen: 'I do not know why I may not keep him as a curiosity, as well as some of my neighbours do lions and tygers at a larger expence than he will probably ever put me to; the amusement I shall have in his future conversation and the benefit he will be of to this ship, as well as what he may if another should be sent into these seas, will I think fully repay me'.[7] As Tupaia and his boy-servant Taiato took their leave Purea burst into tears. She knew what she was losing.

No mere curiosity, Tupaia became the *Endeavour*'s high priest–navigator. He called upon his gods to send a fair wind, and piloted the ship through familiar waters to Huahine and his home island of Ra'iatea. He also guided them through the customs of the Society Islands, orchestrating encounters with other islanders by making speeches; managing a symbolism of bare chests (including that of Dr Monkhouse, the surgeon), plantain leaves and red feathers; and visits to sacred sites. He must also have had to explain what these pale visitors were up to with their flags, military drill and strange incantations as they symbolically took possession of lands new to them. Indeed, Cook and Banks soon found that Tupaia could mediate their arrival in places where he himself had never been before. His language was understood in New Zealand and he was in the forefront in negotiations with the Maori (although he also fired on them when an encounter turned violent). He was useful to the *Endeavour*, but he was not simply its servant. The discussions of religion he had with the Maori served other ends. He had travelled as a Ra'iatean priest from the homeland of Havai'i. They had ancestors and gods in common. The Maori were more interested in Tupaia than they were in the rest of the ship's company. When the second voyage called at New Zealand the people asked after Tupaia, and thought the *Endeavour* had been his ship. Indeed, even those who had not met him had heard of the famous navigator. His name was known throughout the islands.

Tupaia had certainly known his own worth. When he was told that King George III had many children he 'declared he thought himself much greater, because he belonged to the arreoys'.[8] As it was also later reported, he was 'by no means beloved by the Endeavour's crew, being looked upon as proud and austere, extorting homage, which the sailors who thought themselves degraded by bending to an Indian, were very unwilling to pay'.[9] Cook must have had trouble with him too. While he and Banks both valued Tupaia's geographical and ethnographic knowledge, Cook offered an ungracious obituary when the Polynesian, weakened by scurvy, had succumbed to malaria at Batavia and was buried with Taiato on the same small island where William Spavens had been imprisoned by the Dutch only eight years before (see chapter 6). Tupaia, Cook said, was a 'Shrewd Sensible, Ingenious Man' but one who was also 'proud and obstinate which often made his situation on board both disagreeable to himself and those about him'.[10]

The tension between these two navigators and leaders is evident in the map they produced together in the Great Cabin of the *Endeavour* where Cook and Banks's men of science discussed their discoveries (figure 11.5).

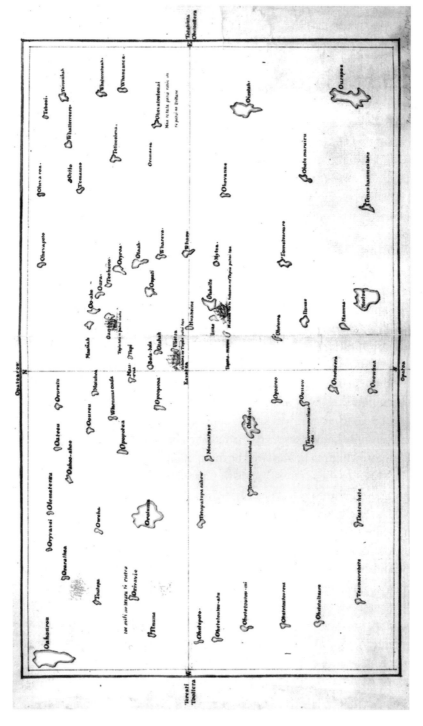

Figure 11.5 Tupaia's map. This chart of part of the Pacific Ocean was drawn on board the *Endeavour* by Captain Cook from information provided by the Polynesian navigator and priest Tupaia. It presents an intriguing meeting of the different way-finding practices of Pacific Island voyagers and European Enlightenment travellers.

It contains more than seventy islands, from a list of over 130 that Tupaia had given to Banks. They are set out in concentric circles around Ra'iatea (Ulietea), covering an area of ocean the size of the United States. It is probably in Cook's hand, copied from a chart that Tupaia had made but which is now lost. It included twelve islands that Tupaia had visited and many that he had heard of from others. On the one hand, it is an appropriation of indigenous knowledge in European form. It puts what would have been contained in oral narratives and the memory work of star compasses and sea-paths down on to that fundamental Enlightenment tool, the map. In doing so it seeks to strip the islands and the paths between them of their stories, preserving only their locations. It prominently marks (with ships) the islands where Europeans had been. It ties it all together with the four points of the compass. On the other hand, however, it is also the indigenous appropriation of a European form of knowledge. Tupaia's home is at the centre of this world. It shows a navigable sea of islands, a familiar world. Tupaia gives the islands their names (no King George's Land here). The map prioritises relative location by sailing time rather than absolute location in space, and organises the whole according to the places to which the prevailing winds blow. It is, in the end, neither one thing nor the other. The map is neither simply a representation of Tupaia's navigational knowledge nor the imposition of Cook's cartographic template. Confusion over the names for directions – *opatoereau* means the point towards which the north wind blows, rather then north itself – meant that some of the islands the British knew are positioned according to a scheme that is different from the one used for those known only to Tupaia. The tension between these proud and austere navigators, both sure of their own way of finding the way, makes the map a record of the shifting path that was drawn out between them.

Seeing the Pacific

Tupaia also produced pictures. A series of watercolours of people, scenes and encounters from the Society Islands, New Zealand and Australia have been attributed to him. One of the most striking represents a moment of exchange on New Zealand. A European, probably Banks, barters Tahitian bark-cloth (*tapa*) for a Maori's crayfish (figure 11.6). Tupaia, who as an *arioi* would have known the stylised production of patterns on bark-cloth and on bodies through tattooing, was engaging with another form of representation, one crucial to European voyages in the Pacific. This was the production of art, of visual images, meant to record the historical details of a scene, but also to show the typical features of people, places and encounters. They

Figure 11.6 Cross-cultural exchange. This drawing by Tupaia shows a Maori dressed in a feathered cloak exchanging a crayfish (held on a string) for a piece of white cloth proffered by a European (possibly Joseph Banks). It is one among a series of pictures drawn by Tupaia while on board the *Endeavour*.

were, in addition, meant to impart some moral lessons too. Tupaia would have learned what he had about drawing and painting from the artists employed by Banks, and he clearly had some access to their precious store of colours.

It was Banks's privately funded group that offered a commitment to the visual record of the first voyage beyond the drawing of charts and coastal profiles to aid navigation. In London, Sydney Parkinson, a young Edinburgh Quaker, had already been employed drawing flowers, birds and insects and was signed up as the *Endeavour*'s botanical and zoological illustrator. In addition, Alexander Buchan had been taken on to depict ethnographic and landscape subjects. When he died shortly after the arrival in Tahiti, Herman Spöring, an untrained draughtsman, took over some of his duties and Parkinson expanded his repertoire. Both men were also to die before the voyage's end, just as Tupaia had, of diseases contracted at Batavia. But their pictures returned to Britain, some of the first European records of the people, nature and landscapes of the Pacific, shaping how they understood these new worlds. Banks had certainly had this metropolitan audience in mind for Buchan's work. When the artist died Banks somewhat selfishly lamented that 'his Loss to me is irretrievable, my airy dreams of entertaining my friends in England with the scenes that I am to see here are vanished. No account of the figures and dresses of men can be satisfactory unless illustrated with figures: had providence spar[e]d him a month longer what an advantage would it have been to my undertaking.'[11] He feared that he would no longer have Buchan's portraits and landscapes, to instruct and entertain, along with the more precise record of plants that Parkinson might provide to set alongside his expanding collection of dried and preserved specimens. Seeing, it seemed, was believing. If those in Europe could not see they would not believe.

This attention to artistic production was continued on the second and third voyages. Banks had originally engaged the portrait artist Johan Zoffany and several draughtsmen for his return to the Pacific. However, when their patron withdrew they were replaced by the young 'Landskip Painter' William Hodges, and by Georg Forster who drew plants and animals for his naturalist father. Several young men on the ship spent some of their time, under the eye of Hodges, learning to draw coastal profiles. By the third voyage, and after constant friction with Johann Forster, Cook had had enough of scientists. Or perhaps he judged he could do enough geography, ethnography and natural history himself. Yet he needed an artist, not least to provide illustrations for the account of the voyage that would be his lasting legacy. John Webber, trained as both a painter and engraver, fitted the bill and produced an impressively comprehensive and readily reproduced record.

As is clear, these artists between them had to produce visual images for an array of different purposes and in a range of different forms. There were sketches done on the spot in pencil, chalk or watercolour (some even in oils). There were worked up versions for publication as engravings. There were also full-scale oil paintings commissioned by the Admiralty and completed in the years after each voyage as its public record. These were exhibited before the critics at the Royal Academy's exhibitions alongside the best of British art. Different genres and forms served different purposes. There was the technical utility and aesthetic precision of coastal profiles and botanical drawings, which brought back the details of geography and botany to be pored over in London. There were the ethnographic drawings which sought both to depict the character of individuals encountered along the way, and to show something of their modes of life to an audience eager to compare the world's peoples and their scales of 'civilisation'. There were the modern history paintings which aimed to depict the heroic significance of moments of encounter and discovery. And there were the large-scale landscape scenes, seeking to recall both the distinctive atmosphere of the Pacific and to lend some classical moral weight to the depiction of such strange places.

Artists on the voyage had to choose what to depict and how to represent it. They had to cut into the flow of events to draw out an enduring image that could stand for much more than just that moment. This was as true of Tupaia as it was of any of the others. In the context of a legal dispute over a farm sale, Banks later remembered, although mistaking some details, that 'Tupia the Indian who came with me from Othaheite Learned to draw in a way not Quite unintelligible... and he drew me with a nail in my hand delivering it to an Indian who sold me a Lobster but with my other hand I had a firm fist on the Lobster determind not to Quit the nail till I had Livery and Seizin [possession] of the article purchasd.' Banks, the wealthy land-owner, insisted that it showed that 'in all Nations the delivery and the Payment is done at the same moment'.[12] Yet it was exactly this point of principle that had repeatedly been a matter of dispute in New Zealand. Maori gift exchange, as Tupaia knew, often involved delayed reciprocity to demonstrate chiefly power. The British, in contrast, quickly turned to violence when exchanges were not immediately fulfilled. Tupaia's picture of Banks, with the Englishman's hands on both crayfish and cloth, perhaps showed not the certainties of the customs of all nations but a European's uncivilised failure to follow the appropriate rituals of recognition and exchange in the Sea of Islands. To make a representation was always to take a position. William Hodges certainly found that out.

The world of William Hodges

The second voyage's landscape painter was born in 1744 to a London black-smith and the sister of a Newgate curate. He was sent to William Shipley's drawing school, where his talent was spotted by the landscape artist

Richard Wilson to whom he was articled as an assistant at fourteen years of age. Wilson, who had shifted away from painting portraits and had spent some time in Italy, was crucial in developing English landscape painting as a serious genre, influenced by the French classical tradition of Claude Lorrain and Nicolas Poussin. Hodges, working in Wilson's studio, would have imbibed these ambitions for the genre along with his master's attention to naturalistic detail. Following periods working in London, and painting theatrical scenery in Derby, he was, through the offices of Lord Palmerston, a member of the Admiralty Board, appointed to replace Zoffany on Cook's second voyage. The order, addressed to Cook, instructed Hodges to 'make Drawings and Paintings of such places in the Countries you may touch on in the course of the said Voyage as may be proper to give a more perfect idea thereof than can be formed from written description only'.[13] If Hodges kept a journal it has not survived. The record of his voyage is in his pictures, and in the words of others on board ship.

As the expedition's artist Hodges had to grapple with all the problems of representation. First, he had to find ways of depicting the unfamiliar. Along with Cook and the Forsters he developed an interest in the distinctive atmospheric conditions of the tropics and the Antarctic, and tried to find ways to depict them. Among the icebergs of the South Pacific there were no precedents for depicting seascapes made up of vast expanses of open ocean and mountains of ice and snow. He approached it with a muted palette of grey watercolour washes and wave crests picked out with a reed pen (figure 11.7). Among the Society Islands, painting in oils, he used thinly applied cool blues and ochres to evoke the hazy light. He always tried to get the clouds just right. Second, the artist could not simply step back from the intimacies of encounter. Hodges drew many of the people with whom Cook dealt, including Tu, who had gained political control in Tahiti; Tynai-mai, the daughter of a Ra'iatean chief; and men and women of New Caledonia unidentified by name but personalised in his pictures. He sketched encounters involving friendship and those involving violence.

Each representation was a moment of intimacy and of distance. After Hodges sketched a Maori girl at Pickersgill Cove she gave him a cloak and tried to tie up his hair as a sign of his power. Yet his intentions were also easily misunderstood. As the naturalist Anders Sparrman reported, Hodges paid a girl to come to the Great Cabin to be painted. She, perhaps through her experience of other members of the ship's company, had other expectations: 'She was astonished when signs were made for her to sit on a chair; such a novel way of doing things struck her as absurd, but she promptly volunteered

Figure 11.7 The *Resolution* passing an iceberg, by William Hodges, 1773–1774. This watercolour is from the second voyage's attempt to explore the far southern reaches of the Pacific Ocean. William Hodges used a restricted palette of grey tones to capture both the atmospheric conditions and the threatening atmosphere of being on a small vessel amongst vast icebergs.

a prone position on the chair for the painter and his companion. To her further surprise she was eventually put in a correct position, just sitting on the chair with nothing to do; whereupon . . . she quickly saw her likeness appearing in a red crayon drawing.'[14] Hodges's images had to negotiate the uncertainties of encounter, and the immorality that so troubled Captain Cook.

Finally, Hodges had to address the audience in Britain. He did so through the encounter images that were engraved for the official account of the voyage. He also did so through a series of dramatic oil paintings of Pacific land- and seascapes that adopted the conventions, and sometimes the figures and motifs, of classical landscape painting to depict warriors in their imposing canoes, the *Discovery* and the *Resolution* in Matavai Bay, and waterspouts during a storm off the New Zealand coast. He later argued that his intention in landscape painting was a moral one: '[I]n the ancient and in many of the modern masters of landscape . . . I confess there seemed very rarely to me

Figure 11.8 *Tahiti Revisited*, by William Hodges, 1776. By applying the conventions of picturesque landscape painting and classical references to an unfamiliar Pacific scene, William Hodges produced a melancholy image of Tahiti as a paradise lost. This painting was produced for the Admiralty after the voyage and displayed to audiences in London.

any moral purpose in the mind of the artist . . . To give dignity to landscape is my object . . . [and] to amend the heart while the eye is gratified.'[15] It is possible to see him pursuing ideas such as this, and grappling with the difficulties that the Pacific posed for him, in one of his best-known pictures: *Tahiti Revisited* (figure 11.8). The island's dramatic landscape, tropical climate and unfamiliar vegetation, along with the naked Tahitian women, one with tattooed buttocks, swimming in the river flowing into Vaitepiha Bay are given a moral, and somewhat melancholy, meaning by their classical treatment. It is a reworking for this earthly paradise of a theme that had been explored by Richard Wilson among others, *Et in Arcadia Ego*: a reminder of the temporary nature of human pleasures.

In London, Hodges was retained by the Admiralty to work up these larger oils. He showed some of them at the Royal Academy, prompting mixed reactions to his use of colour and technique. Following the death of his wife in childbirth within a year of their marriage in 1776, William Hodges packed his brushes and travelled for three years in India under the patronage of Warren Hastings (see chapter 4). Upon his return, with an illegitimate son, his Indian pictures made his name and his fortune. He was elected to the Royal Academy and he married a pianist, Ann Mary Carr, and brought up five children. Yet, with his 'extravagant notions caused by pride and ostentatious liberality', William could not hold on to his money.[16] He unsuccessfully sought patronage in St Petersburg, and, in 1794, hatched an ambitious scheme for an exhibition that would display the moral purpose of landscape painting. However, his theme, displayed on two large canvases entitled *The Effects of Peace* and *The Consequences of War*, came at a bad time. With Britain not only at war with revolutionary France (see chapter 10), but also reeling from a series of military defeats on the continent, the duke of York ordered that the Bond Street exhibition be closed. Hodges gave up on painting, took his family to Devon and opened a bank. Yet that failed too. Hodges died soon after from a fever and gout in the stomach, although some whispered that it was suicide. He had, in his last venture as an artist, been unable to negotiate the demands of the powerful and the morality of landscape painting.

Knowing the Pacific

The pictures that William Hodges and others produced were only one part of the material that was brought back from the Pacific, or that told the tale of the voyages to audiences in Europe. There were also the naturalists' collections of specimens of plants and animals, the curiosities gathered by members of the ships' companies from the islanders, and the journals in which those who took the time and trouble, or were required to do so by the Admiralty, had recorded their experiences. The public display, or publication, of these materials had to find an audience. In part this was a matter of convincing people that the expense and effort of these lengthy maritime undertakings was justified by the discoveries that they produced, especially when their major geographical findings were negative ones: the news that there was no Great Southern Continent and no northwest passage. Joseph Banks, on his return to England in 1771, worked very hard among the great and the good, including King George III, to publicise the first voyage and, of course, himself. Lord Sandwich, First Lord of the Admiralty, gathered together the journals of the voyage and paid Dr John Hawkesworth, an author, critic and writer of essays for literary periodicals, the vast sum of £6,000 to work them up into a narrative that would appeal to a broad audience.

There was certainly a market. Accounts of Cook's voyages became some of the most widely read books of the late eighteenth century. People read them for very different reasons. Among Scottish Enlightenment philosophers such as Adam Smith, David Hume, Adam Ferguson and William Robertson (the author of a history of the Americas) accounts of the Pacific promised to reveal significant truths about human societies and their relationships to nature. As Edmund Burke put it in a letter to Robertson in 1777, 'I have always thought with you, that we possess at this time very great advantages towards the knowledge of human Nature. We need no longer go to History to trace it in all its stages and periods . . . [N]ow the Great Map of Mankind is unrolled at once; and there is no state or Gradation of barbarism, and no mode of refinement which we have not at the same instant under our View. The very different Civility of Europe and China; The barbarism of Tartary, and of Arabia. The Savage State of North America, and of New Zealand.'[17] For Burke, geography replaced history. The different historical stages of human history, the different 'levels' of improvement of human society from savagery to civilisation, could be explored by travelling to distant places or, for those at home, by studying the Great Map of Mankind. The knowledge that Cook had brought back promised to reveal important new truths.

Yet the ideas of these Enlightenment philosophers were just one part of a much broader range of questions about cultural (and natural) differences that were raised by the voyages. There were those who simply revelled in the exotic stories of faraway places. There were those who wanted evidence that mankind was fragmented into different species, and those who sought confirmation of the unity of humanity. There were those who sought in these stories of different societies evidence of abiding and vicious savagery, and others who took these tales as accounts of just the opposite. They read them as descriptions of the noble savage, of the perfection and harmony of humankind in a state of nature untainted by the corruptions and luxury of the modern world. Again and again, however, one set of concerns kept cropping up for all these different audiences: questions of the relationships between men and women, questions of sex and sexuality. As Europeans used these tales of the Pacific to tell them about the world and about themselves the same stories from the voyages were returned to as evidence: Joseph Banks's relationship with Purea; the exchange of nails for sex with Tahitian women; the characterisation of the *arioi* as 'a society, in which every woman is common to every man'; and, especially, the story of what happened at Point Venus on Sunday, 14 May 1769.[18]

Cook reported that on that morning he had held divine service at the fort built to protect the observatory on what they had called Point Venus, and had invited some of the islanders to attend. Later that day the Tahitians had orchestrated a scene of their own. A young man and a girl of ten or twelve years of age performed sexual intercourse at the gate of the fort. Purea and other women had, Cook wrote, 'instructed the girl how she should play her part'. Hawkesworth, reworking Cook's report, and noting the latter's remark that this 'appear'd to be done more from Custom than Lewdness', added that this incident might be of use in 'determining a question which has long been debated in philosophy; Whether the shame attending certain actions, which are allowed on all sides to be in themselves innocent, is implanted in Nature, or superinduced by custom?' Different answers were quickly forthcoming from many different quarters. What was taken to be the revelation of the unnaturalness of sexual shame was celebrated in re-enactments in houses of prostitution frequented by aristocratic libertines and in titillating prose and poetry in print. But others condemned Hawkesworth's descriptions as pornography, and dismissed what they described as fiction. The methodist minister John Wesley (see chapter 10) expressed his disbelief in the lack of God-given shame in his diary: 'Men and women coupling together in the face of the sun, and in the sight of scores of people! Hume or Voltaire might believe this, but I cannot . . . I cannot but rank this narrative with that of Robinson Crusoe.' He was certainly right about Voltaire. The veteran French *philosophe* took the story as confirmation of his long-held opinions, arguing that 'One can be sure that the Tahitians have preserved in its purity the most ancient religion of the world.'[19] Whatever the truth about what happened on 14 May 1769 – whether the boy and girl were willing participants or forced to perform by Purea, and what this was meant to show to the British: a *arioi* rite, or a satire on the British sailors' bizarre willingness to have sex in public – those in Europe took these stories from the Pacific, just as they had taken plants, animals and artefacts, and sought to build them into a bigger account of themselves and their place in the world. They did the same with people too.

The world of Mai

The second voyage also brought back to Britain its first Polynesian visitor. Mai – or Omai, as he was known to the British – was a Ra'iatean of non-chiefly status whose land-owning family had been dispossessed by the same Boraboran invasion of the island that had displaced Tupaia. Mai had been present in Tahiti when the *Dolphin* arrived, but eventually joined the second voyage, on the *Adventure* under Captain Tobias Furneaux, at the nearby island of Huahine. He was keen to visit Britain. It was reported that he sought revenge on his Polynesian enemies, and wanted to enlist British help in regaining his lands. Joseph Banks's housekeeper Mrs Hawley noted that 'Omai says he wants to return with men & guns in a Ship to drive the Bola Bola Usurpers from his property.'[20] Others, however, were less sure of the usefulness of his visit to Britain, and of him to the British. The *Westminster Magazine* welcomed back the second voyage with the opinion that 'I do not find that any good hath accrued to the Community. Numbers of our hardy subjects have died on the passage – many have been roasted and eaten by Cannibals – numbers have drowned – and a great expence the nation hath been put to; and only to bring home a few seeds – some shells – stuffed fish – dried birds – voracious animals – pressed plants – and an Indian – in short, as many rare things as would set up a Necromancer or a Country Apothecary.'[21] Mai was lumped in with the bizarre cargo of a voyage that had not, the author noted, annexed any new territories or islands to the British Empire.

For those who did think the Pacific voyages could tell the British some-thing about themselves and their place in the world, Mai became the focus of attention. He was taken under the wing of Joseph Banks and Lord Sandwich, presented to the king, taken on a tour of the navy's ships and to the theatre, and introduced to high society in London and around the country. Variously described as a Tahitian prince or priest, neither of which was the case, he was scrutinised for the lessons taught by his customs, manners and reactions, and by the ways these changed while he was in Britain. Opinions varied. Fanny Burney, future novelist and sister of one of Mai's shipmates on the *Adventure*, found him possessed of a natural polish and sociabil-ity. She compared him favourably to Lord Chesterfield's illegitimate son Philip Stanhope, judging that Mai 'with no Tutor but Nature . . . appears in a *new world* like a man [who] had all his life studied the Graces, & attended with un[re]mitting application & diligence to form his manners, & to render his appearance & behaviour *politely easy*, & *thoroughly well bred*!' As she concluded, drawing out the philosophical principle from her encounter with Mai, 'I think this shews how much *Nature* can do with-out *art*, than *art* with all her refinement, unassisted by *Nature*.'[22] Others, however, were not so sure. Samuel Johnson thought that any polish and politeness that Mai demonstrated had been picked up by mixing in the finest social circles. In addition, some newspaper commentary presented him as interested only in 'immediate corporeal Gratifications', describing him as 'a *Sensationalist* of the first Kind'. These were the marks of the savage.

Figure 11.9 *Omai*, by William Hodges, c. 1775–1776. This portrait
of Mai, emphasising his strong features, was probably produced
for the prominent London surgeon John Hunter. Hunter had an
interest in comparative anatomy that led him to collect both body
parts and images of peoples from different parts of the world.

Similarly divergent ideas seem to be being worked out through por-
traiture. William Hodges's likeness of Mai (figure 11.9) may have been
commissioned by the leading surgeon John Hunter (who also purchased a
Maori head from one of Mai's shipmates). It first appears in his collection,
and may have been part of his interest in comparative and evolutionary
anatomy. The depiction of Mai is, however, quite different in Sir Joshua
Reynolds's portrait (figure 11.10) where he appears as the epitome of the
noble savage: barefoot, tattooed, but elegant and refined in a costume, pose
and landscape that combines the classical with the Polynesian. In addition,
coming from the Society Islands, being associated with the notorious adul-
terer Lord Sandwich and with Joseph Banks, whose sexual encounters in the
South Seas were the subject of much poetry, prose and gossip in London,

Figure 11.10 '*Omai*', engraving by Johann Jacobé from a painting by Joshua Reynolds, 1780. This engraving from the Reynolds portrait emphasises Mai's nobility and civility. The setting, costume and pose mix imagined versions of the Polynesian, the Oriental and the classical to present Mai as the refined product of nature that many of his London acquaintances wished him to be.

Mai could not escape the discussions of sexuality that interpreted and criticised the peoples of the Pacific and those who voyaged among them. Satirical pamphlets alluded to the pleasures he had enjoyed in London, including those of the adulterous Lady Grosvenor and the notorious brothel-keeper Charlotte Hayes and her 'mystic school'.[23]

Mai stayed two years in Britain. His final part in the process of exploring and knowing the Pacific was to be his return to the Society Islands on Cook's third voyage. Travelling via New Zealand and Tonga, Mai returned to the island of Huahine in October 1777. There was certainly no attempt to restore him to his lands in Ra'iatea, or to offer military support for any battles with the Boraborans. Instead, Mai's return seems to have been part of the notions of 'improvement' that increasingly shaped British designs in the Pacific (see chapter 3). Mai was returned with new seeds, animals and tools. Cook's men built him a cottage, provided furniture and planted a garden. They left him with little models of carriages and animals, as well as tin soldiers, and with maps and globes. He was, it seems, to be an agent for the transformation of the Pacific in European terms. Yet he also brought guns, gunpowder and shot (although more for hunting than warfare), and a more varied set of European items including a barrel organ, an electrical machine and a suit of armour. It proved difficult for Mai to use these varied resources, along with the stories he had and his store of precious red feathers, to work his way back into island society and politics. He died within a few years of fever. His house was burned and his garden was abandoned.

The European encounter with the Pacific has to be understood from both sides. It involved the ideas of Enlightenment philosophy, the development of European arts and sciences, and the imperatives of empire. Europeans were interpreting and representing themselves and others as they traversed this ocean. Yet theirs was not the only work of interpretation and representation. Everywhere they went their actions had to be shaped to the actions, reactions and interpretations of Pacific Islanders, whether this was the indigenous Australians' refusal to engage with them, the violence (and cannibalism) of the Maori or the interest of Polynesians in incorporating the British into their politics, and even – for Tupaia, Mai and others – in travelling to what they called 'Pretane'. By sailing into the Pacific Cook and his crews were sailing into someone else's world. This shaped Cook's death as it had his life.

The third voyage was Captain Cook's last. With Cook overseeing the science and John Webber producing images that were destined for the published narrative, the *Resolution* and the *Discovery* visited now familiar islands – New Zealand, Tonga and Tahiti – but they also explored places new to them too. The far north of the Pacific was charted, involving encounters with the Nuu-chah-nulth people at what was to become Nootka Sound on Vancouver Island, and with Chukchi villages of the Siberian shore. On their way north from Tahiti the *Resolution* had also happened upon the westernmost of the Hawai'ian islands (which Cook named the Sandwich Islands after his patron). In November 1778 the *Resolution* returned to the archipelago, first to Maui and later to Hawai'i itself. Cook was disturbed to find that there was already evidence of the venereal diseases that he had been powerless to prevent his men bringing to the islands on their first visit. He was angry with his men and concerned about what his ship's arrival at these islands meant for their inhabitants.

The islanders were also interpreting this visitation too. Since Mai had been returned to Huahine there were no fellow Polynesians on the ships to mediate the encounter. The Hawai'ians seem, therefore, to have fitted the Europeans into what they knew of the world. The *Resolution* had appeared off the coast early in the Makahiki, a time for the celebration of the return of the ancestor god Lono. This god's symbol was a white *tapa* cloth held aloft on a cross of wood, not unlike the sails of a European ship. The ritual cycle had Lono's symbol carried clockwise around the island. The winds meant that the *Resolution* had to tack in that direction around Hawai'i searching for an anchorage. In the islanders' cosmology Lono came to bring peace and prosperity. At the end of the Makahiki he left to be replaced by Ku, the god of war. Where Cook fitted in was a matter of interpretation. Hawai'ian beliefs did not strictly separate the world of gods and the world of humans. Associating Cook with Lono (or Ku, as some did) did not mean venerating the Englishman as a god. It meant placing him in a line of sacred ancestors descended from the original Lono and carrying their *mana* (sacred power) in the world. It did mean that what Cook meant to the islanders had to be understood in terms of the Makahiki cycle, the sacred geography of the island, and in relationship to the Hawai'ian chief Kalani'opu'u who himself represented the god Ku.

In mid-January the *Resolution* found the perfect place to anchor. They sailed into Kealakekua Bay – the pathway of the gods – to be greeted by thousands of islanders celebrating their arrival. Rituals and celebrations continued. Cook became part of adapted rites for the welcome and worship of Lono. They called him 'Erono' (Lono). He also exchanged names with Kalani'opu'u. There were feasts, dances and displays of martial arts. Eventually it was time for the *Resolution* to leave. They did so on 4 February 1779, just as the Makahiki cycle ended. Unfortunately they soon sailed into a gale which damaged a mast. Cook decided that they had to return to the only safe anchorage they had found, Kealakekua Bay. Their reappearance, however, was not a matter for celebration. The return of the representatives of Lono so soon, and before the annual cycle was complete, could only be interpreted as a challenge to the god Ku, and an upsetting of the cosmological order. They were met with thefts and petty violence. When Cook, as he had done many times before on other islands, attempted to hold Kalani'opu'u hostage for the return of one of the *Resolution*'s boats it seemed he was issuing a direct challenge from Lono to Ku. In a confrontation at the water's edge Captain Cook was clubbed down and killed. His marines, still in a boat offshore, were unable or unwilling to help him.

Cook's life continued to be important after his death. His body was dismembered and parts of it distributed to the high chiefs of the island. Lono's priests returned a part of his thigh to the *Resolution* and asked questions which disturbed the ship's company: when would 'Erono' return, and what would he do to them when he did? In reply, Cook's men exacted their own revenge by killing at least thirty islanders. Back in Britain, when the news of Cook's death was announced, he was elevated to the pantheon of British heroes. As Hannah More's poem shows (see chapter 10), Cook promised the British a model of global empire clothed in the language of humanitarianism and liberty. Cook himself had, however, never been quite so sure that was what he had brought to the Pacific. The islanders that he met had also had their own interpretations of him and his life too.

Further reading

For an overall account of European exploration in the Pacific, see Glyndwr Williams (1998) 'The Pacific: exploration and exploitation', in P. J. Marshall (ed.) *The Oxford History of the British Empire*, vol. II, *The Eighteenth Century* (Oxford University Press, Oxford) pp. 552–575. There are excellent anthropologically informed accounts of Cook's voyages in Anne Salmond (2003) *The Trial of the Cannibal Dog: Captain Cook in the South Seas* (Allen Lane, London) and Nicholas Thomas (2003) *Discoveries: The Voyages of Captain Cook* (Allen Lane, London). Cook's journals are reproduced in J. C. Beaglehole (ed.) (1955–1967) *The Journals of Captain James Cook*, 4 vols. (Hakluyt Society, Cambridge) and in abridged form in Philip Edwards (ed.) (1999) *The Journals of Captain Cook* (Penguin, London). For Tupaia, see David Turnbull (1998) 'Cook and Tupaia, a tale of cartographic *méconnaissance?*' in Margarette Lincoln (ed.) *Science and Exploration in the Pacific: European Voyages to the Southern Oceans in the Eighteenth Century*

(Boydell Press, Woodbridge) pp. 117–131 and Glyndwr Williams (2003) 'Tupaia: Polynesian warrior, navigator, high priest – and artist', in Felicity Nussbaum (ed.) *The Global Eighteenth Century* (Johns Hopkins University Press, Baltimore) pp. 38–51. For well-illustrated accounts of artistic representation in the South Pacific, see Bernard Lewis (1985) *European Vision and the South Pacific*, 2nd edn (Yale University Press, New Haven) and Nigel Rigby and Pieter van der Merwe (2002) *Captain Cook in the Pacific* (National Maritime Museum, London) chap. 5, 'Art and artists on Cook's voyages'. For William Hodges, see Geoff Quilley and John Bonehill (eds.) *William Hodges, 1744–1797: The Art of Exploration* (National Maritime Museum, London). For Mai, see E. H. McCormick (1977) *Omai, Pacific Envoy* (Auckland University Press, Auckland). There are entries in the *Oxford Dictionary of National Biography* for Cook, Hodges and Mai.

Notes

1 Quoted in Anne Salmond (2003) *The Trial of the Cannibal Dog: Captain Cook in the South Seas* (Allen Lane, London) p. 25.
2 Quoted ibid., p. 30.
3 Quoted in J. C. Beaglehole (ed.) (1955) *The Journals of Captain James Cook*, vol. I, *The Voyage of the* Endeavour, *1768–1771* (Hakluyt Society, Cambridge) p. cxxxvi.
4 Quoted ibid., pp. 514–515.
5 Quoted in Salmond, *The Trial of the Cannibal Dog*, p. 305.
6 Quoted in Beaglehole, *The Journals of Captain James Cook*, vol. I, *The Voyage of the* Endeavour, p. 117.
7 Quoted in Nicholas Thomas (2003) *Discoveries: The Voyages of Captain Cook* (Allen Lane, London) p. 81.
8 George Forster quoted in Glyndwr Williams (2003) 'Tupaia: Polynesian warrior, navigator, high priest – and artist', in Felicity Nussbaum (ed.) *The Global Eighteenth Century* (Johns Hopkins University Press, Baltimore) p. 40.
9 John Marra quoted in Salmond, *The Trial of the Cannibal Dog*, p. 112.
10 Quoted in Beaglehole, *The Journals of Captain James Cook*, vol. I, *The Voyage of the* Endeavour, p. 442.
11 Quoted in Salmond, *The Trial of the Cannibal Dog*, p. 68.
12 Quoted in Williams, 'Tupaia', p. 43.
13 Quoted in Nigel Rigby and Pieter van der Merwe (2002) *Captain Cook in the Pacific* (National Maritime Museum, London) p. 103.
14 Quoted in Salmond, *The Trial of the Cannibal Dog*, pp. 187–88.
15 Quoted in Rigby and van der Merwe, *Captain Cook in the Pacific*, p. 105.
16 Joseph Farington quoted in William Hodges's entry in the *Oxford Dictionary of National Biography*.

17 Edmund Burke to William Robertson, 9 June 1777 in George H. Guttridge (ed.) (1961) *The Correspondence of Edmund Burke*, vol. III (Cambridge University Press, Cambridge) p. 351.

18 John Hawkesworth quoted in Gillian Russell (2004) 'An "entertainment of oddities": fashionable sociability and the Pacific in the 1770s', in Kathleen Wilson (ed.) *A New Imperial History: Culture, Identity, and Modernity in Britain and the Empire, 1660–1840* (Cambridge University Press, Cambridge) p. 63.

19 All quotations are from Neil Rennie (2003) 'The Point Venus "scene", Tahiti, 14 May 1769 ', in Nussbaum, *The Global Eighteenth Century*, pp. 239–251.

20 Quoted in E. H. McCormick (1977) *Omai, Pacific Envoy* (Auckland University Press, Auckland) p. 113.

21 Quoted in Harriet Guest (2004) 'Ornament and use: Mai and Cook in London', in Wilson, *A New Imperial History*, p. 317.

22 Quoted in McCormick, *Omai*, p. 128.

23 Quoted in Russell, 'An "entertainment of oddities"', p. 68.

Epilogue

Through the telling of more than forty lives this book has sought to bring to life the history of Britain's place in the world from the coronation of Queen Elizabeth I in the middle of the sixteenth century to the abolition of the slave trade at the beginning of the nineteenth century. Doing so has meant setting out the histories and geographies of the different processes which shaped global history over those two hundred and fifty years. This has involved investigating how activities which stretched across space and time, pulling people, places and things into new configurations, were organised, and to what purpose and with what effects. Although ideas, institutions and forms of resistance changed over time, many of the seeds of what came later can be seen in the tentative, if also belligerently violent, beginnings of Elizabethan England's entry on to the global stage. There was the crucial role of merchants, including slave-trading merchants such as John Hawkins, in the beginnings of a new world of exchange, profit and violence in the Atlantic and beyond. There was the importance of the ideas Europeans such as Walter Ralegh had about the rest of the world, and what happened when those Europeans came up against other peoples with other ideas about how the world was and how it should be. And, finally, there were the varieties of opposition prompted by schemes of colonisation and domination. As Hugh O'Neill's story shows, these took many forms, from shows of deference to the monarch to outright violent rebellion. The chapters have also demonstrated how these beginnings opened out into a multiple and diverse world of global geographies. There were differences between those who traded and those who sought to settle, and differences for those that they sought to trade with and settle among. There were differences, in relationships of power if not in attentiveness to market opportunities, in trading to the East Indies, Africa and the Americas. There were differences between seeking profit and seeking knowledge. There were differences between living from slavery and fighting against it. In each case the chapters have marked out the scale and scope of the histories and geographies of these overlapping and more or less distinct processes which together shaped this world.

Yet there are broader patterns to be discerned amongst all this variety. At the beginning of the period Britain's engagement with the world beyond

Europe was sporadic and unpredictable. It was uncertain whether it would produce spectacular successes or equally spectacular failures. It was, perhaps, only predictable that the uncertainties involved would breed violence. In part, this was a matter of operating in a world that the Spanish and the Portuguese claimed but did not effectively control. In part, it was simply a matter of beginnings. No one on any side of these many encounters knew what was going to happen next. By the end of the period there were still many parts of the world where success, failure, destruction and death were patterned by uncertainty and unpredictability. Captain Cook and the islanders he met in peace or in violence at the end of the eighteenth century did not know what would happen next, and tried to make sure that, whatever happened, they had some control over it. Yet many other places and possibilities had become more certain and more predictable. The relationships which linked parts of the world, if no less violent or exploitative than before, had become more regular and routine. This integration can be seen in the settlement of the Americas, and its displacement of indigenous peoples beyond new frontiers. It can be seen in the forms of organisation of trading companies such as the East India Company, and in the more flexible and self-organised practices of Atlantic merchants. It can be seen in the destruction of piracy and the establishment of wage labour at sea, and it can be seen in the centrality of the massive system of slave trading and plantation slavery to a new global economy. Hard work, violence, danger, fear and uncertainty had not gone away, particularly for those on whom the new arrangements bore down most heavily, but their overall shape and rhythm were more predictable. Encounters had become routines.

The other broader pattern that can be discerned is the increasing centrality of Britain to this world. Of course this depended very much on both geography and history. For many people and places, especially in Africa and Asia, the real encounter with British imperial power was yet to come. However, Britain started the period considered here as a place on the margins of Iberian attempts to construct a universal monarchy, and ended with an 'empire of the seas' which also included a great deal of territory and a large number of people, both enslaved and free. This empire was, as has been shown in various chapters, made (and parts of it lost) through warfare. Wars to defend and extend trade, settlement and security beyond Europe were knitted into European concerns over religion and the balance of power across the seventeenth and eighteenth centuries. The contenders changed over time. Wars were fought against Spain in the early seventeenth century, against the Dutch in the late seventeenth century and against the French across the long eighteenth century. In each case local wars were global, and global wars were local. As they brought lands and peoples under British control in the Caribbean, in Bengal and in North America, and as some slipped from Britain's hands again, the British fought with and against an array of others: Abenakis, Marathas, freed slaves, American colonists, Jamaican maroons and Black Caribs. After each cycle of wars there were the consolidations of peace. New territories offered new opportunities for those who could integrate them into the fabric of trading, voyaging, exchanging and taxing. They offered new troubles for those who might be sent to do the work. There were always disagreements – about forms of rule, and about what sorts of labour and settlement were appropriate – as the empire expanded and contracted. However, if it was not clear what sort of empire the British should have, it had become clear that they would have an empire.

Seeing the global history of these centuries in this way – as made up of a variety of different processes, as increasingly integrated by multiple forms of mental and manual labour, and as contested through wars fought with weapons and ideas – highlights the role of human action in making this world what it was. The biographical sketches – and they can be little more than that – around which each of the chapters is organised seek to give life to this world by showing people in action within it. Once again, these forms of action are diverse. Their multiplicity goes beyond any simple attempts to categorise them. There are forms of self-interested action – merchants making deals, the ambitious seeking advancement and strategists looking for power – as well as action devoted to helping others live. There are those using their heads and hands in different ways for different ends: as traders, translators, lawyers, sailors, thieves, runaways, labourers, writers, activists, warriors, artists, navigators and travellers. There are, therefore, forms of action that used diverse tools and techniques: ropes, sails and ships; hoes, bills and mills; corn, cloth and spices; maps, ledgers and quills; books, speeches and pictures; and guns, knives and whips. There are violent actions in service of profit or power or aiming towards freedom and liberty. There are those endeavouring to make new identities, those struggling to deal with conflicting pressures on who they should be and those struggling to preserve old senses of self. There are failures and there are successes. In each case, the aim has been to show individuals taking action where and how they can, with the sense that this is easier for some than for others.

It is, however, often a long way from individual action to global history and global geography. For some the gap has long been closed. It is common for figures such as Captain Cook, Walter Ralegh, William Jones and Poca-hontas to have their lives presented, albeit in very different ways, on the world stage. Increasingly, others are being put there too. Eunice Williams, John

Sassamon, Radhakanta Tarkavagisa, William Freeman, Richard Oswald, William Dampier, William Kidd, Bartholomew Roberts, Anne Bonny, the Robin Johns, Thomas Thistlewood, Olaudah Equiano, Toussaint L'Ouverture, Tupaia, William Hodges and Mai have all recently had their stories told in ways that put them back into the wider worlds they inhabited.

This book has told other life stories as well. Including them all as 'global lives' – those who stayed put as much as those who travelled; those who had little power as well as those who wielded great influence; those who made a difference to only a few alongside those who shaped the lives of many – means thinking carefully about action in the world. It means understanding how action can be shaped by global processes, global histories and global geographies, even when that action remains more circumscribed. Sarah Affir's life of work and her decisions to become a mother when others did not were shaped by the long, deep and troubling history of plantation slavery and her place within it. Essa Morrison's style of getting by in London's riverside lodging houses was also framed by the worldly relationships of land and sea, men and women, capital and labour, in the Atlantic maritime economy. Their actions may not have had far-reaching consequences in themselves, but they stand for the actions of millions with no large-scale plan and with few resources to realise their intentions beyond their immediate situation. In this they are as important to this history of global lives as the grand actions of the few. As all the chapters have shown, this world was built and changed by small actions with often limited intentions: making a profit, holding a position, finding something out, growing a crop, righting a wrong, avoiding or inflicting pain and suffering, making a truth or taking a voyage. For many there was no overall scheme or plan, but a new world got built. Those who did have a plan to make a world – or break someone else's – needed to try and realise it by using the small actions and limited intentions of other people, or they could see it undone by them instead.

This means that all of these forms of action – great and small – can be understood only as actions taken with and against the actions of others. Focusing on individual lives, rather than on social processes, means that in any particular instance what was true of encounters – the open-ended and uncertain interplay of actions and reactions – continued to be the case as relationships were built that drew many more people into webs of connection linking distant places to each other. No one knew for sure which encounters would lead to violence, and who would prevail. No one knew for certain which profit-making ventures would succeed and which would fail. No one knew which ship would have a good voyage and which a hard one. No one knew whether a treasure ship or a naval frigate would be over the horizon. No one knew if a slave revolt, a speech, a poem or a petition would free the enslaved. There were always enough willing to try. Doing so meant trying to shape a global life by acting with, on and against the actions of others. This book has sought to put the life back into global history by broadening the range of people whom we take to be those who made this world, by populating it with many men and women and by demonstrating the difficult conditions under which they did what they did. It has shown that this world, with all its inequities, injustices and resistances, was made what it was by people living all sorts of global lives.

Index